Supervision and Surveillance
The Powers of the Financial Services Authority

Dr C Chatterjee
LL.M (CAMBRIDGE), LL.M, PhD (LONDON), BARRISTER
LAW DEPARTMENT, LONDON GUILDHALL UNIVERSITY

Anna Lefcovitch
LL.M, SOLICITOR, EC HARRIS

Apart from any fair dealing for the purpose of research or private study, or criticism or review, as permitted under the Copyright, Designs and Patents Act 1988, this publication may only be reproduced, stored or transmitted, in any form or by any means, with the prior permission in writing of the publisher, or in the case of reprographic reproduction in accordance with the terms and licenses issued by the Copyright Licensing Agency. Enquiries concerning reproduction outside those terms should be addressed to the publishers at the undermentioned address:

Financial World Publishing
IFS House
4-9 Burgate Lane
Canterbury
Kent
CT1 2XJ
United Kingdom

Telephone 01227 818687

Financial World Publishing Publications are published by The Chartered Institute of Bankers, a non-profit-making registered educational charity.

The Chartered Institute of Bankers believes that the sources of information upon which the book is based are reliable and has made every effort to ensure the complete accuracy of the text. However, neither CIB, the authors nor any contributor can accept any legal responsibility whatsoever for consequences that may arise from any errors or omissions or any opinion or advice given.

Typeset by Kevin O'Connor
Printed by Watkiss Studios, Biggleswade

Copyright © The Chartered Institute of Bankers 2001

ISBN 0-85297-551-1

Contents

	Table of Cases	xii
	Table of Statutes	xiv
	European Union Legislation	xxii
	Introduction	xxiv
1	**Legal Aspects of the Growth and Development of the Business of Banking until the 19th Century**	**1**
	Introduction	1
	The Early History of Monetary Transactions in England	1
	The Evolution of the Bank of England: 1735 -1801	7
	The Evolution of the Bank of England in the 19th century – Transition to a National Bank	11
	Conclusions	13
2	**The Bank of England vis-à-vis the British Economy and the Government**	**14**
	Introduction	14
	The Bank of England, the British Economy and the Government	14
	The Period between 1800 and 1914	14
	The Period between 1918 and 1945	17
	The Post-1945 Years	18
	Conclusion	20
3	**An Analysis of the Statutory Provisions Governing the Business of Banking**	**22**
	Introduction	22
	PART I	22
	Early Banking Legislation including the Banking Act 1979	22

Bank of England Act 1694	22
Bank of England Act 1716	23
Bank Notes Act 1826	24
Bank Charter Act 1844	24
Bank of England Act 1861	24
Bank of England Act 1946	25
Banking Act 1979	27
PART II	**31**
Banking Act 1987	**31**
An Analysis of the Banking Act 1987 – Certain Important Definitions	32
Deposit	32
Deposit-Taking Business	33
Exempted Persons and Exempted Transactions	34
Essential Features of the Banking Act 1987	35
Grant and Refusal of Authorization	41
The Circumstances in which Restriction on Authorization May be Imposed, and the Procedure thereof	47
Revocation of and Restrictions on Authorization	51
Directions	56
Objections to Controllers	57
Advertisement Regulations as Part of Supervision and Control	60
Supervision and Control by Seeking Information	63
Supervision and Control by Investigations	68
Supervision and Control in relation to Accountants and Auditors	70
Reflecting on the Authorization and Revocation System of the Financial Services Authority	71
Statement Based on Section 16 of the Banking Act 1987	72
Minimum Criteria for Authorization, Section 3 of the Banking Act 1981	72
Prudent Conduct Criteria	74
Adequate Capital	74
Integrity and Skill in Carrying on Business	76

	Supervision of Risk-Based Banking Business by the FSA	79
	The Composition of the Board of Directors	80
	Directors, Controllers and Managers Must be Fit and Proper Persons (Schedule 3 Paragraph 1)	80
	Conclusions	83
4	**The Deposit Protection Scheme**	**84**
	Introduction	84
	The Deposit Protection Scheme	84
	Meanings of Certain Key Terms	85
	Insolvency	85
	Compensation Payments to Depositors (section 58)	86
	Protected Deposits	87
	Trustee Deposits, Joint Deposits, etc. (section 61)	88
	Contributory Institutions	88
	Initial Contributions	89
	Further Contributions (section 54)	89
	Special Contributions (section 55)	90
	Deposit Base of Transferee Institutions	90
	Payments out of the Fund (section 58)	91
	Repayment in respect of Contributions (section 63)	93
	The Board of Banking Supervision (section 64)	94
	Conclusions	95
5	**The Impact of the Second Council Directive on the Coordination of Laws, Regulations and Administrative Provisions Relating to the Taking up and Pursuit of the Business of Credit Institutions**	**96**
	Introduction	96
	A Brief Analysis of the Directive	97
	Harmonization of Authorization Conditions	98
	Harmonization of the Conditions Governing pursuit of the Business of Credit Institutions	99
	Provisions relating to the Freedom of Establishment and the Freedom to Provide Services	102

	Conclusions	106
6	**An Examination as to whether the Bank Collapses were due to the lack of Regulatory Measures**	**107**
	Introduction	107
	An Examination of the Causes Leading to the Bank Failures in Recent Years	107
	The Collapse of Johnson Matthey Bankers Limited	107
	The Collapse of the Bank of Credit and Commerce International (BCCI)	110
	Introduction	110
	Conclusions	132
	The Collapse of Barings	136
	Basic Facts	136
	Specific Issues Relating to the Collapse of Barings Group	140
	Authorized Trading Activities of BFS on Singaporean and Japanese Futures Exchanges	143
	Internal Controls	152
	Internal Audit	155
	External Audit	158
	Issue of Supervision	164
	Conclusions	170
7	**The Financial Services Authority**	**172**
	Introduction	172
	The Memorandum of Understanding between HM Treasury, the Bank of England and the FSA	175
	The Specific Responsibilities of the Bank of England	175
	The Responsibilities of the FSA	177
	The Responsibilities of the Treasury	177
	The Distribution of Responsibility between the Treasury, the Bank and the FSA	178
	The Nature of the Relationship between the Bank of England and the FSA	178
	A Brief Summary of the Nature of Banking Supervision by the FSA	180

	Elements of Supervision	184
	Adequate Capital (see page 74)	186
	Adequate Liquidity	186
	A Viable Business Plan	186
	An Adequate Control System	186
	Adequate Provisions for Bad and Doubtful Debts	187
	Carrying on its Business with Integrity and Skill	187
	Directors, Managers and Controllers to be Fit and Proper Persons	187
	Conclusions	188
8	**The Objectives of the Financial Services and Markets Act 2000, and the FSA's Operating Framework**	**189**
	Introduction	189
	Statutory Objectives and the Principles of Good Regulation	190
	The FSA's Principles for Business	191
	The FSA's Approaches to Regulations	194
	Practitioner Involvement	195
	The FSA's New Operating Framework	197
	Market Confidence	201
	Public Awareness	202
	Disclosure	202
	Consumer Protection	203
	Market Abuse	203
	Financial Crime	205
	Consumer Complaints	206
	Consumer Compensation	210
	The FSA's Regulatory Tools	214
	Activities Directed Towards Commerce or the Industry In General	215
	Activities Directed Towards the Industry	215
	Activities Directed Towards Individual Institutions	215
	The FSA's General Duties	216
	Implementation	218
	Power of the FSA as to Rule-Making	218
	Asset Identification Rules	220
	Endorsing Rules	220
	Specific Rules (Price-Stabilizing Rules)	220

	Financial Promotion Rules	221
	Money-Laundering Rules	221
	Control of Information Rules	221
	Conclusions	223
9	**Financial Services and Markets Act 2000**	**224**
	Introduction	224
	Definitions	225
	The Regulator and Provisions about Regulated Activities and Prohibited Activities	234
	Authorization and Exemptions	237
	Grant of Permission	238
	Exercise of Passport Rights by the United Kingdom	239
	Permission to Carry on Regulated Activities	241
	Performance of Regulated Activities/Prohibition Order	243
	Control over Authorized Persons	247
	Revocation of Authorization Order Otherwise than by Consent	252
	Conclusions	253
10	**Collective Investment Schemes**	**255**
	Introduction	255
	Collective Investment Schemes	255
	Authorized Unit Trust Schemes	258
	Open-ended Investment Companies	261
	Recognized Overseas Schemes	261
	Individually Recognized Overseas Schemes	264
	Recognized Investment Houses and Clearing Houses	266
	Competition Scrutiny	270
	Conclusions	272
11	**Control of Business Transfers**	**273**
	Introduction	273
	Control of Business Transfers	273
	Banking Business Transfer Compensation Schemes	277
	Common Provisions between an Insurance Transfer Compensation Scheme and Banking	278
	Conclusions	280

12	**Official Listing**	**281**
	Introduction	281
	Listing Particulars	283
	General Duty of Disclosure	283
	Dispensation from Disclosure	284
	Discontinuance or Suspension	289
	Conclusions	290
13	**Provision of Financial Services by Members of the Professions**	**292**
	Introduction	292
	Provision of Financial Services by Members of the Professions	292
	Mutual Societies	299
	Auditors and Actuaries	300
	Public Reward, Disclosure of Information and Cooperation	301
	Conclusions	305
14	**The Financial Services Compensation Scheme**	**307**
	Introduction	307
	The Financial Services Compensation Scheme	307
	Other Provisions	313
	Conclusions	314
15	**Insolvency**	**316**
	Introduction	316
	Voluntary Arrangement	316
	Administration Orders	317
	Receivership	319
	Voluntary Winding Up	319
	Winding Up by the Court	320
	Bankruptcy	321
	Provisions against Debt Avoidance	322
	Supplemental Provisions concerning Insurers	322
	Conclusions	324
16	**Lloyd's**	**325**
	Introduction	325
	The Society	326

	The FSA's General Powers	327
	Former Underwriting Members (Sections 320-322)	328
	Conclusions	329
17	**Notices**	**330**
	Introduction	330
	Warning Notice	330
	Decision Notice	330
	Notice of Discontinuance	330
	Final Notice	331
	Publication	331
	Conclusions	333
18	**Investigations and Control**	**335**
	Introduction	335
	Investigations	335
	Information Gathering and Investigations	336
	Investigations in support of Overseas Regulators	339
	The First Set of Conditions	342
	The Second Set of Conditions	342
	The Third Set of Conditions	342
	Conclusions	344
19	**Intervention and Disciplinary Measures by the FSA**	**345**
	Introduction	345
	Intervention of the FSA in respect of the Incoming Firms	345
	Disciplinary Measures	349
	Injunctions and Restitutions	351
	The Enforcement Manual	354
	Conclusions	355
20	**Dispute Settlement Procedures**	**362**
	Introduction	362
	PART I	362
	The Ombudsman Scheme	362
	The Scheme Operator	363
	Jurisdiction	365
	The Compulsory Jurisdiction	365
	The Voluntary Jurisdiction	366
	Comments	367

PART II	368
The Tribunal Procedure	368
Conclusions	372
Overall Conclusions	**386**
Annexes	**389**
Annex 1: Section 187 of the Consumer Credit Act 1974	389
Annotations:	390
Annex 2: Section 183 of the Financial Services Act 1986	390
Bibliography	**392**
Textbooks	392
Consultation Papers Issued by the FSA	392
Index	**394**

Table of Cases

Barrass v Reeve [1980] 3 All ER 705	63
Bracey v Read [1963] Ch 88, [1962] 3 All ER 472	67
Brazier v Skipton Rock Co Ltd [1962] 1 All ER 957	37
British Olympic Association v The Commissioners London VAT Tribunal (1979)	235
Caparo Industries plc v Dickman [1990]	133
Carapanayoti & Co v Comptoir Commercial Andre & Cie SA [1972] 1 Lloyd's Rep 139	61
Cawley v Frost [1976] 3 All ER 744	60
Church of Scientology of California v Customs and	235
Clear v Smith [1981] 1 WLR 399	63
De Beers Consolidated Mines Ltd v Howe [1906] AC 445	41
Dodds v Walker [1981] 2 All ER 609	57
Dorchester Finance Co v Stebbing [1989] BCLC 498	36
E J Riley Investments Ltd v Eurostile Holdings Ltd [1985] 3 All 181	57
Egyptian Delta Land and Investments Co Ltd v Todd [1929] AC 1	41
Gaumont British Distributors Ltd v Henry [1939] 2 KB 711	59
Gibson v Skibs A/S Marina [1989] BLCL 498	37
Greenough v Gaskell (1833) 1 My & K 98	67
James & Son Ltd v Smee [1955] 1 QBD 78	60, 61
Johnson v Jewitt (H.M. Inspector of Taxes) (1961)	235
Jones v Meatyard [1939] 1 All ER 140	63
J W Wilcox v The Commissioners (1978)	235
J W Wilcox v The Commissioners [1976]	235
Kenneth Gordon Coleman v The Commissioners (1976)	235
Knox v Boyd 1941 JC 82	59
Lord Advocate v Huron & Erie Loan and Saving Co (1911) SC 612	41
Lovelace v DPP [1954] 3 Ell ER 481	60
Maaunsell v Olins [1975] AC 373	67
Manorlike Ltd v Le Vitas Travel Agency and Consultancy Services Ltd [1986] 1 All ER 573	57
McLeod (or Houston) v Buchanan [1940] 2 All ER 179	60
Metropolitan Water Board v Paine [1901] 1 DB 285	67

Nakkuda Ali v Jayaratne [1951] AC 66, PC	67
Norman v Theodore Goddard [1991] BCLC 1027	36
Oliver v Goodger [1944] 2 All ER 481	65
O'Sullivan v Truth and Sportsman Ltd (1957) 96 CLR 220	60
R v Banks [1916] 2 KB 6221, [1916-1917] All ER Rep 356	67
R v Bates [1952] 2 All ER 842	62
R v Bishirgian [1936] 1 All ER	62
R v Harrison [1983] 3 All ER 134	67
R v Kane [1965] 1 All ER 705	60
R v Lord Kylsant [1932] 1 KB 442, [1931] All ER	62
R v Wellard (1884) 14 QBD	60
Re D'Jan of London Ltd [1994] 1 BCLC 561	36
Re Bayer Products Ltd's Application [1947] 2 All ER 188	63
Re Hilton, Gibbes v Hale-Hinton [1909] 2 Ch 548	41
Ross Hillman Ltd Bond [1974] 2 All ER 287	60, 61
Shave v Rosner [1954] 2 All ER 280	60
Shulton (Great Britain) Ltd v Slough BC [1967] 2 All ER 137	60
Stevens & Steels Ltd and Evans v King [1943] 1 All ER 314	63
Stewart v Chapman [1951] 2 KB 792	57
Taylor's Central Garages (Exeter) v Roper (1951) 115 JP 445	59
Tesco Supermarkets Ltd v Nattrass [1972] 2 All ER 127	61
Towers & Co Ltd v Gray [1961] 2 QB 351	65
Webb v Baker [1916] 2 KB 753	65
Westminster City Council v Croyalgrange Ltd [1986] 2 All ER 353	59
Whitley v Stumbles [1930] AC 544	67

OTHER PRIMARY SOURCES

The Bank of England Note, The Bank of England and Johnson Matthey Bankers Limited, 1984

The Bank of England Banking Act 1987, Section 16: Statement of Principles, May 1998

The Oxford English Dictionary, Second Edition, prepared by J A Simpson and E S C Weiner, Volume XVII, Clarendon Press, Oxford, 1989

Table of Statutes

12 Anne Stat 2, c.16, s.2	4	Banking Act 1979 – contd.	
13 Eliz. c.8	2	s. 21	85
37 Hy. VIII, c.9	2, 4	s. 23(2)	86
7 Anne, c 7	10	s. 25(2)	89
8 & 9 Wm., c 32	5	Schedule 1	28, 30
		Schedule 2	30, 32
Bank Act 1998	34	Schedule 3	30, 32
Bank Charter Act 1844	24, 25	Schedule 4	30, 32
Bank Notes Act 1826	24	Schedule 5	30, 32
Bank of England Act 1716	23	Schedule 6	30, 32
Bank of England Act 1861	24	Schedule 7	30, 32
Bank of England Act 1946	25	Banking Act 1987	31, 35, 77, 78, 80, 104, 128, 168, 180, 181, 182, 185
s. 1	26		
s. 2	26		
s. 3	26	s. 1	34
s. 4	26	s. 1(4)	34
s. 5	26	s. 3	33, 69, 70, 72
s. 6	26	s. 6(1)	33
Schedule 1	26	s. 8	180
Schedule 2	26	s. 8(5)	35, 70
Bank of England Act 1998	172	s. 11	51, 52, 53, 72
Banking Act 1694	4, 22	s. 12	47, 51, 55
Banking Act 1979	22, 27, 77, 111	s. 12(3)	55
s. 3(5)	113	s. 12(8)	55
s. 4	28	s. 13	47, 51, 54
s. 5	29	s. 13(4)	54
s. 8	29	s. 13(5)	54
s. 13	29	s. 14	47, 51, 53, 54
s. 16	29	s. 15	51, 55
s. 17	29	s. 16	51, 72
s. 18	29	s. 17	51
s. 19	29	s. 18	51, 55, 56
s. 20	29	s. 18(3)	56

Banking Act 1987 – *contd.*	
s. 19	56
s. 20(4)	56
s. 22	52
s. 23	52
s. 24	89
s. 27	56
s. 32	60
s. 33	61
s. 33(5)	60
s. 34	62
s. 35	62, 69
s. 36	63
s. 37	63
s. 38	63, 64, 77
s. 38(1)	65, 165
s. 38(2)	78
s. 39	63, 65, 67, 105, 125
s. 39(1)	70
s. 39(4)	65
s. 39(13)	67
s. 40	63
s. 40(2)	67
s. 41	68, 125
s. 41(3)	69
s. 42	68, 69
s. 42(1)	69
s. 44	68
s. 47	70
s. 47(2)	70
s. 50(1)	84
s. 52(4)	89
s. 53	89, 90
s. 54	89
s. 54(1)	90, 94
s. 54(2)	89
s. 55	90, 94
s. 55(2)	94
s. 56	89
s. 57(3)	91
s. 58	86, 88, 91, 94
s. 58(3)	86
s. 58(4)	92
s. 60	87

Banking Act 1987 – *contd.*	
s. 61	88
s. 61(8)	88
s. 62	92, 94
s. 62(2)	92
s. 63	93
s. 63(5)	94
s. 64	94
s. 89	390
s. 94	82
s. 105	80, 81
s. 105(3)	39, 82
Schedule 2	90
Schedule 3	35, 72, 193
Banking Act 1999	224
Bankruptcy (Scotland) Act 1985	312, 317
Schedule 5	317
Bretton Woods 1946 Act	26
Building Societies Act 1986	193, 278, 316
s. 45	71, 193
Cheques Act 1957	27
Companies (Northern Ireland) Order 1986	85, 256
Art 386(3)	320
Art 389(A)	320
Art 418	318, 319, 321
Art 420A	278
Art 534	85
Companies Act 1985	256
s. 378	320
s. 381A	320
s. 425	310, 318
s. 427A	278
Companies Act 1986	
s. 48(1)(a)	319
s. 67(1)(a)	319
s. 112	319
s. 123	320
s. 135	320
s. 221	320
s. 423	322

Companies Act 1986 – *contd.*		Financial Services and Markets Act 2000	189, 304
s. 425	319, 321	s. 9(1)	236
s. 716	261	s. 19	236
Companies Act 1989	266	s. 20	337
Companies (No 2) (Northern Ireland) Order 1990	266	s. 21	235, 257
Consumer Credit Act 1974	27, 31, 46, 52, 77, 238, 349, 389	s. 21(1)	235, 236
		s. 21(3)	235
s. 21	238	s. 21(6)	235
s. 25(2)	346, 348	s. 24	236
s. 39(5)	238	s. 25	236
s. 147(1)	238	s. 26	236
s. 183	390	s. 27(1)	310
s. 187	31, 389	s. 33	350
s. 203	238	s. 35	319
Contracts (Rights of Third Parties) Act 1999	357	s. 38	241
		s. 39	241
Court and Legal Services Act 1990		s. 39(1)	241
s. 71	369, 370	s. 40	241, 242
Court of Session Act 1988		s. 41	241
s. 45	269, 331, 366	s. 42	241
Credit Union (Northern Ireland) Order 1985	278	s. 43	241
		s. 44	241
Credit Unions Act 1979	278, 299	s. 45	241
Criminal Justice Act 1983	77	s. 46	241
Criminal Justice Act 1993	304, 337, 346	s. 47	241
		s. 48	241
s. 195(4)	346	s. 49	241
		s. 50	241
Data Protection Act 1998		s. 51	241
s. 31	363	s. 52	241
		s. 53	241
Finance Act 1989		s. 53(4)	332
s. 182	304	s. 53(7)	332
Financial Services Act 1986	46, 52, 77, 390	s. 53(8)	332
		s. 54	241
s. 8(1)(a)	318	s. 55	241
s. 9	309	s. 56(3)	243
s. 26	310	s. 56(6)	338
s. 27	310	s. 58	243
s. 183	31, 32, 56	s. 59	245, 246, 339
s 187	31	s. 59(1)	338
s. 262	317	s. 59(2)	338
		s. 59(5)	244

Financial Services and Markets
Act 2000 – *contd.*

s. 60	244
s. 60(3)	244
s. 62(2)	244
s. 64	245, 246
s. 64(8)	245
s. 66	246, 338, 339
s. 66(2)	246
s. 67	246
s. 67(1)	339
s. 68	246
s. 69	245, 246, 379
s. 77(1)	289
s. 77(2)	289
s. 78(2)	332
s. 78(5)	332
s. 80	283, 284
s. 80(1)	284
s. 81	286
s. 82	286
s. 83	288
s. 84(2)	285
s. 85	288
s. 90(1)	286, 287
s. 90(3)	285
s. 90(4)	287
s. 90(8)	286
s. 91	286, 287, 288
s. 91(6)	287
s. 92	287
s. 93	288
s. 97	288
s. 98	288
s. 102(1)	289
s. 104	273
s. 105	274
s. 105(2)	274
s. 105(4)	280
s. 106	277
s. 106(1)	278
s. 106(4)	278
s. 107	276
s. 108	276

Financial Services and Markets
Act 2000 – *contd.*

s. 111	276, 279
s. 111(1)	273, 276, 279, 280
s. 112	279
s. 112(2)	279
s. 114	276
s. 114(2)	277
s. 116	277
s. 116(3)	277
s. 119	347
s. 123	204, 205, 341, 379
s. 124	204
s. 126	204
s. 132	368, 371
s. 132(2)	368
s. 133(1)	331
s. 135	369
s. 137	331
s. 138(4)	218
s. 139(3)	219
s. 141(4)	219
s. 148(4)	222
s. 150	253, 258
s. 153(5)	217
s. 157(1)	373
s. 165	304, 336, 339
s. 166	302, 337
s. 168	304
s. 168(1)	340
s. 168(2)	205, 341
s. 168(4)	340
s. 169(3)	339
s. 170	336
s. 174	336
s. 174(1)	341
s. 174(2)	341
s. 175(2)	341
s. 176	336, 342, 343
s. 177(3)	344
s. 178	249, 250, 252
s. 178(1)	249, 251
s. 178(2)	249, 251
s. 178(4)	247

Financial Services and Markets Act 2000 – *contd.*

s. 179	248, 249, 252
s. 179(2)	248
s. 180	249, 252
s. 180(2)	248
s. 181	249, 252
s. 181(2)	249
s. 183(3)	249
s. 185(3)	249
s. 186	250
s. 186(5)	250
s. 187(1)	250
s. 187(3)	249, 250
s. 189	250, 251
s. 189(4)	251
s. 189(7)	252
s. 190	249, 252
s. 190(1)	249
s. 196	347
s. 196(4)	336
s. 197(3)	332
s. 197(6)	332
s. 197(7)	332
s. 203	348, 349
s. 203(3)	349
s. 203(9)	349
s. 204	350
s. 205	350
s. 206	350
s. 210	379
s. 215	309
s. 215(1)	309
s. 215(2)	309
s. 216(2)	310
s. 216(3)	310
s. 217(3)	310
s. 217(4)	311
s. 217(6)	311
s. 219	312
s. 220	312
s. 222(1)	312
s. 222(2)	312
s. 223(3)	313

Financial Services and Markets Act 2000 – *contd.*

s. 224	312, 313
s. 226(7)	365
s. 230	364
s. 230(3)	364
s. 230(4)	364
s. 233	362
s. 235	255
s. 236	272
s. 236(3)	256
s. 238	272
s. 238(1)	257, 258
s. 240	257
s. 242	258
s. 243	258, 260
s. 244	258
s. 245	258
s. 246	258
s. 247	259
s. 248(3)	260
s. 249	385
s. 250	258
s. 251	260
s. 252	258
s. 253	258, 260
s. 254	252
s. 255	258
s. 256	258
s. 257	253, 258
s. 258	253
s. 259	253, 258
s. 259(3)	332
s. 259(8)	332
s. 259(9)	332
s. 260	253, 258
s. 261	253, 258
s. 262	261, 335
s. 262(2)	261
s. 263	261, 317
s. 264	258, 262, 264, 314
s. 264(2)	262
s. 264(5)	262
s. 265	261

Table of Statutes xix

Financial Services and Markets Act 2000 – *contd.*	
s. 266	261
s. 267	262, 263
s. 267(2)	263
s. 268	263
s. 268(3)	332
s. 268(7)	332
s. 268(9)	332
s. 269	261
s. 270	261, 264, 336
s. 271	261
s. 272	264, 266, 336
s. 273	261, 265
s. 274	261
s. 275	261
s. 276	261
s. 277	261
s. 278	261
s. 279	265
s. 280	261
s. 281	261, 286
s. 282	261
s. 282(3)	332
s. 282(6)	332
s. 282(7)	332
s. 283	261
s. 286(1)	266
s. 286(4)	266
s. 287	267
s. 287(3)	267
s. 288	267
s. 291(1)	267
s. 292	269
s. 293	268
s. 293(3)	268
s. 293(5)-(7)	268
s. 294	268
s. 294(4)	269
s. 296	269
s. 299	270
s. 300(4)	270
s. 301(4)	270
s. 301(10)	270

Financial Services and Markets Act 2000 – *contd.*	
s. 302(2)	270
s. 303	271
s. 304	271
s. 305(6)	297
s. 306	271
s. 308	271
s. 308(8)	271
s. 314	326
s. 315	297, 326
s. 315(5)	326
s. 316	327, 328
s. 316(1)	297
s. 316(3)	327
s. 316(4)	327
s. 317	297, 327
s. 318	327, 328
s. 318(1)	327
s. 319	328
s. 319(7)	328
s. 320(2)	328
s. 321(2)	332
s. 321(5)	332
s. 325	292
s. 325(1)	296
s. 325(4)	294, 298
s. 326	354
s. 327	292, 293, 295, 296, 298, 354
s. 327(1)	293, 294
s. 327(4)	293
s. 328	298
s. 328 (1)	293, 294
s. 328(8)	293, 294
s. 329	294, 295, 298, 299, 354
s. 331(10)	295
s. 332	299
s. 332(1)	298
s. 332(3)	297
s. 334	299
s. 338(1)	299
s. 338(2)	300
s. 339	299

Financial Services and Markets
Act 2000 – *contd.*

s. 343(8)	300
s. 345	384
s. 347	301
s. 347(6)	302
s. 347(1)	355
s. 348	304
s. 348(2)	302
s. 348(6)	303
s. 349	303
s. 349(1)	303
s. 349(2)	303
s. 349(4)	303
s. 349(5)	303
s. 350(7)	304
s. 351	304
s. 351(1)	304
s. 353	305
s. 354	305
s. 356	316
s. 357	317
s. 358	317
s. 359	324
s. 360	318
s. 362	309, 310
s. 366	320
s. 367	320
s. 371	310
s. 374	310
s. 375	322
s. 375(4)	322
s. 376	322
s. 376(10)	323
s. 379(2)	324
s. 380	351
s. 381	205
s. 382	352
s. 382(7)	352
s. 382(8)	352
s. 383	205, 352
s. 384	331, 353, 354
s. 384(5)	331, 354
s. 386	354

Financial Services and Markets
Act 2000 – *contd.*

s. 389	331
s. 391	332
s. 392	332
s. 393	332, 334
s. 393(4)	350
s. 394	330, 332
s. 394(2)	332
s. 394(3)	333
s. 394(7)	332
s. 395	333
s. 395(2)	333
s. 395(4)	333
s. 395(13)	332
s. 404	313
s. 405	313
s. 407	313
s. 408	314
s. 409	314
s. 414	232
s. 418	227
s. 419(1)	226
s. 420	232
s. 422	230, 249, 252
Schedule 3	218, 237, 238, 241, 320
Schedule 4	237, 241, 320
Schedule 5	241
Schedule 7	281
Schedule 8	281
Schedule 10	286, 287
Schedule 12	274
Schedule 13	371
Schedule 17	361, 362, 363, 367, 368

Friendly and Industrial and
    Provident Societies Act   299
Friendly Societies Act 1992
  s. 50   193

Human Rights Act 1998   270, 351
  s. 6(1)   289, 312, 368

	Art 3	98
	Art 4(1)	98
	Art 4(2)	98
	Art 5	98
	Art 6	99
	Art 9(4)	314
	Art 10(5)	51
	Art 11(3)	100
	Art 12(2)	100
	Art 16	101
	Art 16(7)	102
	Art 18	102, 230
	Art 21(7)	183
89/647/EEC	Solvency Ratio Directive 89/647/EEC OJ L386/14 of 30 December 1989	75, 77, 327
90/619/EEC	Council Directive of 8 November 1990 on the coordination of laws, regulations and administrative provisions relating to direct life assurance, laying down provisions to facilitate the effective exercise of freedom to provide services and amending Directive 79/267/EEC – Article 11	274
92/30/EEC	Second Directive on Supervision of Credit Institutions on the Consolidated Basis	78
93/6/EEC	Council Directive on Capital Adequacy of Investment Firms and Credit Institutions	75, 240
	Art 7(5)	314
	Seventh Company Law Directive 1983 which was extended in 1990 to commercial partnerships, limited partnerships and unlimited companies	243
93/22/EEC	Investment Services Directive	44

Introduction

The supervision and surveillance mechanisms, until recently in operation under the Banking Act 1987 (the '1987 Act'), were transferred to the Financial Services Authority (the 'FSA' or the 'Authority') by the Bank of England Act 1998 (the '1998 Act') on 1 June 1998. Soon after the supervision and surveillance mechanisms were transferred to the Financial Services Authority, a new, comprehensive legislation entitled The Financial Services and Markets Act 2000 (the 'FSMA' or the 'Act') was enacted whereby powers of a comprehensive nature have been conferred on the FSA. They are comprehensive because they encompass all kinds of institutions involved in financial services including insurance companies and Lloyd's.

The Act provides for a single regulator for financial services regulation; it empowers the FSA with the full range of statutory powers and establishes a new institution called the Financial Services and Markets Tribunal (the 'Tribunal'), in addition to establishing the framework for single ombudsman and compensation schemes in order to provide further protection for consumers.

The businesses that are to be authorized and regulated under the Act include:

    Banks

    Building Societies

    Credit Unions

    Derivatives Traders

    Friendly Societies

    Fund Managers

Insurance Companies

Investment and Pensions Advisors

Lloyd's

Professional Firms operating in certain types of investment services

Stockbrokers

The Act makes provisions among other things in respect of the definition of the scope of regulatory activities, the constitution and the scope of powers of the FSA, the recognition of investment exchanges and clearing houses, supervision of financial services provided by members of the professions, marketing and regulation of collective investment schemes, powers to impose penalties for market abuse, the authorization scheme for both European Union and non-European Union institutions and the protection of the interests of consumers and professional firms such as accountants, actuaries and solicitors will be regulated directly by the FSA. The FSA will also have powers to regulate Lloyd's insurance market, in addition to powers of Directors of the Council of Lloyd's.

One of the principal purposes of the Act is to coordinate and modernize financial regulatory arrangements that are operational under various Acts, namely:

(a) the Credit Unions Act 1979;

(b) the Insurance Companies Act 1982;

(c) the Financial Services Act 1986;

(d) the Building Societies Act 1987; and

(e) the Friendly Societies Act 1992.

The intention of the Act of 2000 is for business in the financial market to be operated by one principal actor; therefore certain enactments will be repealed or substantially repealed, including the Policy-Holders Protection Act 1975-1997, the Industrial Assurance Act 1923-1948 and the Insurance Brokers (Registration) Act 1977. The Act also provides for the transfer of the remaining functions of mutual societies, building societies' commissions, friendly societies' commission and the registering of the friendly societies. With the coming into force of this Act the responsibility of various bodies will no longer be relevant, the Securities and Investments Board (which is now very much the FSA), the Self-regulatory Organizations, the former supervisory and surveillance powers of the Bank of England, the Building Societies Commission, the Insurance Directorate of the Treasury, the Friendly Societies Commission and the Registry of Friendly Societies. The FSA will, however, work closely with the Treasury in respect of various matters that are explained in this work.

In July 1998 the Treasury published a paper entitled *Financial Services and Markets Bill* (the 'Bill'), the consultation document which explained the future policy for controlling and regulating the institutions in the financial markets. The Treasury also published a number of relevant consultation papers and invited comments from a large number of firms and bodies interested in the regulation of the financial bodies that represent the investors. It is a legislation that attempts to strike a balance between the supervisory and regulated activities of the FSA and the protection of consumers and investors. The Bill received the Royal Assent on 14 June 2000.

The Act contains 30 Parts and will be passing through what may be described as an evolutionary process; indeed, both the FSA and the Treasury are required to develop regulations and procedures in due course in order to implement the provisions of this Act.

The reader is reminded of the fact that since the submission of this work for publication, the FSA has published a number of documents which obviously could not be referred to.

1 Legal Aspects of the Growth and Development of the Business of Banking until the 19th Century

Introduction

The reasons that led to the foundation of the Bank of England (the Bank) in 1694 were primarily wars and various financial crises, including the issue of national debts, the need for the government to raise monies to fund those wars, and the fact that the Goldsmiths' banking system distrusted the King and the Government, a result of Charles II's appropriation of the assets of the London Goldsmiths.

Between 1694 and 1734 the Bank obtained monopoly over financial matters in which the Government was involved, foreign trade and exchange issues. In 1720 the Bank overcame its first crisis when its credits were almost wiped out by the South Sea Bubble.

The Bank gradually became involved in the issues of national debt and restructuring of the national economy, a discounter and lender of last resort. In 1844 the Bank was formally given powers to make and issue banknotes, and after that it began to assume the character of a central bank in a recognizably modern form.

The Early History of Monetary Transactions in England

Although the method of assigning debts by bills of exchange was known in England in the 14th century, the practice was used only by foreign merchants. English participation in banking transactions did not develop until the late Tudor and early Stuart period. There were two main reasons for this: firstly, the expansion of trade during the reigns of Elizabeth I and James I, and secondly the change of public opinion with regard to the ethics of usury. As the result of the latter, the provisions of the Act of 1545 (37 Hy. VIII, c 9)[1] allowed the taking of interest up to 10 per cent and increased the transactions of 'money-master' and 'money-lender'. Although the Act was repealed in 1552, the Elizabethan Act of 1571 (13 Eliz. c.8)[2] revived the maximum interest rate of 10 per cent. Another factor that probably contributed to increasing activity by financial intermediaries was the dissolution of the monasteries by Henry VIII, representing a loss of their lending facilities to farmers who used to borrow money from monasteries on the security of future supplies of goods. Thus, the late Tudor and Stuart periods saw the emergence of *'the pioneers of the banker's trade in England'* – *'the merchant, the broker, the scrivener and the goldsmith'*[3]. It is clear, therefore, that the money-lending trade was institutionalized in the form of brokers, scriveners and goldsmiths. Furthermore, lending was based on guarantees which primarily took the form of promissory notes.

During this period the money market was primarily dominated by private lenders. Logically speaking, however, there were certain instruments that are now in vogue in the money market, but which could not be created without formal authority of the government, such as legal tenders and treasury bills.

The concept of 'Exchange' between units of money and goods was developed, especially between goldsmiths and pawnbrokers assisted by brokers. In order to formalize borrowing and lending, exchange of notes was devised by money lenders as early as the 14th century[4]. This also helped in devising the means of assigning mercantile debts. Bilateral trade between England and foreign traders became a common factor during the reigns of Elizabeth I and James I, in consequence of which English businessmen attained recognition as money changers, money lenders, exchange specialists and financial middlemen[5].

---

[1] R D Richards, op.cit., p.19.
[2] R D Richards, op.cit., p.20.
[3] R D Richards, op.cit., p.2.
[4] In the reign of Edward IV, for example, by the merchants of the Staple; see further R D Richards, op.cit., p.2.
[5] R D Richards, ibid.

Although the concept of a bank as such, did not exist in England at that time, international transactions were performed by money lenders and specialists in exchange, which took the form of exchange of documents or otherwise. The system of offering guarantees by English traders, particularly with Italian traders, was developed during the second half of the 16th century. Historically, it was the Italians and the Dutch who could be regarded as forerunners of the early banking system, but interestingly enough the City of London drew the attention of most of the foreign traders even during the 16th century. It is correct to maintain that the principle of trust in money transactions originated in this period, otherwise the governments, who carried out the transactions, would not have had any credibility.

The transactions carried out by the Martins, Hoares and other goldsmiths of the Elizabethan and Jacobean period clearly suggest that Tudor goldsmiths were important bullion merchants[6], and considerations for loans, which in the contemporary financial markets are known as guarantees and securities, were primarily offered in metals. It could, therefore, be said that metals played an important role in forming the future markets, and metal was accepted as an important element for lending and borrowing because the supply of metal was in abundance at that time. By the Tudor period, metallic[7] coins became an important element in international transactions, and the medium of exchange. Richards maintains that in the last decade of the Tudor period the English Exchange merchants used to transfer coins and bullion from England to France, and from the countries on the European Continent to England. Furthermore, according to Wilson's work, the merchants thus set the price of the currency, making it either high or low, for their own personal gain[8].

It was during this period that the term 'value of money' based on the intrinsic value of the coin was devised, and international transactions were facilitated by units of money rather than by reference to other means of exchange such as gold and silver.

---

[6] E.g. Sir Richard Martin's transactions, P.R.O., Ex. Accs. V., E. 101, Bdles. 296/4, 304/12; and those of Sir Martin Bowes, ibid., Bdles. 302/24 and 27, 303/5, 7 and 8, see further R D Richards, op.cit., p.8.

[7] R D Richards, op.cit., pp.8-9.

[8] *Discourse uppon Usurye*, see further R D Richards, op.cit., p.8.

By the 17th century, if not earlier, the recording system of monetary transactions became a common practice. This facilitated the financial activities of London merchants from the reign of James I onwards. Although 16th-century England made remarkable progress in developing money markets and means of transaction, abuse of the system was also prevalent. Unofficial brokers, local and foreign alike, became players on the market, and the statute of 1697[9] entitled 'An Act to restrain the Number and Ill Practice of Brokers and Stock Jobbers', was passed to deal with unwarranted broking and stock-jobbing. It could be argued, therefore, that by the 17th century there was a demand for setting up regulatory bodies to control malpractice by brokers and stock-jobbers.

By the 17th century scriveners, also known as money scriveners, became active money lenders and custodians of deposits. Indeed, in the Act of 1713 (12 Anne Stat 2, c.16, s.2)[10] scriveners appeared first in the list of financial middlemen. Thus, deposit-taking became prevalent in the 16th century, culminating in an institutionalized form by the 18th century, although no system of what is now known as Investor Protection was available at that time.

The activities on the money markets of the 16th century had a great impact on the future capital market in England. Not only was the concept of interest devised by the 1545 Act (37 Hy. VIII, c.9)[11] but the setting up of joint stock companies also commenced during the 16th century. The concept of shares and dividends originated during this period too, in particular in connection with the Tudor money enterprises. It was again during the 16th century that an identifiable accounting system was developed in England[12].

By the late 17th Century the Goldsmiths were in dispute with each other and the trading community had argued for the need for public institutions. The struggle between the goldsmiths and the idea of institutionalization was finally settled in 1694 when the Bank of England (the 'Bank') was set up[13]. But, it must be pointed out that the Bank was

[9] 8 & 9 Wm. III, c.32, see further R D Richards, op.cit., p.14.
[10] R D Richards, op.cit., p.17.
[11] R D Richards, op.cit., p.19, footnote 5.
[12] *The Brief Instruction and maner how to keep bookes of Accompts after the order of Debitor and Creditor*, see further R D Richards, op.cit., p.21.
[13] The Bank was set up under the authority of The Tunnage Act 1694, now known as The Bank of England Act 1694.

established initially not for the primary purpose of carrying out what may now be regarded traditional banking, but primarily for dealing with a national debt, which was occasioned by the war waged by William III[14]. Since the war, governments had run deeply into difficulties to such an extent that even payment of interest on monies borrowed from goldsmiths could not made. This required the Bank to reflect on the adverse monetary implications for the economy if borrowing and lendings were not carried out prudentially.

During the initial period the Bank struggled through various financial problems, predominantly occasioned by national crises including wars, and the Bank was not allowed to borrow above its original capital of £1,500,000 except with special parliamentary authority[15]. This indicates that even in its early days the constitutional principle of ministerial responsibility was extended to deal with matters relating to the Bank.

The 1697 Banking Act, which was the second banking act, augmented the Bank's original capital and gave the institution a monopoly of banking. By the latter part of the 17th century, it became clear to the government that financial matters of a fundamental nature such as raising of capital, national borrowings and issues of foreign exchange, should be allowed to be dealt with by an expert national institution.

It was in 1694 that the Charter of the Bank established the Corporation of the Governor and company of directors of the Bank which was run by elected governors, directors and cashiers. It soon became evident that the use of paper money would be inevitable, not only to avoid the excessive use of metals, but also for ease of transactions. Again, it was in 1694 that the Bank's methods of conducting the business of its customers were consolidated by referring to notes payable to bearer to be endorsed[16], and running cash notes had to be signed and countersigned by two of the cashiers.

The Bank's rapport with other banks was a close one: its tellers presented to the goldsmiths notes that were accepted by the Bank, and the ledgers of Child and Hoare showed that these banks frequently discounted the Bank's sealed bills and promissory notes.

---

[14] John Giuseppi, *The Bank of England*, London, Evans Brothers Limited, 1966, pp.10-11.
[15] R D Richards, op.cit., pp.145-147.
[16] R D Richards, op.cit., p.153.

Since its early days the Bank has been conscious of developing an appropriate administration whereby its external operations run smoothly and, at the same time, it retains the power to supervise other banks. This may be regarded as the beginning of what is now known as the surveillance system in its rudimentary form.

The Bank suffered a setback when, in 1696, a rival bank was established by the Land Act in an attempt to wind up the Bank. The subscription books were opened at Exeter Exchange but the scheme, however, was exposed when the promoters and subscribers failed to pay their contributions to any significant degree. Soon thereafter, the Land Bank became unpopular because the government lent unnecessary support to it, particularly at a time when its performance was unremarkable. In fact, the depositors were anxious for the security of their funds. The government learnt from the fiasco of the Land Bank that credit was a vital asset and that money could not be obtained as a deposit unless the depositors had confidence in the Bank[17].

In 1696 the House of Commons resolved that during the continuance of the Bank, no other bank would be established by Act of Parliament, and indeed the Royal Assent to this proposal was received on 1 April of that year. This raised the price of Bank stock. By 1697 the Bank saw considerable increase in the number of commercial transactions, and discounting of inland and foreign bills. The Bank once again realized that what was most needed for the commercial world was the confidence that the public placed in the Bank[18].

The period between 1695 and 1734, which is known as the 'Grocers' Hall' period, did not see much development from a legal standpoint, but it was during this period that the South Sea Bubble disaster took place, disturbing financial markets, and putting the Bank's reputation in jeopardy again. The South Sea Company appeared to be a challenger to the Bank's standing; this, however, was unacceptable because then the market would be governed again by a private company. Although the South Sea Company existed for well over a century, its constant rivalry with the Bank ultimately culminated in the Bank's regaining its position, primarily due to the fact that by the 18th century the London Money Market had developed a degree of confidence in the functioning

---

[17] John Giuseppi, op.cit., pp.28-32.
[18] John Giuseppi, op.cit., pp.28-32.

of the central institution – the Bank of England[19].

The Evolution of the Bank of England: 1735 -1801

During Walpole's term of office the relationship between the Bank and the government was congenial and smooth. This type of relationship was necessary for recognition of the Bank as an institution which would have the support of the government to deal with its monetary and financial issues, including the issue of reducing the national debt.

After the end of the Seven Years War in 1764 there followed frantic market activity, especially in the stock of the East India Company. This coincided with the heyday of colonialism. The positive aspect of the market activity was that by the mid-18th century, the Bank became recognized as a trusted and trustworthy institution, and many traders, fearing that cash would not be secure in private hands, transferred it to the Bank. Furthermore, having overcome intermittent difficulties, the Bank managed to consolidate its position as a government representative for financial matters and as a centre for dealing with financial issues relating to international trade[20].

Between 1688 and 1815 England was involved in a number of wars and rebellions, and ironically the demands of the wars proved to be an important factor for defining the terms of reference and the forms of banking activity in which the Bank would be involved. The issue of national debt was a disturbing one, and an institution with public authority was needed to deal with that issue[21]. It fell on the Bank to promote economic stability and make the British economy healthy; thus the Bank was brought into the arena of commercial activities. The Bank was required to act in emergencies, as a discounter of bills and lender of last resort, and thus consequentially attracted a degree of trust in the mind of business community[22].

In 1710 the Bank became the receiver of public money for the state lottery, and in 1715 it became involved in the management of the

---

[19] John Giuseppi, op.cit., pp.33-49.
[20] John Giuseppi, op.cit., pp.50-67.
[21] Edited by Richard Roberts and David Kynaston, *The Bank of England - Money, Power and Influence 1694-1994*, Oxford, Clarendon Press (1995) p.5.
[22] Richard Roberts and David Kynaston (ed.), ibid., p.5.

government debt by acting as both receiver and manager of the subscriptions to the annuity issue; indeed, from then the Bank acted as the manager of government annuities and stocks on a regular basis, maintained the ledgers, supervised transfers, paid out interest and performed specialist tasks in a significant way so that by the 1760s, the Bank managed around 70% of the national debt[23].

Despite the Bank's development no universal recognition within the country was accorded to the Bank during the 18th century; this was perhaps because the activities of private banks, principally, those of goldsmiths and brokers, had made an indelible mark in the minds of the business community. This lack of universal recognition of the Bank seems to have had a profound effect on the acceptance of it as a national institution with the authority to regulate the money market. On the other hand, it was the public sector that became convinced that intervention, by a bank like the Bank, would be essential for developing international trade progressively and for handling national debt and restructuring the economy. Roberts and Kynaston observed that during the 18th century the Bank's future was never assured[24]. Opposition against the Bank also became evident, particularly from the monied companies in the City, on the ground that the Bank was exerting undue influence in high political circles[25]. The opposition was voiced by the private sector for two primary reasons, (i) by the 18th century, particularly around 1781, the private money sector realized that the Bank was gaining ground and that they would lose the business that they had traditionally held for a long time, and (ii) a public bank would obviously have more power in dealing with national financial affairs. The opposition presented by the private merchants was not insignificant in nature, and during the 1790s, when England was involved in the war against France, the question was again raised whether the charter of the Bank should be renewed.

Although the Bank went through public criticisms, ironically perhaps

---

[23] Clapham, *Bank*, I, 102, see further Richard Roberts and David Kynaston (ed.), op. cit., pp.17-21

[24] Richard Roberts and David Kynaston ed., ibid., p.5.

[25] For the Whig and Tory opposition towards the Bank and other City institutions during the first half of the 18th century, see H. T. Dickinson, *Liberty and Property: Political Ideology in Eighteenth-Century Britain* (1977), pp.170-2, 182. For later hostility towards the City institutions see H. V. Bowen, *The Pests of Human Society: Stockbrokers, Jobbers, and Speculators in Mid-Eighteenth Century Britain*, History, 78 (1993), pp.38-53, see further Richard Roberts and David Kynaston, op.cit., p.7.

because it wished to protect the interests of the private sector, the fact remains that the charter of the Bank was renewed every time the renewal was due. By the 18th century the supporters of the Bank sought legislation to remove any doubts as to the Bank's status and the privileges it should enjoy. The country's involvement in various wars necessitated a virtually permanent existence of the Bank. By 1749 the country's debt rose significantly, and in 1781 the Bank's capital had to be increased by making calls upon stockholders in order to bring the stock in line with the government's debt[26].

By the late 18th century, the Bank had become heavily involved in offering long-term credit facilities to the government, and the scope of the government's related business undertaken by the Bank steadily increased because by this time the Bank was clearly able to establish its superiority over the private financial market, particularly when the government needed financial help for the armed forces and other requirements. Effectively, in the final quarter of the 18th century there took place an administrative shift from the Exchequer to the Bank, mainly because the Exchequer lacked expertise in dealing with complex issues of public money. It is to be pointed out that such expertise or acumen in money was not available in the private financial sector.

By the late 18th century, the Bank virtually enjoyed a quasi-monopoly over short-term lending to the government[27]. It was the only public institution that would be prepared to serve the government in times of need, even at little profit, which would be contrary to the practice of the commercial world.

By the 18th century, the Bank seemed to have been involved in most aspects of public finance; it provided credit and deposit for individual government departments beyond the Exchequer, extended loans to the forces and directly managed government departments' accounts and balances. By the 1780s many accounts of government departments were transferred to the safekeeping of the Bank as part of the economic measures of the government[28].

[26] Richard Roberts and David Kynaston (ed.), op.cit., pp.8-9.
[27] Dickson, *Financial Revolution,* 360, see further Richard Roberts and David Kynaston (ed.), op.cit., p.10.
[28] John Ehrman, *The Younger Pitt: The Years of Acclaim,* (1969), pp.90, 302; Binney, *British Public Finance,* pp.145-9, 156, 207, 275. Also, Clapham, *Bank,* ii, pp.46-7, see further Richard Roberts and David Kynaston (ed.), op.cit., p.11.

The 18th century must be regarded as a very constructive century for the Bank of England because, despite the turmoils it went through, this period proved to be a period of consolidation for the Bank. Metaphorically speaking, private opposition surrendered: indeed the private sector is not supposed to be involved in public money which might or might not offer them sufficient profits. Service to the country must be rendered by a public body. That message was clearly stated to the House of Commons by the supporters of the Bank every time the Bank's charter was required to be renewed. The Bank was now regarded as a public bank.

Although the relationship between the state and the Bank had consolidated significantly by that time, the state did not directly underwrite any of the Bank's own note issues or credit obligations. In this regard, the Bank and the government were separable and separate entities. During this period the Bank would not have wished to be involved in transactions in which private individual interest remained paramount; assistance to individuals, primarily, took the form of discounting of notes and bills, but its activities also extended to include commercial houses in the form of extending loans[29]. Even at this time, the directors of the Bank were quite cautious to ensure that bad loans did not jeopardize the Bank's position, and perhaps the money market in general. One of the issues that troubled the private sector during the 17th and 18th centuries was whether the Bank should be allowed to issue paper money and be a place of safe deposit for the public money. An ardent supporter of the Bank being the issuer of notes was Sir Francis Baring, and he advocated that the responsibility for issuing public money must be entrusted to the public body that would work in the interests of the public and remain accountable to the public.

The private financial sector opposed the idea of the Bank being the issuer of paper money because they would lose their importance in the market, and power would shift from the private financial sector to the public financial sector. However, as from 1709 the Bank was granted a near-monopoly of note issue by virtue of a statute (7 Anne, c 7), distinguishing it from its continental counterparts, which predominantly acted as deposit and exchange banks. By the 18th century the Bank

---

[29] Richards, *First Fifty Years*, 253-4, see further Richard Roberts and David Kynaston, op.cit., p.15.

acted as a clearing house for government paper money, issued its own notes, offered credit facilities and thus established a good rapport with the government. The Bank accumulated significant deposits and thus was in a position to put a considerable volume of notes in circulation. The sound financial position of the Bank was reflected in the private stock and in the annual dividend payment to its stockholders[30].

The Bank's contribution to the private sector cannot however be disregarded, particularly its assistance to the East India Company, the Hudson's Bay Company and the South Sea Company, and its promotion of British business, both in domestic and non-domestic arenas. The progress made by the East India Company, in particular, in the British colonies, was very much due to the financial support that the Bank of England provided it[31].

By the 18th century the Bank had a wealth of knowledge in both the private and public sector which proved to be its strength when compared with the private sector. An example of the Bank's prudence came in 1772 with the Bank refusing to assist the ailing and overextended Ayr Bank, other than on the harshest possible terms in consequence of which the bank eventually collapsed[32]. From a legal standpoint it can, therefore, be maintained that the idea of maintaining a dependable and responsible money market came about in the 18th century under the leadership of the Bank of England.

The Evolution of the Bank of England in the 19th century – Transition to a National Bank

The mix of the Bank's public and private roles represented an important aspect of the Bank's status in the country. Perhaps it is this mix of personality that still distinguishes the Bank of England from any other central bank in the world. The Bank, even in the 19th century, was not under government pressure to do anything, nor is it now.

---

[30] W A Speck, *Conflict in Society*, in Geoffrey Holmes (ed.), *Britain after the Glorious Revolution 1698-1714* (1969), p.143, see further Richard Roberts and David Kynaston (ed.), op.cit., p.14.

[31] K N Chaudhuri, *The Trading World of Asia and the English East India Company 1660-1760*, (Cambridge, 1978), p.439, see further Richard Roberts and David Kynaston (ed)., op.cit., p.15.

[32] see further Richard Roberts and David Kynaston (ed.), op.cit., p.16.

In summary, the Bank managed to overcome the difficulties presented by the state and the private financial market, and it is to be appreciated that it volunteered to deal with the most difficult issues of the national debt which were primarily occasioned by wars, and gradually progressed into other functions such as issuance of notes, discounting of bills and consolidating its position both inside and outside the country. During the 19th century the question of developing any form of regulations to control the money market did not arise. Historically, this was the period primarily concerned with the formation and development of the Bank. But it is remarkable that even in the early days of the 17th century the Bank realized what kind of functions it would be required to perform to protect the interests of both the state and the private sector.

This, however, put the Bank's status into a difficult situation – how to split the mix. The government became more and more dependant on the Bank, particularly for borrowing and settling national debts, and for controlling the money supply in order to ensure that the foreign trade of the country was not adversely affected. On the other hand, the state continued to exert considerable controlling influence over the way in which the Bank should function. In the private sector, the Bank by then had already been established as a formidable private joint stock organization, which could not be rivalled by any private financial institution in the City of London.

The Bank sought a free hand to determine monetary policy, whereas the directors denied that the Bank had any responsibility for the regulation of the state's financial affairs. Irrespective of the controversy as to the real status of the Bank, by the 19th century the Bank had become a *de facto* guardian of the gold standard, which standard was internationally recognized when the International Monetary Fund was set up. By the 19th century it became clear that the remit of the Bank's function could not be as limited as it is was in 1694.

Eventually, it was decided that the most satisfactory solution would be to authorize the Bank to act as supervisor for the private sector because in a democratic financial market the participation of the private sector cannot be denied and the most responsible way to maintain a private sector would be to accord to a national institution the power to supervise it.

Conclusions

It is clear, therefore, that by the early 19th century the Bank assumed two identities: as banker to the state and regulator of commercial monetary activities; the latter activities, however, were not clearly spelt out at that time. It also became clear that the state showed the need for an institution that would have supervisory power over banking activities, and thus should be accorded a special status as a national bank.

The Bank's current activities became clearly identifiable with the enactment of banking legislation, particularly during the 20th century. So far an attempt has been made to identify the nature of the conflicting ideas and policies that the Bank went through. Until the 20th century the Bank seems to have been developed in a piecemeal basis. The recognition of the Bank as the nation's bank by the state was steady but slow, particularly because of the interventions made by the private sector.

2 The Bank of England vis-à-vis the British Economy and the Government

Introduction

By the 19th century, the Bank was established as a financial agent of the government. But on the other hand, the Bank assumed the responsibility for controlling the money market, which had a profound impact on the economy. The situation was in fact cyclical because the economy governs the money market or vice versa, but whichever may be the case it became manifest that a controlling body was necessary.

The Bank of England, the British Economy and the Government

The Period between 1800 and 1914

By the 19th century the Bank had virtually become the central banker and its functions included the establishment of a sound currency, issuance of paper notes, the maintenance of the convertibility of the currency into gold, the safeguarding of the financial structure, and the development of investments and techniques of control, however rudimentary in form at that time.

Interestingly enough, the Bank remained a privately-owned joint stock bank with obligations to its stockholders. The Bank has always been required to perform its functions in a dual capacity.

By the 18th century England had become an established colonial power and the City of London an established financial market. The English merchants' involvement in international trade and the Bank's role as a settler of national debts required the establishment of a sound currency. This need for a sound currency was also felt by the fact that during the 19th century, and in particular prior to 1825, a number of banks collapsed, leaving adverse marks on the economy.

The Bank entered into agreements with private banks whereby they discontinued the issue of their notes and used the Bank's notes; they also received notes free of interest; the bills were deposited as security, payable in London and credited as they fell due to the account of private banks with the Bank of England [1]. The private banks were freed from the need to hold gold against their notes and their position was secured because they could obtain additional credit at attractive rates. Eventually, by the middle of the 19th century, provincial banks' notes had been replaced by Bank of England notes.

The Bank had the *de jure* authority to issue banknotes to the exclusion of all others. The 1844 Act aimed to regulate the stock of money almost automatically, by linking issuing of notes to the gold holdings of the Issue Department of the Bank of England. However regulation of money and credit without any reference to domestic needs proved to be the cause of crises which took place in 1847, 1857 and 1866, in consequence of which, the Act was suspended on each occasion. By the middle of the 19th century, the London Capital Market had attained prominence in the world, and after the 1844 Act the Bank concentrated entirely on its London business, emphasizing the functions of the banking department, implying that the Bank had a role to play in commercial banking. The Bank advised all commercial banks to keep their portfolios liquid so that re-discounting would not be necessary. By 1900 the circulation of provincial bank notes fell to a minimum [2].

It became clear to the Bank that it had the responsibility to preserve the convertibility of the currency into gold. The Bank's decision to maintain the gold standard and a fixed rate of exchange proved to be a cause of concern. The Bank of England took action against these

---

[1] Richard Roberts and David Kynaston (eds)., op.cit., p.57.
[2] R S Sayers, *The Bank of England, 1891-1944*, Cambridge, Cambridge University Press (1976), pp.i & 9; see further Richard Roberts and David Kynaston (eds.), op.cit., p.58.

eventualities by raising the bank rate and making it effective. This helped to reduce the outflow of funds or to draw funds from other financial centres. Thus, the high bank rates had a powerful impact on the movement of funds and could cause some liquidation of stocks, thus producing an improvement in the balance of trade. It realized that one of the means of avoiding market disruption would be to collaborate with other central banks in this regard, a forerunner of the principle of collaboration between the central banks of the important economies.

The years preceding World War I witnessed a very remarkable surge in sterling, and this became evident in a substantial balance of payments surplus for a long time, adding to its financial power. However, the inadequacy of the Bank's gold stock and the need for frequent changes in the bank rate provided to be a cause of concern for the commercial banks immediately preceding World War I. One of the primary concerns of the Bank was to ensure that all commercial banks had sufficient capital adequacy and thus it effectively took on a supervisory function in so far as the protection of depositors was concerned. The Bank Charter of 1844 provided for a separation of the Issue Department from the Banking Department in order to encourage the idea that the note issue and the banking issue were separate ones. The Banking Department was considered free to engage in ordinary commercial banking, still not the prime interest of the Bank, in addition to its meeting the needs of the government. But the Bank was cautious enough not to be in direct competition with private and joint stock banks for commercial business, but rather to act as a lender of last resort. The bank failures in the 1880s and 1890s prompted the commercial banks to appreciate the need for a sound banking system to ensure their survival, which entailed the availability of a lender of last resort. During this time the Bank experienced a series of problems emanating from the growing size of the joint stock banks, some of which were bigger than the Bank. Secondly, it faced the difficulty of making the bank rate effective when market rates fell to unusually low levels. In an attempt to maintain its income during the mid-1890s the bank rate was kept unchanged for 2.5 years. Thus, it was able to cut its dividend and draw on hidden reserves. The Bank also paid considerable attention to its lending policies whereby default in servicing the loans would not take place.

Although the Bank was passing through a relatively unsettled financial environment its contribution to the economy in the 19th century was mainly to help to create an economic climate whereby stability in the market could be achieved and the investors would develop confidence by ensuring that sterling was sound and stable both in terms of its internal and external value.

The Period between 1918 and 1945

After World War I, the Bank despite its separate identity found itself increasingly closer to the Treasury; this was primarily due to (a) the need to manage debts, and (b) the link between debt management and the monetary policy.

As government borrowing increased, the government's influence on interest rates also increased. After World War I, the greater weight of debt and its increasing financial needs made the government realize that the issue of debt management and the monetary policy, particularly in relation to borrowing, were interlinked. It was also recognized that by varying the average maturity of outstanding government debts or by replacing debt of one structure by the debt of another maturity, it was possible to influence the structure and even have a limited effect on the level of interest rates.

The interwar years were concerned with the four principal issues, namely the shape that domestic monetary policy should take, how to manage debts, whether to return to the gold standard and the need for industrial reconstruction. It is worth pointing out that the 1930s depression enforced a new type of relationship between the Treasury and the Bank [3], the Treasury exercising the dominant influence, whereas the Bank acted as its agent in the foreign exchange market as well as in the management of debts. The Bank carved out its banking operations but the Treasury took responsibility for the policy. The Governor of the Bank was required to act as a guardian for reconstruction of British industry, contributing to reduced employment. The Bank gradually

---

[3] For details of these issues, see D E Moggridge, *British Monetary Policy, 1924-1932*, Cambridge, Cambridge University Press (1972), pp.27-28; Steven Tolliday, *Business, Banking and Politics: The Case of British Steel, 1918-1939*, (Cambridge, Mass., 1987), p.197; Edwin Green and Michael Moss, *A Business of National Importance: The Royal Mail Shipping Group, (1902-1937)* (1982), pp.118-19; see further Richard Roberts and David Kynaston (eds.), op. cit., pp.64-67.

became involved in the reorganization of the Lancashire cotton industry and other industries, including shipbuilding. It was through the prudence of the Bank that three new bodies were brought into existence, namely the Securities Management Trust of 1929, the Bankers' Industrial Development Company in March 1930[4] and the Special Areas Reconstruction Association Limited a forerunner of the ICFC (Industrial and Commercial Finance Corporation). The Bank, therefore, was the initiator in reshaping banking institutions to the needs of industrial reconstruction and developed policies as to how to raise capital to meet those needs.

Involvement in this type of work on the part of the Bank proved to be so useful for future years that the Bank now claimed to be a reservoir of information and expertise, not only in respect of banking matters but also matters of economy, foreign exchange and international trade. Later statutes, directly or indirectly, provided for the Bank's authority in giving, at least, advisory guidance to both government and industry.

The Post-1945 Years

With the end of World War II, the Bank was determined to establish its new organizational structure and to see itself as a promoter of the economy. Indeed, as from 1945 the Bank's relations with the economy were significantly those of a central bank under government control[5], the first time that the Bank's relationship with the government was clearly established. Its aims were subordinated to those of the government and its policies had to conform to the views of the government, developing a kind of partnership which is still prevalent, and often reflected in statutes, and when harmonious action by the Bank and the government is required to be taken.

The monetary policy of the country is the issue that cannot be dominated either by the Treasury or the Bank. The Bank advises the government as to adverse effects of high bank rates or high borrowing and thus restrains the government from developing a policy the implementation of which would adversely affect the economy and put the Bank's position in jeopardy[6].

---

[4] Richard Roberts and David Kynaston (eds.), op.cit., pp.67-68.
[5] Richard Roberts and David Kynaston (eds.), op.cit., p.69.
[6] John Fforde, *The Bank of England and Public Policy*, 1941-1958 (Cambridge, 1992), pp.37-48, see further Richard Roberts and David Kynaston (eds.), op.cit., p.71.

There was a noticeable conflict throughout the 1950s between the Treasury and the Bank on the issue of whether the country should have adopted a flexible monetary policy whereby no rigid restrictions should be imposed on bank credit. The Bank advocated a strict monetary policy including the tightening up of bank advances [7].

The 1960s were concerned with the issue of limiting inflation, with economic growth and resolution of the balance of payments difficulties. Action was taken in regard to exchange contracts and the Bank played a subsidiary and complementary part alongside the Treasury in the construction of an international system of currency swaps. The Bank made clear to the government the adverse effects of the Bank's exercise of excessive control over other banks, and the Bank devised a new policy whereby expansion in bank credit and deposits would take place. At the same time, the Bank paid attention to the issue of devising a reliable indicator of inflationary pressure so as to be able to take precautionary measures. The Bank was involved in preparing money targets for the purpose of devising a suitable financial policy which could be managed without much interruption by the government. During the 1960s the Eurodollar market grew and sterling deposits increased alongside overseas investments. The Bank was thus constrained to pay attention to the issue of liquidity, removal of exchange controls and organization of a sound and reliable market.

By the 1970s the Bank began removing credit controls; by the end of 1973 the Bank reintroduced control in the form of the 'corset' (the supplementary special deposits scheme), although it was short-lived.

Since its inception in the 17th century, the Bank has never been designated a central bank for the country, and the Treasury has always been involved in the Bank's activities in some way or other. The constructive elements that came out from the interactions between the Treasury and the Bank were that a proper monetary policy must be developed by experts, and at the same time it must not be totally contrary to the aims of the government.

On the international scene, the Bank had already attained a formidable position by the end of World War II. Through its involvement in British industry and by developing a dynamic economic policy, the Bank was

---

[7] For detailed discussion of the issues discussed by the Radcliffe Committee see John Fforde, *The Bank of England and Public Policy 1941-1958*, Cambridge, Cambridge University Press (1992)

able to attract foreign investment, so much so that by the 1960s the London Market became known as the Eurodollar market. This advance necessitated the Bank in developing a sophisticated stock exchange and, at the same time, a mechanism whereby it could be properly regulated, giving security to the depositors.

The Bank was also involved in foreign exchange issues, commodities and equity markets. At the beginning of World War I, the government decided not to suspend the convertibility of sterling with a view to safeguarding the standing of London as an international financial centre. During the postwar era, development in foreign exchange became an important issue because the City market was extremely active. London became the great market for international money[8], regulated by the Foreign Exchange Brokers Association, which adopted a code of conduct in consultation with the Bank.

The London Commodity Market became an important part of the City's activities.

Following the end of World War II, it was on the advice of the Bank that various commodities associations were set up in the City to give protection to the traders and to ensure that the market was not unduly disrupted in the absence of regulatory bodies.

In the 1950s development in the equity market became a cause of concern both to the Bank and the government. The issue of take-overs and mergers often plagued the money market and the Bank again intervened by establishing in 1968 a system of compliance through the Panel on Take-overs and Mergers. The City Code and the Panel still remain an important instrument for controlling acquisitions and mergers.

Conclusion

This Chapter briefly explains the growth and development of the relationship between the Bank and the government. Initially uncertain, a true partnership developed; the Bank primarily operates as advisor to the government and regulator of money market including banks and

---

[8] B M Anderson, Three and a Half Billion Dollar Floating Debt of Europe to Private Creditors in America, *The Chase Economic Bulletin*, 1 (October, 1920), pp.9-10; see further Richard Roberts and David Kynaston (ed.), op.cit., p.171.

other financial services. But, it has always directed its efforts to maintaining the market and developing confidence in the minds of investors and depositors.

Until the enactment of the Bank of England Act 1998 [9], which has transferred responsibility for banking supervision from the Bank to the Financial Services Authority, the Bank considered itself, predominantly, as a coordinator and regulator of financial services.

In the following chapters an attempt is made to examine and analyse the various statutes in accordance with which the Bank has been required to control and regulate the financial market in the UK so as to perform two broad functions: attracting investors and securing confidence in the minds of investors and depositors alike. Chapters 1 and 2 of this work have simply attempted to identify the circumstances that led to the enactment of the future legislation.

---

[9] The Act came into force on 1 June 1998.

3   An Analysis of the Statutory Provisions Governing the Business of Banking

Introduction

Having discussed the growth and development of the Bank of England as a banking institution, it is appropriate now to examine and analyse the statutes relating to the banking business, and to demonstrate how the Bank of England was empowered to implement provisions, as and when necessary, for the regulation of the Capital Market and the protection of depositors and investors.

PART I
Early Banking Legislation including the Banking Act 1979

Bank of England Act 1694

As it has been stated earlier, the Bank of England was officially set up by the Banking Act 1694 as a joint stock company. The company was endowed with perpetual succession and a common seal, and it was prohibited from trading although allowed to deal in bills of exchange and to buy and sell bullion, gold and silver. The 1694 Act did not confer any exclusive privileges on the Bank of England; the first direct privilege of exclusive banking was conferred by the Banking Act 1696.

The development of the Bank of England seems to have taken place on a piecemeal basis, primarily because of the hesitancy of the contemporary commercial world and the governments as to what purpose the Bank should serve. The preamble to the 1694 Act is interesting because it precisely identifies the purpose for which this act was enacted:

> *An Act for granting to theire Majesties severall Rates and Duties upon Tunnage of Shipps and Vessells and upon Beere Ale and other liquors for securing certaine Recompenses and Advantages in the said Act mentioned to such Persons as shall voluntarily advance the sume of Fifteene hundred thousand pounds towards the carrying on the War against France.*

It is clear from this preamble that enactment of this legislation was inevitable in view of the war against France. As stated earlier, the government also found it preferable to deal with foreign debts through recognized institutions rather than leaving it to private commercial bankers.

The 1694 Act did not authorize the Bank of England to trade, primarily for the reason that in so doing, not only would the government have antagonized the contemporary private merchants in the country, but also it did not consider the Bank to be an institution that should engage in profit-making based on private trading.

Bank of England Act 1716

This Act primarily gave the Bank of England power to borrow monies at such rates of interest and terms as the Governor and the Company deemed fit without the obligation to pay interest in exchange for security to the satisfaction of the lenders. This was an Act of necessity in that the government, in the early 18th century, was in need of funds for meeting the unforeseen expenses occasioned by wars and national debts. From a legal standpoint, by this Act the government authorized the Bank to borrow on behalf of the government, a clear indication of what the government wanted of the Bank. The intention is clear that both borrowing and lending by or on behalf of the government must be carried out through an institution which, although it originated as a joint stock company, had the attributes of a public entity. As stated earlier, the precise legal status of the Bank of England may be difficult to determine, at least, in its early days.

Bank Notes Act 1826

This Act prohibited the issuing of promissory notes of low values (i.e. below £5). The Act aimed at minimizing administrative work and prohibited the circulation of promissory notes of lesser values. However, the Act did not prohibit issuance of promissory notes because they had always been treated as one of the most effective ways of raising loans and giving sufficient guarantee to lenders as to the recovery of the money lent. The service rendered by promissory notes cannot be overemphasized by the commercial world, even at the present time.

Bank Charter Act 1844

This Act authorized the Bank of England to establish a separate department, called the Issue Department, for the issue of promissory notes (banknotes) payable on demand. The Issue Department was required to submit to the Governor and the Company in the Banking Department an account of the capital stock, the deposits, and the money and securities belonging to them on specified dates, and these accounts were to be published in the London Gazette. This Act certainly recognized the Bank of England as the government institution and a bank of issue, an important step forward towards recognition of the Bank of England as a public entity. This Act also separated the Issue Department from the Banking Department, emphasizing that the Banking Department would be in effect a policy-making department and thus superior to the Issue Department.

The Act also enabled the Governor and the Banking Department to know the exact holdings of gold coins, gold and silver bullion, and securities. This meant that both the government and the Bank of England by then realized the importance of having healthy reserves and of keeping up to date accounts of money issued and the reserves maintained.

Bank of England Act 1861

This was an act

> ... to make further Provision respecting certain payments to and from the Bank of England and to increase the

Facilities for the Transfer of Stocks and Annuities, and for other Purposes.

This was again a statute of necessity. Section 5 of the Act clearly provided for regulation of balances for the dividend account at the Bank. This Act also evidences the fact that the Bank of England, as a joint stock company, had dealings with the Treasury, and in order to settle deficiencies on its account the national loans fund, an account held by the Treasury at the Bank of England, would be utilized, when possible. The 1861 Act also recognized that the bank was the agent of the government, the parliamentary book-keeper of the fund and that the Bank owed a duty to all individuals who were interested in the fund.

Bank of England Act 1946

By the time this statute was enacted, the world economy was due to take on an entirely new shape, primarily for two reasons: (a) to recover from the adverse effects of World War II, and (b) to be prepared for a new kind of economic interaction with the advent of newly born countries as products of de-colonization. The Bank needed to have an organizational structure and to be endowed with the power of a policy maker. By 1946 the Bretton Woods Agreement was reached and the British Government was an important participant in that agreement. Furthermore, the Bank of England was required to be involved in the establishment of the International Monetary Fund and the International Bank for Reconstruction and Development. The preamble to the Act merely states that its purpose was to

> ... bring the capital stock of the Bank of England into public ownership and bring the Bank under public control, to make provision with respect to the relations between the Treasury, the Bank of England and other banks and for purposes connected with the matters aforesaid.

This Act legitimized the Bank as a bank with public ownership and public control. It also formalized the basis for the Bank's relations between the Treasury and with other banks. It is a very short act with six sections, namely:

section 1	Transfer of Bank stock to the Treasury
section 2	Court of Directors of the Bank
section 3	Consequential provisions as to constitution and powers of the Bank
section 4	Treasury directions to the Bank and relations of the Bank with other banks
section 5	Interpretation
section 6	Short title

The Act has two schedules, Schedule 1 – Incidental and Supplemental Provisions as to the Government Stock and Sums payable by the Bank to the Treasury, and Schedule 2 – Supplemental Provision as to the Court of Directors.

By section 1, the Bank was required to transfer the whole of its existing capital stock to the Treasury. Section 2 provided for the Court of Directors of the Bank consisting of the Governor, Deputy Governor and 16 Directors. Schedule 2 to the Act details the terms of office of various offices including that of the Governor and the Deputy Governor.

One of the most important sections was section 4 whereby the Treasury was to give directions to the Bank after consultation with the Governor on any matter that would protect the public interest. By sub-section 3 of section 4 the Bank was empowered to request information from and make recommendations to bankers on any banking or financial matter, if it deemed it necessary in the public interest, and this power was also to be exercised if the Treasury so authorized the Bank. But this power would not be exercised in respect of the affairs of any particular customer of a banker.

The 1946 Act was supplemented by the Bretton Woods 1946 Act. However, in so far as domestic legislation relating to the Bank of England was concerned, this Act must be regarded as an act that formalized the status of the Bank as the banker to the government. Transfers of bank stock to the Treasury must be evidential of the intention of the legislature as to how the Bank should be allowed to operate. Section 4 of the Act states that both the Bank of England and the Treasury can seek information from private banks and give recommendations to them whenever either of them may deem it necessary to do so in the public interest. Section 3 confirmed that the Bank of England would be one of the most appropriate institutions, like any other department of the government, to decide what would be in the public interest and direct the private banks to do or not to do certain things.

Subsection 4 of section 4 again reaffirms the Bank's position as a judge of the public interest in that even the provisions of the Official Secrets Act 1911 have been made applicable to the recommendations or directions to be given by the Bank of England and/or the Treasury.

Banking Act 1979

Although the 1973 oil crisis made certain rich countries suffer, ironically, after this crisis took place, the foreign investment pattern in the West and, in particular, on the London Capital Market significantly changed. During the 1970s and 1980s more deposits were made by foreign depositors and foreign banks also turned to the United Kingdom.

Whereas the 1946 Act was predominantly concerned with domestic banking, the 1979 Act (which came into force on 1 October 1979, and in part on 19 February 1982) had much broader purposes than the 1946 Act. The preamble to the 1979 Act clearly indicates the remit of the Act:

> ... to regulate the acceptance of deposits in the course of business; to confer functions on the Bank of England with respect to the control of institutions carrying on deposit-taking businesses; to give further protection to persons who are depositors with such institutions; to make provision with respect to advertisements inviting the making of deposits; to restrict the use of names and descriptions associated with banks and banking; to prohibit fraudulent inducement to make a deposit; to amend the Consumer Credit Act 1974 and the law with respect to instruments to which section 4 of the Cheques Act 1957 applies; to repeal certain enactments relating to banks and banking; and for purposes connected therewith.

The Act aimed at prohibiting fraudulent inducements to make

deposits in order to ensure that banking services would be rendered by banks in the most honest and fair manner. From this standpoint, the 1979 Act should be regarded as a landmark in the matter of protecting depositors' interests, at the same time giving legitimate assurances to depositors about their protection which, in turn, would increase the flow of financial investment. No other act in the past had these twin objectives.

The Act has four parts:

Part I   Control of Deposit-Taking

Part II   The Deposit Protection Scheme

Part III Advertisements and Banking Names

Part IV   Miscellaneous and General

Part I of the Act provided for prior authorization and supervision of institutions that took deposits from the public. The Act, therefore, defined deposit and explained how to control deposit-taking. The Act provided for a two-tier system of authorization whereby institutions satisfying a range of difficult criteria would be recognized as banks, while others would be eligible for a licence to take deposits. The Bank of England was given a total authority to supervise the activities of banks and the licensed institutions.

No institution would be allowed to function on the London Capital Market unless it was recognized or licensed, as the case may be, by the Bank of England in order to ensure that depositors did not remain unprotected. Under the Act the Treasury retained its power to add, by means of statutory instruments, persons to the list set out in Schedule 1 of the Act entitled 'Exceptions from Prohibition in Section 1', which was concerned with the control of deposit-taking and the meaning of deposit. Under section 4 of the Act, the Bank of England remained obliged to submit to the Chancellor of Exchequer a report of its activities in a given financial year in the exercise of functions conferred upon it by this Act. The Chancellor of Exchequer was required to submit a copy of every report made by the Bank of England before the Houses of Parliament, making the bank accountable not only to the Treasury, but also Parliament.

A system of transparency was also developed by this Act whereby the Bank was required to make available to any person a list of all the institutions that were recognized or licensed under this Act. The Bank was also required to make a statement to the Chancellor of the Exchequer as to the principles on which it was working and whether the institutions were allowed to function as banks or licensees.

In order to protect the market and depositors, the Act also made clear provisions (section 5) for revocation of recognition or licence. Similar powers were conferred on the Bank of England by the Act in connection with the termination of deposit-taking authority (section 8). This was the first legislation in which the duties of licensed institutions were clearly identified, albeit briefly, and inspection of audited accounts of licensed institutions was made compulsory.

A detailed appeals procedure was included in the Act so as to ensure that no applicant for recognition or a licence was unduly or unfairly denied its right. Section 13 of the Act provided for appeal to the High Court or the Court of Session on points of law.

The essence of control and surveillance can be found in sections 16 to 20. Section 16 ('Powers to obtain information and require production of documents'); section 17 ('Investigations on behalf of the Bank'); section 18 ('Winding up on petition from the Bank'); section 19 ('Confidentiality of information obtained by the Bank'); section 20 ('Information disclosed to the Bank from other sources') evidenced the scope of power that the Act conferred on the Bank of England. It would appear that although these powers were essential for the smooth running of a capital market, the Act did not make any provisions as to how these powers should be exercised.

As stated earlier, one of the most important contributions made by the 1979 Act was the provision for the deposit protection scheme. To this end, the Deposit Protection Board and the Deposit Protection Fund were set up.

Part II of the Act provided for a detailed deposit scheme including, inter alia, the system of contribution to the Deposit Protection Fund, various other contributions, how payments were to be made to depositors when institutions became insolvent, meaning of deposits, the concept of trustee deposits and joint deposits, liability of insolvent institutions in respect of payment made by the Board, repayments in respect of contributions and tax treatment of contributions and payments. Many of these issues were either amended or further developed in the 1987 Act. From this standpoint, the 1979 Act significantly contributed to the development of the 1987 Act.

Part III the Act made provisions for control of advertisements for deposits.

The Act also provided for offences in relation to fraudulent deposit-taking or supply of misleading information, whether to the Bank or to deposit makers; thus an attempt was made by the Act to prevent unscrupulous financial institutions from taking part in the business of banking.

The Act has 7 schedules:

Schedule 1	Exceptions from Prohibition in Section 1
Schedule 2	Minimum Criteria for Deposit-Taking Institutions
Schedule 3	Transitional Provisions
Schedule 4	Revocation of Recognition or Licence
Schedule 5	The Deposit Protection Board
Schedule 6	Consequential amendments
Schedule 7	Enactments Repealed

Of those, Schedules 2, 4 and 5 were of particular importance. Schedule 2, for example, attempted to curtail the number of unscrupulous deposit-taking institutions by setting the minimum criteria for them, whereas Schedule 4, in addition to the principal provisions in the Act, provided for the procedures that the Bank of England was required to follow in respect of revocation of recognition or licence. Schedule 5 detailed the constitution and proceedings of the Deposit Protection Board, and its responsibilities and powers in respect of its annual reports and auditing of accounts.

Historically, the 1979 Act was the first legislation in the United Kingdom to provide for a licensing and recognition system, and protection of depositors. It also embodied clear provisions for control and surveillance by the Bank of England. Ironically, the 1979 Act did not prevent the collapse of Johnson Matthey Bankers Ltd, which will be discussed in a subsequent section. There is thus reason to believe that the 1979 Act did not provide for effective means of control and surveillance as otherwise those bank failures could perhaps been prevented. It would be unfair, however, to underestimate the purposes for which the Act was enacted and the service rendered to the London Capital Market in controlling and governing the business of banking through the leadership of the Bank of England.

PART II
Banking Act 1987

The collapse of Johnson Matthey Bankers (JMB) in 1984 shocked the London Capital Market, particularly in view of the fact that the provisions for the protection of depositors enacted by the Banking Act 1979 were in place. The legal issues of banking supervision in relation to the JMB scandal receive attention in a separate chapter of this work; suffice it to say that the collapse of JMB was, to a large extent, responsible for the implementation of the Banking Act 1987, superseding the 1979 Act. The preamble to this Act makes this point clear:

> *An Act to make new provision for regulating the acceptance of deposits in the course of a business, for protecting depositors and for regulating the use of banking names and descriptions; to amend section 187 of the Consumer Credit Act 1974 in relation to arrangements for the electronic transfer of funds; to clarify the powers conferred by section 183 of the Financial Services Act 1986; and for purposes connected with those matters.*

If one looks at the preambles to both the 1979 and the 1987 Acts, one can easily reach the conclusion that the latter legislation was developed with a view to creating new provision for regulating the acceptance of deposits in the course of a business, and for making more effective provisions for the protection of depositors. The two other important purposes for which the 1987 Act was enacted were: (a) to amend section 187 of the Consumer Credit Act 1974 [1], and to clarify the powers of the

---

[1] See further Annex 1.

Bank of England under section 183 of the Financial Services Act 1986[2].
The 1987 Act consists of six parts:

Part I	Regulation of Deposit-Taking Business
Part II	The Deposit Protection Scheme
Part III	Banking Names and Descriptions
Part IV	Overseas Institutions with Representative Offices
Part V	Restriction on Disclosure of Information
Part VI	Miscellaneous and Supplementary

The following are the titles of Schedules:

Schedule 1	The Board of Banking Supervision
Schedule 2	Exempted persons
Schedule 3	Minimum criteria for authorization
Schedule 4	The Deposit Protection Board
Schedule 5	Transitional provisions
Schedule 6	Minor and consequential amendments
Schedule 7	Repeals and revocations

By Schedule 7 the Banking Act 1979 has been repealed except for sections 38[3], 47[4], 51[4], 52[5] and Schedule 6[7].

The 1987 Act was an improvement on the 1979 Act in many important aspects; it places significant importance on the regulation of the deposit-taking business and on the deposit protection scheme.

An Analysis of the Banking Act 1987 – Certain Important Definitions

Deposit

Whereas the 1979 Act defined 'deposit' in a negative fashion by

---

[2] See further Annex 2.
[3] It amended the Consumer Credit Act 1974, ss 74, 114, 185(2).
[4] Defence of contributory negligence.
[5] Its title was 'Consequential amendments and repeals'.
[6] Its title was 'Short title, commencement and extent'.
[7] It identified the Consequential amendments.

providing what deposits did not include, the meaning of 'deposit' under the 1987 Act is much clearer and it stands for a sum of money paid on terms:

> (a) under which it will be repaid, with or without interest or a premium, and either on demand or at a time or in circumstances agreed by or on behalf of the person making the payment and the person receiving it; and
>
> (b) which are not referable to the provision of property or services or the giving of security;

and references in this Act to money deposited of property and to the making of a deposit shall be construed accordingly. (Section 5(1(a) and (b).)

A deposit under the 1987 Act does not include any sum that may be paid by the Bank of England, or an authorized institution or by a person specified in Schedule 2 to this Act, or by a person other than those mentioned above in the course of carrying on a business in the form of a loan or a sum paid by the company to one of its subsidiaries or when both are subsidiaries of another company, or a sum which is paid by a person who is a close relative of the person receiving it or who is a close relative of a director, controller or manager of that person.

Deposit-Taking Business

The substantive part of the definition of deposit-taking under both the 1979 and 1987 Acts is the same save that the 1987 Act clarifies the position even further by providing that in determining whether deposits are accepted only on particular occasions 'regard shall be had to the frequency of the occasions and to any characteristics distinguishing them from each other' (section 6(4)).

A business is not to be regarded as a deposit-taking business when it may be accepted by a person who is exempt from the prohibition in section 3, that is, a person who is not authorized by the Bank of England for deposit-taking under this Act, and also if it is received for a purpose other than that described in section 6(1) of this Act (that is monies received as a deposit for the principal purpose of lending).

Section 3 of the 1987 Act also provides for restrictions on acceptance of deposits. This provision is activated when the Bank believes that an authorized institution may no longer be allowed to accept deposits if thereby the interests of depositors will be jeopardized. Section 3, however, does not clarify the circumstances in which an authorized institution may be directed not to accept deposits. It may be safely assumed, however, that when the Bank of England would consider the authorization of an authorized institution it would take action under section 3 of the Act. Presumably, the deposits that have already been accepted by an authorized institution may not be refunded to the depositors until the Bank so directs.

Exempted Persons and Exempted Transactions

The Act intends to regulate the deposit-taking business by the Bank of England generally, and in particular, by the Board of Banking Supervision. By section 1 the Bank has the general duty to supervise the institutions authorized by it to be involved in a deposit-taking business. Nowhere in the Act has the term 'supervision' been defined or described. One is thus required to rely upon the literal meaning of the term which, according to the Oxford English Dictionary, means *'general management, direction, control, oversight, superintendance'*[8].

The Bank has the duty to keep under review the operation of the Act and developments in the field of banking that may appear relevant. Indeed, in the exercise of this duty the Bank of England has now created an entirely new division for supervision of banking institutions under the new Bank Act 1998, which receives attention in a separate section of this work.

The Bank remains accountable to the Chancellor of the Exchequer in that after the end of each financial year it is required to submit to the Chancellor a report on its activities over the financial year, although the Bank has the discretion as to the manner in which the report should be prepared.

The Act, however, exempts the Bank of England and its employees and members of its Court of Directors from liability in negligence or any other activity for failing to perform their duties in relation to regulation of deposit-taking business because section 1(4) provides that:

---

[8] *The Oxford English Dictionary* (ed.) by J A Simpson and E S C Weiner, second edition, Oxford, Clarendon Press, 1989, p. 245.

> *Neither the Bank nor any person who is a member of its Court of Directors or who is, or is acting as, an officer or servant of the Bank shall be liable in damages for anything done or omitted in the discharge of the function of the Bank under this Act unless it is shown that the act or omission was in bad faith.*

Essential Features of the Banking Act 1987

Whereas the 1979 Act developed the system of recognition and licensing, the Banking Act 1987 is concerned with authorizations. An application for authorization must be made to the Bank of England, accompanied by a statement setting out the nature and scale of deposit-taking business that the applicant intends to carry out together with a plan for future development of that business, and particulars of the arrangement that it wishes to make for the management of that business. The Bank reserves the right to obtain further information and/or documents for the purpose of determining the application (section 8(5)). The Act is not clear on what grounds applications may be treated by the Bank. There thus remains a large margin of discretion to be exercised by the Bank. An applicant reserves the right to withdraw its application by a written notice to the Bank at any time before authorization is granted or refused.

Schedule 3 to the Act details the minimum criteria for authorization: directors and other responsible officers must be fit and proper persons; business is to be directed by at least two individuals; in the case of an institution incorporated in the United Kingdom the number of directors without executive responsibility for the management of the business may be determined by the Bank, taking into account the circumstances of the institution and the nature and scope of its operations; business must be conducted in a prudent manner; the integrity and professional skills appropriate to the nature and scale of its activities by the officers managing the business must not be questionable; and a minimum net assets requirement must be satisfied[9]. Of these criteria, two of them

---

[9] 89/646/EEC Second Council Directive on the coordination of laws, regulations and administrative provisions relating to the taking up and pursuit of the business of credit institutions and amending Directive 77/780/EEC, 320 O.J. Eur. Comm.1989 (No. L386).

need particular comment: directors and officers to be fit and proper persons and business to be conducted in a prudent manner.

Paragraph 2 of Schedule 3 to the Act provides the criteria for determining whether a director, controller or manager is a fit and proper person:

> *In determining whether a person is a fit and proper person to hold any particular position, regard shall be had to his probity, to his competence and soundness of judgement for fulfilling the responsibilities of that position, to the diligence with which he is fulfilling or likely to fulfil those responsibilities and to whether the interests of depositors or potential depositors of the institution are, or are likely to be, in any way threatened by his holding that position.*

The English courts have developed guidelines on interpretation of some of the expressions.

In *Dorchester Finance Co v Stebbing*[10] Foster J held that diligence meant '...*such care as an ordinary man might be expected to take on his own behalf...*'. This ruling confirmed that the test to be applied in ascertaining diligence was an objective one in that an ordinary man will be diligent in the promotion of his own affairs. Furthermore, in two recent cases[11], Hoffman J confirmed that the requirement of diligence was to be viewed objectively. He adopted as an accurate expression of the common law the test embodied in section 214 of the Insolvency Act 1986 (wrongful trading). This is that an assessment of what a director of company should have done or known is to be based on what would be done by '*a reasonably diligent person having both (a) the general knowledge, skill and experience that may reasonably be expected of a person carrying out the same functions as are carried out by that director in relation to the company, and (b) the general knowledge, skill and experience that that director has.*'[12]

The requirement of competence has not been defined either in the

---

[10] [1989] BCLC 498.
[11] *Norman v Theodore Goddard* [1991] BCLC 1027; *Re D'Jan of London Ltd* [1994] 1 BCLC 561.
[12] section 214(4) of the Insolvency Act 1986.

1987 Act nor in Statement of Principles (below). A competent man was held to mean '... *a man who, on the fair assessment of the requirements of the task, the factors involved, the problems to be studied and the degree of risk ... implicit, can fairly, as well as reasonably, be regarded by the manager, and in fact is regarded at the time by the manager, as competent to perform such an inspection...*'.[13] In *Gibson v Skibs A/S Marina*[14] a competent man was held to mean a man competent for the task, '*a person who is a practical and reasonable man, who knows what to look for and knows how to recognize it when he sees it.*'

Schedule 3 also provides that in determining whether a person is proper and fit, regard may be had to the previous conduct and activities in business or financial matters of the person in question and, in particular, whether any evidence exists of his having committed criminal offences, dishonesty or malpractice, or whether he has been declared a bankrupt.

The criteria for determining that a person is a fit and proper person are set out in *The Banking Act 1987, Section 16: Statement of Principles* which was issued by the Bank of England. This is now the responsibility of the Financial Services Authority[15]. Three sets of criteria are set out in Statement of Principles, one for directors, chief executives, managing directors and managers and the second for shareholders, and the third for indirect controllers[16].

The criteria for assessing whether a person is a fit and proper person to be a director, chief executive, managing director or manager comprise general considerations and the circumstances of the particular position held by such a person and the institution concerned[17]. They include consideration whether a person has sufficient skill, knowledge, diligence, competence and soundness of judgement to perform and discharge duties and responsibilities required by the position he holds. Of particular relevance in this respect will be whether the person has

---

[13] *Brazier v Skipton Rock Co Ltd* [1962] 1 All ER, 955 at 957 per Winn J.
[14] [1966] 2 All ER 476 at 478 per Cantley J.
[15] Section 16 of the Banking Act 1987 requires the Bank of England to publish a statement of principles as to how it interprets the criteria specified in Schedule 3 to this Act.
[16] For definitions see section 105 of the Banking Act 1987.
[17] Banking Act 1987, Section 16: Statement of Principles, paragraphs 2.33 - 2.40.

previous experience of similar responsibilities, his record in fulfilling them, and whether he has appropriate qualifications and training. With regard to soundness of judgement, the Bank will consider '... *the degree of balance, rationality and maturity demonstrated in his conduct and decision-making.*'[18]. The diligence criterion expects the person to devote sufficient time and attention to the discharge of his duties and responsibilities. The probity of the person who has the responsibility for conducting a deposit-taking business is another important factor; it is crucial that he is *of 'high integrity'*. The standards of the above requirements will vary depending on the precise position held by the person concerned. According to the Statement of Principles, '... *a person could be fit and proper for one position, but not fit and proper for a position involving different responsibilities and duties.*'[19] In assessing the above criteria the key consideration remains the interests of current and potential depositors.

Other factors taken into account by the Bank of England include the person's reputation and character, whether he has a criminal record, in particular in relation to fraud and dishonesty, whether the person has contravened any provisions of banking, insurance, investment '*or other legislation designed to protect members of the public against financial loss due to dishonesty, incompetence or malpractice.*' The Bank will also take into account the person's record of compliance with non-statutory codes, such as the Take-over Code and the London Code of Conduct[20].

The application of the fit and proper criterion with regard to shareholder controllers and indirect controllers depends on the position held by such a person and the influence he has on the interests of current and potential depositors[21]. Thus, the higher the influence (in terms of shareholding), the higher the standards that will be required of him to fulfil the criterion. The Bank takes into account two factors in applying the fit and proper criterion. Firstly, the level of influence the person has, or is likely to exercise. If the person exercises a close control over the business, then the Bank will expect that person to have the knowledge, skill, soundness of judgement, and probity expected of

---

[18] op. cit. paragraph 2.37.
[19] op. cit. paragraph 2.35.
[20] op. cit. paragraph 2.38.
[21] op. cit. paragraphs 2.41 - 2.46.

directors, managing directors, chief executives and managers. Conversely, a lower standard will be applied if the person does not influence the management of the authorized institution. The second factor taken into account by the Bank is whether *'the financial position, reputation or conduct of the shareholder controller or prospective controller has damaged or is likely to damage the authorized institution through 'contagion' which undermines confidence in it.'*[22] This will be relevant if a holding company, or a major shareholder, were in financial difficulties which could affect the authorized institution in terms of difficulties in obtaining deposits, other funds or raising new equity from existing and potential shareholders. Again, the higher the shareholding, the higher is the risk of 'contagion', such as publicity about illegal or unethical conduct by the holding company or another member of the group.

With regard to an indirect controller who 'directs' or 'instructs' a shareholder controller, as defined by section 105(3)(d) of the 1987 Act, similar considerations are applied as those relevant to assessing the fulfilment of the criterion for shareholder controllers, and the level of their application will again be dependent on the level of 'directing' or 'instructing' the board of an authorized institution [23].

A person's improper involvement in business such as banking, insurance, investment, financial services or management of companies, will be considered derogatory and is regarded as a ground for making him an unfit and improper person. He must not have been engaged in any business practices which according to the Bank would be regarded as deceitful or oppressive, or otherwise improper or *'which otherwise reflect discredit on his method of conducting the business'* (paragraph 3(c) of Schedule 3). He must not have been engaged in or associated with any other business practices or otherwise conducted himself in such a way that would cast doubt on his competence and soundness of judgement. In other words, a director, controller or manager must be a 'clean' man.

The other important criterion for authorization is that business must be conducted in prudent manner. The Act does not define the term

---

[22] op. cit., paragraph 2.44.
[23] see further op. cit., paragraphs 2.46 - 2.47.

'prudent manner' but paragraph 4(2) of Schedule 3 provides that:

> *An institution shall not be regarded as conducting its business in a prudent manner unless it maintains or, as the case may be, will maintain net assets which, together with other financial resources available to the institution of such nature and amount as are considered appropriate by the Bank, are:*
>
> *(a) of an amount which is commensurate with the nature and scale of the institution's operations; and*
>
> *(b) of an amount and nature sufficient to safeguard the interests of its depositors and potential depositors, having regard to the particular factors mentioned in sub-paragraph (3) below and any other factors appearing to the Bank to be relevant.*

Interestingly enough, the criteria for satisfying 'prudent manner' almost solely relate to the maintenance of minimum assets and other financial resources. Furthermore, the nature and scope of the institution's operations and the risks inherent in these operations are integral criteria for determining whether the business is being conducted in a prudent manner. Another important criterion for satisfying 'prudent manner' according to Schedule 3 is whether an institution is maintaining adequate accounting and other records of its business, in addition to maintaining an adequate system of control of its business and records (paragraph 4(7) of Schedule 3). The 'catch-all' criterion for prudent manner has been embodied in paragraph 4(8) of Schedule 3:

> *Those records and systems shall not be regarded as adequate unless they are such as to enable the business of the institution to be prudently managed and the institution to comply with the duties imposed on it by or under this Act and in determining whether those systems are adequate the Bank shall have regard to the functions and responsibilities in respect of them of any such*

---

[24] The details relating to the composition, duties and operation of the Board of Banking Supervision are set out in Schedule 4 to the Banking Act 1987.

directors of the institution as are mentioned in paragraph 3 above.

The Act also provides for the Board of Banking Supervision [24] which would consist of three ex officio members, namely the Governor of the Bank of England, the Deputy Governor and the executive director responsible for the supervision of an institution authorized under the Act, and six independent members appointed jointly by the Chancellor of the Exchequer and the Governor. It is the duty of the independent members to advise the Board of Banking Supervision as they may think fit. The Bank is required to make regular reports to the Board on matters that the Bank considers relevant to the independent members, which seems to be rather a curious provision. Although the independent members have the authority to ask the Bank to provide such information as they may require, this provision has also been qualified by the word 'reasonably'[25].

Grant and Refusal of Authorization

The Bank of England has total discretion either to grant or refuse any application for authorization, as per Schedule 3 of the Act. In the case of an applicant whose principal place of business [26] is outside the United Kingdom, the Bank may regard itself as satisfied that criteria specified in Schedule 3 (paragraphs 1, 4, 5 – fit and proper persons, adequate liquidity, capability of providing liquidity) are fulfilled if:

(a) *the relevant supervisory authority in that country or territory informs the Bank that it is satisfied with respect to the prudent management and overall financial soundness of the applicant; and*

(b) *the Bank is satisfied as to the nature and scope of the supervision exercised by that authority.*

This provision is puzzling in that it defeats the criteria for

---

[25] For the functions and powers of the Board of Banking Supervision in relation to the Deposit Protection Scheme see Chapter 4, page 94.

[26] As to what is a 'place of business' see *Lord Advocate v Huron & Erie Loan and Saving Co* 1911 SC 612. The question as to what is a principal place of business is one of fact; see *De Beers Consolidated Mines Ltd v Howe* [1906] AC 445; *Re Hilton, Gibbes v Hale-Hinton* [1909] 2 Ch 548; and *Egyptian Delta Land and Investment Co Ltd v Todd* [1929] AC 1.

authorization established in Schedule 3. The Act is not clear on how this discretionary power may be exercised; it may promote an incidence of undue discrimination between supervisory authorities in various jurisdictions or countries. Furthermore, unless there is equivalence in respect of 'prudent management' and a system of judging overall 'financial soundness', the Bank of England might exercise its discriminatory power.

In determining whether to grant or refuse an application, the Bank may take into account any matters relating:

> *(a) to any person who is or will be employed by or associated with the applicant for the purpose of the applicant's deposit-taking business; and*
>
> *(b) if the applicant is a body corporate, to any other body corporate in the same group or to any director or controller of any such other body.* [27]

No application for authorization shall be granted if all the assets are owed by a single individual to prevent insufficient security for depositors. Authorizations for partnerships are granted in the name of a partnership.

Although an application for seeking an authorization is governed by Schedule 3 of the Banking Act 1987, the onus of satisfying the FSA in respect of all the conditions therein rests on the applicant. The principal concern of the FSA would be whether an institution, when authorized, would be a liability on the London International Capital Market and whether it would carry out its business in a prudent manner. The FSA is also governed by the Basle Core Principles for Effective Supervision [28], and the Basle minimum standards [29].

In the case of overseas institutions, the FSA under the terms of section 9(3) of the 1987 Act may regard itself as satisfied that the criteria of a fit and proper person, prudent conduct, integrity and professional skills are fulfilled, if the banking supervisory authority in that country

---

[27] Section 9(4).
[28] These Principles were issued in 1997 by the Basle Committee on Banking Supervision and are reproduced in 37 *International Legal Materials* (1997) 405.
[29] The minimum standards stand for supervision of international banking groups and their cross-border establishment issued in July 1992.

confirms this and the FSA is satisfied as to the nature and scope of the supervision exercised by that authority.

To summarize: section 11 of the Banking Act 1987 is the key section that provides for the grounds for revocation of authorization. As stated earlier, whether or not section 11 should be activated is solely decided by the FSA. In principle, section 11 is activated by the FSA when the interests of depositors and potential depositors are threatened, which may be consequential upon the failure to operate the banking business in a 'prudent manner'. Section 11 of the 1987 Act sets out the principles in accordance with which the FSA may exercise its discretionary power regarding imposition of restrictions or revoking authorization.

Section 11(1)(a)

'If any of the criteria specified in Schedule 3 to this Act is not or has not been fulfilled, or may not be or may not have been fulfilled in respect of the institution.' The criteria specified in Schedule 3 are: (a) directors, managers, shareholders, controllers etc. to be fit and proper persons; (b) business to be directed by at least two individuals; (c) composition of the board of directors; (d) business to be conducted in a prudent manner; (e) integrity and skill; and (f) minimum net assets.

Section 11(1)(b)

'... the institution has failed to comply with any obligation imposed on it by or under this Act.' This gives the FSA a very wide discretionary power. Failure to comply with the provisions of section 39, for example (power to obtain information and require production of documents), is usually considered to be a serious departure from the statutory provisions.

Section 11(1)(d)

An authorized institution giving the FSA false, misleading or inaccurate information would allow the FSA to exercise the power of revocation. The same power is exercisable if it should appear that false, misleading or inaccurate information was provided by the institution concerned *'in connection with an application for authorization, by or on behalf of a person who is or is to be a director, controller or manager of the institution.'*

Section 11(1)(e)

The FSA may revoke the authorization of an institution if in its view the depositors' interests, current or potential, are in any way threatened.

Section 11(1A)

This section sets out the following additional grounds on which the FSA can exercise its powers to revoke or restrict the authorization of a credit institution incorporated in the United Kingdom:

(a) if the institution's principal place of business is or may be outside the United Kingdom, that is, where the central management or direction resides;

(b) if it appears that the institution has carried out impermissible activities, other than deposit-taking from the public, whether within or outside the United Kingdom, without any prior notice to the FSA of its intention to do so;

(c) if certain United Kingdom regulatory authorities notify the FSA of any contravention by an institution of any provisions of the Financial Services Act 1986, or any rules or regulations made under it or any other related provisions;

(d) if the FSA is informed by the Director General of Fair Trading that an institution or certain other persons connected to the institution has or have done any of the things specified in sub-section (a) to (d) of section 25(2) of the Consumer Credit Act 1974;

(e) if an institution has failed to comply with any obligations imposed on by the Regulations, or the Credit Institution (Protection of Depositors) Regulations 1995;

(f) if the FSA is informed by a supervisory body in another member state of the EEA that an institution has failed to comply with their local laws or regulations connected with the implementation of the Second Banking Coordination Directive or any rule of law of another EEA state for purposes connected with the implementation of the Investment Services Directive 93/22/EEC or Directive 94/19/EEC on deposit guarantee schemes.

---

[30] For the definition of 'close links' see Schedule 6 of the Act of 2000.

Section 11(1B)

Where it appears to the FSA that an institution's 'close links'[30] with any person are such as to prevent the FSA from effectively exercising its supervisory function in relation to that institutions.

Section 11(2)

(a) The FSA may revoke authorization of an institution if it appears to it that the institution has not accepted a deposit in the United Kingdom, when so authorized, within a period of twelve months since it was authorized, or has ceased to accept deposits for a period of more than six months.[31]

Section 11(3)

When the supervisory authority of an overseas institution has withdrawn from the institution an authorization corresponding to that conferred by the FSA, then the latter may revoke the authorization, presumably of the branches or subsidiaries operating in the United Kingdom.

Section 11(6)

The FSA *shall* revoke the authorization when an authorized institution wherever incorporated has been subject to a winding-up order or a resolution for a winding-up or for a voluntary winding-up in the United Kingdom has been passed. The FSA *may* revoke the authorization of an institution incorporated outside the United Kingdom if that institution has been subject to a winding-up order in that country or a resolution for its voluntary winding up has been passed.

Section 11(7)

The FSA may revoke the authorization of an institution incorporated in the United Kingdom if it appears to it that:

> *(a) a composition or arrangement with creditors has been made in respect of the institution;*
>
> *(b) a receiver or manager of the institution's undertaking*

---

[31] For the meanings of 'deposit' and 'deposit-taking business' see respectively section 5 and section 6 of the Banking Act 1987.

has been appointed; or

(c) possession has been taken by or on behalf of the holders of any debenture secured by a charge, of any property of the institution comprised in or subject to the charge.

In the case of an authorized institution incorporated elsewhere the FSA may revoke its authorization if an event has occurred corresponding as nearly as may be to any of those mentioned in paragraphs (a), (b) and (c) above.

Section 11(8)

The power to revoke an authorization exists where it may appear to the FSA that an administration order has been made in relation to an institution under section 8 of the Insolvency Act 1986.

Section 11(9)

The FSA shall revoke the authorization of an unincorporated institution when a winding-up order has been made against it in the United Kingdom or when:

(a) the institution has been dissolved; or

(b) a bankruptcy order, an order of sequestration, an order of adjudication of bankruptcy or a composition or arrangement with creditors has been made or a trust deed for creditors has been granted in respect of that institution or any of its members; or

(c) events similar to a winding-up order, bankruptcy order, voluntary winding-up resolution, placing of the institution into receivership or any other similar event has taken place in respect of that institution or any of its members; or

(d) the institution's entire assets have passed into the ownership of a single individual.

These powers may be described as 'enforcement powers' of the FSA, and they are extensive; they extend to include overseas institutions too. Revocation of an authorization is therefore governed by the Banking

Analysis of Statutory Provisions Governing the Business of Banking 47

Act 1987, the Financial Services Act 1986 or the Consumer Credit Act 1974, in addition to the Insolvency Act 1986.

The revocation of an authorization is mandatory under section 11(9) of the Banking Act 1987.

The Circumstances in which Restriction on Authorization May be Imposed, and the Procedure thereof

These circumstances have been included in section 12 of the Banking Act 1987, and the provisions regarding mandatory revocation and restrictions in cases of urgency have been detailed in section 14 of the 1987 Act. Whereas the FSA's intention to impose restrictions on the authorization must be communicated by a written notice (section 13), no such notice needs to be served upon an authorized institution when the FSA decides to exercise its power under section 14 (mandatory revocation and restrictions in cases of urgency). The circumstances in which restrictions upon authorization may be imposed are:

section 13, section 12, section 14 along with section 13.

Section 13: Notice of Revocation or Restriction

Where the FSA proposes: (a) to remove an authorization or (b) to restrict the authorization or (c) to vary the restriction imposed on an authorized institution otherwise than with the consent of the institution concerned (unless it is a situation that warrants section 14 action), it shall give to the institution written notice conveying intention to do so. Obviously, this procedure is activated when it may appear to the FSA that the authorized institution has derogated from one or more of the provisions of Schedule 3 to the 1987 Act, or that in the opinion of the FSA the authorized institution concerned is likely to jeopardise the protection of the depositors' interests.

A notice must specify whether the FSA intends to revoke or restrict or vary an authorization and the grounds thereof, and must also give particulars of the institution's right of representation, which right must be executed by the institution concerned within fourteen days beginning with the day on which the notice was served [32]. Where the notice is based on paragraph 1 of Schedule 3 to the 1987 Act (Directors, etc. to be fit and proper persons) or the proposed restriction *'consists of or*

---

[32] Section 13(3) and (5).

includes a condition requiring the removal of any person as director, controller or manager', a copy of the notice must be served on that person too, with a statement of his/her right to make representations to the FSA.

Upon receipt of the representation, if any, the FSA decides whether:

(a) to proceed with the action proposed in the notice; or

(b) to take no further action; or

(c) where the proposed action was meant for revoking the institution's authorization, to restrict its authorization instead; or

(d) '*...if the proposed action was to restrict the institution's authorization or to vary the restrictions on an authorization, to restrict it or to vary the restrictions in a different manner.*'[33]

In this context, it should be pointed out that the onus is on the authorized institution or person concerned. When a notice is served for this purpose, to clearly state and submit sufficient evidence to justify why the proposed action by the FSA is contested, it is for the person concerned to refute the allegation by evidence. The FSA's notice must state the grounds and give particulars of the rights of the institution or the persons concerned, which rights allow the institution or the person concerned to make a written representation to the FSA within a period of seven days beginning with the day on which the notice was served, and the FSA may, after taking those representations into account, alter the restrictions. This procedure does not apply where the FSA has taken a decision not to take any further action against an authorized institution or its officers [34]. The provisions for right to appeal of an institution or a person have been embodied in section 27 of the 1987 Act [35]. However, after examining the representation made by the authorized institution or person concerned, the FSA has the discretion either to reverse the notice (thus the authorization remains in force) or restrict or vary or reverse any authorization. It is important to bear in mind that where the FSA makes a decision under section 13(7) the time limit for making

---

[33] Section 13(6).
[34] Section 13(9).
[35] See post.

a representation is seven days, and that a notice under sub-section (7) is given within the period of twenty-eight days beginning with the day on which notice under sub-section (1) was given, and if no notice under sub-section (7) is given within that period the FSA *'shall be treated as having at the end of that period given a notice under that sub-section...'*[36].

In the case of mandatory revocation under section 11 or where in the opinion of the FSA restriction on an authorized institution should be imposed or varied as a matter of urgency, no notice needs to be given under section 13 of the 1987 Act. In such a situation, the FSA simply notifies the institution, in writing, of its decision that the authorization has been revoked, or that restriction on the authorization has been imposed or varied, and the reasons therefore. Where a notice imposing or varying restriction is issued, particulars of the rights under sub-section (5) and section 27 must be provided in it.

Where restriction is imposed or varied on an authorization, notice is necessary, except in the circumstances detailed in section 14(2). An institution to which a notice is served under section 14 of imposition of a variation of a restriction may make representation to the FSA within fourteen days from the day on which the notice was served. The FSA determines whether to confirm or rescind its original decision or to impose a different restriction or to vary the restriction in a different manner (section 14(6)(a) and (b)) within twenty-eight days as from the date of service of the notice, taking into consideration any representations made by the authorized institution concerned. Where a notice of the proposed revocation of an authorized institution under section 13 is followed by a notice revoking the authorization under section 14, the latter notice has the effect of *'terminating any right to make representations in respect of the proposed revocation and any pending appeal proceedings in respect of a decision implementing that proposal.'*[37]

The Preamble to section 12 is clear on that point: *'Where it appears to the FSA:*

> *(a) that there are grounds on which the FSA's power to revoke an institution's authorization are exercisable;*

---

[36] Section 13(10).
[37] Section 14(a).

> but
>
> (b) that the circumstances are not such as to justify revocation...'

The FSA may restrict the authorization instead of reversing it. This provision may be regarded as a prelude to revocation. The following are the manners in which the authorization may be restricted:

(a) imposition of such limit on its duration as the FSA thinks fit;

(b) imposition of such conditions as the FSA thinks desirable for the protection of the institution's depositors or potential depositors; and

(c) imposition of both the above mentioned limits and conditions.

Restriction on an authorization must not remain in force for more than three years from the date on which it is imposed, or not exceeding the period which the FSA considers that an authorized institution may require for repaying its depositors in an orderly manner.

Restrictions under this section may take the following forms:

(a) the institution may be required to take certain steps or to refrain from adopting or pursuing a particular course of action or to restrict the remit of its business in a particular way;

(b) limitation on the acceptance of deposits, the granting of credits or the making of investment;

(c) prohibition on the institution from soliciting deposits;

(d) prohibition on entering into any other transaction or class of transactions;

(e) removal of any director, controller or manager; and

(f) other requirements to be fulfilled otherwise than by action taken by the institution [38].

It is for the FSA to prescribe one or more restrictions primarily by reference to Schedule 3 to the Banking Act 1987.

Any condition imposed under section 12(4) may be varied or withdrawn by the FSA as the period of restriction. Failure to comply

---

[38] Section 12(4).

with any of those restrictions constitutes a ground for the revocation of the authorization but shall not invalidate any transaction. However, if restrictions are imposed on an institution for a specific duration, it can apply for a new authorization in accordance with section 8 of the Act.

There is no doubt that under the Banking Act 1987, the FSA can exercise a wide discretionary power in regard to revocation, restrictions and variations of authorization. But, these powers of the FSA are based on two concerns: (a) protection of the depositors' interests; and (b) running of a banking business in an imprudent manner.

Revocation of an authorization is ordered when the FSA considers that there are no reasonable prospects of remedying the situation in the near future, even though there does not exist any immediate threat to the interests of depositors. This is why in its representation the authorized institution is required to convince the FSA by referring to its activities after restrictions are imposed on an authorization, that its chances of recovery are realistic; in this process, the institution concerned must establish its capital adequacy, and the future plans for expanding its business, in addition to showing the corrective measures it has taken. The FSA's actions in regard to revocation are progressive in nature, providing opportunities to an authorized institution to amend its position. A time-limited authorization is one of the most appropriate and effective actions that the FSA takes.

In the event of a United Kingdom incorporated credit institution failing to meet the requirements in paragraph 4(3A) of Schedule 3 [39], the FSA may take action in accordance with Article 10(5) of the EC Second Banking Coordination Directive [40].

Revocation of and Restrictions on Authorization

The Act contains detailed provisions on revocation of and restrictions on authorization (sections 11-18). The FSA enjoys a discretionary power as to whether a licence should be revoked or restrictions should be imposed on a licence. Under section 11 of the Act the Bank may revoke

---

[39] The minimum capital holding – ECU 5m.
[40] Article 10(5). '...if, in the cases referred to in paragraphs 1, 2 and 4, the own funds should be reduced, the competent authorities may, where the circumstances justify it, allow an institution a limited period in which to rectify its situation or cease its activities.'

a licence under certain specified circumstances, namely:

a) if any of the criteria specified in Schedule 3 (minimum criteria for authorization) has not been fulfilled, or may not be or may not have been fulfilled by the institution;

b) that the institution has failed to comply with any obligations imposed on it by or under this Act; or

c) that the person has become a controller of the institution in contravention of section 21 (Notification of new or increased control) or has been assigned the position of a controller, or remains a controller after a notice of objection has been served on him under sections 22, 23 or 24 of the Act[41]; or

d) that the FSA has been provided with false, misleading or inaccurate information by or on behalf of the institution in connection with the application for authorization including its proposed directors or officers; or

e) the interests of depositors or potential depositors of the institution are threatened.

The FSA may revoke authorization if any of the five criteria set out in section 11 is not satisfied.

Sub-section 2 of section 11 provides for further grounds on which the FSA may revoke the authorization of an institution, mainly when it has not accepted a deposit in the United Kingdom in the course of carrying on a deposit-taking business within a period of 12 months commencing with the date of the authorization, or where an intermission of 6 months has taken place as from the date of first deposit-taking. In the event of a foreign institution whose principal place of business is outside the United Kingdom, if the supervisory authority in that country or territory withdraws its authorization from that institution, the FSA may revoke the authorization of that institution in the United Kingdom. Power to revoke the authorization has also been conferred on the FSA by other relevant statutes, and these have been referred to in section 11(4) which states:

In the case of an authorized institution which is an

---

[41] This is discussed in subsequent sections of this work.

> *authorized person under the Financial Services Act 1986 or holds a consumer credit licence under the Consumer Credit Act 1974 the Bank may revoke the authorization if it appears to the Bank that the institution has ceased to be an authorized person under the said Act of 1986 (otherwise than at the request or with the consent of the institution) or that the licence under the said Act of 1974 has been revoked.*

Under section 11 the Treasury has also the power to revoke an authorization after consultation with the FSA, but it must be exercised in pursuance of a resolution of either House of Parliament. Revocation of the authorization should, of course, be almost automatic when a winding-up or bankruptcy order has been made against an applicant, or a resolution for its voluntary winding-up has been passed. The FSA authority to revoke the authorization seems to be extremely wide. Section 11(7) provides that the FSA may revoke the authorization of an authorized institution incorporated in the United Kingdom if it appears to the FSA that a composition or arrangement with a creditor has been made in respect of an institution, or that a receiver has been appointed, or that possession has been taken by or on behalf of the holders of any debenture (secured by a charge on any property) of the institution comprised in or subject to the charge (section 11(7)(c)), or in the case of an authorized institution incorporated elsewhere, any of the above-mentioned events has taken place. The FSA may exercise its power to revoke the authorization if an administrative order has been made in relation to an institution under section 8 of the Insolvency Act 1986.

Section 11 of the Act deals solely with the issue of revocation of the authorization. Revocation of the authorization is justifiable when an authorized institution has been subject to a winding-up order or has run into any other financial difficulties because such an institution would be a liability to the London Capital Market. In so far as the revocation criteria under section 11(1) are concerned, legal controversy may arise, particularly in respect of the criteria in paragraph (e) of section 11(1), which provide that revocation of the authorization may be ordered when it may appear to the FSA that the interests of depositors or potential depositors are in any other way threatened. The determination of whether the interests of depositors, current or potential, are threatened is to be made by means of an objective review of the performance of that institution.

Under section 14 the FSA retains a mandatory power to revoke a licence or impose restrictions on a licence in case of urgency. In such a situation no notice need be given. In the case of imposing or varying a restriction, a notice under section 13(4) is required to give the grounds thereof. An institution that has been subject to a notice of restrictions or variation of restrictions has the right to make a representation to the FSA within a period of 14 days from the date on which the notice was given. The FSA may review its own decision upon receipt of the representation, and then decide whether to confirm or rescind the original decision, or to impose different restrictions or to vary the restrictions. However, where a notice of the proposed revocation of an authorization of an institution under section 13 of the Act is followed by a notice revoking its authorization, the latter notice shall have the effect of terminating a new right to make a representation in respect of the proposed revocation and any pending appeal proceedings.

Revocation or a restriction of an authorization must be preceded by a notice unless revocation of the restriction on an authorization is mandatory (section 14). Under section 13 the FSA is required to give notice as to its intention to revoke or restrict its authorization or vary the restrictions imposed thereon. Usually the FSA is required to specify the nature of the proposed restrictions or of the proposed variation of restrictions. A notice must contain grounds on which the FSA proposed to act and it must also give particulars of the institution's right as to making a representation to the FSA (section 13(5)). Where a notice is initiated by the FSA on the ground that the proposed revocation or variation of restrictions is deemed necessary by virtue of an institution failing to satisfy the criteria in paragraph 1 of Schedule 3, or that it has no prospect of satisfying those criteria, or where a proposed restriction consists of or includes a condition requiring the removal of any person as director, controller or manager, the FSA must give that person a copy of the notice together with a statement of his right to make a representation to the FSA.

After giving notice and taking into account any representations, the FSA is required to decide whether to proceed with the action proposed in the notice, or to abandon the notice, or whether to restrict authorization in any manner, or to vary the restrictions on an authorization, or to vary the existing restrictions in a different manner. The Act is silent on what basis the FSA may do this, presumably after studying the financial situation and the activities of the institution.

Section 12 of the Act deals with restrictions on authorization. When it appears to the FSA that the circumstances are not such as to justify revocation, the FSA may restrict the authorization by imposing time limits on its duration, or by imposing such conditions as it deems desirable for the protection of the depositors, both existing and potential, of the institution. Authorization may be restricted by a period of three years from the date on which the restriction is imposed and a limit on the duration of the authorization may be imposed in a case in which '... *the Bank considers that an institution should be allowed time to repay its depositors in an orderly manner*' (section 12(3)).

The purpose of imposing restrictions on authorizations is to require an institution to take certain steps, or to refrain from adopting or pursuing a particular course of action, or to limit the scope of its business. The FSA can also prohibit the institution from soliciting deposits either generally, or from persons who are not depositors; it can prohibit it from entering into any other transactions or class of transactions, or require the removal of any director, controller or manager and specify the requirements to be fulfilled. An institution that fails to comply with any of the required restrictions or any prohibition imposed on it shall be guilty of an offence and liable to a fine. Failure to comply with conditions imposed under section 12 of the Act shall be a ground for revocation of the authorization. According to section 12(8) an institution whose authorization is restricted may apply for a new authorization, but it must be borne in mind that unless it is a European Union Bank or a financial institution, it is required to comply with the Second European Directive [42]; in other words it must make an application for authorization afresh irrespective of the duration it operated as a bank in the United Kingdom prior to the Second European Directive coming into effect.

An authorized institution has the right to surrender its authorization by a written notice to the FSA (section 15), and the surrender shall take effect on the date specified in the notice.

---

[42] 89/646/EEC Second Council Directive, op. cit.

Section 18 of the Act deals with issues relating to a false statement as to authorized status. According to this section no person other than an authorized institution shall describe itself as an authorized institution, or so hold itself out, or to indicate that it is an authorized person. No person shall falsely state or do anything which falsely indicates that he is entitled to accept a deposit in the course of carrying on a deposit-taking business. Any person who may contravene the provisions of section 18 shall be guilty of an offence and liable on conviction on indictment to imprisonment for a term not exceeding two years or to a fine or both, or on summary conviction to imprisonment for a term not exceeding six months or to a fine not exceeding the statutory maximum, or both (section 18(3)).

Directions

In order to protect the interests of institutional or potential depositors the FSA may give an institution directions under section 19 of the Act when giving a notice of revocation of the authorization, or when voluntary winding-up has taken place, or when an institution serves a notice surrendering its authorization, or at any time after expiry of a restricted authorization of an institution (otherwise than by virtue of section 12(8) – that is when an institution on which a restriction is imposed for a duration of time has applied for a new authorization); at any time after a disqualification has been served on the institution under section 183 of the Financial Services Act 1986 [43].

The FSA has the discretion to exercise a variety of powers in order to protect the interests of depositors and an institution that fails to comply shall be guilty of an offence.

A direction given under section 19 may be varied by further directions or revoked by the FSA by a written notice to the institution concerned. A direction must state the reasons for which it is given and must give particulars of the institution's rights (sections 20(4) [44] and 27 [45]). In the

---

[43] See further Annex 2.
[44] Section 20(4) provides that 'An institution to which a direction is given which requires confirmation under subsection (2) above and a person who is given a copy of it under subsection (3) above may, within the period of fourteen days beginning with the day on which the direction is given, make written representations to the Bank; and the Bank shall take any such representations into account in deciding whether to confirm the direction.'
[45] The right of appeal.

event of a direction requiring the removal of any director, controller or manager of an institution, the FSA must give that person a copy of the direction together with a statement of his rights under section 20(4); the FSA is not obliged to give that person any information which does not relate to him.

The purpose of exercising the power in the form of 'directions' is clear – the institution concerned has failed to perform its duties prudently and the Bank, therefore, adopts measures which would protect the interests of depositors and investors.

Objections to Controllers

No person can become a minority, majority or principal shareholder controller or an indirect controller of an authorized institution incorporated in the United Kingdom unless he notifies the FSA in writing that he wants to become such a controller of the institution. The FSA will either notify the person concerned in writing within a period of three months confirming that there is no objection to his becoming such a controller, or by virtue of not serving any written notice of objection under sections 22 or 23 of the Act, the person concerned becomes eligible to become such a controller[46].

The above provisions also apply to a person becoming a partner in an authorized institution, which is a partnership formed in the United Kingdom. The FSA retains the right to seek more information and documents which it may reasonably require for deciding whether to serve a notice of objection or not. The period of three months for confirming objections may be extended when an additional time period becomes necessary for securing more information and documents. The FSA may enter objections to any new or increased control (section 21) if it is satisfied that the person concerned is not a fit and proper person to become a controller whether as a minority, majority or principal shareholder, or an indirect controller, or that the interests of depositors,

---

[46] It deals with objections to new or increased control.
[47] The general rule has been that in counting the period, the date of the issue of the notice must be diregarded, see further *Stewart v Chapman* [1951] 2KB 792. For a period ending with midnight of the last day see *Manorlike Ltd v Le Vitas Travel Agency and Consultancy Services Ltd* [1986] 1 All ER 573, see also *Dodds v Walker* [1981] 2 All ER 609, *E J Riley Investments Ltd v Eurostile Holdings Ltd* [1985] 3 All 181.

including potential depositors, of the institution might be threatened by virtue of that person assuming new or increased control, and that the person's likely influence on the institution as a controller might jeopardize the interests of the depositors and investors. Prior to the serving of a notice of objection under section 22[47], the FSA serves the person concerned with a preliminary written notice stating that it is considering the service of a notice of objection which shall specify the grounds and give particulars of the rights or representations to the person concerned. The time limit for making written representations to the FSA under section 22 is one month from the date of service of the notice.

The FSA may in compliance with the direction of the Treasury serve a notice of objection under section 23 on a person who has given notice under section 21, or who has become such a controller without giving the required notice. Under this section, if it appears to the Treasury that in the event of his becoming, or as a result of his having become, such a controller, a notice can be served on the institution by the Treasury under section 183 of the Financial Services Act 1986[48] (disqualification or restriction of persons connected with overseas countries which do not afford reciprocal facilities for financial business). All notices of objections under this section must state the grounds on which they are served but no direction shall be given by the Treasury in a case after three months following the Treasury's becoming aware of the fact that the person concerned has become a controller of a relevant institution.

Where it appears to the FSA that the person who is the shareholder or controller of an authorized institution incorporated in the United Kingdom is no longer a fit and proper person, the FSA may serve him with a written notice of objection to his becoming such a controller of the institution, only after serving the preliminary written notice stating that it is considering the service on that person of a notice of objection and that notice shall also specify the reasons thereof.

The right of representation of a person concerned shall not be taken away, and representations must be made within a period of one month from the date of service of notice. Where such representations are made the Bank shall take them into account in deciding whether to serve a

---

[48] See Annex 2.

notice of objection. The usual grounds for serving such notice are that the person is not or is no longer a fit and proper person. Any offence occasioned by the contravention by the controller of sections 21 to 24 has been detailed in section 25 of the Act. According to this section, a controller may not be deemed to have contravened the section, when he may be able to establish that he had no knowledge [49] of the Act; but if he subsequently becomes aware of the fact that he has become a controller within the meaning of the Act, then he shall be guilty of an offence unless he gives the Bank of England a written notice to the effect that he has become such a controller within 14 days of his becoming aware of the fact.

Section 26 of the Act authorized the Bank to impose restrictions on a sale of shares, exercisable by the Bank when a person has contravened the provisions of section 21 having been served with a notice of objection to his becoming a controller, or has become a shareholder controller of any description in contravention of section 21 and continues to be one after such notice has been served on him, or that he continues to be a shareholder controller after being served with a section 24 notice [50].

The Bank may serve a written notice on a person directing that any specified shares to which section 26 applies shall, until further notice, be subject to one or more of the following restrictions:

a) any transfer of shares or, in the case of unissued shares, any transfer of the right to be issued with them shall be void;

b) all voting rights in respect of the shares shall be withdrawn;

c) no further shares shall be issued;

d) except in liquidation, no payment shall be made of any sum due from the institution on the shares whether in respect of capital or otherwise.

On the application of the Bank, the court may order sale of any specified shares which are subject to restrictions under section 26, and

---

[49] Knowledge of the Act and circumstances are the essential ingredients of the offence, see further *Gaumont British Distributors Ltd v Henry* [1939] 2 KB 711. Any deliberate attempt to avoid making inquiries of a fact may constitute in law actual knowledge, see further *Knox v Boyd* 1941 JC 82 at 86, *Taylor's Central Garages (Exeter) Ltd v Roper* (1951) 115 JP 445 at 449, 450 per Devlin J; and *Westminster City Council v Croyalgrange Ltd* [1986] 2 All ER 353.

[50] Objection to existing shareholder controller.

if these are already subject to restrictions under section 26(2), they shall cease to be so. No court order, however, shall be made in a case where a notice of objection was served under sections 22 or 24 until the expiry of the period of an appeal against a notice of objections, and if the appeal has been brought, until it has been determined or withdrawn. The Bank has the right to make further applications to the court for orders relating to the sale or transfer of the shares, as it thinks fit. Where shares are sold in pursuance of a court order, the proceeds of the sale less costs of the sale, shall be paid into the court for the benefit of the 'beneficiary interested in them', and any such person may apply to the court for payment of the whole or part of the proceeds.

Advertisement Regulations as Part of Supervision and Control

Financial institutions usually invite customers, current and potential, to make deposits or increase their existing deposits by means of various advertisements. In order to regulate such advertisements or publicity the 1987 Act provides for regulation of advertisements and incidental issues, sections 32 to 35. Advertisement in this context would also include fraudulent inducement to make deposits.

Under the 1987 Act it is for the Treasury to make regulations after consultation with the FSA and the Building Societies Commission.

Section 32 provides for 'deposit advertisements' which are advertisements which contain an invitation to make a deposit or information which is intended to, or *'might presumably be intended to lead directly or indirectly to the making of a deposit'* (section 33(5)(b)).

[51] The terms 'caused' entails a degree of dominance or control from the person 'causing', see further *McLeod (or Houston) v Buchanan* [1940] 2 All ER 179 at 187, HL, per Lord Wright; *Shave v Rosner* [1954] 2 All ER 280; *Lovelace v DPP* [1954] 3 All ER 481; *Shulton (Great Britain) Ltd v Slough BC* [1967] 2 All ER 137; *O'Sullivan v Truth and Sportsman Ltd* (1957) 96 CLR 220 at 228, 229. A person cannot be said to have caused another to do or not to do something unless he either knows or deliberately chooses not to know what the other is doing or failing to do about the relevant subject; *James & Son Ltd v Smee* [1955] 1 QB 78; *Ross Hillman Ltd v Bond* [1974] 2 All ER 287.

[52] Public place stands for a place where the public go or can go irrespective of whether they have a right to go; *R v Wellard* (1884) 14 QBD 113, or a place where the public have access whether they come to that place at the invitation of the occupier, or with someone's permission, or whether access is allowed on payment, or even upon signing a visitor's book, *R v Kane* [1965] 1 All ER 705 at 709, per Barry J; see also *Cawley v Frost* [1976] 3 All ER 744.

For the purpose of the above provision, an advertisement includes any means of bringing about such an invitation to the notice of the person or persons to whom it is addressed. If an advertisement is issued or caused [51] to be issued by any person by way of display or exhibition in a public place [52] it shall be governed by the provisions of section 32 of the Act. For a corporation to be liable for causing or permitting it to be caused, it must be shown that some person for whose criminal acts the corporation would be liable caused or permitted the commission of the offence; knowledge on the part of an ordinary employee is not sufficient, there must be someone to direct the mind of the other party [53].

For the purposes of section 32 an advertisement issued outside the United Kingdom shall be treated as issued in the United Kingdom if it is directed to a person in the United Kingdom, or is made available to him, otherwise than in documents in the public domain such as newspapers, journals, magazines and other periodicals circulated principally outside the United Kingdom, or by means of television, radio broadcasts outside the United Kingdom.

If in the opinion of the FSA any deposit advertisement already issued or proposed to be issued by or on behalf of an authorized institution is misleading, the FSA may by a written notice give the institution a direction under section 33 which may contain all or any of the following prohibitions or requirements:

a) a prohibition on the issue of the advertisement of a particular type;

b) a requirement that the advertisement be modified in a specified manner;

c) a prohibition on the issue of an advertisement which is wholly or substantially a repetition of an advertisement which has been already issued and identified in the direction;

d) a requirement to take all practical steps to withdraw from display any advertisement or any advertisement of a particular

---

[53] *James & Son Ltd v Smee* [1955] 3 All ER 273; *Ross Hillman v Bond*, see above; *Tesco Supermarkets Ltd v Nattrass* [1972] 2 All ER 127, HL.

[54] The day on which the notice is issued is excluded from the calculation of the period; there must be seven clear days for giving a warning notice, *Carapanayoti & Co v Comptoir Commercial Andre & Cie SA* [1972] 1 Lloyd's Rep 139.

description specified in the direction.

The FSA must issue a warning notice to the institution concerned at least seven days[54] before giving a section 33 direction stating the reasons for the proposed direction in addition to pointing out the particulars of rights or representations by the person to whom the notice is addressed. Any breach of section 33 provisions may make the institution guilty of an offence and liable in law.

Section 34 of the Act deals with unsolicited calls. According to this section the Treasury may, after consultation with the FSA and the Building Societies Commission, make regulations for regulating the making of unsolicited calls on persons in the United Kingdom, or from the United Kingdom on persons elsewhere, with the view to procuring the making of deposits. According to this section, an unsolicited call means '... *a personal visit or oral communication made without express invitation.*' (section 34(4)).

The institution must be prohibited from soliciting deposits and making agreements with the view to accepting deposits from persons on whom unsolicited calls are made. Under this section regulations can be made by the Treasury to specify the persons to whom or the circumstances in which unsolicited calls may be made, and under the regulations the Treasury may require specified information to be disclosed to persons on whom unsolicited calls are made.

Section 35 of the Act deals with fraudulent inducement to make a deposit and provides that:

> *Any person who*
>
> *(a) makes a statement, promise or forecast which he knows to be misleading*[55]*, false or deceptive, or dishonestly conceals any material facts; or*
>
> *(b) recklessly*[56] *makes (dishonestly or otherwise) a statement, promise or forecast which is misleading, false or deceptive, is guilty of an offence if he makes the statement, promise or forecast or conceals the*

---

[55] For the definition of what is misleading see *R v Lord Kylsant* [1932] 1 KB 442, [1931] All ER Rep 179, and *R v Bishirgian* [1936] 1 All ER 586.

[56] For the interpretation of 'reckless' see *R v Bates* [1952] 2 All ER 842 where it was held that 'reckless' should be given its ordinary meaning and not restricted to recklessness involving dishonesty.

Analysis of Statutory Provisions Governing the Business of Banking

> facts for the purpose of inducing, or is reckless as to whether it may induce, another person (whether or not the person to whom the statement, promise or forecast is made or from whom the facts are concealed)
>
> (i) to make, or refrain from making a deposit with him or any other person; or
>
> (ii) to enter, or refrain from entering, into an agreement for the purpose of making such a deposit.

Information may not be treated as misleading unless there is a reasonable probability of confusion [57].

Supervision and Control by Seeking Information

Sections 36 to 40 deal with the responsibility of institutions for notifying the Bank of England of various changes in the structure of the business and the power of the FSA to obtain information. These provisions have, therefore, two aspects: firstly, the responsibility of the institution to notify the FSA of change of directors, controllers or managers, notification of acquisition of significant shareholdings, and involvement in large exposures, and secondly, the power of the FSA to obtain information by various means which has been discussed in this section. It is for the institution concerned to notify the FSA by a written notice if any person has become or ceased to be a director, controller or manager of the institution before the end of the period of 14 days beginning with the day on which the institution becomes aware of the relevant facts. The FSA, however, has the authority to exonerate the institution from performing this obligation, wholly or partly, if the principal place of business is outside the United Kingdom.

A person who becomes a significant shareholder, 5-15% of voting rights, section 37(2), in relation to an authorized institution incorporated

---

[57] See *Re Bayer Products Ltd's Application* [1947] 2 Al ER 188 at 190, CA, per Lord Green MR. It is immaterial whether false or misleading information has proved advantageous or gainful; *Jones v Meatyard* [1939] 1 All ER 140; *Stevens & Steels Ltd and Evans v King* [1943] 1 All ER 314; *Clear v Smith* [1981] 1 WLR 399, *Barrass v Reeve* [1980] 3 All ER 705.

in the UK must notify the FSA in writing within seven days from his becoming such.

Breach of any of the obligations will render the person guilty of an offence.

Unless an authorized institution's principal place is outside the United Kingdom, it is obligatory for it to report to the FSA whenever it may enter into a transaction relating to any one person in consequence of which it is exposed to the risk of incurring losses in excess of 10 per cent of its capital resources, or if it proposes to enter into a transaction relating to any one person, which either by itself or along with other previous transactions entered into by it in relation to that person would expose it to the risk of incurring losses in excess of 25 per cent of those resources. The term 'transaction' in this context includes transactions relating to different persons if they are connected and the cumulative effect of it might affect the financial soundness of the other(s).

In the event of an authorized institution having one or more subsidiaries that are not authorized institutions, the FSA may by a written notice to that institution direct that the provisions as to reporting of large exposures under section 38 of the Act shall apply to it as if *the transactions and available capital resources of a subsidiary or subsidiaries or such of them as are specified in the notice, were included in those of the institutions'* (section 38(3)). For the purposes of this section a transaction entered into by an institution relates to a person if it is:

(a) a transaction that entails an obligation for that person to the institution, or in consequence of which he may incur such an obligation;

(b) a transaction under which the institution will incur or may incur an obligation if that person defaults on an obligation to a third party; or

(c) a transaction under which the institution acquires or incurs an obligation to acquire or in consequence of which it may incur an obligation to acquire an asset the value of which depends wholly or mainly on the performance of the obligation by that person or on his financial soundness;

and the risk of loss attributable to the transaction emanates from the default by the person, or to his obligations under (a) or (b), or that the risk emanates from his defaulting on his obligations under paragraph (c), or due to a deterioration in his financial soundness.

An institution that fails to make a report as required by section 38 of the Act shall be guilty of an offence.

The Treasury has a discretionary power to amend section 38(1) after consultation with the FSA in order to vary the percentage mentioned in that paragraph.

Section 39 gives the FSA almost unrestrained power to obtain information and to require the production of documents. Under this section the FSA has the authority to require an authorized institution to provide such information as the FSA may reasonably require for the performance of its functions; it may also require the institution to provide the FSA with a report by an accountant or other person with relevant professional skill, or on any aspect of any matter in regard to which the FSA may decide to obtain information. The accountant or other person appointed by the institution for this purpose shall be a person nominated or approved by the FSA, and the FSA may require his report to be in such form and manner as may be specified in a notice. The phrase *'reasonably require for the performance of its functions'* creates controversy in that one is required to rely on the judgement of the FSA, and it will be extremely difficult for an institution to question the validity of that judgement [58].

The FSA may by a written notice require an authorized institution to produce document(s) which may be specified by it within such time and at such place as the FSA may decide.

This power of requiring production of documents extends to persons who appear to be in possession[59] of them, but where any person when *'such production is required claims a lien on documents produced by him the production shall be without prejudice to the lien.'* (section 39(4)).

Production of documents under this section includes power to take copies of and extracts from them, and even require a person who is a

---

[58] See also section 1(4) of the Act.
[59] A term 'possession' is required to be given a broad interpretation to cover more than actual physical possession; see further *Webb v Baker* [1916] 2 KB 753; *Oliver v Goodger* [1944] 2 All ER 481; *Towers & Co Ltd v Gray* [1961] 2 QB 351.

present or past director, controller or manager of, or was at any time employed by, or acting as an employee of the institution, to provide an explanation of any of them, and to inquire of the person the location of the documents if they are not produced by the person who was so required to do. If, in the interests of depositors or potential depositors, the FSA deems it desirable, it may exercise this power of obtaining information and production of documents in relation to any body corporate that is or has at time been:

> *(a) a holding company, subsidiary or related company of that institution;*
>
> *(b) a subsidiary of a holding company of that institution;*
>
> *(c) a holding company of a subsidiary of that institution; or*
>
> *(d) a body corporate in the case of which a shareholder controller of that institution, either alone or with any associate or associates, is entitled to exercise, or control the exercise of, more than 50 per cent of the voting power at a general meeting; or in relation to any partnership of which that institution is or has at any relevant time been a member (section 39(6)).*

Again, if the FSA deems it desirable in the interests of depositors or potential depositors of an institution which is an authorized partnership, it may exercise the power to obtain information and require production of documents in relation to:

> *(a) any other partnership having a member in common with the authorized partnership;*
>
> *(b) any body corporate which is or has been at any relevant time a member of the authorized partnership;*
>
> *(c) any body corporate in the case of which the partners in the authorized partnership hold more than 20 per cent of the shares or any partner in the authorized partnership, either alone or with any associate or associates, is entitled to exercise, or control the*

> exercise of, more than 50 per cent of the voting power at a general meeting; or
>
> (d) any subsidiary or holding company of any such body corporate as is mentioned in paragraphs (b) or (c) above or any holding company of any such subsidiary (section 39(7)).

The FSA may also exercise this power in order to determine whether a director, controller or manager of an authorized institution is a fit and proper person to hold the particular position, or whether he may be allowed to hold such a position. The FSA may also exercise this power in relation to any person who is a significant shareholder of that authorized institution. Any person, who without reasonable excuse, fails to comply with the requirement of section 39 shall be guilty of an offence. However, 'nothing in section 39 shall compel the production by a barrister, advocate or solicitor of a document containing a privileged communication[60] made by him or to him in that capacity' (Section 39(13)).

Any officer, servant or agent of the FSA may enter any premises[61] occupied by a person on whom a notice has been served under section 39 of the Act for the purpose of obtaining the information or documents required by the FSA. Although this power extends where a section 39 has been served on a person who occupies the premises, the FSA shall not authorize any person to act under section 40(2) unless 'it has reasonable cause to believe[62] that if such a notice was served it would not be complied with, or that any documents to which it would relate

---

[60] Communications made to and from a legal adviser for the purposes of obtaining legal advice and assistance are protected from disclosure in the course of legal proceedings; see *Greenough v Gaskell* (1833) 1 My & K 98 at 102 et seq. See further, as to legal professional privilege, 14 Halsbury's Laws (4th edn) paras 71 *et seq.*

[61] For the definition of the term 'premises' see further *Metropolitan Water Board v Paine* [1907] 1 KB 285; *Whitley v Stumbles* [1930] AC 544, HL; *Bracey v Read* [1963] Ch 88, [1962] 3 All ER 472; and *Maaunsell v Olins* [1975] AC 373, [1975] 1 All ER 16, HL.

[62] It is difficult to determine on what bases the FSA may have reasonable cause to believe; perhaps it would reach this conclusion on the basis of the information that it may receive from various sources, be they official or unofficial, or by reference to the performance of the authorized institution; see further; *R v Banks* [1916] 2 KB 6221, [1916-17] All ER Rep 356, and *R v Harrison* [1938] 3 All ER 134, 159 LT 95; and *Nakkuda Ali v Jayaratne* [1951] AC 66, PC.

would be removed, tampered with or destroyed.' Any person who intentionally obstructs a person appointed by the FSA to exercise these rights shall be guilty of an offence.

Supervision and Control by Investigations

If information obtained arouses suspicion in the mind of the FSA then it has the right to activate its power to investigate the affairs and conduct of an authorized institution under section 41 to 44. It is to be emphasized, however, that the powers are meant to be exercised by the FSA to protect the interests of depositors, actual or potential, of an authorized institution.

The FSA may appoint one or more competent person(s) to investigate and report on the nature, conduct or state of the institution's business or any particular aspect of it or the ownership or control of the institution but the FSA must give written notice of any such appointment to the institution concerned. Any of the appointed persons may also investigate the business of any body corporate, or a partnership which is or at any relevant time has been:

> *(a) a holding company, subsidiary or related company of the institution under investigation;*
>
> *(b) a subsidiary or related company of a holding company of that institution;*
>
> *(c) a holding company of a subsidiary of that institution;*
>
> *(d) a body corporate in the case of which a shareholder controller of that institution, either alone or with any associate or associates, is entitled to exercise, or control the exercise of, more than 20 per cent of the voting power at a general meeting; or the business of any partnership of which that institution is or has at any relevant been a member* (section 41(2)).

In the case of a partnership such persons have the right to investigate the business of:

> *(a) any other partnership having a member in common with the authorized partnership;*

(b) any body corporate which is or has at any relevant time been a member of the authorized partnership;

  (c) any body corporate in the case of which the partners in the authorized partnership hold more than 20 per cent of the shares or any partner in the authorized partnership, either alone or with any associate or associates, is entitled to exercise, or control the exercise of, more than 20 per cent of the voting power at a general meeting; or

  (d) any subsidiary, related company or holding company of any such body corporate as is mentioned in paragraph (b) or (c) above or any holding company of any such subsidiary (section 41(3)).

However, such person(s) must give written notice to the body corporate or partnership to the effect that it would conduct an investigation into the affairs and conduct of the business.

During the investigation process every person who is or was a director, controller, manager, employee, agent, banker, auditor, solicitor, or a significant shareholder, is required to produce by the stipulated time and place all documents relating to the body concerned which are in his custody or power, to attend before a person so appointed if necessary, and to cooperate with the appointed person(s) carrying out the investigation. Any person who without reasonable excuse fails to produce any document which it is required to produce, or to attend before an appointed person for questioning, or fails to answer questions which may be put to him, or intentionally obstructs a person in the exercise of the rights conferred by this section, shall be guilty of an offence. Any statement that may be made by a person in compliance with a requirement imposed by virtue of section 41 may be used in evidence against him. A barrister, advocate or solicitor may not be compelled to produce a document under this section which may contain privileged communication made by him or to him in that capacity.

A similar kind of power to that under section 41 has been conferred on the Bank by section 42 in cases of suspected contraventions of sections 3 and 35 of the 1987 Act. If the FSA has reasonable grounds to believe that a person has contravened the provisions of section 42, it may apply to a Justice of the Peace for a warrant to enter and search the premises, take possession of any documents specified in section 42(1)(c), take copies thereof and require any person named in the warrant to answer questions relevant to determine whether that person is guilty of any contravention of section 42.

Supervision and Control in relation to Accountants and Auditors

The 1987 Act makes it obligatory for authorized institutions when they accept deposits to keep a copy of the most recent audited accounts which must be available for inspection by any person on request during normal business hours. Failure to comply with this provision (section 45) shall make an authorized institution guilty of an offence. An authorized institution incorporated in the United Kingdom is obliged to give written notice to the FSA if it proposes to remove its auditors before the expiration of their term of office, or replaces its auditors, or if the auditors resign the auditor must notify the FSA. The auditors or a person appointed to make a report in section 8(5)[63] or section 39(1)(b) of the 1987 Act shall not be deemed to have contravened the provisions of section 47 provided they(he) have(has) communicated with the FSA in good faith, whether in regard to making a response to a request made by the FSA for providing information or otherwise. This applies to any matter of which *'he becomes aware of in his capacity as auditor and which relates to the business or affairs of the institution or any associated body'*[64] (section 47(2) of the Act).

Where restrictions have been imposed on acceptance of deposits under section 3 of the 1987 Act and an authorized institution contravenes the provisions, the FSA has the power under section 48 to seek an order of the court to compel the institution to repay the deposits forthwith, or at such time as the court may direct. In Scotland, such deposits will be recovered by a receiver. However, in issuing such an order the court must pay regard to the effect that repayment may have on the solvency of the person concerned, or on his ability to carry on

---

[63] This subsection relates to applications for authorization.
[64] See also section 39(6) of the 1987 Act which also defines an associated body.

his business in a manner satisfactory to his creditors. If the court is satisfied that the authorized institution has earned profits on deposits, which were accepted in contravention of section 3, it may order him to pay into court *'such sum as appears to the court to be just having regard to the profits appearing to the court to have accrued to him'* (section 49(1)). Any amount paid must be paid as the court may direct.

Where section 3 has been activated by the FSA, the authorized institution has an obligation to comply with that order in order to give protection to the depositors; such orders are issued when the credibility of an authorized institution is questioned. The Act, therefore, provides for the relief and compensation that may be provided to the depositors and, therefore, authorizes the FSA to seek an order of the court.

Reflecting on the Authorization and Revocation System of the Financial Services Authority

As explained in the previous sections, the primary features of the Banking Act 1987 are: (a) authorization, (b) investigation procedures and (c) the deposit protection scheme.

In Schedule 3 of the 1987 Act it is intended to give a schematic view of the authorization system and the stages involved in the restriction and revocation of authorization.

As stated earlier, in supervising banks and credit institutions, the FSA is primarily concerned with how the banks operate and whether the depositors' interests could be jeopardised. In fact, when these two aspects of supervision are examined and analysed, the other related aspects, namely the criteria of fit and proper person, integrity and skill, liquidity and capital adequacy also come under those major headings.

In performing its supervisory functions, the FSA is guided primarily by three Statements of Principle, in addition to which the FSA is required to pay attention to the Guide to Banking Supervisory Policy because this Guide provides for giving information to authorized institutions of the approach that the FSA adopts in respect of particular supervisory issues. The Guide is updated and the authorized institutions are informed accordingly.

The Building Societies Commission published its own Statement of Principles in accordance with section 45AA(a) of the Building Societies

Act 1986 which applies to the supervision of all building societies incorporated in the United Kingdom and authorized by the Building Societies Commission.

The FSA Statements of Principle referred to above are now discussed.

Statement Based on Section 16 of the Banking Act 1987

This Statement applies to all institutions authorized by the FSA under the Banking Act 1987. Of course, variations in application may take place depending on whether an institution is to be designated as a credit institution or not[65].

In deciding whether to authorize an institution or restrict or revoke its authorization, the FSA is guided by the Principles in the Statement in addition to the criteria established by Schedule 3 to the 1987 Act, which have already been discussed. After an institution has been authorized by the FSA it remains under its supervision and if at any time in the future the activities of an authorized institution are deemed to be unacceptable, the FSA would usually initiate a discussion with the authorized institution concerned and any failure to correct its position might lead to restriction on authorization and in appropriate circumstances may lead to revocation of the authorization. The legal powers of the FSA are exercised when an authorized institution persistently fails to correct its position and/or leaves its depositors unprotected.

Statement 1 under section 16 of the Banking Act 1987 provides for correct interpretation of each of the minimum authorization criteria embodied in Schedule 3 to the 1987 Act; it explains the FSA's approach to risk management and supervision, the scope of its discretionary power as to the grant of authorization including authorization to overseas institutions, that is, the institutions outside the EEA; interpretation of the various grounds for revocation which may be found in section 11 of the 1987 Act; and the principles governing the exercise of the FSA's discretion to restrict or revoke an authorization.

Minimum Criteria for Authorization, Section 3 of the

---

[65] A credit institution is an 'undertaking whose business is to receive deposits or other repayable funds from the public and to grant credits for its own account' as defined in the First Banking Coordination Directive which applies for the purposes of the Banking Act and the Regulations.

Banking Act 1981

(a) directors and other officers must be fit and proper persons;

(b) the business must be directed by at least two individuals;

(c) the business must be conducted in a prudent manner;

(d) the business must be carried on with integrity and the professional skills appropriate to the nature and scale of its activities; and

(e) there must be minimum net assets in addition to having an appropriate board of directors.

'Fit and proper persons' has been discussed earlier in this chapter. Determining whether a director or any officers is a fit and proper person or not is a value judgement. However, the FSA is required to pay attention to the criteria that appear at (a) to (d) of paragraph 3 of Schedule 3. These criteria generally refer to the honesty of the officer, that is, whether he has committed an offence involving fraud or dishonesty or violence or contravened any provisions of any legislation designed to protect members of the public against financial loss due to dishonesty, incompetence or malpractice, or has engaged in any business practices which would appear to be deceitful or oppressive or otherwise improper or *'which otherwise reflect discredit on his method of conducting business'* or has engaged in or been associated with any other business practices or conducted himself in such a way as to cast doubt on his competence and soundness of judgement.

In determining whether a director or an officer is a fit and proper person to hold any particular office, regard is paid to his probity, competence and soundness of judgement, diligence and whether *'the interests of depositors or potential depositors of the institution are likely to be in any way threatened by his holding that position'*.

In the case of an overseas institution the same criteria are applied to consider whether directors and officers are fit and proper persons or not. It may be unfair to apply the same criteria to officers from different backgrounds, although the criteria that they are honest and possess soundness of judgement must be satisfied by everybody. The issue of competence might present a problem in that competence in the technology of advanced societies and in the technology of not so advanced societies must be different and this has a bearing upon the other criterion of 'diligence'. It is accepted that the fit and proper person criterion under Schedule 3 seems to be appropriate but a uniform application of this criterion to persons of different financial and economic backgrounds may present legal difficulties.

Prudent Conduct Criteria

The list of the criteria to be satisfied for 'prudent' conduct cannot be exhaustive; in fact certain other relevant issues pertaining to institutions are required to be considered for determining whether an institution conducts its business in a prudent manner; the institution's management including overall control and direction by the board of directors, the institution's general strategy and objectives, lending exposures, bad debt, valuation of methods of securities, interest rate policy, training of staff etc.

Adequate Capital

The protection of the depositors is one of the main aspects of prudential banking supervision. In the event of a bank running into financial difficulty, losses must be borne by its shareholders and not by its depositors. Therefore, they must have adequate capital to return to their depositors in the event of an emergency arising. A bank's capital is usually formed of the following:

(a) shareholders' equity and accumulated profits, known as the 'core' capital;

(b) general provisions which the bank set aside for meeting unidentified future losses occasioned by medium- and long-term debts, usually known as 'supplementary' capital;

(c) subordinated term debt of at least two years' maturity, which cannot be repaid without the FSA's permission and therefore is subject to a 'lock-in' clause; and

(d) the accumulated profit arising from its trading activities.

In practice, future losses occasioned by medium- and long term-term debts (supplementary capital) is not allowed to exceed 50% of the capital at (a); at least 50% of a bank's capital must be of the type as at (a); subordinated term debt may not exceed 50% of the capital at (a); and general provision as at (b) must not exceed 1.25% of a bank's total risk-weighted assets. Total debts at (b) and (c) (subordinated debt) in the trading book may not exceed twice the total capital at (a). The term 'risk-weighted assets' means the risks that have been 'weighted' – measured or attached to a type of asset held by a bank at a particular period of time; but the degree of risks to which a type of an asset may be subject depends upon market conditions; however, generally, cash held by a bank is weighted at 0% and personal loans at 100%.

The Second Solvency Ratio Directive [66], which was implemented in the United Kingdom in December 1990, and the Capital Adequacy Directive [67], which was implemented in January 1996, related to the issue of capital adequacy of banks precisely for the purpose of protecting depositors. However, whereas the Solvency Ratio Directive measures credit risk, measurement for market risks [68] is the objective of the Capital Adequacy Directive. This Directive also introduced the system of allocating positions between the *trading book* and the *banking book*. No financial instrument can be simultaneously held in both books; when an instrument is to be held for short-term gain it is then placed on the trading book; the banking book holds long-term instruments, and is subject to the Solvency Ratio Directive. The instruments in the trading book which are subject to the Capital Adequacy Directive accrue capital charges which are calculated by reference to the nature of the risk, e.g. foreign exchange risks. The bank risk asset ratio is usually calculated by dividing its capital base by the sum of the banking book risk weighted assets and the trading book Notional Risk Weighted Assets. All banks incorporated in the United Kingdom are required to set a target 'capital adequacy' requirement for both their trading books and banking books and must maintain those targets.

In considering the issue of assessment of capital adequacy the FSA generally refers to the relevant chapters of the Guide and the method of

---

[66] 89/647/EEC, Council Directive on a solvency ratio for credit institutions.
[67] 93/6/EC, Council Directive on Capital Adequacy of Investment Firms and Credit Institutions.
[68] Market risk stands for risk that is occasioned by the movement in the price of financial instruments, e.g. derivatives.
[69] See further, the Guide to Banking Supervisory Policy.

assessing capital adequacy is mainly found in chapters CA, CO and BC [69]. These chapters implement the relevant EC Banking Directive, namely own funds, Solvency Ratio Directive and Capital Adequacy Directive. Under these Directives authorized institutions must maintain a minimum standard of capital adequacy throughout the EEA in consistence with the Basle Accord, International Convergence of Capital Measurement and Capital Standards 1988, which was subsequently amended by the member countries of the Basle Committee on Banking Supervision [70]. In assessing a bank's capital adequacy the FSA takes into account the level of an institution's own funds, liquidity and large exposures. An institution's capital is considered to be adequate when the amount commensurate with the nature and the scale of the institution's operations is sufficient to safeguard the interests of its depositors, both current and potential, taking also into account the risks inherent in these operations including the operations of an undertaking belonging to the same group [71].

In the case of a United Kingdom incorporated credit institution, at least ECU 5m or equivalent must be maintained, although this criterion may be relaxed on a discretionary basis by the FSA in respect of overseas institutions. Credit institutions that are authorized prior to legislation implementing the Second Banking Coordination Directive [72] coming into force are required to maintain own funds of at least ECU 5m or the highest level an institution attained at any time after 22 December 1989, whichever is the lower [73].

Integrity and Skill in Carrying on Business

This Principle entails two elements: (a) whether an institution's business

---

[70] Members of the Basle Committee are: Belgium, Canada, France, Germany, Italy, Japan, Luxembourg, the Netherlands, Sweden, Switzerland, the United Kingdom and the United States.

[71] Capital has been defined in the Own Funds Directive 89/299/EEC and amended by the Capital Adequacy Directive 93/6/EEC) and consists of the following:
Tier 1 - Own Funds (intangible assets such as goodwill are deducted in calculating own funds)
Tier 2 - Supplementary Capital
Tier 3 - Short-dated Debt Capital to support a trading book.

[72] 89/646/EEC.

[73] See further Statement 1, the Banking Act 1987, section 16 paragraph 2.9; where there has been a change in the parent controller of the institution after 1 January 1993 the requirement is generally ECU 5m.

is carried out with integrity, and (b) whether it is carried out with the professional skills befitting the nature and scale of the activities of the institution concerned.

Integrity stands for high ethical standards but does not prevent a banking institution from maximizing its profits in a business manner but in carrying out its business it must not be involved in criminal activities, dishonesty, malpractice or incompetence. Examples of some of the statutes and regulations that must not be violated by a banking institution are the Theft Acts 1968 and 1978. The Criminal Justice Act 1983 in particular deals with issues relating to insider dealing, the Money Lending Act 1993, the Consumer Credit Act 1974, The Financial Services Act 1986, the Banking Act 1979 and 1987. In addition, there are certain codes of conduct such as the London Code of Conduct for the Wholesale Market in Sterling, the Foreign Exchange and Bullion, the Code of Banking Practice and the Takeover Code.

Although the level and skills may vary according to the nature of the banking business, integrity can never be compromised irrespective of the size and scope of activities of the institution.

The Solvency Ratio Directive [74] adopts a 'risk-weighed assets' measure which stands for the credit risk for which a bank remains responsible. The Solvency Ratio Directive recommends a minimum risk asset ratio of at least 8%; the FSA follows the same principle, but in relation to the nature of the operations, the range of this ratio may be significant – sometimes to the extent of 40%.

The quality of the on- and off-balance sheet exposures also becomes a reference point in assessing the capital adequacy of an authorized institution and the reasons thereof. Under the EC Directive on the Monitoring and Control of Large Exposures of Credit Institution [75] and section 38 of the Banking Act 1987 an authorized institution other than those the principal place of which is outside the United Kingdom shall make a report to the FSA if it has entered into any transaction relating to one person which exposed the authorized institution to risk in excess of 10% losses of its available capital resources, or it proposes to do so whether as an isolated transaction or as a transaction linked to previous transactions which would expose the authorized institution to a risk of

---

[74] 89/647/EEC.
[75] 92/621/EEC.

incurring losses in excess of 25% of its available capital adequacy.

The reporting obligation also applies to transactions which related to different person *'if they are connected in such a way that the financial soundness of any one of them may affect the financial soundness of the other or others or the same factors may affect the financial soundness of both or all of them.'* (section 38(2) of the Banking Act 1987).

The FSA also takes into account other risks, namely, operational risks (the risks emanating from negligence or incompetence of the management) which risk may also arise from irresponsible acts of the holding company or subsidiaries or other connected companies and/or foreign exchange position risk. In accordance with the EC Second Directive of Supervision of Credit Institutions on the Consolidated Basis [76], the FSA examines the capital adequacy issue on a consolidated basis.

The FSA adopts both qualitative and quantitative criteria in assessing the capital adequacy issue. Whereas the quantitative aspect of assessment refers to CAMEL factors (capital, assets, market risk, earnings, liabilities), BECOM factors (business, controls, organization, management) are referred to as qualitative risks.

The financial ability of an institution is judged by reference to various factors, namely, its ability to renew or replace its deposits and other funding, the quality of liquid assets, quality of management, internal control system, nature of its business, whether progressive or not, its position in the market, and of course, by referring to broad criteria whether the business is being carried out in a prudent manner. The burden is on each institution to justify the criteria laid down in Schedule 3 Banking Act 1987 and each must comply with, among others, the requirements of the Guidelines on liquidity, mismatches it may run, whether it involves a comparison of its assets to liabilities and its other commitments in addition to in- and out-flows of cash.

Although usually in the case of a non-UK incorporated bank, the FSA is satisfied with the scope of home country supervision but it has the power to evaluate the parent's liquidity and capital adequacy position on a global basis. If the global liquidity position of the holding company is not satisfactory, the FSA has the authority to advise that the UK operation be transformed into a subsidiary or even a finance house.

[76] 92/30/EEC.

Analysis of Statutory Provisions Governing the Business of Banking 79

Another aspect of determining the assets position is to take account of the depreciation and diminution in the value of an authorized institution's assets so that its total assets and liquidity position may also be determined. Furthermore, provision for doubtful and bad debts, expected losses and contingent liabilities, tax liabilities and their determination in accordance with accepted accounting standards is essential[77]. The progress in debt recovery made by an authorized institution, its loan policy and its system of valuation of security are very carefully looked into by the FSA. All authorized institutions are required to maintain an adequate level of provision against debts. As stated earlier, given the freedom to authorized institutions as to how to run their business, each institution is nevertheless bound by the provision of the Banking Act 1987 and the relevant EC Directives.

What the FSA would like to see is that an authorized institution maintains a standard of control, management and business policy, not only in a prudent manner coupled with integrity and skill, but also so that business standards are higher than the minimum level prescribed by the statutes, Code of Conduct and EC Directives.

Supervision of Risk-Based Banking Business by the FSA

Supervision of this type of business by the FSA is confined to the authorized institutions that are incorporated outside the EEA, as authorized institutions incorporated elsewhere in the EEA with branches in the UK are primarily supervised by their home country supervisors. However, with regard to this kind of supervision the Rate Framework is followed[78] by a formal risk assessment of every authorized institution or group of institutions during each supervisory period but the length of the period varies according to the risk profile[79]. A formal risk assessment entails nine evaluation factors – capital, assets, market risks, earnings, liabilities, business, controls, organization, management (CAMEL and BECOM), and the assessment is performed by the FSA on the basis of the information it receives from an authorized institution during the normal cause of supervision. In the case of an overseas

---

[77] The Accounting Standards stand for the standards recommended in the Statements of Standard Accounting Practice and Financial Reporting Standards.
[78] Risk assessment, tools of supervision, evaluation.
[79] This period can be as short as six months if the risk profile is considered to be very high, otherwise the usual supervisory period is two years.

institution, the FSA also receives information from its overseas home supervisors. It is to be pointed out, however, that the purpose of such assessments are twofold: (a) to secure the depositors' interests, and (b) to allow the authorized institution to amend its position.

After each risk assessment the FSA, when necessary, suggests remedial action and in the event of an authorized institution failing to take any action, the FSA has the authority to take action under the Banking Act 1987 which progresses from warning to suspension and ultimately to revocation of authorization.

The Composition of the Board of Directors

The number of directors to be elected depends on the nature of the institution and the scale of its operations. Directors may be executive or non-executive; the FSA maintains that non-executive directors may play a valuable role in bringing an independent perspective to the running of the business and can be a source of expertise. According to the FSA the United Kingdom incorporated institutions and UK-based banking groups should have an audit committee on which suitable non-executive directors should be placed and they should be required to audit committee functions [80]. The FSA does not however maintain a rigid policy as to the appointment of non-executive directors or an audit committee if an institution's holding company satisfactorily fulfils the role of an audit committee.

Directors, Controllers and Managers Must be Fit and Proper Persons (Schedule 3 Paragraph 1)

Section 105 of the Banking Act 1987 provides that every person who is or is to be a director, controller or manager of an authorized institution must be a fit and proper person to hold such a position. In determining 'fit and proper person' the FSA considers whether that person has sufficient skills, knowledge and soundness of judgement to undertake his duties and responsibilities. Presumably, the past records, current conduct and the manner in which a person of such a status discharges his responsibilities are considered by the FSA, along with a degree of value judgement.

---

[80] In regard to an audit committee see Chapter R3 of the Guide to the Banking Supervision.

However, a person's probity and integrity may not be questioned. As to soundness of judgement, the FSA considers the capacity to make decisions in emergency as well as normal situations, maturity of mind and the capacity to rationalize issues and problems by the officer concerned. Of course, such an officer must not have a criminal record, in particular convictions for fraud and dishonesty, namely in banking, insurance, investment business or in breach of other legislation, the purpose of which is to protect members of the public against financial losses [81]. Such a person must not be involved in any business practices which would appear to be deceitful or improper, and which may in any other way arouse suspicion as to the skill and integrity of the person in conducting a business. The FSA may refer to the person's record of compliance with various codes such as the London Code of Conduct for the Wholesale Markets in Sterling, the Joint Money Laundering Steering Group's Guidance Notes, the Code of Banking Practice, and the Takeover Code in so far as these are relevant to such person's activities. Depending upon the nature or the value of banking business that an authorized institution does, the standards required of such a person must seem to be commensurate.

As stated earlier, there are three stages in banking supervision: (a) authorization; (b) surveillance after authorization has been granted; (c) restrictions on authorization leading to revocation of authorization if during surveillance the FSA has become convinced that any of the Schedule 3 criteria has been persistently violated by an authorized institution.

After authorization, therefore, an authorized institution remains under the surveillance of the FSA and whenever imprudence becomes evident or adequate capital has not been maintained, or depositors' interests prove to be in jeopardy, or the probity, competence or professional skills of an officer may be questioned, the FSA can activate its enforcement measures, after discussing issues first with the

---

[81] Exception 95 of the Banking Act 1987 permits the FSA to have regard to certain spent convictions under the Rehabilitation of Offenders Act 1974.

[82] For the UK incorporated credit institutions, the thresholds of shareholding at which the fitness and properness of shareholders controllers must be assessed at 10%, 20%, 33%, 50% and 75% together with shareholdings of less than 10% where the person is a minority shareholder, as defined in section 105(4)(a) of the Banking Act 1987. For other authorized institutions, the thresholds are 15%, 50% and 75%.

responsible officers of the authorized institution concerned. Shareholders and controllers (the latter whether direct or indirect), as defined in section 105 of the Banking Act 1987, may also be required to pass the test of a fit and proper person; again the reason being that they must not be instrumental in damaging the depositors' interests. The standards of a fit and proper person must be commensurate with the level of shareholding[82].

With a branch of an overseas authorized institution, the FSA takes special care of whether shareholders and controllers in the parent company might present any threats to the depositors' interests, whether by virtue of inadequacy of capital, operational business with persons who are not deemed to be fit and proper persons, and whether an institution is involved in high risk-based lending or investment. Other factors such as skills, integrity and probity are also considered. Where shareholders do not exert influence by virtue of not holding a high level of shares (between 10% to 20%) the FSA may not be strict in satisfying all the factors usually included in determining whether a person is a fit and proper person. The FSA also takes into account the issue of conflict of interests. The possibilities of causing damage to an authorized institution's interests are contagious which undermines confidence in the institution, is taken seriously by the FSA, and in practice it is believed that the higher the shareholding the greater the risk of contagion if the shareholder(s) encounter(s) financial difficulties. Of course, the risk of contagion relates to publicity with regard to illegal or unethical conduct by the parent company, or another member of the group of the authorized institution.

In the case of non-voting shareholders who in effect exert substantial influence over an authorized institution for whatever reasons, the degree of their influence and its impact on the authorized institution is also considered by the FSA. In other words, the principles of a fit and proper person may also be applied to them. The same argument applies to minority (less than 10%) shareholders controllers of a UK incorporated authorized institution.

In the case of an indirect controller who directs or instructs[83] shareholders controllers in accordance with section 105(3)(d) of the Banking Act 1987 the FSA applies similar considerations to those for

[83] See Statement 1 Banking Act 1987, section 16 paragraph 2.63.

shareholders controllers. Any new development that may occur within an authorized institution must be reported to the FSA; section 94 of the Banking Act 1987. A responsible officer of the authorized institution must not knowingly or recklessly provide the FSA with information which is false or misleading in a material particular, and if he does so then he shall fail to satisfy the criterion of a fit and proper person.

Conclusions

The 1987 Act is an improvement on the 1979 Act, paying more attention to the issue of control and supervision of authorized institutions by adopting elaborate but essential machinery. This includes: directions, objections to controllers, the procedure for seeking information, instituting investigations and making accountants and auditors more accountable to the FSA than ever before. Part I of the Act, which is concerned with the regulation of deposit-taking business, also provides for the procedures for authorization including suspension/withdrawal and deposits which have been accepted as unauthorized ones.

The 1987 Act gives the FSA discretionary powers to a significant extent, presumably because the legislation is based on the assumption that in view of the wealth of its experience the FSA will not abuse its position; both the 1979 and 1987 Acts place emphasis on the protection of depositors, and this explains why the Act has allowed the FSA such wide powers. What is disturbing, however, is that the Act exonerates the FSA, including its officers and staff, from any liability in damages for anything done or omitted to be done in the purported discharge of its functions [84].

The London Capital Market must protect its reputation and efficiency; the FSA, therefore, is required to be allowed extensive powers to ensure not only that the Market, by virtue of its regulatory measures, may increase the flow of investment into it, but also that it may afford sufficient protection to its depositors.

---

[84] Section 1(4) of the Banking Act 1987.

4 The Deposit Protection Scheme

Introduction

The Deposit Protection Scheme was first initiated by the 1979 Act, although the protection system in a rudimentary form was on the mind of the Bank of England even prior to the 1979 Act coming into force. The 1973 oil crisis disturbed the money market in many ways, but ironically the oil-producing countries increased their investment in the West and in London. The 1979 Act was, therefore, timely legislation incorporating the provision for a protection scheme but soon after the coming into force of the 1979 Act, the first bank failure, after a long interval, took place in the United Kingdom. The Johnson Matthey Bankers (JMB) episode prompted the Market and the legislative authorities to review the banking legislation, and the 1987 Act was enacted with extensive provisions for control and supervision of authorized institutions together with an elaborate provision for a deposit-taking scheme. It is again ironical that soon after the 1987 Act came into force, the BCCI episode took place. However, one is required to affirm that the deposit protection scheme came to the rescue of many unfortunate depositors, although the 1987 Act could not have prevented the collapse of the Barings Bank. It is a purpose of this chapter to analyse critically the deposit protection scheme under both the 1979 and 1987 Acts.

The Deposit Protection Scheme

Part II of the 1987 Act deals with the Deposit Protection Scheme (the 'Scheme'), which in many ways is similar to that established by Part II of the 1979 Act. Indeed, section 50(1) of the 1987 Act confirms that the Deposit Protection Board (the 'Board') and the Deposit Protection Fund (the 'Fund') established by section 21 of the 1979 Act shall continue to exist.

The Board shall in the main hold, manage and apply for the Fund in accordance with the provisions of this Part of the Act [1], levy contributions from authorized institutions and perform such other functions as may be conferred on the Board by the Act [2]. The Board's constitutional functions are detailed in Schedule 4 of the 1987 Act and it is appropriate to deal with the meanings of certain key terms which have received attention in the following section.

Meanings of Certain Key Terms
Insolvency

A UK bank becomes insolvent in the following circumstances:

(a) if a winding-up order has been made against it;

(b) if a resolution for a voluntary winding-up has been passed and no statutory declaration of solvency has been made under section 89 of the Insolvency Act 1986; or Article 534 of the Companies (Northern Ireland) Order 1986; or

(c) if a creditors' meeting has been held in accordance with section 95 of the Insolvency Act 1986, or under Article 541 of the 1986 Order.

A bank incorporated outside the United Kingdom becomes insolvent *'on the occurrence of an event which appears to the Bank to correspond as nearly as may be'* to any of the circumstances mentioned above.

An English partnership is to be regarded as insolvent on the making of a winding-up order against it under any provisions of section 420 of the Insolvency Act 1986. A partnership in Northern Ireland will be regarded insolvent when an order of adjudication of bankruptcy against any of the partners has been made. A partnership formed under law of a member state, other than the United Kingdom, becomes insolvent when an event occurs which, in the opinion of the Board, corresponds

---

[1] See post.
[2] See post.

very nearly to one of these mentioned above; and the same criterion is to be satisfied for declaring insolvent an unincorporated association formed under the law of another member state.

Compensation Payments to Depositors (section 58)

If at any time an authorized institution or a former authorized institution [3] becomes insolvent, the Board shall as soon as possible pay out of the Fund to each depositor who has a protected deposit with that institution *'an amount equal to three-quarters of his protected deposit'* [4].

The same is also true in the event of an administration order being made under section 8 of the Insolvency Act 1986, or an institution which comes under section 58 of the 1987 Act.

The amount paid may be reduced if the depositor is also covered by a guarantee given by a government or other authority; the Board may make a payment in full and recover from that authority such contribution to it *'as may be specified in or determined under the agreement'* (section 58(3)(b)).

Where the Board makes such a deduction, it may agree with the authority responsible for the Scheme, or by which the guarantee has been given, to reimburse that authority the deducted amount or any lesser amount. The Board has the discretion not to allow a person any payment who, in its opinion, has any responsibility for or may have profited directly or indirectly *'from the circumstances giving rise to that institution's financial difficulties'* (section 58(5)). Where the Board has not been made liable to make a payment under section 58(1), it can nevertheless receive any notice or other document required to be sent to a creditor of an authorized institution whose debt has been proved. A duly authorized representative of the Board shall be entitled to attend any meeting of creditors of the authorized institution and to make representations as to any matter for decision at that meeting, or be a member of any committee set up. When the Board has not been made liable to make a payment under section 58(2) of the 1987 Act in relation to an institution falling within that subsection, the Board shall nevertheless be entitled to receive any notice or document required to

---

[3] An institution that is not a recognized bank or licensed institution becoming insolvent is excluded under section 23(2) of the Banking Act 1979.

[4] For the meaning of 'protected deposit' see page 87.

be sent to a creditor of the institution under Part II of the Insolvency Act 1986. The duly authorized representative of the Board shall be entitled to attend any creditors' meetings of the institution summoned under Part II of Insolvency Act 1986 and make representations as to any matter for decision at that meeting. Such a duly authorized representative of the Board may also be a member of any committee established under section 27 of the Insolvency Act 1986.

Protected Deposits

A protected deposit under section 60 of the 1987 Act stands for the total liability of an authorized institution in respect of the holder of the deposit immediately prior to its becoming insolvent but limited to a maximum of £20,000 in respect of the principal amounts and accrued interest on sterling deposits that may have been made by such a person with the United Kingdom officer of an authorized institution. A principal idea is that because they are 'protected deposits' the authorized institution, even if it went into liquidation, must remain liable to the depositors for reimbursing them. In order to take advantage of the protected deposit scheme, the beneficiary must lodge a proof of debt with the liquidator of the insolvent institution, or in the event of an institution formed under the law of a country or territory outside the United Kingdom, an act must have been done which would be regarded by the Board as an act which corresponds as nearly as may be to the proof of debt and lodging with the liquidator.

In determining the total liability of an authorized institution to a depositor, whether under subsection (1) or (2) of section 60, no account shall be taken of any liability in respect of the deposit if:

(a) it is a secured deposit; or

(b) it is a deposit which had an original term to maturity of more than five years; or

(c) the institution is a former authorized institution and the deposit was made after it ceased to be an authorized institution or a recognized bank or licensed institution under the Banking Act 1979 unless, at the time the deposit was made, the depositor did not know and could not reasonably be expected to have known that it had ceased to be an authorized institution, recognized

bank or licensed institution. (Section 60(6)).

Trustee Deposits, Joint Deposits, etc. (section 61)

Under section 61 of the 1987 Act a person may be entitled to a deposit as a trustee, and if the same person is entitled as a trustee to different deposits made under different trusts, he shall be treated as a separate and distinct body in respect of each of those trusts. Where a deposit may be held for a person individually, or for two or more persons jointly by a bare trustee then that person(s) must be treated as entitled to the deposit without any intervention of the trust. A deposit held by a partnership shall be treated as a single deposit. In the case of a deposit to which two or more persons are jointly entitled and if section 61(2) does not apply, then each of them shall be treated as having a separate deposit, and it must be divided between them. Where a person, whether a trustee or otherwise, is entitled to a deposit made out of a client's account, to which one or more person(s) are entitled, then each of them shall be entitled to the deposit corresponding to the proportion of the money in the account to which each of them has entitlement. According to section 61(8):

> *Where an authorized institution is entitled as trustee to a sum which would be a deposit apart from section 5(3)(1) above and represents deposits made with the institution, each of the persons who made those deposits shall be treated as having made a deposit equal to so much of that sum as represents deposit made by him.*

The Board retains the right to refuse to make any payment under section 58 in respect of a deposit until the claimant informs the Board of the capacity in which he is entitled to the deposit and provides sufficient information in support of his claim.

Contributory Institutions

All authorized institutions are required to contribute to the Fund, and thus they are known as 'contributory institutions'. The Board has the discretion to levy contributions from a contributory institution and specify the amount to be paid by each institution. The deposit base of each authorized institution becomes a reference for determining the amount of contribution that each authorized institution will be required to pay. The Board places emphasis on sterling deposits with the United Kingdom officers of that institution other than secured deposits, which had an original term to maturity of more than five years, and the deposit in respect of which the authorized institution has issued a sterling certificate of deposit (section 52(4)).

Not less than £10,000 and a maximum of £300,000 can be levied. It will not be necessary for any contributory institution to pay more than 0.3% of the institution's deposit base. An institution is not entitled to repayment of any contributions made, nor is the Board prevented from levying contributions from other contributory institutions in respect of which the limit in section 56 has not been reached. The Treasury retains the right to amend the limits of maximum and minimum contributions after consultation with the Board.

Initial Contributions

Unless the Board waives an initial contribution, a contributory institution will be subject to a levy for an initial contribution as soon as possible after the day on which it becomes a contributory institution (section 53). Where an institution has a deposit base, *'the amount of an initial contribution levied under [section 53] shall be such percentage of the deposit base as the Board considers appropriate to put the institution on a basis of equality with other contributory institutions'*, but regard must be had to the initial contributions previously levied under this section or under section 24(1) of the Banking Act 1987, and any increase in the size of the Fund resulting from an order under section 54(2) of the 1987 Act, or section 25(2) of the Banking Act 1979[5]. When an institution has no deposit base, the amount of an initial contribution levied under section 53 shall be the minimum amount for the time being which will be determined by the provisions of section 56 of the 1987 Act.

Further Contributions (section 54)

Should the amount standing to the credit of the Fund be less than three million pounds at the end of any financial year, the Board may, with the approval of the Treasury, levy further contributions from

---

[5] This section is concerned with further contributions.

contributory institutions in order to restore the amount standing to its credit to a minimum of five million pounds and a maximum of six million pounds. If, however, in the opinion of the Treasury, the size of the Fund should be increased in the interests of depositors, it may, after consultation with the Board, by order amend the provisions of further contributions, but no such order shall be made unless a draft of it has been approved by a resolution of each House of Parliament.

Special Contributions (section 55)

If, in the opinion of the Board, compensation payments to depositors are likely to exhaust the Fund, the Board may, with the approval of the Treasury, levy special contributions; where, however, at the end of any financial year there may be a surplus in the Fund arising from special contributions and no more compensation payments to depositors would be required to be made, the Board shall repay to contributory institutions such amounts which would not reduce the amount standing to the credit of the Fund below the maximum amount for the time being and specified in section 54(1) ('Further Contributions'). The Board may also repay to contributory institutions such payments which would not reduce the amount standing to the credit of the Fund below the minimum amount for the time being specified in section 54(1) of the 1987 Act. Repayments to institutions under section 55 shall be made pro rata, according to the amount of the special contribution made by each of them, but the Board has the authority to withhold the repayment whether in its entirety or in part to an institution that has become insolvent, or that has ceased to be a contributory institution. In the case of the latter, the Board may make such repayments to any other contributory institution which, in the opinion of the Board, is its successor.

Deposit Base of Transferee Institutions

Where the liabilities of an exempted person [6] are transferred to an institution which is not an exempted person, it is called a 'transferee institution'. If such an institution becomes a contributory institution, it shall be treated for the purpose of section 53 ('Initial Contributions') as having such deposit base as it would have if:

---

[6] For exempted persons see Schedule 2 to the Banking Act 1987.

(a) *sterling deposits with the United Kingdom offices of the exempted person at any time had at that time been sterling deposits with the United Kingdom offices of the transferee institutions; and*

(b) *sterling certificates of deposit issued by the exempted person had been issued by the transferee institutions* (section 57(2)(a) and (b)).

Where, however, a transferee institution is already a contributory institution at the time of the transfer, the Board shall levy from it as soon as possible after the transfer, a further initial contribution of an amount equal to the initial contribution which it would have been liable to make if:

(a) *it had become a contributory institution on the date of the transfer;*

(b) *its deposit base were calculated by reference (and by reference only) to the sterling deposits with the United Kingdom offices of the exempted person, taking sterling certificates of deposit issued by the exempted person as having been issued by the transferee institution; and*

(c) *the amount specified in section 56(2) above were reduced by the amount of any initial contribution which the transferee institution has already made* (section 57(3)(a)-(c)).

Payments out of the Fund (section 58)

Payments out of the fund are known as compensation payments. If an institution becomes insolvent or an administration order is made under section 8 of the Insolvency Act 1986, as an authorized institution, whether under the 1987 Act or the 1979 Act, the FSA shall as soon as practicable pay out of the Fund to each depositor (who has a protected deposit with that institution) an amount equal to three-quarters of his protected deposit (section 58)[7]. Where, however, a depositor receives compensation under a government guarantee or other authority, the

---

[7] For any late payment the administrator's approval under section 24 of the Insolvency Act 1986 is required.

Board may deduct that amount from payment which would have been made to him under the Deposit Protection Scheme. When the Board makes such a deduction it may agree with the authority responsible for the scheme or by which the guarantee was given *'to reimburse that authority to the extent of the deduction or any lesser amount'* (section 58(4)).

In the event of a person having profited, directly or indirectly, from the circumstances occasioning the institution's financial difficulties, the Board may decline to make any payment to that person. Any amount of payment made by the administrator in respect of a deposit shall be taken into account by the Board in making payment in respect of that deposit, i.e. the payment shall not exceed three-quarters of that deposit. Section 58 also makes provisions for deductions of payments in certain circumstances which have already been explained. Section 62 applies to an institution which is insolvent and provides that:

(a) *the institution shall become liable to the Board, as in respect of a contractual debt incurred immediately before the institution became insolvent, for an amount equal to the compensation payment;*

(b) *the liability of the institution to the depositor in respect of any deposit or deposits ('the liability to the depositor') shall be reduced by an amount equal to the compensation payment made or to be made to him by the Board; and*

(c) *the duty of the liquidator of the insolvent institution to make payments to the Board on account of the liability referred to in paragraph (a) above ('the liability to the Board') and to the depositor on account of the liability to him (after taking account of paragraph (b) above) shall be varied in accordance with subsection (3) below* (section 62(2)(a)-(c)).

The variation in subsection 2 of section 62 may be explained in the following way:

i. in the first instance the liquidator shall pay to the Board any amount which would be payable on account of the liability to the depositor unless the liability relates to the deposit referred to in section 60(6) which provides that:

In determining the total liability of an institution to a depositor for the purposes of subsection (1) above, or the liability or total liability of an institution to a depositor for the purposes of subsection (2) above, no account shall be taken of any liability in respect of a deposit if:

(a) it is a secured deposit; or

(b) it is a deposit which had an original term to maturity of more than five years; or

(c) the institution is a former authorized institution and the deposit was made after it ceased to be an authorized institution or a recognized bank or licensed institution under the Banking Act 1979 unless, at the time the deposit was made, the depositor did not know and could not reasonably be expected to have known that it had ceased to be an authorized institution, recognized bank or licensed institution.

and,

ii. if at any time the total amount paid to the Board is equal to the amount of the compensation payment made to the depositor, the liquidator shall pay to the depositor any amount which would be payable to the Board in respect of the liability to the Board.

Where the issue of liability in respect of compensation payment applies to an institution in respect of which an administration order is in force: (a) the institution shall (if at the time of making the compensation payment in respect of the deposit fails to be made with the Board) become liable to the Board for an amount equal to the payment; and (b) the liability of the institution to the depositor shall be reduced by an amount equal to that payment. Where the compensation payment is to be made by the Board to a trustee, any liability of the institution must be construed as a liability to the trustee.

Repayment in respect of Contributions (section 63)

'Recovered money' (that is the money received by the Board under section 62) shall not form part of the Fund. But for the remainder of the financial year it shall be placed with the Board in an account with the Bank of England (now the FSA) which shall as far as possible invest the money. Any income arising from money shall be credited to the Fund. Repayments of recovered money under section 63 shall be made pro-rata according to the amount of the special or further contributions made by each of them. If, at the end of a financial year, the money recovered by the Board and any amount standing to the credit of the Fund after any repayments made under section 55 ('Special Contributions') exceeds the maximum amount for the time being specified in section 54(1) ('Further Contributions'), the Board shall, as soon as possible, make further repayments under the scheme, but such further repayments shall not reduce the amount below the minimum amount for the time being specified in section 54(1).

The Board of Banking Supervision (section 64)

Section 64(1) empowers the Board, after consultation with the Treasury, to borrow up to £10 million or such larger sum if it may find it necessary. Such borrowed amounts shall not be included in ascertaining the amount standing to the credit of the Fund for the purposes of sections 54(1), 55(2) and 63(5).

The Board has also the power to obtain information with the approval of the Bank of England from an institution including an insolvent institution, and to produce such documents as the Board may reasonably require for the purpose of determining the contributions of the institution.

Where in respect of an insolvent institution any document has come into the possession of the Official Receiver or in the Northern Ireland, the Official Assignee, he shall permit any person duly authorized by the Board to inspect the documents with a view to establishing the identities of the institution's depositors to whom the Board is liable to make a payment under section 58 ('Compensation Payments to Depositors'), and the amount of the protected deposit held by each of the depositors.

Conclusions

The Banking Supervision mechanism is much more comprehensive under the 1987 Act than that under the 1979 Act. Whereas the 1979 Act was concerned with the granting of licences to financial institutions, the 1987 Act is concerned with granting authorizations to institutions. There exists a distinction between licensing an institution, and authorizing it; whereas licensing entails a degree of discretion, authorization requires a thorough study of the institution on the basis of its projected activities although in effect the grant of a licence may also entail that process.

The 1987 Act is also more categorical about the meaning of certain terms, namely deposit, compensation payments, protected deposits etc. than the corresponding provisions of the 1979 Act.

It would be correct to maintain that perhaps the JMB episode prompted legislation for a more elaborate mechanism for supervision and surveillance, and to make further provisions for the protection of deposits. It is unfortunate that despite the elaborate mechanism adopted by the 1987 Act two more bank failures, BCCI and Barings, took place; the issues pertaining to these failures receive attention in Chapter 5 of this work.

It must, however, be pointed out that the Banking Act 1987 exonerates the FSA from any of the consequences of any negligent act, and this issue is certainly disturbing in the sense that the FSA may not even be amenable to the jurisdiction of English courts unless *'it is shown that the act or omission was in bad faith'* (section 1(4) of the 1987 Act).

The Bank of England Act 1998 simply consolidates the supervision and surveillance functions of the Bank of England under one authority, namely the Financial Services Authority. In whatever form the FSA may perform its duties, it is basically going to implement the supervision and surveillance mechanism adopted by the 1987 Act.

5 The Impact of the Second Council Directive on the Coordination of Laws, Regulations and Administrative Provisions Relating to the Taking up and Pursuit of the Business of Credit Institutions [1]

Introduction

As its principal purpose, the Preamble to the Directive states that:

> '...this directive is to constitute the essential instrument for the achievement of the internal market, a course determined by the Single European Act and set out in timetable form in the Commission's White Paper, from the point of view of both freedom of establishment and the freedom to provide financial services, in the field of credit institutions;'

In order to achieve a harmonized internal European Union market in the field of financial services and credit institutions, the Directive

---

[1] This Directive which was issued on 15 December 1989 (No. 89/646/EEC) came into force on 1 January 1993. See OJ No. L/386/5 dated 30 December 1989. This Directive also amended the First Council Directive 77/780/EEC of 12 December 1977 (OJ No. L.322.17.12.1977).

provided for a system of mutual recognition, authorization, the responsibilities of home and host states, the criteria that each deposit-taking credit institution must satisfy for its operation in a host state and other related matters. It is to be borne in mind that the principle of free movement of capital combined with the right of establishment under the Rome Treaty, made inevitable the issue of this 'Coordination Directive'. Along with the coordination related matters and activities theory the Directive also aims at improving the basic fundamentals of the services to be rendered by credit institutions: prudent management of business and the protection of depositors' interests. The Preamble to the Directive further provides that:

> *'Whereas the harmonization of certain financial and investment services will be effected, where the need exists, by specific Community instruments, with the intention, in particular, of protecting consumers and investors;...'*

In sum, therefore, the Directive sets a common view to attaining a reliable standard to generate confidence and protection to depositors, and enforcement or corrective measures against those of the credit institutions which may derogate from the established standards within the European Union. The Directive also provides for 'Relations with Third Countries'.

A Brief Analysis of the Directive

Title I gives definition of certain essential terms, Title II deals with the issue of harmonization of authorization conditions; whereas relations with third countries is the subject of Title III. Title IV deals with the issue of harmonization of the conditions governing pursuit of the business of credit institutions, provisions relating to the freedom of establishment and the freedom to provide services have been embodied in Title V. Final provisions, which do not relate to the substantive aspects of the Directive have been included in Title VI. The Annex to the Directive provides a list of activities which are subject to mutual recognition.

All member states of the European Union must implement this

Directive; in so far as the United Kingdom is concerned this is via the Financial Services Act 1986 and the Banking Act 1987, including in particular, Schedule III to the Act. Most of the aspects of the enforcement powers of the FSA have already been discussed in Chapter 3 of this work. As a matter of principle:

> 'The Member States shall prohibit persons or undertakings that are not credit institutions from carrying on the business of taking deposits or other repayable funds from the public.'[2]

Harmonization of Authorization Conditions

Instead of using the traditional term 'licence', the Directive uses the term 'authorization'. Under the system, an authorization issued by the relevant host Member State's competent authorities must be recognized and allow that European Union credit institution to operate in the chosen host state(s).

The general rule is that no authorization shall be granted by any competent authority unless an applicant credit institution has an initial capital of at least ECU 5 million[3]. The Member States have the option however of granting authorization to particular categories of credit institutions the initial capital of which is less than the minimum, but in no case shall it be less than ECU 1 million[4]. In this latter event, the Member State concerned is required to notify the Commission of its reason for exercising this option.

No authorization shall be granted unless the competent authorities have been informed of the identities of shareholders or members, *'whether direct or indirect, natural or legal persons, who have qualifying holdings, and of the amounts of those holdings.'*[5] In order to protect the interests of depositors as well as the reputation of capital markets, Article 5 also provides that:

---

[2] Article 3 of the Directive. This provision does not apply to the taking of deposits or other funds repayable by a Member State or by a Member State's regional or local authorities or by public international bodies of which a Member State is a member.
[3] Article 4(1).
[4] Article 4(2).
[5] Article 5.

> 'The competent authorities shall refuse authorization if, taking into account the need to ensure the sound and prudent management of a credit institution, they are not satisfied as to the suitability of the above mentioned shareholders or members.'

Host Member States may no longer require authorization or endowment capital for breaches of credit institutions authorized in other member States [6].

Harmonization of the Conditions Governing pursuit of the Business of Credit Institutions

A credit institution's own funds must not fall below the amount of initial capital (ECU 5 million); however credit institutions that were already functioning in the European Union prior to 1 January 1993 may continue to carry on their activities even though they do not attain the minimum level of initial capital. But, in any event, their own funds may not fall below the highest level reached after the date of notification of this Directive. In the event of the merger of two or more credit institutions, their own funds in the new institution may not fall below the total owned funds of the merged institution at the time of the merger. The competent authorities have inherent power to derogate from the minimum capital requirement rule if circumstances so justify, but only for a limited period during which time the credit institution concerned is required to rectify its situation or cease its activities.

The Member States must ensure the competent authorities are informed of the size of the intended qualified holding in a credit institution. Likewise, such a person and the credit institution must inform the competent authorities if it proposes to increase its qualifying holding so that its voting rights would reach or exceed 20%, 33% or 50% so that the credit institution would become its subsidiary. The competent authorities have the discretion to oppose such a plan within the maximum period of three months from the date of notification on the ground that sound and prudent management of the credit institution may not be guaranteed and that they are not satisfied as to the suitability of the person(s) mentioned above. In the case of acquisitions the

---

[6] Article 6.

assessment of the acquisition must be a matter of prior consultation between the competent authorities of the member states concerned. Where a person proposes to dispose of a qualifying holding in a credit institution, the competent authority must first be informed of the size of the intended holding. The same obligation falls on the credit institution, i.e. a proportion of the voting rights or of the capital held by him would fall below 20%, 33% or 50%, or so that the credit institution would cease to be his subsidiary [7]. Credit institutions have an obligation to inform the competent authorities at least once a year of the names of shareholders and members possessing qualifying holdings and the size thereof, in order to ascertain the extent of influence a person may exercise by virtue of a holding. This may work to the detriment of the prudent and sound management of the institution, and in that event the competent authorities must take appropriate measures to bring that situation to an end. This may be achieved by various means – in the form of injunction, sanctions against directors and managers or the suspension of exercise of voting rights attached to the shares held by the shareholders in question.

No credit institution may have a qualifying holding exceeding 15% of its own funds in an undertaking that is neither a credit institution nor a financial institution.

> *'The total amount of a credit institution's qualifying holdings in undertakings other than credit institutions, financial institutions or undertakings carrying on activities referred to in the second subparagraph of Article 43(2)(f) of Directive 86/635/EEC may not exceed 60% of its own funds.'* [8]

In all cases of exceptions or exemptions the competent authorities may be allowed to exercise their discretionary powers but supervisory monitoring must also be carried out over such activities. Article 12(8) provided that:

> *'The Member States may provide that the competent authorities shall not apply the limits laid down in*

---

[7] Article 11(3).
[8] Article 12(2).

> *paragraphs 1 and 2 if they provide that 100% of the amounts by which a credit institution's qualifying holdings exceed those limits must be covered by own funds and that the latter shall not be included in the calculation of the solvency ratio. If both the limits laid down in paragraphs 1 and 2 are exceeded, the amount to be covered by own funds shall be the greater of the excess amounts.'*

The prudential supervision of a credit institution shall be the responsibility of the competent authorities of the home member states, unless provided otherwise, ensuring sound administration, accounting procedures and an adequate internal control mechanism. Host member states in conjunction with the competent authorities of the home member states have responsibility for the supervision of the liquidity of the branches of credit institutions pending further coordination but host member states will have complete responsibility for the measures resulting from the implementation of the monetary policies.

Where a credit institution authorized in another member state carries on its activities through a branch, the competent authorities of the home member state must inform the competent authorities of the host member state so that when necessary on-the-spot verification may be made of the information referred to in Article 7(11) of the First Council Directive on Banking. The Directive provides for confidentiality of professional secrets ensuring that no confidential information is divulged to any person or authority except in summary or collective form. However, where a credit institution has been adjudicated bankrupt or is being compulsorily wound up, confidential information, which does not concern third parties involved in attempts to rescue that credit institution, may be divulged in civil or commercial proceedings [9]. Confidential information may be used by credit authorities only in identified situations, namely, in checking the conditions governing the taking up of a business of credit institutions, to facilitate monitoring, to check the manner in which the business is conducted, or to impose sanctions or in the case of appeal against a decision of a credit authority or in court proceedings. Confidentiality of information can be breached

---

[9] Article 16.

in accordance with the law of a member state, such as disclosure to inspectors acting on behalf of governments. However, such disclosures may be made only where necessary for reason of prudential control. Disclosure of information must take place with the consent of the credit authority which disclosed the information or of the credit authority of the member state in which on the spot verification was carried out [10].

Provisions relating to the Freedom of Establishment and the Freedom to Provide Services

Member states are required to allow the activities listed in the Annex [11] to be carried on within their territories either by the establishment of a branch or by way of providing services by any credit institution (or subsidiary) authorized and supervised by the competent authorities of another member state provided that such activities are covered by authorization [12] provided that it fulfils each of the following conditions:

a) the parent undertaking must be authorized as a credit institution by the member state's competent authorities and its subsidiary must be governed by the law of the same member state;

b) the activities of the credit institution must be carried out within the territory of the same member state;

c) the parent undertaking must hold 90% or more of the voting rights in respect of shares in the capital of its subsidiary;

---

[10] Article 16(7).
[11] Annex – List of Activities Subject to Mutual Recognition
(1) Acceptance of deposits and other repayable funds from the public. (2) Lending. (3) Financial leasing. (4) Money transmission services. (5) Issuing and administering means of payment (e.g. credit cards, travellers' cheques and bankers' drafts). (6) Guarantees and commitment. (7) Trading for own account or for account of customers in: (a) money market instruments (cheques, bills, CDs, etc.); (b) foreign exchange; (c) financial futures and options; (d) exchange and interest rate instruments; (e) transferable securities. (8) Participation in share issues and the provision of services related to such issues. (9) Advice to undertakings on capital structure, industrial strategy and related questions and advice and services relating to mergers and the purchase of undertakings. (10) Money broking. (11) Portfolio management and advice. (12) Safekeeping and administration of securities. (13) Credit reference services. (14) Safe custody services.
[12] Article 18.

d) the parent undertaking must satisfy the competent authorities as to prudent management of the subsidiary and must declare the consent of the relevant member state's competent authorities that they jointly and severally guarantee commitments entered into by the subsidiary; and

e) that the subsidiary must be included in the consolidated supervision of the parent undertaking, in particular for the calculation of the solvency ratio, for the control of large exposures and for the purposes of limitation of holdings.

Although the competent authorities of the home member state must ensure compliance with the requirements in respect of its subsidiaries, in the event of any failure in this regard, the home member state is required to notify the competent authorities of the host member state and the activities carried out by such an institution shall be subject to the legislation of the host member state.

The credit institution wishing to set up a branch within the territory of another member state must notify the competent authority of its home member state. Usually within three months of receipt of the request, decision of the competent authority must be communicated to the applicant institution unless the competent authorities of the home member states have reason to doubt the adequacy of the administrative structure or the financial status of the applicant institution.

The host member state concerned must be notified in sufficient time (usually two months) that a branch of the credit institution will be entering the host member state in order to prepare itself for supervision of the competent authority and indicate the conditions under which the activities must be carried out.

A host member state may require all credit institutions having branches within its territorial boundaries to report periodically on its activities, and if found to be in breach of an obligation to provide services, will require the institution concerned to put an end to the irregular situation, and if it should fail to do so, the host member state can notify the competent authorities of the home member state accordingly. If the irregularities are not corrected promptly, the host member state has the authority to take appropriate measures to prevent or prohibit further irregularities and even prevent the institution from initiating further transactions within its territory, in order to protect the interests of the depositors and the general good. A credit institution has the right of appeal against such decision to the courts of the member state's authorities that adopted such measures. A host member state may take any precautionary measures in emergencies necessary to protect the interests of depositors, investors and others to whom services are provided. In such an event the Commission and the competent authorities of the other member state concerned must be notified of the measures taken as soon as possible. The Commission has the authority to consider whether the member state concerned must amend or abolish these measures after consulting the matter with the competent authority of the host member state. Where, however, the competent authorities of a home member state withdraws the authorization from a credit institution, the competent authorities of the host member state must be informed and shall take as soon as possible appropriate measures to prevent the institution concerned from initiating any further transaction in order to safeguard the interests of depositors.

The Banking Act 1987 provides for the kind of protective measures in the UK that the Directive prescribes. Although under the Directive the competent authorities in the home member state have primary responsibility for supervision of credit institutions incorporated in these states, under the Directive the host member states have been allowed a good measure of power over such credit institutions. The Financial Services Authority (FSA) is required to cooperate with the home state authority to ensure that the EU credit institutions maintain adequate liquidity and avoid risks that might disturb the financial market here. When a problem arises with regard to a EU credit institution, under the Directive the primary responsibility for remedial measures lies with the competent authorities of the home member state, although, as stated earlier under the Directive, the FSA has considerable power in this regard. The FSA has already agreed the Memorandum of Understanding with all other EU authorities where by home states have agreed to exchange information with the FSA. Under Regulations 9 and 10, the FSA has the power to impose prohibition or restriction on an EU institution in appropriate circumstances.

However, a successful implementation of the Directive requires an effective degree of cooperation between the competent authorities of the host and home member states in regulating capital adequacy, solvency ratio requirements, maintenance of the minimum criteria of operations and exchange of information. It is possible for the FSA to exercise powers on an EU credit institution if the latter should fail to comply with the requirement imposed under section 39 of the Banking Act 1987. The FSA may require the institution to remedy the situation, and may impose a prohibition or restriction only if it is satisfied that the competent authority in the home member state has failed or refused to take measures for remedying the situation or that the measures taken have proved inadequate for that purpose. The FSA can also take action under section 39 of the Banking Act 1987 notifying the home member state authorities. The EU Commission has the power under the Directive to require the FSA to amend or withdraw any measures it has taken under Regulation 11(6). According to the Memorandum of Agreement between the FSA and other EU authorities, the FSA will assist the home member state authorities by providing information on request on the United Kingdom financial markets. The FSA usually exercises its powers where either the competent authorities in the home state have failed to take remedial measures or when the credit institution is in breach of the relevant laws and regulations prevalent in the United Kingdom. But in all situations, the FSA is expected to take up the matter first with the competent authorities of the home state concerned. The FSA may be required to intervene unless it may have reasons to believe that the activities of an EU credit institution might jeopardise the depositors' interest and the general good of the financial markets. The FSA can take action against a credit institution if it appears that it has been provided with false, misleading or inaccurate information by or on behalf of an EU credit institution. In taking any measures the FSA must take up the matter first with the competent authorities of the home member state and actual measures will be taken only if they have failed to take appropriate remedial measures or unwilling to take such measures. The initiative may be taken by the FSA if EU credit institution derogates from the criteria of Schedule 3 of the banking Act 1987. The other major powers of the FSA are exercisable under Schedule 7 of the Directive, Regulations 192 and 193, the latter for the purpose of imposing restrictions in relation to any of the activities listed in the Annex to the

Regulations carried on in the United Kingdom by United Kingdom subsidiaries.

Conclusions

The EC Second Banking Directive came into being as an instrument for coordination in culmination of the principle of free movement of capital and services and the right of establishment throughout the EU.

Although the objectives of the Directive are in line with those of the EU in regard to creating one united capital market, in view of the current disparity between the capital markets in the EU coupled with the disparate banking system, it might take some time to achieve the desired objectives.

As stated earlier, advanced capital markets such as those of Germany and the United Kingdom will have no difficulty in implementing the Directive, and the United Kingdom has already taken steps for implementing it.

The Directive, when combined with the Basle Core Principles for Effective Banking Supervision, 1997 [13] gives a comprehensive programme, including the supervision mechanism, for operating a uniform banking system throughout the European Union.

---

[13] The text of the Core Principles has been reproduced in 37 *International Legal Materials* (1997) 405.

6 An Examination as to whether the Bank Collapses were due to the lack of Regulatory Measures

Introduction

As has been stated earlier, the Bank of England over the years adopted a variety of regulatory measures, culminating in the Bank of England Act 1998, the need for which regulatory measures for banks, particularly in a market like the London International Market, cannot be overemphasized. The purposes of such measures are not only to adopt a system whereby accountability must be established between the regulator and the institutions authorized by it, but also to develop a degree of voluntary reporting whenever an authorized institution may find itself in a difficult situation.

This chapter attempts to explain the limits to regulatory and supervisory measures by referring to the three bank failures in recent years, namely Johnson Matthey Bankers Limited, BCCI and Baring. Curiously enough, through all the three bank failures one common element runs, the inadequacy of the audit system and lack of responsibility on the part of the management.

An Examination of the Causes Leading to the Bank Failures in Recent Years

The Collapse of Johnson Matthey Bankers Limited

Johnson Matthey Bankers Limited (JMB) was one of the five London bullion banks and a subsidiary of Johnson Matthey & Co Limited (JM), gold refiners of Hatton Garden. It was established in 1965 to conduct the banking and bullion business of JM. JMB was authorized to deal in foreign exchange in 1967 under the Exchange Control Act and exempted from the Protection of Depositors Act in 1970. Thus, JMB was already being supervised by the Bank of England when the 1979 Act came into effect, and in April 1980 was granted authorization under this Act as a recognized and authorized bank.

The balance sheet of JMB, set out in its annual accounts, more than doubled between March 1980 and March 1984 [1]. JMB's total assets rose from £874 million in 1980 to £2,089 million in 1984. However, commercial lending, in the form of loans and overdrafts, increased rather rapidly from £34 million in 1980 to £309 million in 1984. In 1981 JMB diversified its portfolio, to some extent, into other financial services such as soft commodities broking, insurance broking and asset management (mainly in the United Kingdom and the United States). It did not, however, expand its business into other banking services such as corporate finance or investment management. Its core finance business tended to be based on connections with the Middle East, Nigeria and Pakistan.[2]

Although regular prudential interviews took place between the Bank and JMB and the Bank was apparently satisfied with the performance of JMB, during 1983 it drew JMB's attention to problems about the adequacy of its liquidity position. This, however, was rectified promptly.

However, JMB entered into several large exposures, each of them equivalent to 10% of its capital base. In 1984, problems arose with two large exposures, which compelled JMB to make a choice whether to advance more funds to enable its debtors to trade out of its problems, or to refuse further credit. JMB chose the former. By June 1983 the exposures to these debtors were equivalent to 26% and 17% of JMB's capital base respectively, by December 1983 they increased to 51% and 25%, and by June 1984 they grew rapidly to 76% and 39%[3].

In August 1984 the Bank launched a rescue operation which involved the cooperation of Johnson Matthey plc, other members of the gold market and major commercial banks. It ultimately resulted in the

---

[1] The Bank of England Note, 1984, *The Bank of England and Johnson Matthey Bankers Limited*, p.3.
[2] ibid., p.3.
[3] op. cit., p.4.

purchase of JMB by the Bank for £1. The investigation initiated by the Bank revealed that, apart from the two large exposures, the reasons for the collapse included the rapid growth of the loan book, the inadequacy of internal controls and systems, shortcomings of the organization and management of the commercial banking and credit monitoring activities, and insufficient attention to the accumulated risks. Furthermore, contrary to the usual banking practice, no security was taken from the borrowers, the need for provisions against bad and doubtful debts was not assessed with the proper degree of caution and the judgement of management in approving loans was defective. No evidence of fraud by the directors or staff of JMB was found [4]. The Bank of England apparently relied upon the auditors' reports.

The Bank's assessment of JMB's loan book was seriously hindered by significant understatement of the level of JMB's large exposures. For example, in December 1983 these exposures were reported to amount to 27% and 18% respectively, whereas the actual figures were 51% and 25%; similarly in June 1984 the reported figures were 38% and 34%, whereas actual figures stood at 76% and 39% of JMB's capital base. Although the figures reported in December 1983 were in line with the size of exposures carried out by other banks, the levels reported in March 1984, 38% and 34% respectively, would have resulted in the Bank requesting a meeting with JMB. However, the report for March, which was due in April, was not received by the Bank until June, notwithstanding repeated requests by the Bank for its submission. Eventually a meeting took place in August 1984 following which the Bank requested its auditors to examine the loans in greater depth. The examination revealed the extent of the provisions required, and on 25 September 1984 JMB's management advised the Bank that required provisions would substantially reduce the bank's net worth [5].

The JMB crisis and the resultant investigation thereof highlighted a number of problems with the then supervision system. The Bank placed reliance on a bank's external auditors to cover these matters whose task it was, and still is, to assess the basis on which the directors arrive at their valuation of a bank's assets. It is for the auditors to review the adequacy of a bank's internal controls and systems during the course of

[4] op. cit., pp.4-5.
[5] op. cit., pp.5-6.

an audit and to comment on any aspects they consider unsatisfactory.

Other features that transpired during the investigation of JMB's affairs were failure, both by JMB and its parent company, to appreciate the problems caused by deficient internal systems, poor lending judgements and inadequate monitoring and control, and the inaccurate and misleading reporting system of JMB.

Whereas it cannot be disputed that the collapse of JMB was caused by the loan concentration and that the Bank of England was misinformed by JMB's management about the size of the loans, Stephen Fay[6] takes the view that there were flaws in the manner in which JMB was supervised. The Bank had been aware that the two largest exposures increased in size. However, the approach adopted by the Bank was based on the principle of trust that governed the relationship between the Bank of England and authorized banks.

The collapse of JMB also sparked heated exchanges in the House of Commons, where The Chancellor of the Exchequer, Mr Nigel Lawson, directly criticized the Bank's supervision of JMB and said that *'The Bank did not on this occasion act as promptly as they should have done. They did to some extent fall down on the job'.*[7] A Bank-Treasury committee was set up by the Chancellor of the Exchequer to reconsider banking supervision, to examine the flaws in the supervision system and to identify the need for any legal changes to the system. The committee put forward some thirty-four recommendations; perhaps the most important one was the abolition of the division between full banks and licensed deposit-takers (the two-tier system). JMB was an authorized bank and as such was liable to the limited scrutiny; unfortunately, events proved that this was insufficient.

The Collapse of the Bank of Credit and Commerce International (BCCI)
Introduction

BCCI was set up in London in 1992 as a branch of BCCI International Holdings (Luxembourg) SA ('BCCI Holdings') by Mr Agha Hasan Abedi,

---

[6] Stephen Fay, *Portrait of an Old Lady, Turmoil at the Bank of England*, Hamondsworth, Middlesex, Penguin Books Ltd, 1987, pp.148-155.
[7] House of Commons, Hansard, vol. 81, 20 June 1985 cols.454-65; see further Margaret Reid, op. cit., p.229.

according to the Bank an experienced and successful banker, and the Bank did not have any reason to believe that he was not a fit and proper person to initiate such a proposal. The proposed manager of the new branch, also known to the Bank, had proved himself reliable and trustworthy. At the time BCCI was established, the Bank had no power to block entry although it could withhold exchange control authorization. BCCI grew rather rapidly, but most of its investments were made by a number of wealthy shareholders. The speed of growth first became a cause for concern in the summer of 1974 but no concrete evidence was available to establish that BCCI expanded illegally. Informal inquiries as to its rapid expansion were nevertheless carried out by the Luxembourg Banking Commission (LBC) and the Bank of America, but their reports were favourable. By 1976 rumours as to BCCI's business integrity were available but again the contemporary evidence did not suggest that market opinion in the United Kingdom was strongly hostile at that time [8].

During 1977, a number of issues became dominant:

(a) Mr Abedi's ambition to expand the Group remained unabated;

(b) much of the expansion of BCCI took place through overseas operations which were subject to little or no supervision;

(c) more important issues, such as ratios and debt provisions, were perhaps neglected;

(d) the UK branches of BCCI were thought to be overtrading at a loss;

(e) that the bank had too many branches in the UK although it did not have any sizeable banking business in Luxembourg or in the Cayman Islands; and

(f) criticisms, although unofficial, about the manner of banking and its unabated growth became rampant.

The supervision, if at all carried out, was carried out by LBC; indeed there was no single regulator responsible for overseeing BCCI's worldwide operations until the Banking Act 1979 came into force in the UK.

---

[8] Inquiry into the Supervision of The Bank of Credit and Commerce International, London, HMSO, 1992, op. cit., p.31.

According to the Inquiry into the Supervision of The Bank of Credit and Commerce International (the Bingham Report), the manner of carrying out its business and the speed of its growth became points of concern but they could not be justified or affirmed by evidence. The LBC continued to give the Bank a clean bill of health; the auditors also gave an unqualified opinion on the Group's accounts; there was no concrete evidence of malpractice [9]. However, a scheme was proposed for combining the UK business and the overseas business into a single UK subsidiary, which would be directly subject to the supervision of the Bank, and BCCI made an application to the Department of Trade and Industry (the DTI). The Bank was required to obtain letters of comfort from ultimate owners of the proposed subsidiary share capital, affirming the support for it; in the case of BCCI the comfort letters should have come from the Bank of America, but it declined and decided to withdraw from BCCI. Even the LBC expressed its reservations about the proposal. Finally unless a UK subsidiary of BCCI was recognized as a bank in the United Kingdom, BCCI could not use a banking name. Before the 1979 Act came into force, the Bank of England was concerned about the rapid growth of BCCI in the United Kingdom, and indeed, Mr Abedi was questioned by the Bank regarding the overall number of UK branches. Under the Banking Act 1979 authorization for all banks became necessary. No major objections were raised against BCCI's authorization; the shareholders appeared to be supportive and willing to provide more capital, the auditors gave unqualified opinion on the accounts, the Group appeared to be profitable, and both the LBC and the Basle Concorde gave favourable opinions on the performance of the bank, and the Bank of America indicated no ground for concern [10]. No concrete evidence of malpractice was established. At this point, however, a few negative factors became evident:

(a) the complex structure of the Group prevented any supervisor from examining the Group's real operations;

(b) unclear ownership structure (the largest block of shares was owned by a Cayman company, ICIC Holdings) [11];

---

[9] op. cit., p.32.

[10] op. cit., p.35; The Bank of America, however, showed a degree of uneasiness as it proved to be difficult for them to discover what was really going on within the Group.

[11] op. cit., see further p.35.

(c) the Group lacked a lender of last resort;

(d) it lacked a natural home; the Group did much of its business in the jurisdiction in which supervision was at a rudimentary level, or non-existent.

The Group attained its credibility through the reputation of only one person. In other words, the bank's strengths and weaknesses could be identified with those of Mr Abedi.

Under the 1979 Act, it became necessary to draw a distinction between institutions whose principal places of business were in the United Kingdom, and those in foreign jurisdictions. Supervision of overseas units could be carried out by overseas supervisors, and the Bank would be notified of the results of the relevant overseas supervisor. Unfortunately, the Bank never made an inquiry to ascertain where was the principal place of business of BCCI. BCCI was denied recognition because it failed to satisfy the section 3(5) criteria [12]. Although BCCI satisfied the four criteria, its application for recognition as a bank was rejected by the Bank for various reasons:

(a) that the institution had not enjoyed for a reasonable period of time a high reputation and standing in the financial community;

(b) the structure of the Group was unclear;

(c) no one supervisor was able to take an overall view of the Group's operations; and

(d) it was more or less one individual's bank.

The Bank, therefore, decided to license BCCI as a deposit-taking institution, primarily on the basis of the judgement formed on the BCCI's ability by the LBC. In reaching its decision, the Bank heavily relied on the criteria, in Part 2 of Schedule 2 to the 1979 Act, for granting and refusing a full licence to an institution. The issue of the responsible officers being fit and proper persons is fundamental on the list of the criteria. Under the 1979 Act, it was not the function of the Bank to impose any structure on a bank, but it was for the bank concerned to satisfy the Bank that its existing structure would entitle it to a licence.

The refusal of recognition under the 1979 Act was formally

[12] See section 3(5) of the Banking Act 1979.

communicated to BCCI in June 1980, causing unhappiness within the Group, but BCCI never formally reapplied for recognition under the 1979 Act. Although the Bank carried out consultation exercises in 1981 and 1982, BCCI submitted rather favourable accounts to the Bank in 1981. However the Bank still had concerns about persistent imprudent banking by BCCI and that a larger part of BCCI's activities remained unsupervised. BCCI made efforts to satisfy the Bank by making a few changes, and in January 1984 a revised programme was submitted to the Bank in order to seek a full licence. The Bank still found the structure of the Group highly unsatisfactory, LBC lacked reason to supervise the Group effectively, and no one had any clear overall view of the Group's activities. According to the Bingham Committee Report, during 1984 and 1985, BCCI sustained substantial losses in Hong Kong. Mr Abedi tried his best to devise alternative schemes and to restructure the bank, but they did not materialize. Thorny questions simply remained about the location of the headquarters and its structure, which prevented effective consolidated supervision. It is to be emphasized that under the 1979 Act these would prove to be hindrances to giving a licence to any bank.

Between September 1983 and January 1985, the Bank received eight reports on BCCI's activities in the financial and commodity markets. The Bank received letters of concern from various players on the commodities market, but did not take any positive action about it because it believed that it was a matter for the Institut Monetaire Luxembourg (IML) to take action as BCCI's primary supervisor. In October 1985 the IML caused BCCI to commission Price Waterhouse (PW) to review the Central Treasury investment activities. PW were at the same time auditors of BCCI's overseas units. According to the accounts, the overseas units made substantial losses on option contracts and they attributed those losses to incompetence and errors made by '... *unsophisticated amateurs venturing into a highly technical and sophisticated market*'[13]. BCCI never volunteered information about the considerable losses ($400 million) to the Bank, which must be regarded as a serious departure from the obligations under the 1979 Act. These incidents naturally caused the Bank to review the position of BCCI and visit the Central Treasury of BCCI in December 1985. Three conclusions

[13] op. cit., 44.

were drawn; firstly that the Central Treasury should not be part of the UK subsidiary, secondly that in view of the lack of trust then already developed between the Bank of England and BCCI, any continuation of such activity should not allowed, and thirdly that BCCI's continued presence in the United Kingdom called for consideration [14]. The Bank, even in 1986, did not find it necessary to revoke BCCI's licence as, in its opinion, there was no immediate danger to depositor, nor to order closure of forty-five branches in the United Kingdom. Furthermore, it was the perceived belief of the Bank that closure of the branches would cause '... *substantial and diplomatic problems.*' The Bingham Report, however, observed that:

> '*Since one of the Banking Act criteria was that the business should be conducted prudently, and since the business had on any showing been conducted with serious imprudence (even if the losses were attributed to incompetence and lack of sophistication, since management had overridden the intended safeguards), it is not easy to understand how grounds to revoke were thought unlikely to exist.*'[15]

One gets the impression from the Bingham Report that there were sufficient reasons for revoking the BCCI's licence, but this was not done; perhaps the Bank was too concerned with the political and diplomatic repercussions of the revocation of the licence. The dilemma about the revocation of licence and its continuation was clearly brought out by the Bingham Report when it stated that:

> '*That was unfortunate. The statutory power to impose conditions was designed to cover cases where the drastic power of revocation was judged inappropriate but where it was necessary to exert some formal control over the way a business was run. If revocation was inappropriate, it is hard to think that SA [BCCI Holdings] in the summer of 1986 was not such a case. To the extent that the Bank's supervisory plans had been thwarted in April 1984 by lack of leverage on BCCI, such leverage now existed. In*

[14] op. cit., p.45.
[15] op. cit., p.45.

> *this highly judgemental field, it cannot be fairly said that there is any single solution which the Bank should have adopted. The imposition of conditions undoubtedly raised practical and legal problems. But given the formal sanctions now available, it may very well be that agreement on changes acceptable to the Bank could have been reached.'* [16]

In October 1986 BCCI relocated its Central Treasury to Abu Dhabi, primarily for tax reasons, but the Bank was not notified of this move in sufficient time.

The vagueness of the location of BCCI's headquarters and the suggestions put forward by Mr Abedi as to alternative locations became an issue, particularly during the latter part of 1986. BCCI was largely present in the United Kingdom, and Luxembourg was a formal statutory headquarters. It was almost impossible for Luxembourg to supervise the world-wide Group of BCCI. It was at this point that the issue of consolidated supervision by the Bank of England arose. But, the Bank was strongly against undertaking this responsibility due to the complex organization and structure. The Bank had a clear idea by 1986 that BCCI's effective base, apart from the Central Treasury, was in the United Kingdom; it was widely perceived as a British bank, and the United Kingdom's depositors stood to lose much more than those of Luxembourg if things went wrong. In February 1987 the Governor made it clear to BCCI that the Bank would not undertake the world-wide consolidated supervision of the Group [17]. IML reiterated that it lacked the ability to monitor the activities of BCCI on a consolidated basis. The BCCI Group traded in over 70 countries in many of which supervision was weak or non-existent. In those circumstances, implementation of a new supervisory system would also prove to be costly and rather difficult in the sense of finding qualified people to perform that task.

The Bingham Report pointed out that:

> *'The demands on trained supervisory personnel would have been very difficult to meet. But this was by far the most hopeful solution, possibly the only hopeful solution. If it could not be undertaken, urgent steps were needed*

[16] op. cit., p.46.
[17] op. cit., p.47.

> *to reduce the group to a shape and size where supervision could be and would be effectively undertaken by someone, or the group had to rundown."* [18]

Until 1987 the responsibility for auditing BCCI's accounts was divided between Ernst & Whinney (E&W) (for auditing consolidated accounts of the Group), and Price Waterhouse (PW) (for overseas and BCCI Emirates) producing divided audits and potentially unclear Profit and Loss Accounts. This divisional responsibility was not only unsatisfactory, but also objected to by E&W, particularly in May 1986, and in August 1986 PW advised BCCI that for the sake of effective and efficient audit a single firm of auditors should be appointed [19]. In June 1987 PW were appointed as Group auditors. While E&W were auditors, they drew the attention of BCCI to a number of prudential and management concerns; similar concerns were also expressed by PW in respect of BCCI's overseas operations. But neither firm entertained '... *the slightest suspicion of fraud and malpractice which were ultimately revealed.'* [20]

The issue of consolidated supervision kept returning, and the Bank continued to decline the proposal for the reasons stated above. But the issue of whether the depositors' interests were in jeopardy did not seem to be a matter of concern for anybody. Comforting investigations carried out in the late 1980s were on a superficial basis because of the complexity of the structure [21]. During the latter part of 1987, the new proposal for cooperated supervision was considered according to which national supervisors responsible for BCCI would meet twice a year along with the management and auditors of BCCI to discuss relevant issues. This proposal was accepted by all parties, but the mandate of this body was unclear, and eventually it proved to be a rather inefficient method of carrying out effective supervision of a bank the structure of which was vast and complex. By January/February 1988, the Bank received critical reports on BCCI's operations from a number of quarters including one from the City of London Fraud Squad, who felt that BCCI departed from standard banking practice, and the Bingham Report stated, inter alia, that:

---

[18] op. cit., p.47.
[19] op. cit., p.50.
[20] op. cit., p.50.
[21] This point is developed in the subsequent sections of this work.

> 'BCCI management appeared to have colluded with a customer (who was suspected of perjury) to defeat by deception the enforcement of a judgement. The police were contemplating contempt proceedings against BCCI on the ground that it had obstructed their investigations...'[22]

The Bank also received reports through British diplomatic sources in the Gulf, and information on BCCI's activities was also provided by a British chartered accountant working there. However, according to the Bingham Report, it was hard to understand '... *the Bank's apparent lack of interest in establishing the truth*'[23], and the Bank also seemed to have discounted the reliability of such reports because of other suggestions they contained. The allegations against BCCI also pointed to the lack of integrity, fitness and competence of the bank's management. The Bingham Report went on to state that:

> 'In 1988 neither the Bank, nor the IML, nor the auditors suspected BCCI senior management of fraud. But the Bank did not feel it could trust the management and it was well aware of the distrust the group aroused elsewhere. Galpin and the Banking Supervision Division had given doubt about the management's integrity as a reason for reluctance to contemplate a UK subsidiary. In that situation it was in my view incumbent on the Bank to see that serious and apparently credible allegations capable of investigation (other than customer complaints suitable for resolution in the civil courts) were fully investigated.'[24]

By April 1988, BCCI's leadership changed, Mr Abedi's successor, so to speak, being Mr Naqvi. It was around that time that PW published the 1987 Audited Accounts of BCCI and the new cooperated management also submitted its report in May 1988. According to this report, BCCI concentrated on lending to certain customer groups, several of which were BCCI's shareholders. Those loans were secured on shares

[22] op. cit., p.56.
[23] op. cit., p.56.
[24] op. cit., p.57.

in Credit and Commerce American Holdings, the parent company of First American Bank. In 1983 BCCI acquired a minority interest in a Colombian bank with 24 retail branches in Colombia. According to the Bingham Report, one of the BCCI's customers was General Noriega against whom allegations of drug-trafficking had been brought and that because of the US authorities' interest in General Noriega, they began to take an active interest in BCCI's business in Colombia, Pananama and the USA, and in May 1996 launched an operation called 'Operation C – Chase' to ascertain whether BCCI was directly involved in drug-based funds. The Bingham Report stated about a BCCI account in Florida that:

> '... [it] was used for holding cash before its transfer to a BCCI account in Panama. In due course local BCCI officials suggested to the undercover agents that very much more sophisticated procedures should be used to launder these funds, and BCCI accounts in Paris, Luxembourg and London were used for the purpose. Among those who agreed to cooperate in this exercise, with knowledge of what the funds represented, were Mr Asif Baakza, manager of the corporate unit of SA's UK Region at 100 Leadenhall Street, and Mr Ziauddin Akbar, manager of BCCI's Central Treasury at the time of 1984-86 losses and now the moving spirit in Capcom, a company thought in 1985 to have been involved in BCCI's speculative trading activities...'[25]

In October 1988 seven officials of BCCI were arrested at Tampa on drug-trafficking and money-laundering charges. Whether the allegations were sustainable or not, the incident became a matter of concern for the Bank in that widespread adverse publicity would take depositors away from BCCI. The Bank, therefore, promptly made arrangements for monitoring closely the liquidity of BCCI in the UK Region. It received daily statements of liquidity and weekly analyses of deposits and advances. It also held weekly meetings with the management of the UK Region and imposed caps on the Region's funding for the rest of the Group.

[25] op. cit., p.61.

The 1987 Accounts submitted by PW provided certain information which was not provided by earlier reports, and the report of the Co-operative Committee (otherwise known as the College), clearly suggested that it did not have a firm supervisory grip on the Group, nor did it provide any suggestion as to how the structural problem of BCCI could be resolved.

By the beginning of 1989 the Bank successfully maintained a close supervision over BCCI's activities. BCCI seemed to have been involved in further illegal activities such as money laundering for the Abu Nhield organization and was subject to surveillance by the intelligence services. Whether these allegations were substantiated or not, suspicion about BCCI's integrity was aroused, which obviously had an adverse effect on the banking world, and in particular its depositors. PW also gave a qualified opinion on BCCI Group's 1988 accounts because of uncertainty attached to the Tampa proceedings, and their uncertain effect on the operations of the Group. The accounts also showed a loss to the tune of $40 million for the year after loan loss provisions of $145 million. Losses on loans were related primarily to a certain limited number of borrowers [26]. Supervision over the largest exposures and attempts to reduce such exposures proved unsuccessful because of the lack of resources to monitor those exposures efficiently. PW requested an improved control system and a restructure of Central Treasury operations; the only change made was a move of the Central Treasury to Abu Dhabi. The Bingham Reports stated:

> *'The likelihood of involvement in handling the proceeds of drug-trafficking could scarcely have eluded a competent and diligent banker contemplating such an investment, particularly if he had branches in Panama and agencies in Florida. While it is true that money laundering became an increasingly high-profile subject throughout the 1980s, it was not an activity in which a banker of probity would knowingly have engaged in in 1983. Whether BCCI failed to recognize the risk, or recognized and discounted it, or recognized and accepted it, or recognized and took what were thought to be adequate precautions, I do not know. This enquiry was never made. I think it was a pertinent enquiry, to*

[26] op. cit., p.64.

> *which a rigorous supervisor would have wished to know the answer.'* [27]

On 18 April 1990 PW's report on BCCI's 1989 Accounts was submitted to the directors of BCCI holdings. It stated (1) questionable loans were made to borrowers in the Gulf, and certain sums had been credited to non-performing loans in the United Arab Emirates; unauthorized loans were also made on the CCH accounts. (2) The Group required financial support to the tune of $18 billion, and PW declined to sign off the accounts as they stood. (3) Uncertainties relating to major loans, namely those made to the Gulf group ($350 million at the end of 1988 and $400 million to the end of 1989). (4) Despite management assurances that the CCH loans would be reduced during 1989 they had, in fact, increased, interest remained unpaid, additional unsupported drawdowns had been debited and there was an estimated shortfall of $200 million in the value of the security [28]. (5) Their inquiries indicated that certain accounts and transactions which were principally booked in Cayman Islands and other offshore centres were either false or deceitful [29].

Although the Board of Banking Supervision was told of BCCI's financial problems, no mention was made, formally or informally, of the existence of PW's report of 18 April 1990 or its contents. Thus, the Governors and the Board of Banking Supervision were unaware that serious doubt was thrown by PW on the integrity of BCCI's most senior management. According to Bingham LJ, perhaps the Treasury and the Treasury ministers were not informed either [30].

PW's position on the 1989 accounts was clear – that the Government should not commit to support BCCI without a full understanding of the unresolved issues. The audit opinion of PW became a source of public discussion, PW being absolutely certain that without proper support from major shareholders the inevitable would take place. The Bingham Report suggests that the picture, in reality, was perhaps even worse because '*... management might very well have made substantially greater losses in running the business than the accounts disclosed.*' [31]

[27] op. cit., p.73.
[28] op. cit., p.77.
[29] op. cit., p.77.
[30] op. cit., p.79.
[31] op. cit., p.84.

It was around this time that the Abu Dhabi [32] shareholders came to the rescue of BCCI, and the imminent collapse of BCCI was averted. There still existed financial, managerial and structural problems, but at least the immediate collapse was tackled. The Bingham Report stated that:

> 'It is, however, unfortunate in retrospect that the supervisors did not, at this critical juncture in BCCI's affairs, seize the opportunity to establish direct personal contact with the top levels of the Abu Dhabi Government: had senior representatives of the Bank and the IML succeeded in discussing the existing situation and the future at this stage, all involved might have had a clearer understanding of the others' position over the months ahead and it is to be hoped that more detail of Mr Naqvi's revelations would have emerged.' [33]

However, the acquisition of majority control by the Abu Dhabi Government produced two results: (a) it caused the Bank of England to reconsider the longer-term plans for undertaking the consolidated supervision of the Group; and (b) it produced implementation by the majority shareholders of the programme to rationalize the UK operations, resulting in reductions in large number of branches and employees, and to put the bank on a commercial footing. However, because of the majority position of the Abu Dhabi Government, the question arose that if the natural home were at Abu Dhabi would the United Arab Emirates have the capacity to conduct the consolidated supervision of the Group? The Bank of England was, however, inclined to see that the UK subsidiary was set up in order to protect the UK depositors. In 1990 the Bank faced another problem: the Group left Luxembourg but could not go to Abu Dhabi. The Bank was also clear that there should be a legitimate structure reflecting the new principal shareholding, the need for consolidated supervision, and the continuation of the College and to help the United Arab Emirates Central Bank in supervising an Abu Dhabi-registered bank. These issues apparently were not vigorously pursued.

---

[32] For a detailed account of Abu Dhabi interests, see BCCI Report, op. cit. pp.80-81.
[33] op. cit., p.85.

Whether Bank Collapses were due to Lack of Regulatory Measures 123

On the 1990 audit report PW suspected that the previous management must have colluded with some of its major customers to disguise the underlying purpose of significant transactions [34]. According to the Bingham Report, certain major loan accounts which totalled $3.56 billion at 31 December 1989 rose to $4.233 billion by 31 August 1990 of which $2.479 billion were thought to be recoverable [35]. The shortfall in the value of the CCH securities was then estimated at $300 million, and PW thought that the shareholders would be unlikely to accept liability. The projected net loss of $311 million was shown from 1990 and was based on management accounts adjusted by PW, but it excluded the estimated provisions and the income-handling cost and major loss. Additional provisions for financial support to the extent of $1.5 billion was found necessary. PW delivered a copy of the report to the Bank of England on 3 October 1990, but there still existed a belief that the majority shareholders would provide support. PW's report was not widely circulated within the Bank but the Board of Banking Supervision, including the Governors, learnt that PW had reported further problems about BCCI's financial position. But '... *received no indication that PW had made a report which reflected in any way on the honesty of the BCCI's business or the integrity of its manager. Of that the Board and the Governors were entirely unaware. The Treasury and the Treasury minister received no information that the report had been made or of the financial and other problems it revealed, although the Treasury were told in the following spring of the bank's need for large financial support.*' [36] The Bingham Report showed its astonishment that the fitness and propriety issues made so little impact on the minds of those who read PW's report within the Bank of England. The Bingham Report stated that:

> 'In failing to appreciate and react to the implications of this report the Bank was in my view at fault. But it was not solely at fault. The report did not convey in a blunt and unmistakable way, the full extent of PW's concerns...' [37]

---

[34] op. cit., p.95.
[35] op. cit., p.95.
[36] op. cit., p.96.
[37] op. cit., p.96.

In the early part of October 1990, the Board of Banking Supervision was informed of PW's findings on the BCCI's loan book, including malpractice that was carried out by the bank. The Bingham Report suggests that the Board did have power to impose a solution and that the Bank of England should have exerted its supervisory muscle [38]. The period between October and December 1990 was primarily concerned with the financial package that was necessary for supporting the bank's position which was mainly created by its loan portfolio [39]. In so far as the problem loans were concerned, an Investigating Committee was set up in Abu Dhabi by the majority shareholder to ascertain the causes of those loans. According to the Bingham Report, the irrecoverable loans *'were not simply the result of bad lending but were the result of collusion, through joint venture or nominee arrangements with BCCI'.* [40]

During 1990 and 1991 the Bank continued to receive statistical and prudential returns from the UK Region, and regular monthly meetings took place with BCCI. The Bingham Report concludes that *'.... In its supervision of the UK Region the Bank encountered nothing to cause serious concern.'* [41] It was only in June 1990 that the Bank learnt from the Federal Reserve Board in Washington DC of the problems about loans made by BCCI for the purchase of shares in CCAH. The Bank also learnt of the investigations that had been carried out by the New York District Attorney against BCCI. It was not until 16 November 1990 that the Bank came to know of the long-standing suspicion held by the Federal Reserve Board about BCCI's dealings, and in particular the covert financing of the purchase of CCAH shares by BCCI's Middle Eastern shareholders. By January 1991 it became clear that the loans which had accrued to the extent of $600 million were irrecoverable. It was also revealed around this time that BCCI had some unrecorded deposits and that suspicion was raised by the auditors that the deposits had been misappropriated. The Bank knew that it would be difficult to recover the $600 million loan portfolio, but were not aware of the fact that the loans were fictitious. It was only on 10 January 1991 that the unrecorded deposits were reported to the Board of Banking Supervision,

---

[38] op. cit., p.97.
[39] For detailed information on this issue please see the Bingham Report, op. cit., pp. 99-102.
[40] op. cit., p.101.
[41] op. cit., p.103.

but BCCI's authorities maintained that those deposits would not affect the UK operations, although the Bank treated the matter seriously and wanted to investigate it. However, any possible investigation was hampered by the need to preserve confidentiality as to the outcome of the investigation, in that if the result of the investigation went against BCCI then it would be subject to a section 39 or 41 procedure of the Banking Act 1987, but the Bank did not wish to alert the then General Manager of the UK Region to the investigation because his own conduct would be in question. The Bank, ultimately, upon legal advice, decided to issue a notice under section 41 on the condition that the terms of the notice would not be too explicit. In other words, the investigation could not be properly conducted and the Bank, therefore, remained unaware of many important issues that the investigation could have revealed.

The period between 1 February and 1 March 1991 was dominated by the issue of whether the Abu Dhabi Government would support BCCI as to the level of finance required. During this period the issues of restructuring, recruitment and a financial package all received attention, but no concrete decisions were taken.

The majority shareholders made complaints about PW's appointment by the Bank under section 41 of the Banking Act 1987. They also accused the Bank of *'duplicity by encouraging the majority shareholders to pursue restructuring and re-financing of the Group, while secretly harbouring the thought or intention of using PW's duty as advisors to the majority shareholders on the restructuring and refinancing of the Group ... .* [According to them] *PW's ability to make a fair and objective report under section 41 was compromised by this knowledge that if the Group were to collapse as to close their own record as auditors would be called in question.'*[42] According to the majority shareholders, accountants other than PW should have been appointed to report under section 41. The complaints that were brought against PW were considered to be unfounded by the Bingham Inquiry, but the relationship between PW and BCCI deteriorated.

By April 1991 the liquidity problem for BCCI became even more acute. This was primarily due to the reduction in intra-group lending, and the withdrawal of $250 million by the Abu Dhabi Investment Authority. On the issue of restructuring the bank, the Bingham Report

[42] op. cit., p.115.

clearly suggested that BCCI did not pay much attention to it although PW reminded BCCI several times of the need for it. The Bingham Report clearly states that the attention of BCCI's supervisors was dominated during 1989 by the activities and reports of various US authorities; in other words restructuring, recruitment and investigation of outstanding financial problems were relegated to a secondary position. After a section 39 notice was served on BCCI for the purpose of discovery of documents, BCCI held against the Bank on the grounds that the Bank had become unreasonable. The Bank was in a dilemma in that it was fully aware of BCCI's involvement in alleged dishonest activities in the USA, and on the other hand it was required to ensure that BCCI had done some fundamental work to rectify its position in respect of restructuring, refinancing and improving its liquidity position. Furthermore, the Bank's formal responsibility was limited to supervision of the UK branches, and compliance with the criteria of fitness and propriety of shareholders and senior management.

The supposed restructuring of BCCI did not advance. By May 1991 the Group was suffering critical problems and the financial package remained outstanding. According to the Bank's calculations by that time the cost to the majority shareholders supporting BCCI would have been $10.1 billion. On 22 May 1991 the Bank and PW learnt that the majority shareholder's financial support package had been finally signed at about $5.1 billion made up of promissory notes, a guarantee, subscriptions for new shares and replacement of unrecorded deposits. The period between 23 May 1991 and 22 June 1991 showed some progress towards the formation of a new UK subsidiary and some progress towards restructuring of the rest of the Group. PW was very anxious to ensure that the majority shareholders were fully aware of the continuing uncertainties affecting the financial position of BCCI and sought written confirmation that the Abu Dhabi Government intended to continue its support for the bank, and that it was prepared to meet its liabilities as they fell due. But no such undertaking was submitted by the Government. PW's draft section 41 report confirmed that there were genuine liabilities and that there was evidence of fraud and deception which had been practised in the Group over a substantial period of time. The draft report made references of falsification of accounting records, fraudulent use of the Ruling Families funds, collusion with third parties' banks to make loans to BCCI's customers in order to avoid disclosure of such lendings of BCCI's bank sheets, Central Treasury losses, collusion of customers and others to give false confirmation to the auditors of fictitious and non-recourse loans [43].

In June 1991 the Governor of the Bank agreed that in the light of what PW had revealed, the proposed restructuring of BCCI was no longer appropriate, instead the Bank should explore as a matter of urgency how to protect depositors. Indeed, on 1 July 1991 a meeting of the Board of Banking Supervision was held to inform the IML and the Federal Authorities, both in Washington DC and New York, and to alert the Treasury.

On 4 July 1991 the final bell rang, the Governor of the Bank reported to the Board of Banking Supervision that it would seek an orderly winding down of BCCI. Then events took their natural course despite to-ing and fro-ing of officers between London and Luxembourg. At one point on 5 July 1991 a petition by the Bank to the High Court of Justice in London appointed three partners of Touche Ross to be joint provisional liquidators of BCCI SA. The closure of the bank was strongly supported by the Board of Banking Supervision, primarily on the ground that the depositors' interests must be protected as far as possible. With reference to the closure of BCCI, the Bingham Report concluded that:

> *'In the latter stages the Bank came to rely to an excessive extent, in my opinion, on the auditors: under the British system of supervision the auditors have a crucial role to play but the duty to supervise is placed on the Bank and it is a duty which cannot be delegated. It is the Bank, not the auditor, which is the supervisor. In these respects the Bank's supervisory approach to BCCI was in my opinion deficient. How different the course of events would have been had these deficiencies not existed, one can only speculate.'* [44]

Further Reflections on the BCCI Episode

It would seem appropriate to discuss the relevant government

---

[43] op. cit., p.140.
[44] op. cit., p.150.

departments that were involved either peripherally or extensively in this episode.

The first important government department to be discussed in this context must be HM Treasury which is primarily responsible for the integrity and stability of the financial system in the UK. It is important to remember that under the Banking Act 1987, the responsibility for supervising individual banks in the UK was given to the Bank of England. Indeed, the Bank had no obligation to consult or inform the Treasury about any particular financial institution. The Treasury's function, as stated earlier, is to enact legislation and it is not supposed to encroach upon the Bank's function. There exists an understanding that the Bank would not commit its own resources to a rescue operation without informing the Treasury in advance. The Bingham Report states that if support is required in excess of a range permitted by the Bank reserves and involves use of the Issue Department funds or a Treasury guarantee or indemnity, the Treasury's explicit agreement would be required [45]. There exist other situations in which the Bank should alert the Treasury, namely when the financial situation of an institution might lead to its failure with implications for the UK economy as a whole, or when diplomatic or foreign relations problems might arise, or when closure would cause hardship and losses to a significant number of retail customers or when the ownership of a major bank raises some issue of public interest.

In practice, however, communications between the Treasury and the Bank take place on a regular basis and in particular in relation to any of the items mentioned above. In the BCCI's case apparently discussions between the Bank and the Treasury took place a few times. The Bingham Report confirms that in the late 1970s the Treasury became aware of the unease about the BCCI through the Bank but nothing specific was brought to its attention [46].

The Treasury was not alerted *'to the critical view which this episode caused the Bank to entertain of BCCI's management.'* [47] In November 1987 the Bank told the Treasury of the supervisory problems which BCCI presented. The Treasury was always anxious to ensure that it

---

[45] op. cit., p.151.
[46] op. cit., p.153.
[47] op. cit., p.153.

would not in any way encroach upon the Bank's supervisory responsibility; it did, however, request the Bank to keep it fully informed.

According to the Bingham Report, the Treasury was kept informed in fairly general terms of events during 1989 as well as the Bank's plan for restructuring of the Group. In relation to the Tampa episode the Treasury was fully involved in drafting coordinated drafts of ministerial speeches and answers[48]. On 23 April 1990 the Treasury was informed of the difficulty in signing-off BCCI's 1989 accounts. Again, the Bingham Report confirmed that at no time before the closure of BCCI was any reference, direct or indirect, made by the Bank to PW's report of 30 October 1990 in any communication with the Treasury at any level[49]. The Bingham Report states that:

> 'The Treasury received no indication of the financial and other problems which that report revealed, although it did learn in the following spring of BCCI's need for large financial support. It was not told of the unrecorded deposits reported to the Bank on 4 January 1991 or the theft from the Ruling Family's investment portfolio...'[50]

In fact, by 5 April 1991 the Treasury was informed by the Bank that the latter was happy about the financial position of BCCI, and an account was given of the three bank restructuring proposals and of hostile articles published in the US press about money laundering in the First American Bank. On 26 April 1991 the Governor of the Bank told the Chancellor of investigation by the New York Federal Authorities and said that there was no evidence of money laundering by the British arm of BCCI and that this view was fully endorsed by HM Customs & Excise.

In May 1991 the Bank notified the Treasury of the possibility of a large and very public scandal erupting in the USA and its possible consequences on the existing owners and managers who might be regarded as fit and proper persons for running the bank. In other words, until May 1991 the Bank of England seems to have been convinced that the BCCI scandal in the USA was not entirely true and that the performance of the bank in the UK gave no cause for alarm.

---

[48] op. cit., p.153.
[49] op. cit., p.154.
[50] op. cit., p.154.

The Bingham Report pointed out that the Prime Minister first heard about BCCI's problems only on 22 June 1991. It was only on 28 June 1991 that the Bank told the Treasury of its decision that it could not continue to authorize BCCI to operate [51]. On 4 July 1991 the Governor notified the Prime Minister at a meeting of ministers and officials of the Bank's proposed action and the reason for it; the Bank did not seek approval from the Prime Minister.

Apparently the boundaries of responsibilities between HM Treasury and the Bank were clearly maintained in the BCCI's case. On balance, it is for the Bank to guide the Treasury and not the other way round, on such issues. The Bingham Report states that:

> *'Most of the Treasury witnesses who gave evidence to the Inquiry made no complaint that the Bank had failed to keep them fully informed: since the practical conduct of banking supervision was the responsibility of the Bank, there was in the view of these officials no need for the Treasury to be informed until action was called for or there was an apprehension of immediate problems. On this view the Treasury did not need to know the details of BCCI's position until the end of June 1991, which is when the Bank told them.'* [52]

The Bingham Report maintains that although this responsibility structure is understandable, it was not very satisfactory. The Bank failed to give to the Treasury any hint of fraud and the gravity of the Group's financial position was never conveyed [53]. It was not possible for the Treasury to deduce any inference as to the losses that BCCI sustained on the basis of the information it was provided by the Bank; on the contrary, even in April 1991 the Treasury was told that the Bank was happy about the financial position of BCCI. Thus, it was not possible for the Treasury to appreciate that BCCI was technically insolvent.

The Bingham Report also maintains that the Bank had no intention to mislead. According to this Report:

> *'It had no reason or wish to withhold information, and*

---

[51] Authorized the restructuring which was under negotiation, op cit., p.155.
[52] op. cit., p.156.
[53] op. cit., p.156.

motives of self-protection would have made for greater disclosure, not less. The fault lay in the Bank's failure to appreciate the import of the messages it was given by PW, in a deep-rooted reluctance to believe ill of BCCI, in a hope that the past abuses in the group would be put behind it and in a failure to ensure that the matters reported by PW were known to and understood by the top echelons in the Bank.' [54]

The Bingham Report further maintained that:

'The collapse of BCCI was never at all likely to have serious adverse effects on the UK financial system or economy as a whole. But there was from early 1990 onwards an obvious risk that it would cause diplomatic and foreign relations problems, hardship and loss to a significant number of retail customers and political outcry. If that is so, Treasury officials and minister should have been alerted, not because any immediate action was called for but because it is preferable for thought to be given to potential problems before they become emergencies. As it was, the conduct of Treasury officials and minister is not in my view open to criticism in any respect.' [55]

Involvement of the Crown Prosecution Service (CPS) was peripheral and it never prosecuted BCCI for any offence or had grounds for doing so [56].

The Home Office, the Bingham Report confirmed, received no evidence showing that the bank was involved in drug and money laundering or in the commission of any other criminal offence [57].

The Inland Revenue never prosecuted BCCI for any revenue offence nor did it at any time disclose evidence of any non-revenue offence. There was no record of any discussion of BCCI between the Inland Revenue and the Bank of England at any time [58].

[54] op. cit., p.156.
[55] op. cit., pp.156-157.
[56] op. cit., p.170.
[57] op. cit., p.170.
[58] op. cit., p.171.

The records of the Metropolitan Police contained no evidence pointing to the commission of criminal offences by BCCI or its management [59].

The Office of Fair Trading was minimally responsible in respect of BCCI's activities and the Bingham Report confirmed that it was properly mindful of its responsibility but was entitled to take its cue from the Bank, which in huge measure it did [60].

Although BCCI featured in a number of cases that the Serious Fraud Office handled between 1 April 1988 and 1 July 1991 there was no evidence in any of these cases that BCCI itself had committed any criminal offence [61].

Conclusions

The primary reasons for the closure of BCCI have been identified and discussed in this chapter. It has been established that although in certain respects the Bank seemed to have failed to pay much attention to what went on within the BCCI Group; on the other hand the truth remains that the BCCI Group failed to maintain the minimum standard of banking. There therefore remains the question as to how to strike the balance between these two elements: (a) maintenance of a minimum standard by a bank, and (b) the minimum supervision by the supervisory authority.

It has been suggested that a US-style supervision might be more effective whereby a corps of professional examiners would visit and inspect the records of a bank instead of pursuing current practice which is basically based on dialogue with management and prudential returns, but there has been high incidence of bank failures in the USA. The Bingham Report also confirms this when it stated that:

> *'The Bank's traditional techniques of supervision, based as they are on trust, frankness and a willingness to co-operate, seem to me on the whole to have served the community well. The US record does not of itself demonstrate the superiority of the system employed there, which (quite apart from expense) has its own*

---
[59] op. cit., p.172.
[60] op. cit., p.174.
[61] op. cit., p.177.

> *drawbacks. But one of the virtues claimed for the Bank's supervision is its flexibility. This should mean that a quite different supervisory approach is adopted where trust and frankness are lacking. In such cases also special qualities are required of the supervisor.'* [62]

BCCI adopted such a complex organizational structure and administration, and in such circumstances it is not possible for any supervisors to carry out supervision effectively when transparency in respect of deposits, loans, management decision and administrative activities is not available. These were precisely the reasons why BCCI failed.

The need for adopting an effective international supervisory system in addition to the national level in accordance with the recent Basle Committee Core Principles [63] has received attention in a different section of this chapter. But, irrespective of whatever system of supervision a country may adopt for keeping a bank under a proper control, the fact remains that it is for the bank itself to ensure that depositors' interests are protected. By following the Bingham Report one might maintain that the Bank, on many occasions, took a relaxed view of BCCI even though its attention was drawn to the financial state of BCCI by its auditors, PW. Auditors owe a duty of care to their client company and shareholders. One is required to consider whether auditors should report to and/or owe a duty directly to depositors [64]. In relation to auditing of banks, The Bingham Report points out that on the issue of appointing auditors there exist two views: that complex international banking groups should always have a sole joint auditors and that auditors should change after a specific period. According to the Bingham Report no absolute rule should be established and followed in this regard. The Report states that:

> *'The object must be to achieve as thorough and reliable an audit as is reasonably practicable, in the interests of the group, its depositors, its shareholders and its*

---

[62] op. cit., p.182.
[63] The text of the Core Principles has been reproduced in *37 International Legal Materials* (1997), p.405.
[64] op. cit., p.188; see also *Caparo Industries plc v Dickman* [1990] 2 AC 605.

employees. Ordinarily, it would seem to me that this object is most likely to be achieved by employing a single well-qualified firm, which would itself deploy staff so as to achieve the optimum blend of continuity and freshness. But cases vary infinitely and uniformity of practice is not in my view a desirable end.' [65]

In relation to auditors' duties the Bingham Report stated the following:

'(iii) *It is desirable that the duty should be:*

(a) to report to the Bank any information or opinion which the auditor knows or should reasonably know to be relevant to a bank's fulfilment of the criteria in Schedule 3 of the 1987 Act;

(b) to provide information reasonably requested by the Bank for purposes of its supervisory duties.

This is a wider duty than that imposed by the present Guideline. It might be possible to amend the Guideline to similar effect, but a statutory duty could be imposed by regulations made under section 47(5) of the 1987 Act and this would avoid the need for full statutory amendment if changes were thereafter found to be necessary.

(iv) A statutory duty would clarify the position of foreign auditors of UK branches not subject to the Institute's disciplinary jurisdiction.' [66]

Although the Bingham Report on certain occasions criticized the Bank, in so far as auditors were concerned the Report said that there was no reason to recommend any change in the Bank's existing practice under which cases are judged on their merits and '...*appointments made with a view to securing as thorough, expeditious and as fair an investigation as possible. Any accountant who questions whether a conflict may exist is well-advised to heed the detailed guidance given by the Institute on this subject.'* [67]

[65] op. cit., p.188.
[66] op. cit., p.189.
[67] op. cit., p.190.

The importance of internal audit and the role of the Audit Committee were emphasized by the Bingham Report. In so far as auditing of the UK branches of an overseas bank is concerned, the Bingham Report considered that the Bank should have the power to require separate audit in any case where it thinks fit, at least in respect of banks domiciled outside the European Union[68]. This issue also became important in respect of the Barings episode.

Although the Bingham Committee did not have the mandate to review the existing Depositor Protection Scheme, it received a considerable quantity of material on the subject and which showed support:

'(i) *for giving full protection to qualifying deposits up to a certain, relatively modest, level;*

(ii) *for giving protection above that figure, either as now on a percentage basis or on a sliding scale;*

(iii) *for raising the current ceiling figure of £20,000 to a figure more closely in line with the limit on other similar UK schemes;*

(iv) *for alerting the law to provide for speedier payment to depositors where a provisional liquidator is appointed, if the court approves;*

(v) *for requiring banks to notify depositors (perhaps by a notice printed on pass sheets) of the ceiling figure for protected deposits and (if a Community Directive is made) of the Deposit Protection Fund which applies to their deposits.*'[69]

Upon reflection the Bingham Report prompts the following conclusions:

(a) that failures of banks are often caused by negligent and irresponsible acts of banks;

(b) that supervisory authorities have limits to their functions;

(c) that trust and faith in banks should still be treated as the best means of ensuring that they are operating properly on capital markets; and

---

[68] op. cit., p.191.
[69] op. cit., p.192.

(d) that complex organizational structure often creates difficulties for effective banking supervision.

Perhaps a consolidated supervisory system should be adopted and the system of international cooperation between supervision in various foreign jurisdictions should be considered seriously[70].

The Collapse of Barings
Basic Facts

The Barings Bank was set up in 1762 as a partnership, which was privately controlled, and in 1890 Baring Brothers & Co (BB&C) was founded to continue with the business of the bank in succession to the partnership venture. In 1985 Barings plc acquired the share capital of BB&Co and became the headquarters company of the Barings Group. In 1991 the Barings Group acquired a 40% equity interest in Dillon Read & Co Inc, a US investment bank based in New York[71]. BB&Co was the largest authorized bank with branches in foreign jurisdictions, in particular in Singapore and Hong Kong. Two other corporate units, namely Baring Investment Bank (BIB) and Baring Securities Limited (BSL) also became relevant in the Barings' episode. Although BSL was incorporated in the Cayman Islands, its principal office, management and accounts were based in London. BSL expanded widely in various foreign jurisdictions in the form of subsidiaries; the two most relevant ones in the context of this discussion were Baring Futures (Singapore) Pte Ltd (BFS), and Baring Securities (Japan) Ltd (BSJ).

At the outset it must be pointed out that like all other subsidiaries, BB&Co was subject to the banking legislation and supervision and surveillance of the Bank of England. However, by virtue of being a truly transnational bank, it was also subjected to the supervision of a number of different supervisors, and the absence of a coordinated system of supervision among all the supervisors seems to have presented a fundamental problem as to how to measure the performance of the entire group.

BFS, which was a company registered under the law of Singapore, became an indirect subsidiary of BSL. The intention behind the setting

---

[70] This issue has also been discussed in relations to Barings Bank.
[71] See further Report of the Board of Banking Supervision Inquiry into the Circumstances of the Collapse of Barings, London HMSO, 1995, p.4.

up of BFS was to allow Barings to trade on the Singapore International Monetary Exchange (SIMEX). In addition to BFS, Baring Securities (Singapore) Pte Ltd (BSS) was also operating on the Singapore market. BSS was a subsidiary of BSL. Because Mr Leeson became a principal agent to the collapse of Barings, it is worth pointing out that he joined BB&Co in July 1989 to work in Futures and Options Settlements with two years' prior experience in a similar capacity with Morgan Stanley in London. In 1991 he joined the Business Development Group within BB&Co in London. His application for a licence was not pursued by BB&Co because he would not pass credit checks, and he was recommended by Barings to work in Singapore. Barings' application to the Securities and Futures Authority on behalf of Mr Leeson for a licence was withdrawn in September 1992. Soon after he arrived in Singapore (March 1992), he was selected to head Barings' SIMEX operations in Singapore, in addition to acting as a floor manager. Mr Lesson was responsible to the Futures and Options Settlements in London. In late 1992 Mr Leeson passed the SIMEX examinations and began trading on the floor of SIMEX. Around the same time, he was appointed General Manager and Head Trader of BFS.

There was a controversy as to whom Mr Leeson would report about his activities on SIMEX because his reporting lines were never clearly defined [72]. Although he reported to Barings' management in Singapore for the BFS's office, and in particular to the then Divisional Manager (Mr James Bax) and a director of BFS, he also reported to (a) Regional Operations Manager South Asia (Mr Simon Jones) and Chief Operating Officer of BSS, and (b) a Director of BB&Co (Mr Ron Baker) and Head of Financial Products Group of Baring Investment Bank (BIB). According to the *Report of the Board of Banking Supervision into the Circumstances of the Collapse of Barings* ('The Report of the Board of Banking Supervision'), conflicting views existed as to Mr Leeson's precise reporting lines within Barings [73]. BSL went through its reorganization in 1992-93, and it was during this period that BIB was set up. The systems of management and internal control within BSL were known to have been weak as indentified by Cooper and Lybrand, the bank's external auditors, in 1992; it was a business that was led by its front

---

[72] op. cit., p.31.
[73] op. cit., p.7.

office with poor lines of communication between the front office and the back office. BSL also had a strong presence on the Japanese securities market. One of the reasons why BIB was set up was to consolidate all investment banking business of Barings into a single business in one central office. During the second half of 1993, the Board of Banking Supervision decided that, despite different business cultures, BB&Co and BSL must work closely together as a first step towards the formation of BIB. The restructuring of BSL and the formation of BIB were based on a matrix reporting structure whereby profit responsibility was on a product basis, and the local office management would perform an important role in managing the office infrastructure which comprised systems, controls, accounting, settlements and administration [74]. According to Peter Norris, Chief Executive Officer of BIB and a Director of Barings plc, individuals who ran businesses in various locations reported to both the person who managed a particular location and to the relevant product manager, and in his view the roles of the local manager and the product manager were *'equally important'* [75]. Although some members of Barings' management (including Peter Norris) considered the reporting lines as clear, there were others who did not share this view. Indeed, the interviews held by the Board of Banking Supervision Inquiry show that *'...reporting lines and responsibilities were not fully understood by a number of individuals, especially concerning FPG* [Financial Products Group] *headed by Ron Baker, and BFS, of which Leeson was General Manager.'* [76]. One of the consequences of this organizational structure was that some members of management assumed that the responsibilities for certain activities rested with certain managers, who denied having such responsibility [77]. According to the Board's Report this situation *'... resulted in confusion and a pervasive lack of management control over these activities.'* [78].

In July 1992 Mr Leeson opened an account number '88888' in BFS as

---

[74] op. cit., p.21.
[75] op. cit., p.22.
[76] op. cit., p.22.
[77] The Inquiry of the Board of Banking Supervision revealed that there was some confusion and disagreement as to whom Mr Leeson reported to. Some members of the management believed he reported to Ron Baker, whereas Ron Baker thought that other individuals were Mr Leeson's reporting managers. For details see further op. cit., pp.22-23.
[78] op. cit., p.23.

a client account, used to conceal unauthorized trading activities of BFS from 1993 until the collapse of Barings. Having qualified as a trader on SIMEX floor, Mr Leeson started trading heavily, and appeared to make significant profits from his trading. Thus the dynamic approach to investments adopted by Mr Leeson coupled with unclear lines of responsibilities and the profits earned for Barings apparently convinced the Headquarters that everything was in order.

In July and August 1994 BSL's internal auditors carried out a review of Barings' operations in Singapore and its neighbouring countries. The report confirmed that there existed a lack of segregation of duties between BFS's front and back offices. By January 1995, the management of Barings in London had causes for concern with regard to Barings' trading activities on Osaka Securities Exchange (OSE), and even the Bank for International Settlements drew the attention of Barings' Headquarters to the losses in the Nikkei contracts.

In 1995 the discrepancies between the deposits of BFS and its margin [79] on SIMEX became increasingly irreconcilable as the funds of SIMEX and the bank were significantly less than the amount recorded in the BFS's accounting records as owing to BSL, or other institutions such as BSJ. Mr Leeson did not apparently cooperate in discussing this matter with the authorities, either in London or in Singapore, but on 24 February 1995 he notified his employer of his resignation. On 1 March 1995 Mr Leeson flew to Frankfurt where, on 2 March 1995, he was detained by the German authorities. He was charged with offences under the Criminal Procedures Code of Singapore and the Singaporean authorities sought his extradition from Germany. On 26 February 1995 Baring plc was placed in administration. Just over a week thereafter, the majority of the assets and liabilities of the Barings Group was purchased by Internationale Nederlanden Groep NV (ING), the large Dutch banking and insurance group.

Mr Leeson's episode points to several important issues:

a) the nature of supervision and surveillance by the Bank of England and other authorities concerned;

---

[79] Margin means cash or securities deposited with an exchange as a form of collateral and a way of settling realized and unrealized profits and losses on positions. Secondly, its purpose is to ensure that clearing members have sufficient resources to support open positions.

b) the lack of segregation between departments;

c) the lack of reporting by Mr Leeson;

d) a degree of indifference on the part of some of the authorities as to what took place in the name of trading on SIMEX and Japanese Stock Exchanges.

The Report of the Board of Banking Supervision pointed out that during the inquiry the members of the Board of Banking Supervision did not have unfettered access to all the relevant directors and employees of the Barings Group and its records, whether held by Barings or third parties. Apparently, the Board was unable to verify with Mr Leeson the strategy which lay behind the unauthorized trading conducted by BFS, and the entries on account number '88888' against records held by SIMEX. The Board of Banking Supervision was unable to make inquiries of third parties who might have been involved in unlawful trading or of any employees of Barings, it was unable to investigate whether funds remitted by BSL, BSJ and Baring Securities London Ltd (BSLL) were misappropriated, nor to inquire of the adequacy of the work performed by BSF's auditors and the adequacy of SIMEX's supervision of BSF's activities.

Specific Issues Relating to the Collapse of Barings Group

Risk Management

Risk management is a fundamental issue in the banking business, even more important when the organization structure of an institution becomes complex. Each unit of such an organization should, ideally, assess risks according to its own objectives and in relation to the jurisdiction in which it operates its business. The reporting system is crucially important in managing and controlling risks. Foreseeable risks are often taken with sufficient protection; hence the need for assessing risk in the financial sector in particular. Unforeseeable risks may never be assessed, and all institutions may be subject to such risks at any time; they are the real risks.

In relation to the Barings Group what one ought to consider is whether any responsible risk strategy was carried out for each of the units operating in various jurisdictions and what kind of risk management system the Group adopted. Barings business in Japan and Singapore was risk-laden related; thus a viable risk study procedure should have been adopted. In relation to Barings' management in Singapore, the most relevant unit with reference to which it should be considered was BIB. Risk control stands for the preventative stage, whereas management of risk is the stage at which actual risks that have taken place must be managed in such a manner as to minimize the consequential damage. What needs to be considered is whether Barings and BIB had adopted any risk control strategy in order to avoid exposure to unnecessary and, perhaps, self-induced risks, rather than being involved in the management of risk. A risk created at the Japan and Singapore Stock Exchanges must be treated as a risk for the entire Group including the Headquarters, unless the organization maintains that each unit must be entirely independent, not only in terms of management but also in respect of its profits and losses. But, in the case of a transnational corporation that cannot be, because in the final analysis they are one economic unit.

The Barings' collapse (and perhaps the BCCI episode) should remind one of the difficulties that a transnational corporation may encounter if it is vast, and from the standpoint of organization structure extremely complex. When one considers the issue of risk management in relation to BIB, one can easily conclude that the issue of risk should not be exclusively associated with BIB. BIB was an integral unit of Barings Bank and, therefore, a risk for BIB must be treated as a risk for BB&Co too. According to the Board's Report, the risk management in BSL was under the supervision of the Risk Committee constituted in October 1992 and met daily to discuss the risks in BSL. The Risk Committee was provided information on gross positions, on proprietary trading, counter-party excess reports and daily profit and loss figures. Although a procedure for risk identification and a strategy was adopted by BIB, it is reported that most of the officials involved lacked experience in the discipline. It is also stated in the Report of the Board of Banking Supervision that:

> *'The Risk Committee started off and there was a lack of financial information for them to use at that time. They somehow just petered away.'* [80]

[80] op. cit., p.33.

The Report of the Board of Banking Supervision also states that one of the objectives of the Barings's Treasury and Risk Group '...was to establish independence over the monitoring of risk on a global basis'[81]. Risk studies should be localized and their impact must be studied for the organization as a whole. In the case of Barings, although risk controllers were appointed in Tokyo and Hong Kong, no risk controllers were appointed in the Singapore office, which contributed to the collapse of Barings. Most of the 'switching'[82] business managed by Mr Leeson in Singapore was booked in the name of BSJ. But BSJ relied on information provided to it by BFS and did not carry out any independent verification. Perhaps one could assume that BFS either provided inadequate information or provided information that would protect its position and would not give a high risk exposure.

The internal audit report of BFS issued in October 1994 recommended that the risk management element in BFS should be subject to the scrutiny of an independent risk and compliance officer, but by the time of the collapse the risk strategy was not carried out by any such officer. The Report of the Board of Banking Supervision also points out that it was the responsibility of each product group to manage the risks arising from the group's activities. There was no proper risk study, let alone management of risk for the product group in Singapore.

The Report of the Board of Banking Supervision stated that:

> 'The independent monitoring and control of risk in respect of the activities of BFS was inadequate. Also, the risk control function in BSJ was rendered ineffective because it relied wholly on information provided by BFS.'[83]

Risk becomes even riskier when responsibilities within the unit are not clearly demarcated or when responsibilities are unduly dispersed. In both situations, risk remains unmanaged and, therefore, the question of there being control would not arise. In the Barings' case, Mr Leeson created risks but there was nobody to manage them. Apparently, there

---

[81] op. cit., p.33.
[82] Switching entailed the simultaneous purchase and sale of the same futures contracts on the different futures exchanges.
[83] op. cit., p.34.

Whether Bank Collapses were due to Lack of Regulatory Measures 143

was no need for Mr Leeson to be concerned with the issue of risks because he satisfied headquarters that he was a good trader.

Authorized Trading Activities of BFS on Singaporean and Japanese Futures Exchanges

This section briefly examines the types of trading that Barings authorized BFS to carry out in Sinagapore and Japan, and the way in which these trading activities were monitored by the Group for the purpose of managing risks.

Briefly, financial future contracts are agreements to buy and sell a quantity of specified financial instruments at a predetermined future date and at a cost agreed through a transaction on an exchange. All futures and exchange trading options must have a margin posted with a clearing house of the exchange concerned, in order to provide financial protection in the event of a member of a clearing house failing to honour its obligations under such contracts. All such contracts are eventually traded between members of the exchange and the clearing house of that exchange. Trades executed by non-clearing members are 'given up' to a clearing member to clear in order to show that non-clearing members have efficiently traded with the clearing members.

BSL was a full clearing house and a trading member of several exchanges including SIMEX, Tokyo Stock Exchange (TSE), Osaka Securities Exchange (OSE), and Tokyo International Financial Futures Exchange (TIFFE). As an agent for its clients, BFS executed transactions on SIMEX, primarily in respect of the following main future contracts:

a) the Nikkei 225 contracts traded on SIMEX and OSE[84]

b) the 10-year Japanese Government Bonds contracts traded on SIMEX and TSE, and

c) the 3-months Euroyen contracts traded on SIMEX and TIFFE.

---

[84] BFS's trading business comprised both Nikkei 225 futures contracts and some options contracts. These contracts are structured on the Nikkei 225 index which is based on 225 Japanese stocks traded on the Tokyo Stock Exchange and forms the basis for the major Japanese equity derivatives contracts. Whereas a Nikkei 225 futures contract is based on a multiple of times the Nikkei Stock Index trades on OSE and SIMEX, a Nikkei option contract is based on the Nikkei 225 futures traded on OSE and SIMEX. In both types of contract, the contract specification is different between the two stock exchanges.

It is interesting that the margining process between exchanges differs in the nature of characteristics of house (clearing house's own account) and client accounts. Whereas SIMEX and TIFFE require clearing members to keep separate house accounts for clients in order to maintain distinction between the margins posted for clients and margins posted for the clearing members trading accounts [85], clearing members on both OSE and Tokyo Stock Exchange (TSE) need maintain only one account. The Report of the Board of Banking Supervision pointed out that SIMEX margins both the 'house accounts' and 'client accounts' on a gross basis, whereas TIFFE margins only the 'client account' on a gross basis, and the 'house account' on a net basis. Although clearing members on the OSE and TSE can post net margin to the exchange, clients are margined on a gross basis by their clearing members. [86]

SIMEX's margining procedures is the most relevant to the collapse of Barings, and risks related to futures and options contracts traded on SIMEX need, therefore, be considered. Buyers are required to pay a full premium and not a variation margin in order to recoup any value on the sale or exercise of the option. The seller of an option thus receives the full premium as cash but is, nevertheless, required to post an initial margin. This is primarily done for the purpose of offsetting an open risk position [87] through the span of capital system, but an unhedged short option position [88] would normally incur initial margin which is almost equal to the market value of an option. Initial margin changes manifest movements in the market value on short option positions, which is similar in effect to the variation margin arising on future contracts [89]. The Report of the Board of Banking Supervision rightly pointed out that the ability to generate cash flow through selling options on SIMEX in order to receive premium income was limited, unless

---

[85] op. cit., p.40.
[86] op. cit., p.40.
[87] An open position is a position in futures and options, which can be either long or short, and which is not matched by offsetting transactions or satisfied by delivery.
[88] A short position is held by a net seller of an instrument. It appreciates in value when the underlying market price declines (e.g. selling a future). A seller of a put option benefits from an increase in the price of the underlying instrument. Conversely, a long position is held by a net holder or buyer of an instrument, and it will appreciate in value when the market price increases. A holder of a put option will profit when the underlying market declines.
[89] This aspect of future and option contracts has been clearly explained on p.40.

there were offsetting positions whereby margins would be posted in the form of a collateral such as government bonds. According to the same report, none of these possibilities was used to a significant extent by BFS to raise actual funding of margin calls '...*although the receipt of premium income from options sales was used to mask losses through accounting entries over month ends*'.[90] Incidentally, trades that were executed on the Japanese and Singaporean Exchanges were booked in the name of BSLL for proprietary trading, and in the name of BSL for clients. The only business that was registered as a 'house' business on SIMEX was a business booked in the name of BSLL. However, BSL was the primary booking entity for almost all external clients of BFS and BSJ, who executed or cleared through BFS for SIMEX or BSJ for Japanese exchanges. Although BSJ apparently operated a limited type of agency business, according to the Report of the Board of Banking Supervision, the agency business conducted through BSJ was a main contributor to the total revenue for the global interexchange arbitrage in 'switching' activity until October 1994. But the trading decisions were delegated to Mr Leeson in BFS on the understanding that he would be the best person to conduct such business from the floor of SIMEX. Indeed, during 1993, using the Nikkei 225 contracts, BFS found opportunities to improve futures hedges initiated by BSJ's traders, and the futures hedges were switched between Singapore and Osaka for the purpose of profiting from temporary price differences between the SIMEX and Osaka Nikkei 225 contracts. During mid-August 1994 Mr Leeson was allowed a separate Nikkei arbitrage trading book with the specific purpose of identifying the profitability of Nikkei switching activity separately from the profitability of the volatility of trading activity. Lower margins for the Nikkei 225 and Euroyen contracts traded on SIMEX were permitted under the SIMEX rules if these were shown to be offset by related contracts on the Osaka Stock Exchange and TIFFE. Whereas the inter-exchange arbitrage business on the SIMEX was recorded in BFS under account number '92000', BSJ proprietary trading book futures activities were recorded under account number '91000'.

The unusual arbitrage profits were justified by Mr Leeson on the ground that such profits might arise from the normal price differences arising from a functioning of the different exchanges or because SIMEX

[90] op. cit., p.40.

was generally a cheaper exchange.

The management seems to have viewed the arbitrage activities as risk free, but it must be maintained that this could never be so, because it was inevitable that some time difference between executing transactions at two different stock exchanges would occur. According to the internal audit report, BFS traded unhedged risk positions intra-day purely on the basis of its own assessment of market conditions, which was presumably done by Mr Leeson. The internal audit report also pointed out that intra-day positions, particularly in Tokyo, were not monitored, in consequence of which it was not possible to determine whether the limits to those positions had been broken. It was only in the latter part of October 1994 that concern over Mr Leeson's activity was expressed to the Risk Committee, but the Committee simply noted that the limit was applicable only when Mr Leeson would be trading and that a lower limit should be set when he was absent. But intra-day limits were never checked. Again, in October 1994 the Risk Committee discussed Mr Leeson's activities but drew the inference that there was no indication of any breach of intra-day limit by Mr Leeson.

Interestingly enough, during 1994 the strategies operated by Mr Leeson in relation to 'switching' business were reported to have been extremely profitable; indeed according to the Report of the Board of Banking Supervision, Mr Leeson's 'switching' activities contributed at least £28.5 million of revenue. The management maintained that the Nikkei arbitrage was the main revenue generator. The profits earned by Mr Leeson, whether by authorized or unauthorized trading on these exchanges, seemed to have produced a blinding effect on the management of the Barings Group. The extent of the risks was never studied properly; indeed the need for studying risks seem to have been almost totally disregarded by BFS and Barings in London. It was only after the inquiry that it was revealed that BFS had five main accounts, namely BSLL for proprietary business, BSL for agency business, BSJ for proprietary and agency business, Baring Securities (Hong Kong) Ltd (BSHK) for a small amount of Hong Kong agency business, and BNP Japan. As stated earlier, there were also error accounts, namely '99900' and '99902', in addition to the hidden account number '88888', which subsequently came to be known as the BSL client account. Ironically, in September 1994 BFS was awarded the title of *'Number One Volume*

House' by the management of SIMEX at the SIMEX dinner.

Apparently, the trading activities of BFS were treated by Barings Group as 'authorized', thus the question of carrying out illicit or unauthorized business under the guise of authorized business did not arise. The establishment seems to have placed total confidence in Mr Leeson as a fit and proper person whose integrity should not have been questioned.

Unauthorized Trading and Concealment of Trading Activities

During the investigation relating to the preparation of the Report of the Board of Banking Supervision, it was revealed that BFS also engaged in unauthorized activities to a significant extent by taking proprietary positions on SIMEX in respect of both futures and options contracts and various means were used to conceal those positions, but unauthorized trading activities were carried out by Mr Leeson under account '88888'. The Report, however, entered a caveat that in addition to Mr Lesson, others might have been involved in unauthorized trading activities and concealment of such activities.

The losses on account number '88888' were allowed to grow, and apparently the cumulative losses were not recognized until the collapse of Barings in February 1995. The Report of the Board of Banking Supervision maintains that had the unauthorized positions and losses been discovered much earlier, the collapse of Barings could have probably been avoided, raising the question of supervision and risk study.

The Board of Banking Supervision rightly pointed out that '...*Leeson was active in the option products available on SIMEX and this would not, therefore, of itself have been inconsistent with the business objectives authorized by management.*'[91]. From the end of 1992 Mr Leeson also sold options on the Nikkei 225 futures contracts until the collapse of Barings, and these were proved to be unauthorized transactions, which were booked to the account number '88888'. Leeson adopted the strategy of a volatility trader [92]. Believing that the Nikkei 225 futures contracts

---

[91] op. cit., p.67.
[92] Broadly, participants in option markets fall into three categories: hedgers, speculators and volatility traders. Volatility traders take advantage of what they regard as mispriced options. It is clear that when a market is volatile options on that market become more expensive, and conversely when a market becomes stable options become cheaper.

would not move substantially from its trading range, he traded at levels which could not be sustained; known as consistently short volatility. Apparently, using one of the most aggressive techniques for short volatility he was subject to a considerable risk in markets which move in a sudden and unexpected fashion. This kind of risk, which is unexpected and takes place suddenly, is associated with short volatility known as 'Delta', and its rate of change is known as 'Gamma'. Delta and Gamma are the indices for traders to know what the equivalent exposure is and the volatility attached to it. In the case of trading by Mr Leeson in respect of the Nikkei options, both Delta and Gamma were expressed in terms of the equivalent future contracts, revealed only after the collapse of the Barings Group. The Report of the Board of Banking Supervision concluded that the size of the exposure and Leeson's failure to use a pricing model and a risk management system capable of calculating the sensitivities, became questionable. From this standpoint, the responsibility, to a certain extent, may be described as 'personal', although the supervision system within the Barings Group was not a coordinated one and, perhaps, too relaxed.

The Report clearly stated that the fact that Mr Leeson was able to conceal the positions and losses recorded in the account number '88888' caused the collapse of the Barings Group on 26 February 1995 [93]. This should raise the question of how was Mr Leeson able to conceal. There may be two possibilities: either he decided to conceal, or there was no means of detecting the concealment of unauthorized business by Mr Leeson because of the lack of supervision or checking within the Group. Perhaps an element of camouflage existed in concealing unauthorized activities because account number '88888' was originally opened as an error account. Therefore, it was likely that this account would be operated by Mr Leeson rather than by a person who established BFS's operational system [94]. Moreover, the Report suggests that sometime in July 1992, Mr Leeson gave instructions to a system consultant to BFS to exclude account number '88888' from all reports with the exception of the margin file, and this practice continued until the collapse of the Barings Group. According to Barings' management, they were not aware of this fact until 23 February 1995. But, according to the Report of the

[93] op. cit., p.78.
[94] op. cit., p.78.

Board of Banking Supervision, the margin file sent to London did include account number '88888', but apparently was not noticed or appreciated by them. In Singapore, SIMEX made a reference to account number '88888' in that it expressed its concern that BFS might be financing the margins of customers, which was against the rules of SIMEX. The London office maintained that they were not aware of SIMEX's concern expressed in the letter dated 11 January 1995 addressed to Regional Operations South Asia, which proves that at least the office of Regional Operations South Asia was aware of account number '88888'. It may also be inferred that a significant number of members of the trading team on the SIMEX floor were aware of the account. In other words, perhaps indirectly by the unusual nature of some of the transactions Mr Leeson attempted to reveal that he was trading in an unauthorized fashion but because of his meteoric success as a trader, nobody initiated any investigation into his unauthorized tradings.

The Report of the Board of Banking Supervision maintains that Mr Leeson made unauthorized adjustments to the price of transactions concluded on the floor of SIMEX, and '*...caused trades to be entered into books and records of BFS which were not genuine transactions.*' [95]. Mr Leeson managed to do this by what is known as 'cross trade' [96], which involved two traders of the same firm taking either side of the trade in order to transfer the position through the exchange between two customer accounts of the same firm. BFS entered into a significant volume of cross trade between accounts number '88888' and '92000'. (BSJ - Nikkei and JGB arbitrage), account number '98007' (BSLL - JGB arbitrage) and account '98008' (BSLL - Euroyen arbitrage). [97]

A cross trade must be executed at the market price and not at the off-market price, or at the price at a post-settlement period. Many of the cross transactions by BFS seem to have taken place in the post-settlement period, that is after the close of trading is allowed only at the official price. According to the Report of the Board of Banking Supervision '*...it was likely that Leeson chose this period as being one when other*

---

[95] op. cit., p.80.
[96] Cross trade is a transaction concluded across the floor of the exchange by a member who happens to have matching buy and sell orders for the same contract and the same price for two different customer accounts. See also the Board's Report, p.80.
[97] op. cit., p.80.

market operators were least likely to wish to participate in the transaction, which they are entitled to do under the rule of SIMEX'[98]. Leeson instructed settlement staff to break down the total number of contracts into several different trades and change trade prices to show profits by 'switching' accounts with losses having been charged to account number '88888'. By showing profits, the cross trades on the Exchange appear, on the face of it, to be valid and genuine and within the rules of the Exchange; the books and records of BFS maintained a settlement system used by SIMEX's members and reflected pairs of transactions *'...adding up to the same number of lots at prices bearing no relation to those executed on the floor.'*[99] Alternatively, he entered into a trade of smaller size but, at the same time, in the Contac system maintained by SIMEX he arranged for a price to be amended so that profit was credited to the 'switching' account and losses were charged to account number '88888'.

Manipulation of accounts became evident in Mr Leeson's trading activities, and according to the Report of the Board of Banking Supervision, the profit of the Nikkei 225 'switching' book (account number 92000) between 20 January 1995 and 26 January 1995 was £5.3 million. Cross trades in the Nikkei 225 futures markets between account number '92000' and account number '88888' created profits to the extent of £14.2 million on account number '92000'[100]. The Report of the Board of Banking Supervision also pointed out that

> *'The effect of this manipulation was to inflate reported profits in account '92000' at the expense of account '88888', which was also incurring substantial losses from the unauthorized trading positions taken by Leeson.'*[101]

In addition to cross trades on SIMEX between account number '88888' and 'switching' accounts, Mr Leeson also entered fictitious trades between these accounts which were never crossed on the floor of the Exchange, i.e. 'off-market' crosses, which were disallowed by SIMEX. The effect of those, as the Report of the Board of Banking Supervision pointed out, was to credit the 'switching' accounts with profits while

---

[98] op. cit., p.80.
[99] op. cit., p.81.
[100] op. cit., p.81.
[101] op. cit., p.82.

charging account '88888' with losses. Barings' management realized that Mr Leeson's 'switching' activities involved taking a position in SIMEX and taking an equal opposite position on Osaka Stock Exchange, Tokyo Stock Exchange and TIFFE, depending on the nature of a contract. Many of the positions, which should have been placed in SIMEX were never concluded with other market participants, but were simply crossed between the opposite 'switching' accounts and account number '88888'. The Report of the Board of Banking Supervision, therefore, pointed out that as the result *'Barings did not match-off most of its market risks arising on the Japanese exchanges by 'switching' on SIMEX'.* [102]

SIMEX rules required the clearing house to call margin from its members on each customer and house account, known as 'gross margin', forcing members to account separately for the trading positions of their customers and for their own house positions [103]. For computing the total amount of margin payable by the member, a Position Charge Sheet is submitted by each member to SIMEX at the end of a trade day [104], showing the Reported Final Long Position of customers and house accounts as a total figure for each commodity and each delivery month. Mr Leeson apparently departed from most of the rules of SIMEX and instructed BFS settlement staff to make adjustments between positions in the accounts '88888' and '92000' (both set up as customer accounts), offsetting the long Nikkei 225 position in the former against the short position in the latter, against SIMEX rules. A similar situation took place in respect of the Japanese Government Bonds position on account number '88888' and account number '92000'. In the Position Change Sheet entries were reversed so that the daily activities statement for account number '92000' sent to BSJ did not include evidence of these adjustments. The Report of the Board of Banking Supervision concludes that the effect of falsification of the Position Change Sheet was to deceive SIMEX as to the total amount of margin requirement on the customer and house positions of BFS, and until 23 February 1995 the margin requirement made by SIMEX was underestimated by an amount in excess of £250 million [105].

[102] op. cit., p.82.
[103] op. cit., p.85.
[104] The clearing house under this system relies upon the open long positions reported by the member.
[105] op. cit., p.86.

As a direct result of the unauthorized trading activity undertaken by Mr Leeson in account number '88888', an equity balance arose on the account which he concealed '...*by creating false journal entries, fabricating transactions and writing options*'[106]. In doing so, according to the Report of the Board of Banking Supervision, he also deceived external auditors and management of Barings '*either by effecting alterations to the books and records of BFS, or by altering and manufacturing documents*'[107]. Manipulation of documents and receivable balance also took place in respect of 1994, details of which can also be found in the Report of the Board of Banking Supervision [108].

It appears that due to lack of supervision, whether because of complex organizational structure or otherwise, Mr Leeson directly contributed to the downfall of Barings by his unprofessional activities, particularly on SIMEX and the Japanese Stock Exchanges.

Internal Controls

If the organizational structure of a transanational institution becomes complex, the internal control system might not be effectively operated. Furthermore, through decentralization of an organizational structure, the units in various foreign jurisdictions may have to be allowed a degree of independence in terms of control according to the requirements of the local legislation. As explained earlier, this issue became extremely important in the case of Barings Bank in that there did not exist any co-ordinated system of control between the headquarters and its units, particularly in Singapore.

According to the Report of the Board of Banking Supervision:

> '*The internal control environment in the years and months leading up to the collapse was in a state of considerable change as Barings Group management tried to combine the entrepreneurial, and somewhat loosely managed business of BSL with the relatively conservative, tightly managed business of BB&Co.*'[109]

---

[106] op. cit., p.86.
[107] op. cit., p.86.
[108] op. cit., p.88-91.
[109] op. cit., p.120.

Furthermore, between 1992 and 1994 a number of reorganizations took place which had a bearing upon the reporting lines. There was no clear line of authority in the minds of the staff and proper management supervision. The Report maintains that no one in the management accepted responsibility for Mr Leeson's activities between October 1994 and 1 January 1995.

The lack of clarity in Mr Leeson's reporting lines stemmed from two aspects of the matrix structure, firstly 'switching' business, and secondly, the integrity of each local office's operations was intended to be preserved by local office management. Exchange of information and coordination between various units and the control authorities would be essential for the effective operation of such a system. This was clearly lacking in Barings Group.

It has been stated earlier that in the Signapore office there was a lack of segregation of duties for Mr Leeson, and that he was responsible for both the front office and the back office. This is unacceptable for two reasons: firstly, the functions of the two offices must be carried out separately, and secondly where segregation does not exist, manipulation becomes easier. According to the Report of the Board of Banking Supervision, although the management was given a number of warning signals, insufficient action was taken by the management[110]. No risk studies by the management were conducted in respect of the Singaporean operations, although risk studies were carried out for London, Tokyo and Hong Kong entities. Briefly, the main causes for the failure of the internal control system included: (a) lack of system of credit control for identifying margin advanced on behalf of customers; (b) inadequate follow up of key internal audit recommendations; (c) ineffective compliance function of BFS; and (d) inaccurate reporting to regulators.

The Report also commented on the relaxed attitude adopted by Barings Management Committee (MANCO) and Asset and Liabilities Committee (ALCO), particularly regarding 'switching' activity, the risk involved in Mr Leeson's activities, and the way in which Mr Leeson acted in SIMEX. It was only on 30 January 1995 that ALCO agreed on a new strategy:

'The meeting the following day, 27 January 1995, was

[110] op. cit., p.121.

attended in person by the same members as on the previous day (Ron Baker was not present or on the telephone). ALCO agreed the following dealing strategy for Monday 30 January 1995:

(a) There should be no increase in the Nikkei position;

(b) If the market rises the position should be cut;

(c) May increase the JGB/Euroyen position up to the agreed amount of available initial margin;

(d) Intra-day delta limit increased to 500 OSE lots;

(e) If the market falls Leeson is authorized to leave the position to expiry in March.' [111]

At their meeting on 26 and 27 January 1995, ALCO agreed not to increase the Nikkei position. However, the summary sheets presented at ALCO meetings showed that Nikkei increased during February 1995. According to the Report if ALCO's recommendations had been implemented a significant margin from SIMEX could have been made. Furthermore, had Mr Leeson reduced the size of the short position, the amount of margin due to the Exchange would have increased. The SIMEX position was a cause of concern for ALCO, but apparently it was too late to take such action when the concealment technique was carried on by Mr Leeson.

In regard to internal controls, the Report of the Board of Banking Supervision concluded that:

'Management of BIB may initially have been justified in taking no steps with regard to these market concerns, given their perception that the positions in respect of the 'switching' activities were fully matched; nevertheless we consider that at the beginning of February 1995, when other operational issues relating to BFS had also arisen, it would have been appropriate for urgent steps to have been taken to investigate the foundation for these market concerns and to ensure that the positions were fully matched. [112]

---

[111] op. cit., p.125.
[112] op. cit., p.138.

Internal Audit

Internal audit on BFS account was carried out first in July and August 1994 by BSL's Internal Audit Department. The audit identified a few key points of concern: (a) that Mr Leeson's combined agency and trading roles were contrary to the local rules; (b) that Mr Leeson was allowed too dominant a role in looking after both trading (agency and proprietary) and settlement aspects of the business without any provision for challenging his work, and that he was involved in handling large amounts of money in a very fast moving and complex market; (c) that the level of margin calls in futures was paid for by BSL without knowing on whose behalf cash was being paid; and (d) that it was not clear how much of the payments was for house positions and how much was for customers. The initial draft of Internal Audit Report on BFS stated, inter alia, that:

> '*BFS must deposit both initial margin and, if appropriate, variation margin on all contracts open with SIMEX on behalf of clients, which are mainly Baring Securities offices. BFS in turn requests margin deposits from the clients.*
>
> *Leaving aside certain timing differences and other minor exceptions, all figures should agree. If they do not it is possible that either SIMEX or BFS are calling incorrect margin amounts ... there is no check to ensure that the amounts called by SIMEX [on BFS] and BFS [on Barings London] are, leaving aside known reconciling differences, the same.*'[113]

In the final Internal Audit Report on BFS it was mentioned that the BFS back office should have been reorganized so that the general manager (Mr Leeson) was no longer directly responsible for the back office as well as the front office. The growth in size and complexity of the business also became a matter of concern, particularly from risk management and compliance points of view. The executive summary of the Internal Audit Report stated, inter alia:

> '*The audit found that while the individual controls over*

[113] op. cit., pp.144-145.

> *BFS's system and operations are satisfactory, there is a significant general risk that the controls could be overridden by the General Manager. He is the key manager in the front and the back office and can thus initiate transactions on the Group's behalf and then ensure that they are settled and recorded according to his own instructions.'* [114]

The need for checks and balances was also recommended by the Report when it stated that:

> *'Key accounting and settlements controls should either be preformed or reviewed outside BFS's back office area; and*
>
> *BFS's trading activities should be independently reviewed to ensure that regulations are followed and risk limits observed. A suitably experienced manager should be appointed to review the records, perform some tests of detail and discuss activity with BFS's traders.'* [115]

The Internal Audit Report clearly stated that there was an excessive concentration of powers in BFS, whereas companies usually divide responsibilities for initiating, settling and recording transactions among different departments and areas. It became clear from the final Internal Audit Report on BFS that BFS's back office staff were relatively junior and inexperienced, and perhaps this was one of the reasons why Mr Leeson himself took charge of both the back and the front offices contrary to the usual practice. Throughout the final report emphasis is placed on the division of powers in respect of most matters, and that the settlement and recording processes were to be adequately supervised.

As regards risk and compliance monitoring, the Internal Audit Report stated that:

> *'The growth in size and complexity of the business make it now appropriate for BFS's trading to be subject to the security of an independent Risk and Compliance Officer.'* [116]

---

[114] op. cit., p.146.
[115] op. cit., p.146.
[116] op. cit., p.148.

As to the funding arrangements, the Internal Audit Report noted that:

> '...BFS was often left short of funding on a day-to-day basis due to timing differences and a requirement to fund certain clients such as FCT, and that any deficit was made by the Group Treasury in London at a very short notice.'[117]

It further recommended that:

> '"London's Group Treasury should perform a comprehensive review of BFS's funding requirements" to which Tony Hawes' subsequent official response was: "A review of BFS' funding requirements and those of the Japanese derivatives business as a whole will be one of the tasks undertaken by the new International Treasury Department over the coming year".'[118]

Finally, it also identified the lack of proper limits on gross positions on SIMEX and recommended that:

> '...the BSL Risk Committee should consider whether it was appropriate to introduce such limits. James Baker told us: "The risk of not having gross limits to me appeared that they could run into funding difficulties and the positions might be so large that when they actually came to unwind them, the lack of market risk would not necessarily mean that we could avoid any problems getting out of them."'[119]

The Final Internal Audit Report was not seen by MANCO nor was it sent to the external auditors in London, nor was there any formal follow up[120].

There was an assumption on the part of the recipients of the Internal Audit Report that the segregation of Mr Leeson's duties had happened, which was not the case and a risk compliance officer was not appointed.

[117] op. cit., p.148.
[118] op. cit., p.148.
[119] op. cit., pp.148-149.
[120] op. cit., p.149.

The Internal Audit did not uncover account number '88888' although it did address important control issues and made important recommendations. According to the Report of the Board of Banking Supervision, the recommendations were not followed up, pointing out that if after the audit was completed the segregation issue had been taken up then, perhaps, the unauthorized trading of Mr Leeson would have been uncovered; alternatively, if gross trading limits had been imposed, or an independent risk and compliance officer had been appointed, then Mr Leeson's unauthorized trading could have been uncovered. Perhaps, according to the Report of the Board of Banking Supervision, the draft recommendation for a reconciliation of margin accounts should have been adopted and implemented [121].

External Audit

Under the Companies Act an audit of the financial statements of a company incorporated in the UK must be carried out so that the company's auditors are able to submit a report on the performance of the company to its shareholders, as required by the Companies Act. An auditor should assess the company's system of recording and processing transactions by reference to which financial statements have been prepared, he may rely on the operation of internal controls but he should evaluate those controls and perform compliance testing to obtain reasonable assurance that the controls on which he relies are valid and reliable [122]. Guidelines issued by a Trading Practices Board mean a good audit plan would be able to detect material misstatements in financial statements or accounting records arising from irregularities or fraud.

Both internal and external audits must reveal the true state of affairs, otherwise they will not only mislead the shareholders but also the regulatory bodies. Auditors have a responsibility not to mislead investors and shareholders, whether current or future. Audit reports based on misleading information will also have a bearing on the Stock Exchange in that the real strength of a company will not be revealed on the Exchange, thus trading on that company would be contrary to the rules of the Exchange too. At this stage, it would be appropriate to analyse the status of audit of financial statements of BFS for the years 1993 and 1994.

[121] op. cit., p.148.
[122] op. cit., p.152.

1993 Audit

The consolidated financial statements for Baring plc, prepared on 28 January 1994, were based on the financial statements of BFS for the five-month period ending 31 December 1993, and reported by Deloitte Touche to Coopers & Lybrand London. Deloitte Touche's audit was stated to have been conducted in accordance with the United Kingdom's auditing standards. BFS was reported to have earned a profit for the period in the sum of Singapore $20 (£9 million). The Report of the Board of Banking Supervision became convinced that the profits arising from the activities within BFS '...*must have been materially overstated for this accounting period as there were concealed realized and unrealized losses for that period of about £19 million to be offset against the reported profit.*' [123]

It became apparent to the Inquiry Committee into the circumstances of the collapse of Barings that the consolidated profits for Baring plc for 1993 were overstated. The Inquiry Committee had no access to any papers of Deloitte & Touche nor were they able to interview any of the personnel who performed the audit or to the records and explanations that were provided by BFS's personnel to the auditors.

1994 Audit

It is important to point out that at the date of the collapse of Barings, Coopers & Lybrand's 1994 audit of the consolidated financial statements of Baring plc remained incomplete. In a letter addressed to the Inquiry Committee, Coopers & Lybrand advised the Committee that there were outstanding audit items at 25 February 1995:

'*(a) The Preliminary announcement of results was planned for Monday 13 March. At the time of the collapse, the subsidiaries' financial statements had not been agreed and the signing by us of a working copy of the group financial statements was planned for 10 March. Furthermore, we only received a first, incomplete draft of the group financial statements on the afternoon of Friday 25 February.*

(b) We had not started our subsequent events review in London. This is clearly a vital part of the audit and it would be wrong ...

---

[123] op. cit., p.153.

> to conclude that these enquiries would not have led to the identification and questioning of the significantly increased funding requests from Singapore that we now understand to have arisen post 31 December 1994.
>
> (c) At the time of the collapse both our management letters and work relating to regulatory reporting were outstanding'. [124]

Coopers & Lybrand informed the Inquiry Committee that the profits for the year before tax would have been £102 million and that another £1 million was anticipated by way of a provision; furthermore Baring's Board approved the accounts on 22 February 1995, but the recollections of the directors of Baring plc, who were interviewed by the Inquiry Committee, differed as to the state of the 1994 accounts, although these were approved by Baring's Board on the day the collapse took place. The Audit Strategy Memorandum prepared by Coopers & Lybrand Singapore stated in November 1994 that:

> 'No major issues were raised by the Corporate Internal Auditors from London during their visit in August 1994'.

Coopers & Lybrand internal control environment of BFS, BSL Futures and Options Settlements etc. and their assessment of these items are briefly discussed below.

BFS

As part of the 1993 audit Deloitte & Touche confirmed the of adequacy of controls within the accounting systems and that reliance could be placed on these controls. Furthermore, '...that they had performed *sufficient testing to provide audit evidence that internal control procedures were in place and were effective; and that there were no weaknesses in the company's systems which were of sufficient significance to bring to C&L's* [Coopers & Lybrand] *attention.*' [125]

Coopers & Lybrand Singapore carried out an assessment of the BFS's control environment in November 1994 and the assessment stated that:

> 'We have completed our assessment and concluded that

---

[124] op. cit., p.153.
[125] op. cit., p.155.

> *its control environment is satisfactory ... Internal control procedures in place are assessed to be adequate.'* [126]

If the control environment was satisfactory, and if the internal control procedures were adequate, then it becomes hard to justify the collapse of Baring's. Indeed, the Board of Inquiry stated that:

> *'This conclusion as to internal controls is on the face of it not readily compatible with the lack of segregation of duties. We do not know the basis for this conclusion.*
>
> *C&L Singapore [Coopers & Lybrand] had informed C&L London on 27 January 1995 of one potential point for the management letter of BFS. This related to the frequency of the calculation of Adjusted Net Capital for local regulatory purposes.'* [127]

The statements and assessments made by Deloitte & Touche and Coopers & Lybrand Singapore were disturbing in that they pointed to two serious possibilities: (a) either they did not carry out the assessment correctly and competently, and thus failed to comply with the professional requirements for complying with auditing standards and guidelines issued by the Auditing Practices Board; or (b) that they deliberately did so.

BSL

In planning their 1994 audit, Coopers & Lybrand stated, inter alia that:

> *'Prior year experience, preliminary planning and control testing to date...indicates that the control environment is good and that good computer and application controls exist. Therefore, our audit work will primarily consist of tests of application and computer controls for the systems as shown in the flow of accounting records'.* [128]

Their reports for 1992 and 1993 were also consistently appreciative

---

[126] op. cit., p.155.
[127] op. cit., p.156.
[128] op. cit., p.156.

of the control environment and operational controls existing in BSL. The assessment carried out by Coopers & Lybrand London in 1992 stated, inter alia, that:

> 'There is a good attitude towards control and in general the control environment can be relied upon, although the depth of this attitude is in some doubt. However, due to the increased importance of First Futures...there is a need for good manual controls where information is moved between systems, more attention is required in this area'. [129]

Although the 1992 assessment identified certain weaknesses in the company's attitude towards control, the question remains what action was taken to improve this control system. In the assessment of the 1993 audit, Coopers & Lybrand concluded that:

> 'There is a good attitude to control and the general control environment can be relied upon. The environment appears to have strengthened in the year and operational controls operated more effectively as a result'. [130]

In three consecutive assessment reports for 1992, 1993 and 1994 the term 'control environment' appears in a positive manner. Hindsight suggests this was not really the case.

The Board of Inquiry was notified by Coopers & Lybrand London that no draft management letter had been prepared at the time Barings collapsed. The management letter prepared by the Barings Group after the 1993 audit stated that:

> '...reconciliations of intercompany accounts were reviewed monthly but a formal review was only performed annually'. [131]

Although in 1993 the management agreed to adopt a monthly reconciliation system as a Group policy, it was implemented only in London in November 1993, and was never done so in overseas offices.

[129] op. cit., p.156.
[130] op. cit., p.156.
[131] op. cit., p.156.

Incidentally, in 1992 the management letter, which identified control weaknesses in the area of derivatives settlement, observed that:

> 'The areas of internal control weaknesses which we believe require immediate attention are detailed below:
>
> **Derivatives Settlements**
> The Derivatives Controller has not acted in a review capacity due to high staff turnover, and lack of resources on the desk.
>
> Since most of the derivatives business originates in the Far East the Derivatives Controller, who is London based, has found it difficult to exercise the degree of global control required'. [132]

Therefore, at least since 1992 lack of control in respect of derivatives business became manifest, and it is in the light of this background that the system of control adopted by Barings' Board should be considered, particularly in relation to derivatives settlements.

The Audit of Futures and Options Settlements

In 1994 Coopers & Lybrand (C&LL) London adopted an audit approach to BSL including an assessment of the operation of the internal control system to ensure that they were performing effectively. In relation to margin calls, CLL work included a test of the procedures used by Capital Futures and Options Staff to ensure that margin calls were reasonable and payments were authorized within the appropriate limits [133]. CLL were convinced that the manager had the experience to judge in general terms whether margin calls were within the expected range [134]. However, in respect of margin payments to BFS no specific tests were carried out, nor was it explored whether it would be difficult to reconcile margins paid to BFS with the margins collected from the clients of BSL. It was not ascertained either whether BFS was able to provide a precise breakdown in reporting the daily requests of funds [135]. It was also a

[132] op. cit., pp.156-157.
[133] op. cit., p.157.
[134] op. cit., p.157.
[135] op. cit., p.157.

mystery why BSL's staff did not use the specific Standard Portfolio Analysis of Risk (SPAN) margining software for SIMEX. In September 1994 controls over payment of cash from BIB to other Baring's Group companies were audited and the Report of the Board of Banking Supervision stated, inter alia, that: '...*there is no evidence of strong monitoring controls by management. Therefore at the year end we will test the process over reconciliations*'[136]. The inter-company reconciliations until December 1994 were tested by Coopers & Lybrand London and no discrepancies were identified by them.

External Audit

It seems that external audits heavily relied on the reports of internal auditors, presumably because they placed trust in the authenticity of those reports. The Report of the External Auditors in the case of Baring's clearly points to the fact that internal audits and external audits must be carried out independently of each other, although external audits often refer to reports of internal audit, but not total reliance. The causes of Barings collapse were manifold, but the Report of the Inquiry Committee clearly reveals that auditors also failed to reveal control systems prevalent within the Barings Group, and in particular within BFS. Much more specific reference to weaknesses should have been made by the auditors. The windfall profits earned through the false account number '88888' maintained by Leeson were not drawn to the attention of most officers; neither they did attract the attention of the auditors.

Issue of Supervision

In this section an attempt is made to discuss the issue of supervision in two parts (a) reporting by Barings Bank, and (b) duties of supervisors and regulators.

Reporting Duty of Barings to Supervisors and Regulators

It has been stated earlier that Barings adopted what is known as a consolidated supervisory system which entails an assessment of a number of sources and information including consolidated details for the whole Barings Group. The Bank of England authorized BB&Co to

---

[136] op. cit., p.157.

act as the consolidated supervisor of the entire Barings Group. In view of the complex organizational structure of the Barings Group of companies [137] innumerable committees were set up which were entrusted with a variety of functions. Where the linkage between an authorized institution and one of its subsidiaries is sufficiently strong, the Bank of England was entitled to allow the subsidiary to be treated effectively as a divisional institution provided that certain other criteria were met. This is known as the 'solo consolidation' process, and it entails monitoring capital adequacy and large exposures. The Bank of England would permit a bank, which is a member of a group of companies, and subject to consolidated supervision, to act as the 'treasury' for the companies. A bank subject to such a regime would be allowed maximum level of exposure in the form of treasury concessions. Barings Group was allowed treasury concessions twice, but these were subsequently withdrawn when BSL was provisionally solo consolidated with BB&Co.

Section 38(1) of the Banking Act 1987 requires UK authorized institutions to notify the Bank before incurring any large exposures, that is when a loan or a transaction will exceed 25% of its capital base. In determining capital base the link companies' capital bases are also taken into account. Apparently following the 1993 European Union Large Exposure Directive UK banks are required to file large exposure (exposures over 10% capital base) returns with the Bank of England on a quarterly basis.

BB&Co submitted to the Bank of England returns on large exposures but it failed to report proper exposures and true exposures to BFS in the group companies exposures [138]. The unauthorized trading activities conducted under account '88888' were funded in part by top-up account and this was omitted from solo consolidated large exposure account. In so far as consolidated account was concerned, large exposures were reported only in respect of the exchanges in Japan and Singapore. In so far as OSE was concerned, Barings reported only in respect of the house account and non-segregated local clients, but it did report exposures related to segregated clients. Furthermore, reported exposures to SIMEX and OSE at times exceeded the 25% limit. According to the Report of

---

[137] For the details of the organizational structure see the Board's Report, pp.290-293, 309-311.
[138] op. cit., p.165.

the Board of Banking Supervision, there were potentially certain errors in the reporting exposures to OSE and SIMEX in the consolidated large exposure returns [139]. The Report of the Board of Banking Supervision stated that:

> 'At the consolidated level, the "top up" account was mostly represented on the balance sheet as an exposure to SIMEX, as BFS had used the money advanced by BSL, BSLL and BSJ to fund margins placed with SIMEX. The consolidated LE figures in respect of SIMEX reported by Barings to the Bank were provided by BFS. It is not known how, if at all, the balances arising out of account "88888" were reported by BFS to Barings in London for LE reporting purposes.' [140]

With reference to solo consolidation, the Report of the Board of Banking Supervision stated, inter alia, that:

> 'During 1992 and 1993 the activities of Barings' securities businesses were placing considerable strain on Barings' financial resources and the Bank's restrictions on connected lending limits restraining the amounts that could be lent by BB&Co to fund these activities (paragraph 2.8). In the unconsolidated BB&Co LE returns for the quarters ended June and September 1993, the maximum in the period exposures of BB&Co to BSL were £162 million and £151 million respectively, compared to the relevant treasury concessions of £150 million. This demonstrates that the concession was being fully utilized.' [141]

Apparently, the Bank showed its concern at the way the Barings Group was doing its business but the minute of the meeting on 4 February 1993 between the senior Manager of the Bank of England, officers of the SFA and officers of Barings concluded that:

---

[139] op. cit., p.167.
[140] ibid.
[141] ibid.

> '*It appears that the Bank was reassured ... and now has a far better understanding of our business, our recent past and our future plans.*'[142]

BB&Co also failed to report large exposures either to its clients or to BFS, the details being available in the Report of the Board of Banking Supervision[143]. According to the Report either there existed misunderstandings by Barings as to what to report and when to report, or there was failure to comply with regulatory measures. It has already been explained that the issue of risk did not seem to have received much attention from the management. In so far as the possibility of negligence or indifference as to how Barings was performing was concerned, with reference to internal audit the Report of the Board of Banking Supervision audit stated:

> '*[Valerie Thomas, the BIB Compliance Officer] received a copy of the internal audit report on BFS which contained matters relevant to compliance. She told us: "I did not look at this report in any detail at all until later in February 1995 after all the problems had occurred" Also: "I had not read all of the report; I have now but I had not at the time."*'[144]

Apparently, the Bank conveyed its concerns to Barings London, but they seemed to have either disregarded them, or omitted to notify a considerable number of discrepancies to the Bank, or it suffered from misconception about the reporting system, which assumption may be difficult to confirm.

Supervisors and Regulators

The Bank of England was responsible for the consolidated supervision of the Barings Group as it authorized BB&Co. 'Authorization and supervision' in this context must be used to include all aspects of their connotations. The Bank was not responsible for the supervision of any individual Barings entities other than BB&Co and its gilt-edged market, a unit called BSB. The Bank had no power to supervise other companies

---
[142] op. cit., p.168.
[143] op. cit., pp.162-191.
[144] op. cit., p.190-191.

in the Group to which a bank belonged. In other words, its duty of supervision predominantly related to BB&Co. Nevertheless, the Bank was required under the Banking Act 1987 to take into account risks that may be prevalent in a group and which might adversely affect an authorized institution. In theory, the Bank was required to take into account the activities of the other parts of the Barings Group in so far as they might affect the reputation and financial soundness of BB&Co [145]. The Bank is required to analyse risk on a consolidated basis but it can only supervise the institution that it has authorized.

Under the solo consolidation system the management of the solo consolidated subsidiary must be under the effective direction of Barings Bank provided, of course, real linkage exists between the authorized institution and its subsidiary. The Report of the Board of Banking Supervision clearly points out that the Bank views consolidated supervision as a complement *'rather than a substitute for supervision of the bank alone it sets limits for the exposure of the Bank to the rest of the group of companies of which a bank is a member'.* [146]

In England the practice has always been for each UK financial group to be supervised by a recognized regulator too, known as a lead regulator. In the case of Barings, the Bank of England was a lead regulator. The Bank co-ordinated with the relevant Self-Regulatory Organizations (SRO) in order to ensure that a prudent judgement could be taken in respect of an authorized institution. In the case of Barings, its activities in Singapore and in other foreign jurisdictions presented a novel kind of difficulty. It was beyond the remit of the Bank to deal with the warnings or the danger to which they were exposed; in addition many of the warnings could not have been known to the Bank unless it was informed by the Barings Group or by another regulator. The Report of the Board of Banking Supervision states that the Bank was unaware of the issue of lack of segregation in BFS between the front and back offices and of the failure to act on the internal audit recommendations. Hence there was no channel of communication whereby the Bank would receive internal audit reports from the Group. According to the Report of the Board of Banking Supervision, the Bank of England was, however, aware that a high level of funding was required to finance Barings' Far East

---

[145] op. cit., p.193.
[146] op. cit., p.193.

activities and that those activities were virtually risk-free. The Bank was also aware of the issues and questions arising out of Barings' reporting of its consolidated large exposures in respect of the OSE and SIMEX to the Bank [147].

One is required to appreciate that when the remit of supervision is thus limited (the Securities Division of Barings also had its own regulation – SFA) it is not possible for the lead regulator to consider the entire group accounting system, which in this case was particularly complex because of its organizational structure. The options transactions, the accounts of which were not easily available, presented another problem. At the time the Barings Group collapsed, the Bank of England's understanding of the business of BSL was confined to broking. In other words, nobody seems to have notified the Bank of England of the extent of the business the Barings Group was carrying out. The problem related to large exposures. Remember, an authorized institution is required to notify the Bank of England before it or a member of its group enters into a transaction as a result of which the authorized institution of the group will be exposed to risk of incurring losses in excess of 25% of its capital base. In the case of Barings, this criterion did not seem to have been satisfied, the management having had the strange perception that the exposures were not large enough to create any suspicion as to whether Barings took unnecessary risk. The Bank of England maintained that Barings had a reputation for being slightly cavalier in its attitude to internal controls [148].

Barings Group companies that were members of the SFA (Securities and Futures Authority), were BSL, BSLL [LONDON], BB&Co and BSB. Both BSL and BSLL were authorized by the SFA to carry out certain types of investment business in the UK. The SFA was the regulatory authority for monitoring that BSL and BSLL had adequate financial resources and the capacity to protect their customers' assets.

The SFA maintained that it did not have any obligations with regard to subsidiaries other than notification obligations which were explicitly set out in its rules. According to the SFA it did not undertake consolidated supervision of a member firm and its subsidiaries in the way the Bank of England did. The SFA was under no duty, and indeed

---

[147] op. cit., p.196.
[148] op. cit., p.216.

it had no power, to regulate the business of subsidiaries unless those subsidiaries were themselves member firms.

The SFA's method of regulating firms consisted of monitoring financial returns, that is monthly reporting statements (profit and loss account, balance sheets, segregation of accounts). By analysing reports, the FSA would ensure that entries were internally consistent and that there were no unexpected trends. The Report of the Board of Banking Supervision clearly indicates that the management of Barings failed to appreciate the significance of indicators identified by the SFA. Furthermore, the SFA did not receive internal audit reports, nor was it made aware that there was a lack of segregation of Mr Leeson's duties, nor did Barings notify either the SFA or the Bank of large exposure problems. According to the Report of the Board of Banking Supervision, in the absence of information the SFA could not make inquiries of the unauthorized trading of Barings.

Conclusions

The Barings saga is complex, and this complexity seems to stem predominantly from a complex organizational structure adopted by the Group and the unauthorized trading that was carried out by Mr Leeson. Of course, the issue of lack of supervision will always provide controversy. The Report of the Board of Banking Supervision raised two questions in the form of conclusions: (a) how the massive losses incurred; and (b) why the true position was not noticed earlier [149]. The conclusions reached by the Report of the Board of Banking Supervision were inevitable: (a) unauthorized and concealed trading activities within BFS were responsible for the losses incurred by the Group; (b) serious failure of control and managerial confusion within the Group were responsible for the true position not being noticed earlier; and (c) the true position was revealed only after the collapse.

The Barings Headquarters did not have direct control over the activities of the other units of the Group in various jurisdictions. In view of the past performance of Mr Leeson, whether legitimate or not, it was difficult for the Headquarters to believe that something drastically wrong might be done by Mr Leeson.

[149] op. cit., p.232.

Briefly, lack of segregation of Mr Leeson's duties, lack of supervision of BFS, lack of study of risks, failure to report to regulators, and the way the external auditors were rendered unable to look into the real business mechanisms adopted by Barings Group, and in particular Mr Leeson's on SIMEX and OSE, all contributed to and subsequently caused the collapse of the Barings Group. It has to be added that the remit of the SFA was also limited and consequently many of the activities of Barings could not be investigated nor could they be properly controlled.

The Barings' episode clearly highlights what kind of powers should be given to the regulatory bodies and the need for clear coordination and cooperation between regulatory bodies both abroad and at home. The Barings episode also clearly suggests that the internal auditors are required to alert, at an early stage, the authorities concerned, and prompt action by management is required to effect remedial measures so that the investors' interests are protected. The unethical, concealed and unauthorized business that Mr Leeson carried out was known only to Mr Leeson; apparently he decided to pursue it recklessly; law is helpless in rectifying such recklessness. It can only punish the wrongdoer.

7 The Financial Services Authority

Introduction

By the Bank of England Act 1998, which came into force on 1 June 1998, the responsibility for banking supervision in the United Kingdom was transferred from the Bank to the Financial Services Authority (the FSA). The Banking Act 1979 established a supervisory and surveillance system of the Bank of which was further supplemented by the Banking Act 1987. The elaborate Deposit Protection Scheme which was set up by the 1979 Act was further developed by the 1987 Act. The purpose of the transfer of the supervision and surveillance powers from the Bank to the FSA is primarily to entrust a separate and independent expert body with these powers. Based on the principles of transparency and accountability, the Bank of England Act 1998 gives the Bank the total responsibility for monetary policy; the Bank is also required to meet the government's inflation targets. Of course, the idea that an independent supervisory body would be better for banking supervision was introduced by Bingham LJ in his report on BCCI.

The Bank of England Act 1998 significantly changes the position of the Bank in that it clearly provides that the conduct of the monetary policy must be outside direct political control. But the Bank is not a forerunner in this respect; independence of central banks has been achieved by other countries, namely Argentina, France, Germany, the Philippines, Switzerland and the United States; the UK joined the list of such countries on 1 June 1998.

The transformation of the Bank into an independent body was inevitable. Until the 1970s postwar British governments regarded monetary policy as subsidiary to fiscal policy in their belief that the latter mainly governed the economy and stimulated investment by having a directing influence on interest rates. The emphasis on monetary policy was largely due to John Maynard Keynes, a proponent of demand management – the management of demand for money. The failure of the demand management ideology became manifest particularly during the 1970s when governments throughout the developed world found it difficult to control rising unemployment and rising inflation. From the 1970s onwards the concept of 'price stability' was promoted whereby decisions on productivity and supplier goods may be taken by a firm in the most appropriate environment. Monetary policy is now regarded as the principal instrument to achieve price stability[1]. The functions to promote and deliver an appropriate monetary policy has now been given to the Bank. One of the primary purposes of this policy is to regulate interest rates and control inflation. Of course, pressure on the UK to ensure the central bank's independence was brought to bear by the Treaty of European Union 1992 (the Maastricht Treaty) which promotes the idea of the independence of the central banks of the members of the European Union[2]. In other words, the transformation of the Bank may be regarded as a consequential effect of the plan to have monetary union within the European Union.

With the coming into force of the Banking Act 1979, the Bank was engaged in two broad types of functions: debt management and supervision of banks. Banking supervision became an integral part of the Bank's function in that in order for it to act as the 'lender of last resort' it would require access to information that would allow it to decide on whether or not to offer liquidity support to a troubled bank. In recent years the Bank has been criticized for three bank failures which adversely affected its reputation, in that such criticisms might politically and psychologically undermine the credibility of the Bank's monetary policy[3]. The decision that the Bank would be the best institution to adopt and implement an effective monetary policy is based on the assumption that its monetary policy would be above all criticism and will never fail.

1 See further Michael Taylor, *'Central Bank Independence; the Policy Background'* in Bank of England Act 1998, Blair, London, Blackstone (1988) 10-21 at 11.
2 Article 108 of the European Union Treaty requires the member states to adopt legislation whereby independence of the national central banks would be achieved.
3 Michael Taylor, op. cit., at p.20.

Fortunately, the Bank of England Act 1988 does not make the Bank entirely remote from supervision process.

An analysis of the Act reveals certain of its themes which are:

(a) to confer on the Bank the sole operational responsibility for monetary policy;

(b) independence of the Bank from the Government;

(c) transfer from the Bank to the FSA the responsibility for banking supervision and other related tasks;

(d) transparency and accountability of the Bank; and

(e) the merger of the National Savings Stock Register into the Bank Registrar's Department along with the transfer of the responsibility for debt management from the Bank to the Treasury.[4]

The 1998 Act deals with an internal balance within the governance of the Bank including the Monetary Policy Committee and external balance as between the Bank, the Treasury and Treasury Ministers[5]. The Bank of England Act 1998 primarily transfers the powers enjoyed by the Bank under the Banking Act 1987 to the FSA, in addition to transferring the relevant powers under various other related statutes.

The 1998 Act introduces a new organizational structure for the control and supervision of the UK financial market, and the principal powers, objectives and criteria of supervision and surveillance adopted by the Bank are transferred to the FSA. As the FSA is bound by the legislative provisions of the 1987 Act, it is not clear, at least in its early days, in what way(s) other than as a specialized body it can be radically different from the Bank. The principal features of the regulatory process under the FSA regime are not different from what the Bank's regime was: authorization, surveillance, enforcement (sanctions against financial institutions and individuals employed by them when they were involved in malpractice, alleged or proven), developing of rules for business conduct, assessment of risk management policies and practices in the relevant financial institutions, and the available capital for covering risks.

4   See further M Blair, QC 'Introduction and Overview' in *Blackstone's Guide to the Bank of England Act 1998*, London, Blackstone Press Ltd, 1998, pp.1-2.

5   op. cit., p.3.

It is the purpose of this chapter to examine the new organizational structure of the FSA and the justification for setting it up.

The Memorandum of Understanding between HM Treasury, the Bank of England and the FSA[6]

In 1997 the Memorandum of Understanding was issued by the Bank of England with a view to establishing a framework of cooperation between the three institutions: HM Treasury, the Bank of England and the FSA in the UK financial world, to promote the common objective of financial stability. The division of responsibility between these three institutions is based on four guiding principles:

(a) *Accountability*
With well-defined responsibilities, each institution must remain accountable for its actions.

(b) *Transparency*
The remit of authority and responsibility for each of these institutions must be clear to the public, the markets and Parliament.

(c) *Absence of Duplication of Work*
By virtue of having a clear-cut remit of authority and responsibility, duplication of efforts and work between these institutions must be avoided; and

(d) *Exchange of Information*
Regular exchange of information between these institutions should improve their efficiency and should also avoid duplication of efforts and work.

The Memorandum of Understanding has identified the responsibilities of these three institutions. The fact remains that save for the supervision and surveillance functions, the Bank remains responsible for the overall stability of the financial system in the UK as a whole.

The Specific Responsibilities of the Bank of England

The Bank is responsible for monitoring the stability of the monetary

---

[6] Press Release at http://www.sib.co.uk/pressrel/jointmou.htm

system as part of its monetary policy function. The issue of fluctuations in liquidity will be one of its prime concerns, and it will act daily in the markets. The Bank is thus entrusted with the task of an actor in the market and the stability maker of the market. This latter function of the Bank necessarily entails supervision and surveillance of the markets.

As the bankers' Bank it is responsible for developing and maintaining the financial system infrastructure (the payment system). It is for the Bank of England to advise the Chancellor of the Exchequer on any important issues inherent in the payments system.

Broadly, the Bank's responsibilities will entail maintenance of monetary stability; the Bank will have a high level of representation at the institution responsible for financial regulations[7]. In exceptional circumstances, in order to limit risk, which may affect particular interests and gradually spread to the other parts of the financial system, the Bank will undertake official financial operations in accordance with the following arrangement.

> In the event of a genuine threat to the stability of the financial system being posed which would require support operations to avoid a serious disturbance in the UK economy, the Bank may be required to intervene, but of course if the need for a support operation is identified by the Bank or the FSA, they will immediately consult each other.
>
> (e) To maintain the efficiency and effectiveness of the financial sector with particular regard to international competitiveness, the Bank will, of course, acts as the catalyst for improving the financial system infrastructure of the City of London and take the leading role in promoting the cause of the City.

The Bank will concentrate on three important matters:

i) stability of the monetary system;

ii) improvement of the financial system infrastructure; and

iii) maintaining a broad overview of the system as a whole.

The supervision and surveillance system is thus transferred to the new institution, the FSA.

---

[7] Incidentally the Deputy Governor for Financial Stability is also a member of the FSA Board.

The Responsibilities of the FSA

The supervision and surveillance powers of the Bank under the Banking Act 1987 have, under the Bank of England Act 1988, virtually been transferred to the FSA. The responsibilities of the FSA may broadly be categorized in the following way:

i) The grant of authorizations and prudential supervision of banks, building societies, investment firms, insurance companies and friendly societies;

ii) The supervision of financial markets and of the clearing settlements system;

iii) the carrying out of rescue work within its responsibilities for affected firms, markets, clearing and settlements system, whether alone or in conjunction with the Bank;

iv) such other operations as may fall within the remit of the Bank, in addition to issues such as changing capital or other regulatory requirements and facilitation of resolution of a market-related problems; and

v) the development and implementation of regulatory policy in these areas including advice, regulatory implications for firms, markets, clearing systems in both domestic and international markets and new banking institutions whether of domestic or international nature.

Virtually all banking-related issues starting with authorization including suspension and withdrawal thereof, surveillance or regulatory policies, and banking market development matters have now been allocated principally to the FSA. These are not matters of monetary policy which come within the ambit of the Bank. The grey and overlapping areas of activity between the Bank of England and the FSA will be dealt with by either of them after consultation with each other. Both the Bank of England and the FSA will be acting as specialized bodies in their respective specialist fields of activity.

The Responsibilities of the Treasury

The Treasury has no operational responsibility for the activities of the

Bank and the FSA, but it is responsible for the legislation that governs it, i.e. it initiates and promotes regulatory legislation. However, the Bank and the FSA may alert the Treasury about potential problems whether they relate to economic disruption, support operation or change in the law or even cases likely to give rise to questions to ministers in Parliament.

The Distribution of Responsibility between the Treasury, the Bank and the FSA

The Treasury's primary responsibility is that of the government's finance department, and it cannot be expected to be involved in the specialized responsibilities of the Bank or the FSA. Actual or potential financial monetary crises must be notified to the Treasury in sufficient time. It is through the Standing Committee, which consists of the representatives of the Treasury, the Bank and the FSA, that the means of fostering co-operation between these institutions had been devised. This Committee meets on a monthly basis to discuss particular issues or issues of general nature relevant to financial stability. Special meetings for some purposes may also be convened by one of the participating institutions. Furthermore, the Bank and the FSA have a responsibility to give the Chancellor of the Exchequer the option of refusing support action in emergencies. Any major policy changes to be made by the Bank or the FSA that might have an effect on the monetary or financial systems of the country must be discussed with the Treasury. The FSA and the Bank must keep the Treasury informed of developments that may take place in the international regulatory community (e.g. the European Union, the International Monetary Fund, the OECD or the Basle Committee) which are relevant to its responsibilities.

The Nature of the Relationship between the Bank of England and the FSA

The nature of the relationship may be described under the following subheadings:

Acquisition and Exchange of Information

Through its authorization and supervision process, the FSA gathers a wide range of information and data which may be shared between the two institutions, thus avoiding duplication of work and minimizing the burden on firms. The Bank, of course, retains its right to collect the information it may need to discharge its responsibilities; where, however, both the institutions may need access to the same information, one will collect and transmit it to the other in accordance with the agreement reached between them.

Exchange of information may take place at different levels: firstly, close and regular contacts between the Bank and the FSA through the Deputy Governor (Financial Stability), who is a member of the FSA's board, and the chairman of the FSA who is a member of the Court of Directors of the Bank; secondly, in order to strengthen the links and promote a culture of cooperation, a programme of secondments between the two institutions has been established; thirdly, a free flow of information between the two institutions.

Cooperation between the two Institutions and Consultation with each other on Policy Changes

The Bank and the FSA are separable and separate institutions.

Each institution will make its best efforts to facilitate contacts by the other with overseas central banks and/or regulators. Although the FSA is the custodian of all supervisory records, the Bank has free access to them and in the event of one of these institutions being involved in litigation, the other will cooperate fully with it. As regards data on domestic and overseas financial markets or any other information that may be utilized by both institutions, service from the one is to be availed of by the other on the basis of service agreements between them.

Relationship through the Standing Committee

Each institution takes the lead on all problems arising in its area of responsibility and the 'lead institution' (the institution that may take the lead in managing the situation) must coordinate the action of the other institutions, including support operations. From this standpoint there does not exist any hierarchy between the three institutions. In fact, the three institutions together make a composite unit working towards financial stability and the making of a stronger financial system.

Membership of the Committees

Both the Bank and the FSA have representatives on various international and intergovernmental regulatory groups and committees, including the Basle Supervision Committee, the EMI Banking Supervision Sub-Committee and any other such committee on which representation may be necessary in the future. Where only one of these institutions is represented, it seeks contributions and/or information from the others in advance in connection with any meeting and reports fully to the others after the meeting. This is also another source of cooperation and coordination of work between them.

The following represent the current arrangements for chairing domestic market committees:

(a) Sterling Joint Standing Committee: the FSA;

(b) Foreign Exchange Joint Standing Committee: the Bank;

(c) Derivatives Joint Standing Committee: the FSA; and

(d) Stock Lending and Repo Committee: the Bank.

A Brief Summary of the Nature of Banking Supervision by the FSA

The FSA is the supervisor of banks, and the legislation governing its activities relating to safety and soundness of banks is the Banking Act 1987. Save the institutions, namely building societies, which are authorized and supervized by the Building Societies Commission, no institution in the UK may act as a deposit-taking institution without being authorized by the FSA[8] and the criteria which every institution seeking authorization is required to satisfy have been embodied in section 8 of the Banking Act 1987. However, after being authorized, a bank is monitored by the FSA's Financial Supervision Directorate. Like the Bank, supervision under the FSA regime must also be 'prudential'[9]. In order to remain authorized, an institution must conduct its business in a prudent manner which entails the following elements:

(a) adequate capital;

---

[8] Further exemptions have been allowed in respect of the branches of banks incorporated in the European Economic Area, EEA, and other non-European member states: (Liechtenstein and Norway) which may accept deposits in the United Kingdom on the basis of the authorization granted by their home supervisors.

[9] The meaning of 'prudential' has already been explained in Chapter 3.

(b) adequate liquidity;

(c) viable business plan;

(d) adequate control system;

(e) adequate provision in respect of accounts for bad and doubtful debts;

(f) carrying on its business with integrity and skill; and

(g) directors, managers and controllers to be 'fit and proper' persons[10]

Those institutions that satisfy the FSA's criteria are known as 'authorized institutions' under the 1987 Act and the title 'bank' is reserved for the institutions that have more than £5 million of capital (or institutions which are incorporated abroad) although generally all authorized institutions are known as 'banks'.

With the coming into force of the European Community Second Coordination Directive[11] on 1 January 1993, the banks and credit institutions incorporated in other European Union member states no longer require the FSA' s authorization to accept deposits in the UK because authorization for this purpose is provided by the supervisory body in the home state.

Under the European Communities Council Directive, the responsibility for supervision of various aspects of banking lies at three levels:

(a) the responsibility for supervising the financial soundness of a credit institution and, in particular, its solvency rests with the home member state;

(b) the host member state's competent authority retains its responsibility for the supervision of liquidity and monetary policy; and

---

[10] The interpretation of all these terms have been set out in the Statement of Principle originally issued by the Bank of England, shortly after the Banking Act 1987 came into force and which was updated in 1998.

[11] Second Council Directive, 15 December 1983 on the Coordination of Laws, Regulations and Administrative Provisions relating to the Taking Up and Pursuit of the Business of Credit Institutions and Amending Directive 77/780/EEC, Official Journal of the European Communities, 30 December 1989, No. L389/1.

(c) the supervision of market risks is the subject of close co-operation between the competent authorities of the home and host member states[12].

The Second Directive does not, however, define the meaning of 'prudent' supervision. It is believed that the criteria of 'prudent' supervision must be determined by the courts in each member state, but it seems that there will be harmonized criteria for this purpose. Prudent supervision under the Directive seems to be a necessary ingredient for protecting the 'general good' in the host member state. Of course, the underlying philosophy behind prudential supervision in the Directive is to protect the interests of depositors in addition to maintaining a good and reliable market. The Directive must appropriately emphasize the need for cooperation between the member states of the European Union.

The Directive also provides that a credit institution wishing to establish a branch within the territory of another member state must notify the competent authorities of its home member state; furthermore in the event of establishing a branch in another member state, the home state requires every credit institution to notify the host state of its plans to establish a branch including its programme of operations, the structure of organization and the names of those responsible for the management of the branch. In other words, in addition to other criteria, the criterion of 'fit and proper' person under the Banking Act 1987 must be satisfied and corresponding provisions of other member states' legislation must be met too. Under the Second Council Directive transparency of information is an essential ingredient for effective supervision. Article 19(4) provides that:

> *'Before the branch of a credit institution commences its activities the competent authorities of the host member state shall, within two months of receiving the information mentioned in paragraph 3, prepare for the supervision of the credit institution in accordance with Article 21 and if necessary indicate the conditions under which, in the interest of the general good, those activities must be carried out in the host member state.'*

[12] See Preamble to the Second Council Directive.

The authenticity and reliability of information provided by the home member state's competent authority constitute important criteria for effective supervision and in the event of any change in any of the information provided the credit institution concerned is required to give written notice of the change to the competent authorities to the home and host member states in sufficient time (at least one month) before making the change so as to enable the competent authorities of both home and host member states to make a decision on the basis of the change of information, if necessary.

Under Article 21 host member states have the authority to require all credit institutions having branches within their territories periodically to submit reports on their activities to competent authorities of host member states. Article 21(2) provides that if the request is not complied with the authorities can require the institution concerned to put an end to that irregular situation; and if the institution concerned fails then the competent authorities of the host member state can inform the competent authorities of the home state and the latter are required to take all appropriate measures at the earliest opportunity to ensure that the situation is corrected and after the correction of the irregular situation, the home member state must notify the competent authorities of the host member state. Where the institution concerned persists in violating the legal rules prevalent in the host state concerned, the latter may after notifying the competent authorities of the home member state take appropriate measures to prevent or impose sanctions on that credit institution.

Article 21(5) provides that:

> *'The foregoing provisions shall not affect the power of host member states to take appropriate measures to prevent or to punish irregularities committed within their territories which are contrary to the legal rules they have adopted in the interests of the general good. This shall include the possibility of preventing offending institutions from initiating any further transactions within their territories.'*

Under the Second Council Directive (Article 21(7)) the competent authorities of host member states have the power to take any measure during emergencies that they may deem necessary for protecting the interests of depositors, investors and other to whom services are provided and the commission of the competent authorities of other member states concerned must be informed of such measures at the earliest opportunity. It is for the Commission, after consultation with the competent authorities of the member states concerned, to decide whether the member state in question may be required to amend or abolish those measures. Again, this is necessary for maintaining the principle of the freedom of establishment of and the freedom to provide services by a credit institution of the member states within the European Union. The competent authorities of the host member states have the power to penalize a credit institution of another member state for irregularities committed within its territory which may include the possibility of preventing the institution from being involved in further transactions in its territory. If the competent authority of a home member state withdraws authorization from the credit institution, then the competent authority of the host member state must be informed and they shall take appropriate and necessary measures to prevent the institution concerned from initiating further transactions within its territory and to safeguard the interests of depositors. The Commission is required to submit a report on such cases to the Banking Advisory Committee every two years. The supervision and surveillance provisions of the Banking Act 1987 are in line with but exceed those of the Second Council Directive. The free movement of the UK banks within the European Union and the performance of banking functions by them have been secured within other European Union member states. With the exception of ensuring the liquidity of their branches there is the responsibility of the FSA to carry out supervision of the branches of all UK banks that may be operating within the European Union.

Elements of Supervision

The term 'supervision' stands for overseeing the functions of an institution and the manner in which they are exercised. Under the Banking Act 1987 supervision stands for prudential supervision and the role of the FSA in this regard may be compared with that of a watchdog: overseeing, monitoring and enforcing sanctions and measures. The purpose of supervision is to ensure that the market remains undisturbed and depositors and investors do not lose confidence in the market.

Indeed, after granting authorization to a bank the FSA is required to monitor its progress and activities; supervision from this standpoint is a continuing activity. The FSA has various means of continuing its supervisory activities: by collecting information from the statistical returns submitted to it by banks; through accountants' reports, informal interviews and even by paying visits to banks. It is not for the FSA to make any commercial decisions on behalf of an authorized bank, nor is it its function to encroach upon the business plans of a bank. The primary objective of supervision is to ensure that the risks in running a bank's business are minimized and that depositors' interests are protected. The FSA thus has the authority under the Banking Act 1987 to suspend or even revoke an authorization.

The Banking Supervisory Board, which was set up by the Banking Act 1987, comprises the chairman of the FSA and the Managing Director of Financial Supervision, and six independent members who are experienced in banking, accountancy and law. The FSA must inform the Board of Banking Supervision of all new supervisory developments and it is supposed to follow such advice as may be given to it by the Board's six independent members.

The FSA is also involved in what is known as International Supervisory Arrangements, because of the activities of the London International Capital Market in which a significant number of foreign banks participate. The FSA is also a member of the Basle Committee, which issues guidelines for international supervision of those of the banks that operate in multiple jurisdictions, e.g. the Basle Concordat 1975, which recommended a consolidated supervisory system whereby one supervisory authority takes primary responsibility for assessing the financial soundness of the group as a whole[13]. The Basle Committee recently published its set of Core Principles for effective banking supervision[14] in the hope that its member countries would implement

---

[13] This view was not upheld by the Report of the Board of Banking Supervision Inquiry into the Circumstances of the Collapse of Barings; instead it recommended a coordination system between supervisors in various jurisdictions.

[14] The text of the Core Principles has been reproduced in 37 *International Legal Materials* (1997) 405.

them. The FSA maintains relationships with overseas supervisors to ensure that certain common elements of supervision are implemented.

The elements of supervision are briefly discussed.

Adequate Capital (see page 74)

Adequate Liquidity

'Liquidity' means ready money. Each bank must have adequate liquidity to meet its obligations, current and future, without delay. Cash or high-quality capital, such as government bonds, are included in liquidity. Instead of imposing a common liquidity requirement on all banks, the FSA, after consultation with each bank in regard to its capital base, and the prospects of developing a diversified deposit base, sets the appropriate liquidity requirement.

A Viable Business Plan

A viable business plan is essential for maintaining an adequate capital and adequate liquidity base. This requirement is particularly adhered to when a bank fails to do well, although it has not presented any risk to a capital market and its depositors. The viability of a business plan is examined by reference to a bank's track record and the feasible future plans. The bank's liquidity position, debt position and any high risk-based activity are carefully studied.

In the case of banks operating as overseas branches, a global picture of the bank is taken and the viability of the business plan is examined by reference to the bank's global performance.

An Adequate Control System

Keeping and checking of all records is a vital element of a bank's control system, and the management of a bank must keep itself informed of the bank's performance and the risk, whether potential or actual, to which it may be subject. An effective control system would include both internal and external controls. Internal controls should ensure that assets are safeguarded and that Bank's obligations are met at once. External audits (reporting of accountants/auditors) ensure control by reporting periodically on the system of controls maintained by a bank. The Reporting Auditors are required to refer to the FSA any situation of concern pertaining to a bank's performance or activities, which may put the FSA on alert in regard to the performance of the bank and the FSA can then take appropriate action under the Banking Act 1987.

The FSA also operates its own control system, primarily based on Schedule 1 to the Banking Act 1987. Its Review Teams consist of its own specialist staff and professional bankers and auditors (the latter being seconded to the FSA), a Markets Team which examines treasury and capital market activities of banks and an Enforcement Division for carrying out investigations of suspected criminal activities in a bank. The FSA has the authority to seek help from external investigating and enforcement agencies.

Adequate Provisions for Bad and Doubtful Debts

In an ideal world, banks should not incur bad and doubtful debts, but in reality they often do, although in most cases not in alarming proportion. Debt recovery and the operation of a prudent credit policy are the important matters for each bank but any failure to recover bad debts or to make adequate provisions for them presents a risk for its depositors. The FSA, therefore, must satisfy itself that each bank has made adequate provisions for such debts based on a realistic valuation of its loans and assets.

Carrying on its Business with Integrity and Skill

The Banking Act 1987 requires banks to run their business with integrity and skill, criteria which should not be confined only to statutory provisions. Banks themselves know best when they fail to maintain integrity and skills. Statutory provisions authorize the supervisory authorities to investigate doubtful and suspicious cases of dishonesty only when they are exposed or reported.

Directors, Managers and Controllers to be Fit and Proper Persons

If directors, managers, and controllers of a bank are fit and proper persons the likelihood of the bank performing badly is remote. A Statement of Principles issued by the FSA explained how it interprets 'fit and proper' – probity, competence, diligence and soundness of judgement; financial soundness is an additional component in the case of shareholders/controllers which refers to a company and not an individual. Judicial guidelines are also available in England to determine the criteria of fit and proper person. These have already been explained in Chapter 3.

Conclusions

The Maastricht Treaty, which promotes the idea of the independence of the control banks of the members of the European Union, required the setting up of the Financial Services Authority in the UK. As explained, this new body virtually takes over the functions of the Bank save those in regard to the monetary policy and other related matters. Indeed, the Bank of England Act 1998 is, in reality, a power-transferring Act.

The FSA, although broadly an independent body, shares responsibility with the Treasury and the Bank of England; this does evidence the fact that the powers and functions of the Bank and the FSA may not be compartmentalized in a watertight fashion.

The FSA was born out of the wealth of experience of the Bank of England, and as the supervision and surveillance functions are now allocated to a separate institution and against the background of the JMB, BCCI and the Barings episodes, it is expected that it will perform even better.

8 The Objectives of the Financial Services and Markets Act 2000, and the FSA's Operating Framework

Introduction

In January 2000 the Financial Services Authority issued a document entitled 'A New regulator for the new millennium' detailing four essential factors for regulating the financial market.

(a) statutory objectives and the principles of good regulations;

(b) the FSA's new operative framework,

(c) the FSA's regulatory tools; and

(d) implementation.

This document also contains four Appendices addressed to four different issues:

(a) Appendix 1; The costs of regulations in the United Kingdom and Overseas;

(b) Appendix 2; Performance evaluation;

(c) Appendix 3; How the FSA would assess success and failure in its regulation of firms and markets; and

(d) Appendix 4; Case studies illustrating regulatory success and failure.

Statutory Objectives and the Principles of Good Regulation

The FSA has identified four statutory objectives in the new legislation entitled 'The Marketing and Financial Services Act'

- to maintain market confidence;
- to promote public awareness;
- to protect consumers; and
- to reduce financial crime.

The FSA acknowledges that market confidence is fundamental to many successful financial systems and for this purpose two criteria must be preserved: the actual stability in the financial system and the reasonable expectation that it will remain stable. In order to achieve this the FSA aims to prevent material damage to the UK financial system that may be caused by the conduct or collapse of firms, markets or financial infrastructure.

In order to achieve market confidence the FSA aims to maintain a regime that ensures a minimum degree of failure of regulated firms and markets such that public confidence is not jeopardized, automatically entailing careful evaluation of the probability of any collapse.

Under a regulated system it is inevitable that the public will have an expectation of a higher degree of protection of their investment than is achievable or desirable. The FSA appreciates what is achievable or not achievable on the basis of the market experience. The volatile nature of the financial market must be clearly explained to the public so that it is able to appreciate that despite all protective measures some market collapses are inevitable and that no market can be fully risk-free.

The FSA therefore realizes that public awareness of this eventuality is necessary; hence it wishes to pursue two main aims:

The Objectives of the Financial Services and Markets Act 2000 191

(a) to improve generally financial literacy, and

(a) to improve the system of disseminating information and providing advice to consumers.

Priority will be given to filling a number of existing gaps in public understanding of retail financial products and as a measure of improving public awareness a financial education system will be promoted.

Consumer protection is another avowed objective of the FSA. This will be achieved by identifying the risks, namely, prudential risks, bad-faith risks, complexities/unsuitability risks and performance risks. Prudential risks arise because of weak or incompetent management or lack of capital, whereas deliberate failure to disclose relevant information on the selling or advising of financial products, and misrepresentation of financial products, constitute bad-faith risks. Complexities/unsuitability risks arise from the lack of understanding on the part of the consumers of contractual terms in relation to financial products or services; performance risk is the risk attached to the expected returns for investments. The FSA plans to play an active role in identifying and reducing those risks. However, protection of consumers from performance risks is not a responsibility for the FSA. It is for the firm recommending the product to explain to the consumer the risks involved in relation to a particular investment.

Prevention of financial crime is also one of the objectives of the FSA, and to this end three main types have been identified: money laundering; fraud and dishonesty, including electronic financial fraud and fraud in marketing of investments; and criminal conduct of the market, including insider dealing. In respect of other forms of financial crime such as credit card fraud, the FSA is taking a secondary role and will work with other organizations, namely, the police, the Serious Fraud Office and the Department of Trade and Industry.

The FSA's Principles for Business

In order to formulate clear high-level precepts identifying the fundamental obligations of regulated businesses, in September 1998 the FSA adopted eight principles:

1. Integrity	Firms must conduct their business with integrity.
2. Skill, Care and Diligence	Firms must conduct their businesses and organize their affairs with due skill, care and diligence.
3. Management and Control	In order to organize and control its affairs effectively, a firm must ensure that: (a) it has directors and senior managers who are fit and proper for their roles, and operate adequate arrangements for securing the suitability of individuals who may carry out functions on its behalf; (b) it has apportioned responsibilities among its senior managers and directors in such a manner that their individual responsibilities are clear and that its business and affairs are adequately monitored and controlled; (c) that the standards and requirements of the regulatory system are met, and adequate action is taken for guarding against market abuse or financial crime; and (d) that it maintains adequate and orderly records of its business and internal organization.
4. Prudence	Firms must conduct their businesses and organize their affairs with prudence, that is, maintain (a) adequate financial resources and liquidity; and (b) adequate risk-management systems.
5. Market Conduct	All firms are required to observe proper

	standards of market conduct.
6. Customers' Interest	Due regard must be paid to the interests of customers and they must be treated fairly. These aims may be achieved by paying attention to customers' information needs, communicating information in a non-misleading way and managing aspects of interest fairly.
7. Faith with Customers	Firms must keep faith with their customers who are entitled to rely on their (firm) judgement.
8. Relations with Regulators	Firms must deal with their regulators in an open and cooperative way, including notification to the FSA promptly of any matter about which the FSA would expect prompt notice.

These principles, which will apply only to persons authorized by the FSA, were adopted with a view to developing public understanding and maintaining confidence in the UK financial system, protecting customers' interests and reducing financial crime. These principles are not only primarily based on the existing UK models[1], but also are in conformity with the relevant international standards, in particular those of the European Union and the Basle Core Principles for Effective Banking Supervision (1997).

These Principles will not apply to industrial, provident and mutual societies because the FSA has no regulatory functions with such institutions. They will apply, however, to those group companies which are authorized by the FSA or have automatic authorization by virtue of being European firms. However, in appropriate cases, the position of unauthorized companies in a group may have to be taken into account in determining the overall position of the group.

---

[1] E.g. SIB Principles (the minimum standard criteria in Schedule 3 to the Banking Act 1987); the criteria of prudent management in section 45 of the Building Societies Act 1986; the criteria of prudent management in section 50 of the Friendly Societies Act 1992; and the criteria of sound and prudent management in Schedule 2A to the Insurance Companies Act 1982.

According to the FSA, it should not be possible for private persons to institute actions for damages on the Principles alone; these Principles are to be regarded as a statement of regulatory expectations. Because these Principles are not designed to create rights or liabilities in civil law, they do not provide a basis for payments under the compensation scheme[2].

The FSA's Approaches to Regulations

The FSA has adopted several principles of good regulations:

(a) Efficiency and economy. The FSA plans to go beyond the statutory requirement to consult on fees and on its budget by explaining how it plans to use the funds levied through the regulated firms, overseen by a non-executive committee of the board which will report annually to the Treasury.

b) Management in compliance with regulatory requirements, designed *to avoid* an unnecessary intrusion by the regulator into firms' business and to hold the senior management responsible for risk management and controls within firms.

c) Proportionality. This will require the FSA to impose restrictions on firms and markets in proportion to the expected benefits for consumers and the industry, and the FSA will take into account the cost incurred by firms and consumers and undertake a cost benefit analysis of the proposed regulatory requirements.

d) Innovation. This is addressed to avoidance of unreasonable barriers to entry or restrictions on existing market participants who may launch new financial products and services.

e) It must ensure that the competitive aspect of the United Kingdom is maintained by cooperating with overseas regulators for achieving international standards.

f) Finally, the FSA must avoid distorting or impeding competition by dismantling unnecessary barriers to entry or business expansion.

---

[2] See FSA, *The FSA Principles for Business* (September, 1998) at 11.

The FSA aims at becoming the world-leading regulator, respected for its effectiveness, integrity and expertise, to maintain an efficient, orderly and clean financial market, and in particular to help consumers to achieve fair treatment. The new approach to regulation will consist of getting a fair deal for consumers by emphasizing the importance of disclosure of information in the marketplace for achieving market discipline; improvement of industry performance by creating incentives for firms; adoption of flexible and pro-active regulation and by maintaining a bias towards its pro-activity in order to identify and reduce the risks before they cause significant damage. This will include disclosure of major issues publicly by highlighting both good and bad practice among regulated firms and by identifying potential problems for consumers.

The FSA aims at focusing its work more on targeted inquiry into specific issues rather than open-ended information gathering and routine interpretation. In order to achieve these purposes, it aims at recruiting high-quality staff and, where necessary, providing them with the appropriate skills. Full advantage of technology will be taken to improve efficiency and to analyse and comprehend markets better in order to obtain early warning of emerging risks.

Practitioner Involvement

In order to develop its own distinctive approach to regulation in a new statutory framework, the FSA identified, inter alia, in the Consultation Paper entitled *Practitioner Involvement*[3], the role of practitioners in the regulatory system. The FSA's primary aims are:

(a) *'to protect consumers of financial services;*

(b) *to promote a clean and orderly market; and*

(c) *to maintain confidence in the financial system.'*[4]

The FSA seeks practitioner involvement in order to derive help *'to understand and be close to the regulated markets and the firms which operate in them'*[5]. Specific assistance will be sought to:

---

[3] Published in October 1997.
[4] *Practitioner Involvement* at p.4.
[5] ibid., at p.5.

(a) formulate sustainable policies and improve its decision-making;

(b) respond promptly and appropriately to new products or practices and to market intelligence;

(c) practise efficient, cost-effective, practicable regulation in the interests of regulated firms, markets and their customers;

(d) avoid impeding firms in seeking customers;

(e) create industry confidence; and

(f) *'help to secure the understanding and commitment of the regulated community and thereby to achieve an industry culture of high standards.'*[6]

Practitioners are to be chosen for their personal experience and qualities and they must act as independent experts rather than representatives of the FSA.

Practitioner involvement will be secured through a variety of channels:

(a) consulting publicly on important proposals for regulatory change;

(b) maintaining close relations with trade associations, interest groups (including consumer groups) and with any other organization that may have an interest in the FSA's work; and

(c) by establishing a high-level practitioner group, which will comprise senior individuals drawn from the regulated industry and other persons of a high calibre.

The FSA does not consider it appropriate or practicable to provide *'"structured mechanisms" for involving practitioners in day-to-day supervision ...'*[7] but the group would be able to comment to the Board on the FSA's proposed budget, management plan and priorities.

This will obviously involve a degree of accountability for the FSA to an independent group of experts.

---

[6] op. cit., at p.5.
[7] op. cit., at p.11.

The FSA's New Operating Framework

The FSA's new operating framework is concerned with two major aspects: fulfilment of statutory objectives and its own regulatory activities. There now follows a brief description of the elements constituting the FSA's regulatory activities.

The first stage entails *identification of risk* to the fulfilment of statutory objectives. A wide range of sources is drawn on including the information gathered in the cause of supervision of firms, direct contact with consumers, reviews of industry and consumers, market research, consultation with a wide range of stakeholders including market participants and The Consumer and Practitioners Panels, and information supplied by the Ombudsman on industry trends.

Risk assessment and prioritization is the next stage, the FSA using a standard risk-assessment procedure across all its activities. This process of risk assessment will help to prioritize the risk and help to determine resource allocation. Firm-specific risks, products-specific risks or risks relating to the macroeconomic process will all be taken into account, plus:

(a) the level of confidence in the information on which the risk assessment is based;

(b) the standards of the home-regulatory regime in the case of overseas firms; and

(c) foreseeable changes in impact and probability gradings.

Impact factors for firm-specific risks, the first step according to the FSA, would be to assess the impact if an event were to take place. Impact relates to the damage that a regulatory problem within a firm such as a lapse of conduct or collapse would cause to the FSA's objectives. Impact may be low or high, and is assessed by referring to the following criteria: the adverse effect which the collapse of a firm would have on the industry as a whole; how the public perceive the impact of the firm's collapse on the market and its consequences on market confidence; the nature of customers' exposure to the firm; and the prospect of receiving compensation or redress for consumer loss.

The cumulative effect of problems in a number of similar firms will also be taken into account in assessing impact factors. On the other hand, the probability of the risk recurring is to be assessed under three risk headings:

(a) **business risk**

Risk arising from the underlying nature of the industry and the firm's decision-making policy and strategies.

The collapse of a firm often becomes inevitable if its capital and controls are inadequate. The FSA, therefore, views business risk as a risk relating to capital adequacy to cope with:

(i) volatility and losses (risk of portfolio assets);

(ii) liabilities and exposure to external risk (volatility of balance sheet);

(iii) historical trends and patterns of the business (the nature of growth of earnings); and

(iv) strategy (sustainability of earnings and ability to be dynamic, when necessary).

(b) **control risk**

Control risk stands for the risk that a firm cannot and will not evaluate because the firm's controls are not adequate. Control risk is to be considered in the light of the following:

(i) internal system and controls that would entail a study of information flow;

(ii) decision-making process;

(iii) risk control and risk management;

(iv) management skill and competence of the board;

(v) management and staff; and

(vi) compliance records (controls structure).

(c) **consumer relationship risk**

Risk that causes damage to consumers by providing unsuitable products and services. This risk is to be assessed by reference to the nature of customers and products; compliance culture;

record keeping and the way the firm gives advice to its consumers.

The FSA has plans to carry out a more detailed assessment of high-impact firms than the of low-impact firms. Risk assessment entails the following:

- determination as to which entities are subject to risk assessment;
- preliminary risk assessment;
- detailed risk assessment;
- validation panel for review;
- letter to firm suggesting any necessary remedial action; and
- ongoing revision of risk assessment, if necessary.

The FSA does not wish to take the role of a custodian in assessing risks. It will attempt to ensure that the firm understands the reason for undertaking risk evaluation, communicating to the firm the outcome of the risk assessment, but it does not wish to make the assessment public.

For the purposes of analysing impact and risk firms are classified, affecting the FSA's relationship with the firm. In this regard the FSA will adopt two approaches:

(a) **intensive research**
Applicable to firms with the 'high-impact' grading, maintaining regular working relationships with the firm's senior management team in order to have total comprehension of the firm's systems and controls and potential risk.

(b) **remote monitoring**
Small firms with which contact will be maintained by both remote monitoring system and visits, where necessary, enabling the FSA to investigate cross-industry risks and the firms concerned would be expected to submit to the FSA periodic returns and to inform it of any major strategic developments. The FSA, in turn, will consider how best to offer guidance to firms with which it may not have a regular supervisory relationship. However, if a firm finds itself in a

situation of heightened risk, the FSA will render its supervisory assistance until the events causing the crisis have been addressed and successfully dealt with whether by intervention or otherwise.

One of the most important aspects of this supervisory relationship is to develop an understanding on the part of a firm, aided by the FSA, of when and in what circumstances the FSA should be notified of new situations, be they risk-related or otherwise having a bearing on the future stability of the firm. Clearly, the firms with sophisticated risk-assessment procedures will require less attention from the FSA than a firm that lacks such a system.

In so far as consumer and industry-wide risks are concerned, the FSA has identified both impact and probability factors. In assessing the impact of consumer and industry-wide risks, the following will be taken into account by the FSA:

- a systematic study of a problem to determine the effect on consumers and industry as a whole;
- the perceived importance of the product or industry sector to the financial market and consumer generally;
- the quantity of retail consumers involved and how they may be affected; and
- whether compensation be available either from the firms responsible for the loss or from the Compensation Scheme.

The probability factors that could indicate the prospects of a retail problem, such as mis-selling of a product, would include:

- the extent of the mismatch between the complexity of a product being sold and the knowledge and sophistication of the target consumers, assessed through consideration of the structure of the product and the volume of consumer complaints.
- how aggressively the product has been sold by sale forces (the charging structure of the product);
- how persistently the product has been sold (the persistency rates);

- the volume of consumer complaints; and
- the extent of external comment, e.g. from the industry, consumer groups and the media.

The FSA plans to build a range of probability measures in order to cover situations that may arise in the future.

The next stage is the stage of *decision* or *regulatory response*. The available means of responding to a given risk would include the use of the principles of good regulation in order to determine which regulatory tools would be the most appropriate. The FSA appreciates that over a period of time performance evaluation should help to build understanding of the most effective way to combine different regulatory tools to address specific roles. The FSA's performance evaluation is designed to assess whether its activities, in general, have proved to be effective in achieving its statutory objectives and also whether its activities, in general, comply with the principle of good regulation. The FSA plans to set success criteria for individual projects, to evaluate its own performance. The FSA plans to develop 'clusters' of performance indicators which, when taken together, will give a composite and comprehensive picture.

In measuring this performance the FSA aims to use third-party information when available, namely, the international service produced by the World Economic Forum.

In summary the framework for the FSA's operating framework is that it starts with the Risk Identification, Risk Assessment and Prioritization moving onto Decision or Regulatory Response, use of Regulatory Tools and finally Programme Evaluation.

For the time being the FSA plans to assess its achievements of the objectives by reference to the following:

Market Confidence

According to the FSA an overall picture of market confidence can be built by taking into account some of the following:

(a) survey data representing the confidence of the public and regulated firms in the financial markets;

(b) net inflows into personal savings products over time;

(c) the extent of transactions of markets and exchanges;

(d) where regulation is a factor, London's share in internationally-traded products;

(e) in order to give an impartial view of investors' perception of stability of financial firms, bond spreads for financial institutions in regard to other sectors; and

(f) the number and nature of failure of firms and failure in conduct taking into account the zero-tolerance policy.

Public Awareness

This would include survey data of the understanding of the products by retail consumers or their understanding of their financial needs or financial services in general. The FSA is extremely interested in knowing whether its efforts will actually reach its target audience in each case and how consumer behaviour changes over time as a result of the FSA's initiatives.

Disclosure

However, a person may not be required to produce, disclose or permit the inspection of protected items. *'Protected items'* mean:

> *'communications between a professional legal adviser, his client or any person representing his client and any other person which fall within subsection (3)...'* [8];

Subsection (3) defines the nature of communication as:

> *'A communication or item falls within this subsection if it is made:*
>
> *(a) in connection with the giving of legal advice to the client; or*
>
> *(b) in connection with, or in contemplation of, legal proceedings and for the purposes of those proceedings.'*

---

[8] Section 413(2)(a) and (b).

A communication or item is not to be regarded as a protected one if it is held with the intention of furthering a criminal purpose.

Access to information and disclosure of information are now regarded to be two major factors needed for consumers protection. Whether a party has made a full disclosure of facts or not will depend upon the circumstances of each case. Non-disclosure of facts or wrongful disclosure for the purpose of producing the effect of misleading the consumer is a punishable offence.

Consumer Protection

The FSA wishes to meet its consumer protection objective by considering the following:

(a) survey data on retail consumer attitudes, including the issue of whether they have adequate information and understanding to assess products they are buying;

(b) incidences of mis-selling;

(c) the extent of losses suffered by consumers, both compensated and non-compensated;

(d) the volume, nature and outcome of complaints made to the Ombudsman; and

(e) the extent of intervention on disciplinary action taken by the FSA.

Market Abuse

Market abuse stands for a behaviour, whether by one person alone or by more persons jointly in concert, in relation to qualifying investments traded in the market under Part VIII of the Act, which satisfies any one or more of the following conditions:

(a) the behaviour is based on information that is not generally available to market users but which if available to such users would or would be likely to be treated as relevant to the transaction in investments concerned; or

(b) the behaviour is likely to give a regular user of the market false or misleading information as to the supply of or demand for; or

(c) a regular user of the market would or would be likely to regard the behaviour as behaviour which would or would be likely to distort the market of the kind in question.

Market abuse also stands for a behaviour that a regular user might regard as a departure from standard behaviour 'reasonably expected of a person in his or their possession in relation to the market'. The Treasury may by order prescribe the markets to which section 118 applies and the investments that are qualifying in relation to those markets. 'Behaviour' must occur in the UK or in relation to qualifying investments traded on a market in the UK or which is electronically accessible in the UK and includes an act or inaction. It does not amount to market abuse if it confirms a rule that does not constitute a market abuse. The FSA is required to prepare and issue a code of conduct containing provisions and guidance determining whether behaviour amounts to market abuse and may, at any time, alter or replace this code. It is believed that a code of conduct will be crucially important to discipline the market. However, if the Authority is satisfied that an authorized person is or has been engaged in market abuse, or 'by taking or refraining from taking any action has required or encouraged another person or persons to engage in behaviour which, if engaged in by A, would amount to market abuse' (section 123(1)(b)), it may impose on him a penalty of such amount as it may consider appropriate. According to section 124, the Authority must prepare and issue a statement of its policy in regard to the imposition and amount of penalties. The proposed statement of policy must indicate the circumstances in which the FSA may regard a person as having a reasonable belief that his behaviour did not amount to market abuse, or may be considered to be a person who having taken reasonable precautions and exercised due diligence in order to avoid engaging in market abuse. Before publishing the final version of the statement of policy, the FSA must publish a draft version of the policy in order to seek responses from the public.

Section 126 details the procedure for imposing penalties for market abuse. A decision notice must be preceded by a warning notice if the FSA proposes to take action against a person for market abuse under section 123. The warning notice and decision notice must detail the terms and actual amount of the penalty. A person subject to a decision notice may refer the matter to the Tribunal.

The FSA may direct a recognized investment exchange or recognized clearing house to terminate or suspend or limit the scope of any inquiry it is conducting, or not to proceed with a proposed inquiry. The FSA's power relating to market abuse include imposing penalties under section 123, appointment of persons to conduct investigations under section 168(2)(d) and an application to the court under section 381 or 383 requesting it to consider whether the circumstances indicate that a penalty should be imposed. The court has the power to make an order requiring the person concerned to pay to the FSA such amount as it considers appropriate. The imposition of a penalty for market abuse does not rule any transaction void or unenforceable.

Financial Crime

In order to assess the achievement of its objectives, the FSA would like to consider incidences of money laundering and referrals to the National Criminal Intelligence Service.

In relation to its compliance with the principles of good regulation, the FSA aims to develop the following indicators:

- efficiency and economy by comparing the total regulatory costs in the UK with those imposed by overseas regulators and by looking at trends in the FSA's costs;
- proportionality – that is, analysis of the costs benefits of proposed regulatory benefits;
- innovation – introduction of new products over a given period in a particular sector or the number of innovatory start-ups;
- international character of financial services;
- the number of overseas firms carrying out business in the UK and the percentage of trading volume transacted in the UK for important exchange programmes or products; and
- competition – the new authorization in a given period, the trend in the price of key products and the firm's perception of market competition.

The primary objective of performance evaluation is to place increasing emphasis on consumer-orientated or industry-wide activities rather than firm-specific activities.

Over a period of time the FSA plans to shift the balance more towards thematic regulation and to carry out a number of selected projects each year. The portfolio of the selected items must satisfy the following criteria:

- the risk should be such as must be addressed immediately;
- the project should have some public output so that firms can take their own steps to deal with the risk in conformity with the responsibility of the firms' management;
- there must be clear benefit in dealing with a particular risk on an overall basis rather than in a particular division;
- these should be sufficiently important to justify the attention of the senior management in regulated firms;
- appreciable outcomes should be delivered by the project.

In the course of the year 2000 the FSA planned to include topics in relation to regulatory response on e-commerce and the implications of a low-inflation environment and will be provided with resources by the board to work its own timetable for this purpose. In respect of changes in regulatory scope and major new product developments, the first step would be to analyse the risks, the development of options for addressing the risk using different combinations of the regulatory means would be included in the second stage. The FSA will then finally consult on its proposed approach and prepare its plan accordingly.

Consumer Complaints

The protection of consumers of financial services is one of the statutory objectives to be activated by the FSA. In order to consolidate the complaints-handling schemes, in December 1997 it was proposed that a single Financial Services Ombudsman Scheme be set up, which would be comprehensive in its coverage, accessible to consumers, fair and impartial as between consumers and firms, capable of making binding decisions, transparent and accountable, flexible, simple, prompt and efficient and able to provide appropriate feedback to the regulator[9].

---

[9] See further, FSA Consultation 4 entitled *Consumer Complaints*, December (1997). The more up-to-date version of it (Consultation Paper 33) is discussed in the conclusion of this work.

The Scheme was based on views sought from a wide range of institutions and experts on the following:

(a) jurisdiction of awards, an Article 6 Convention for the Protection of Human Rights and Fundamental Freedoms (as amended by Protocol No. 11);

(b) basis of awards;

(c) information sharing;

(d) governance of the Scheme;

(e) funding for the Scheme;

(f) interaction with the compensation process; and

(g) powers and procedures of the Scheme.

The Scheme's compulsory remit should be limited to financial services: the consultation demonstrated support for a separate voluntary jurisdiction for non-authorized firms as such a system would enable the Scheme to cover mortgage-related complaints, general insurance intermediaries (currently within the Insurance Ombudsman scheme on a voluntary basis); and the mortgage intermediaries (currently within the voluntary arbitration scheme operated by the Council of Mortgage Lenders). The idea is to create a 'one-stop-shop' for disputes relating to financial services.

It has also been proposed that the scheme be restricted to complaints from private individuals, unincorporated bodies, partnerships and trade companies.

The limits of awards should be capable of review from time to time (the usual level is in the region of £100,000); the Ombudsman will have discretionary power to go beyond any fixed limit in this regard.

The FSA prefers to accommodate Article 6 requirements within the proposed Scheme[10] whereby it should be possible to ensure that the

---

[10] *'In the determination of his civil rights and obligations or of any criminal charge against him, everyone is entitled to a fair and public hearing within a reasonable time by an independent and impartial tribunal established by law. Judgement shall be pronounced publicly but the press and public may be excluded from all or part of the trial in the interests of morals, public order or national security in a democratic society, where the interests of juveniles or the protection of the private life of the parties so require, or to the extent strictly necessary in the opinion of the court in special circumstances where publicity would prejudice the interests of justice. (continued on p.208)*

great majority of cases are resolved through the informal procedures.

The basis of awards may vary from business sector to business sector: for example, in the deposit-taking and insurance areas, firms are subject only to prudential supervision and complaints are dealt with by the relevant Ombudsman by reference to standards of good industry practice and relevant codes of conduct drawn up by the industries themselves. With the exception of building societies, other firms voluntarily agree to allow an Ombudsman to make awards, and the FSA paid attention to the issue of compulsory membership whereby awards may be made against those firms that are not subject to the FSA conduct of business regulations. The FSA believes that the existing voluntary codes should be allowed to be applied by the Ombudsman for redress purposes.

The Scheme will be established as a limited company to be set up by the FSA, but independent of it. The board members and chairman will be appointed in the public interest, having appropriate industry expertise with a broad consumer perspective rather than being representative of any particular consumer group or sector of the industry. The Draft Bill provides that the Board of the Scheme will appoint a Panel of Ombudsman, including a Chief Ombudsman in addition to any deputy Ombudsman. The budget for the Scheme's Board will need approval by the FSA, based on the following approach:

(a) that the overall costs of the Scheme be met from a levy pro-rated to the FSA subscription costs, which would be charged against all FSA firms[11];

1. Everyone charged with a criminal offence shall be presumed innocent until proved guilty according to law.
2. Everyone charged with a criminal offence has the following minimum rights:
   a. to be informed promptly, in a language which he understands and in detail, of the nature and cause of the accusation against him;
   b. to have adequate time and facilities for the preparation of his defence;
   c. to defend himself in person or through legal assistance of his own choosing or, if he has not sufficient means to pay for legal assistance, to be given it free when the interests of justice so require;
   d. to examine or have examined witnesses against him and to obtain the attendance and examination of witnesses on his behalf under the same conditions as witnesses against him;
   e. to have the free assistance of an interpreter if he cannot understand or speak the language used in court.' (Article 6 – Right to a fair trial, Convention for the Protection of Human Rights and Fundamental Freedoms as amended by Protocol No. 11).

[11] See FSA, *Consumer Complaints: The New Financial Services Ombudsman Scheme*, August 1998, at p.9.

(b) that case fees be generally charged only for those complaints which are upheld;

(c) that no case fee should be charged to a complainant but the Ombudsman be allowed the discretion to order a complainant to pay towards the costs of a complaint where the complaint is deemed to be frivolous, vexatious or unreasonable; and

(d) that there be no exemption from case fees for small firms[12].

Consultation Paper 4 proposal received a considerable degree of support according to which the work to be carried out by the Ombudsman in investigating a complaint should be available to the Compensation Scheme; that the Compensation Scheme, where appropriate, should be able to rely on the Ombudsman awards *'having had regard to the differences in scope between the two Schemes and the need for equity of tribunal for complaints;'*[13] and that there were no persuasive reasons for harmonizing the basis for calculation and the limits of individual payments under the two processes[14].

The Draft Bill provided that awards of the relevant complaints should be reinforced through the courts. Guidance will be available to complainants who experience difficulties in enforcing awards.

In November 1999 the FSA and Financial Services Ombudsman Scheme Limited (FSOS) jointly issued the Consultation Paper 33 entitled *Consumer Complaints and the New Ombudsman Scheme*. Consumer protection and consideration of their complaints is one of the essential features of the new legislation.

Consultation Paper 33 sought views on certain important issues, namely: that the Financial Services Ombudsman Scheme (the Scheme) should be made available to all private individuals and certain small businesses, subject to the compulsory jurisdiction of the Scheme. The FSA proposed that the long-term objective of the Scheme should extend the coverage to all kinds of financial services activities of authorized firms. The FSOS proposed, however, that the voluntary jurisdiction of the new Scheme should initially be open to authorized firms in respect of any of their financial services activities that are not covered by the compulsory jurisdiction, and to unauthorized firms in respect of

[12] ibid.
[13] ibid.
[14] ibid.

mortgage-lending, voluntary jurisdiction being extended to cover other financial services conducted by unauthorized firms in a phased way.

This Paper wanted to replace the eight existing dispute resolutions in the financial services area[15].

In accordance with the Consultation Paper the legislation has accepted that both private individuals and small businesses will have access to the Scheme. The current legislation is quite extensive in that in a case of insurance policies third parties will also have access to the Scheme. In so far as the limit of awards is concerned, the recommendation of the FSA that £100,000 should be the maximum limit seems to have received recognition from all concerned.

Consumer Compensation

The FSA recommended a single compensation scheme, which should be independently managed but which should remain available to the FSA. Within this single scheme, there would be three sub-schemes: deposit taking; insurance; and investment.

One of the primary objectives of this unified Compensation Scheme is to ensure that the compensation arrangements focus more directly on private individuals and smaller firms. Funding of the scheme will be provided by authorized firms. The primary objectives of the Compensation Scheme are: to provide financial remedies, as much as possible, to investors, depositors and policy-holders, when firms fail to meet their liabilities, and to help to *'reduce the systematic risk that a single failure of a financial firm may trigger a wider loss of confidence in the rest of the financial sector concerned.'*[16]

The compensation arrangements are aimed at operating as a safety net for all consumers against any hazard or losses, yet encouraging

[15] *'The existing dispute resolution schemes that will be replaced by the new single scheme are:*
- *The Office of the Banking Ombudsman (OBO);*
- *The Office of the Building Societies Ombudsman (OBSO);*
- *The Office of the Investment Ombudsman (OIO);*
- *The Insurance Ombudsman Bureau (IOB);*
- *The Personal Investment Authority Ombudsman Bureau (PIAOB);*
- *The Personal Insurance Arbitration Service (PIAS);*
- *The Securities and Futures Authority Complaints Bureau and Arbitration*
- *'The FSA Complaints Unit and Independent Investigator.'* (Consultation Paper No 33, at paragraph 2.2).

[16] Consultation Paper 5, *Consumer Compensation*, op, cit., at p.6.

consumers to act responsibly. The FSA maintains that the *'compensation arrangements should also achieve a balance between a level of protection which is reasonable, given the nature of the consumer and the nature of the transaction...'*[17]. A system of *co-insurance* is advocated whereby individual consumers will be required to bear part of any financial loss themselves; however one of the main tenets of the Scheme is to take into account the damage that may occur to a consumer as a result of being poorly advised on products. The FSA recognizes that not all individual consumers will have the same level of understanding about the transactions they enter into. In developing this Scheme the FSA is mindful of the obstacles it may encounter, particularly in what is a computer market, but it wishes to achieve a balance between caveat emptor and complete protection.

However, in the opinion of the FSA, the arrangements for providing compensation should be:

(a) transparent in their structure and operation;

(b) easily accessible to claimants;

(c) fair to both claimants and contributors;

(d) efficient and responsive in operations; and

(e) simple and cost effective.[18]

Since 1997, the FSA attempted to improve consumer protection in relation to investment in the world of banking. In October 1997, it published a Consultation Paper *'Consumer Involvement'* setting out proposals for ensuring effective consumer involvement in the work of the FSA, through a consumer panel, to advise the FSA on matters of policy affecting consumers. The Paper also proposed establishing direct links with consumers and voluntary groups; setting up ad hoc advisory panels, where necessary, in order to assist the FSA on specific policy issues; arranging consumer representation on permanent panels which the FSA may establish, namely, training and competence; establishing mechanisms for gathering information on matters affecting consumers; and *'commissioning research to monitor consumer issues and the effectiveness of the FSA'*.[19]

[17] op. cit., at 7.
[18] op. cit., at 8.
[19] FSA, *Consumer Involvement*, October 1997 at j4.

The Paper also clearly identifies three aims in regard to consumer involvement to protect consumers of financial services; to promote clear and orderly markets; and to maintain confidence in the financial system.[20]

The FSA aims at ensuring that consumers are not exposed to undue risks. Determined to maintain good working relations with consumer bodies, trade associations, interest groups and other institutions with an interest in the FSA's work, in addition to maintaining the principle of transparency of its activities, the FSA also aims at providing consumers with the benefits of competition and innovation in markets for financial products.

According to the FSA, the principal objectives of consumer involvement would be:

(a) to assist it to understand fully and take appropriate account of consumer needs in its policy development;

(b) to be aware, at the earliest possible opportunity, of problems that consumers may be experiencing in the financial services marketplace;

(c) to keep consumers informed of its activities and policies, current and future;

(d) to pay attention to consumer feedback on the effectiveness of its regulatory requirements; and

(e) to facilitate consumer education to assist them make informed decisions.

The FSA appreciates that a multi-faceted method will be necessary to secure consumer input in order to achieve its objectives which are:

(i) to consider the varied interests consumers may have in the work of the FSA;

(ii) to develop the technical expertise of consumer representatives by allowing involvement on a regular basis in the policy issues under consideration; and

(iii) in recognition of the fact that consumers and consumer interest

---

[20] ibid.

groups may not have resources that are available to practitioners and trade associations, to set up a group to which the FSA may provide financial and other resources.

In 1994, the Personal Investment Authority (PIA) Consumer Panel was set up. The original terms of reference of this Panel were the following:

(a) to advise the PIA on the interests and concerns of private investors;

(b) to consider the issues that might affect investor protection and the appointment of public interest directors to the Board;

(c) *'to propose a basis for commissioning and managing consumer research on the effectiveness of PIA'*;

(d) to evaluate the effectiveness of PIA in meeting its objectives to regulate and protect members' investment business;

(e) to seek information from PIA on aspects of their work and responsibilities;

(f) to make reports and recommendations to the PIA Board and to publish annual reports dealing, in particular, with the effectiveness of PIA's regulations;

(g) to consider the trends in complaints received and determined by PIA Ombudsman and their implications for PIA and make appropriate recommendations;

(h) to agree an annual budget with the Board; and

(i) to review the terms of reference, when necessary, and recommend appropriate changes to the Board.

The PIA Consumer Panel has already been active in ensuring that consumers and consumers organizations are kept informed of regulatory initiatives, and that consumers' views, concerns and interests are taken into account in formulating PIA's policy. It has already proved to be an effective voice for consumer issues.

The FSA, however, proposed that its consumer panel should have an essentially advisory role in two principal areas: advising and commenting on policy development by the FSA and reporting to the

FSA, after review, on the effectiveness of its policies in relation to consumers. According to the FSA, the consumer panel should be reasonably free to determine its own work programme including issues falling outside the FSA's regulation boundaries, although it would be advisable to work on a mutually agreed set of terms. The remit of the insurer panel should extend to include almost any consumer issue, e.g. retail banking, life assurance and pensions, etc.

The FSA proposed that appointments to the consumer panel should be made by the Board of the FSA; each member would sit in his/her personal capacity. The Consumer Panel will have a separate budget to cover staff costs, the commissioning of research, and the fees and expenses of the members.

In order to ensure adequate consumer involvement, the FSA proposed to develop direct links with consumer, voluntary and other groups who may be affected by the FSA's activities.

Consumer complaints should be an indicator as to the issues in respect of which more work would be necessary. Analysis of complaints has already proved to be useful, and the FSA intends to establish mechanisms for ensuring that this type of information is effectively used.

Consumer research, regarded as another method of monitoring consumer issues and the effectiveness of the FSA itself, will primarily be carried out through surveys of consumers' needs and views, including:

(a) evaluation of regulations by ascertaining consumer confidence and purchasing behaviour;

(b) operation of quality control mechanism, for example, by setting objectives, through ascertainment of consumer satisfaction;

(c) policy development, for example, by setting objectives, identifying problems and monitoring industry needs; and

(d) costs budget analysis.

The FSA's Regulatory Tools

The range of the FSA's objectives is much wider than that of the Bank of

England; it is therefore necessary for it to use a wider range of tools and responses. Its tools can be divided into two categories:
- the tools designed to monitor and influence the behaviour of consumer groups of regulated firms or exchanges or the financial services industry; and
- the tools designed to monitor and influence the behaviour of the individual institution, namely, regulated firms, exchanges, clearing houses, in addition to approved individuals and firms.

Activities Directed Towards Commerce or the Industry In General

The principal tools suggested by the FSA for influencing consumers, in general, include disclosure of relevant information on products; consumer education and building of public awareness for the purpose of improving the public's understanding of financial systems and understanding of the benefits and risks of particular types of products; the mechanism for complaints handling and the Ombudsman service for the purpose of contributing to consumer confidence; the Compensation Scheme; public statements by the FSA on criminal activities for the purpose of alerting the public and market participants to specific risks; and product approval in accordance with the European Union law for collective investment Compensation Scheme.

Activities Directed Towards the Industry

The principal tools for influencing the industry as a whole include: a training and competence regime with the view to raising standards and improving compliance in the industry, thus bringing benefits to consumers; rule-making for the purpose of setting regulatory standards; market-monitoring; sector-wide projects which include activities such as firm visits and other forms of contact with firms; and international activities.

The latter two will be used for information-sharing for the understanding of specific firms, regulators and markets, and for the purpose of promoting best practice.

Activities Directed Towards Individual Institutions

These include firms, exchanges, clearing houses and approved individuals. The regulatory tools, designed to influence the behaviour of individual institutions, will be used in connection with authorization of individuals and firms in accordance with the standard set for entering into the market; they include prosecution measures where the activity of a firm has caused losses or other adverse effects for consumers. Supervision of firms, including desk-based reviews and on-site visits, may have to be used when an institution may be required to change its capital structure in response to a changing risk profile, or focused reviews of a particular business or control area.

The other tools that the FSA wishes to use for this purpose are investigation and intervention, particularly when risks are immediate and continuing and where the FSA is convinced that the firm concerned will not take appropriate remedial measures.

FSA discipline will include private warning of firms or individuals by public censor, financial penalties in addition to exercising its power of withdrawal or suspension or authorization, and restitution of loss even by means of court orders.

The FSA's General Duties

Section 2 of the Act identifies the regulatory objectives of the FSA as: market confidence; public awareness; the protection of consumers; and reduction of financial crime.

In discharging its functions the FSA is required to pay attention to:

(a) the need to use its resources in the most efficient and economic way;

(b) the responsibilities of those who manage the affairs of authorized persons; and

(c) whether if the burden of restrictions imposed on a person is proportionate to benefits which may be expected to result from the imposition of that burden or restriction;

(d) facilitation of innovation in connection with regulatory activities;

(e) to maintain the competitive position of the UK by referring to the international character of financial services;

(f) the need to minimize the adverse effects on competition that may arise from a discharge of its functions; and

(g) the facilitation of competition between those institutions that are subject to any form of regulation by the Authority.

The general functions of the FSA are: making rules under this Act; preparation and issuance of codes; providing general guidance[21]; and determining the general policy and principles by reference to its particular functions.

Under the Act the FSA has the general duty to consult practitioners and consumers to ensure that its general policy and practices are being appropriately implemented. For this purpose a practitioners' panel is established consisting of individuals who are authorized persons, persons representing authorized persons, persons representing recognized investment exchanges, persons representing recognized clearing houses and a chairman appointed by the FSA.

On the other hand, in order to protect the interests of consumers, there exists a consumer panel. The FSA must appoint a chairman and such consumers or persons representing the interests of consumers as it considers appropriate. The membership must allow a fair degree of representation to those who may use or may contemplate using it in respect of chairmen of both practitioners and consumer panels; the Treasury's approval is required for the appointment or dismissal.

The Treasury has the power to appoint an independent person, authorized to conduct a review of the efficiency, effectiveness and cost-effectiveness with which the FSA has used its resources in discharging its functions, but must not be concerned with the merits of the FSA's general policy or principles. The result of the review (ensuring accountability of the FSA) will be submitted to the Treasury with the recommendation of the reviewer, a copy to each House of Parliament, published in such manner as the Treasury may consider appropriate and all expenses must be met by the Treasury. In order to allow the reviewer to carry out the review effectively his right of access at any reasonable time to documents is assumed provided such documents are reasonably necessary for the carrying out of the review.

---

[21] The meaning of *'general guidance'* appears in section 153(5) of the FSMA.

Implementation

In order to implement a new approach the FSA plans to do the following:

- develop a risk model and apply it across the whole of the FSA regulated community unless modification for a particular sector is necessary;
- oversee the allocation of authorized firms to different risk categories;
- determine the details of supervisory relationship needed in each category; and
- carry out a number of pilot theme projects.

The FSA planned to implement these for the financial year 2000/01 and it hoped that by the end of March 2001 it would be able to use its new risk-assessment approach.

Power of the FSA as to Rule-Making

The FSA has the authority to make such rules (general rules) as should be applied to authorized person in regard to activities, whether regulated or otherwise by them, as may appear to be necessary or expedient for the purpose of protecting the interests of consumers. The FSA's power to make general rules is unlimited and may be applied to authorized persons even though

> '...there is no relationship between the authorized persons to whom the rules will apply and the persons whose interests will be protected by the rules.'[22]

The general rules may not prohibit an EEA firm from carrying on, or holding itself out as carrying on, any activity for which it has permission under Part II of Schedule 3, nor may they pertain to such firms about any matter the responsibility for which is reserved to the firm's home state regulator.

---

[22] Section 138(4).

The FSA may make rules in relation to client's money when it is held on trust[23] or in a single account for specified purposes and also rules regarding the distribution of interest which is or is not to be retained by an authorized person.

The FSA has been given rule-making powers in relation to matters of a certain specific nature, including the manager of an authorized unit trust Compensation Scheme from carrying on particular activities, presumably when such activities would run counter to the interest of the unit trust; on the other hand, such rules may specify an activity which is not a regulated activity, such as insurance. These rules are referred to in this Act as insurance business rules and includes contracts of long-term insurance too. This is, in particular, for the purpose of avoiding making misleading information on the valuation of the property. The FSA may also make rules which would protect the interests of policy-holders

> '...for the substitution of one description of property, or index of value, by reference to which the benefits under a contract are to be determined for another such description of property or index.'[24]

The FSA's powers to make specific rules relate to the following:

(a) asset-identification rules;

(b) endorsing rules;

(c) specific rules (price-stabilizing rules);

(d) financial promotion rules;

(e) money-laundering rules.

These are now discussed below.

[23] In Scotland the reference to money being held on trust is to be read as a reference to its being held 'as agent for the person who is entitled to call for it to be paid to him or to be paid on his direction or to have it otherwise credited to him', see section 139(3)).

[24] Section 141(4)(b). For the purpose of preventing a person who is not an authorized person, and in order to supplement the FSA's rules, where necessary, the Treasury may make regulations to prevent that person, if that person is a parent of an authorized person who has permission to effect or carry out insurance contracts and if it falls within a prescribed class from doing anything to lessen 'the effectiveness of asset identification rules'.

Asset Identification Rules

The FSA requires an authorized person[25] to identify assets belonging to him and which are maintained in relation to a particular aspect of his business. The FSA's regulations may prohibit payment of dividends or the creation of charges, or make charges void. The Treasury also may by regulation declare such charges as void. The Act does not provide the circumstances in which the Treasury may be required to supplement the regulations made by the FSA.

The primary purpose of this rule is to ensure that an authorized person contract has sufficient assets to protect the interests of policyholders. If the financial position of an authorized person is deemed to be precarious then it must be prohibited from paying dividends and creation of charges on its assets, protecting the interests of policyholders and the reputation of the insurance market.

Endorsing Rules

These are the rules that will allow the FSA to endorse the City Code on Takeovers and Mergers and the rules governing institutional acquisition of shares issued by the Panel on Takeover and Mergers (section 143), in respect of all authorized persons or a specified kind of authorized person.

Failure to carry out an endorsed provision may be regarded as a ground entitling the FSA to exercise its powers under Part IV or section 66, if so asked by the Panel at any time when endorsing rules are in force. Similar powers will be exercised by the FSA under Parts XIII, XIV or XXV.

Specific Rules (Price-Stabilizing Rules)

Section 144 of the Act gives the FSA the power to make rules (price-stabilizing rules) for the purpose of stabilizing the price of investments of specified kinds. Price-stabilizing rules are to be applied only to authorized persons although they make different provisions in relation to different kinds of investments.

The Treasury has the power to impose limitations on the power of the FSA to make rules under this section. An order of the Treasury under section 144 *(Price-Stabilizing Rules – Specific Rules)* may, in

---

[25] An authorized person in this context would mean a person who has permission to effect or carry out contracts of insurance.

particular, specify the kinds of affected. One of the reasons why the Treasury has been given superseding authority is that it is also concerned with the monetary policy of the country. Furthermore, the Treasury has the overall duty to ensure that the price of investments is stabilized.

Financial Promotion Rules

The FSA may make rules applicable to authorized persons about communication by them in regard to invitations or inducements either to engage in investment activity or to participate in a collective investment Compensation Scheme and under section 145 make provision about the form and content of such communications. The Treasury retains its right to impose limitations on the power of the FSA to make rules under this section, which would arise only if any communication has been made by a person other than an authorized person without the approval of an authorized person or when communications have been made by an authorized person without contravening section 238(1)[26].

Money-Laundering Rules

Under section 146 the FSA may make rules 'in relation to the prevention and detection of money laundering in connection with the carrying-on of regulated activities by authorized persons'. The section does not provide for any curative function of the FSA.

Control of Information Rules

The FSA has been given authority to make rules whereby an authorized person will be required to disclose information and the circumstances in which an authorized person may withhold information.

Section 148 states that the FSA may, on the application or with the consent of an authorized person, direct that all or any of the rules to which modification or waiver applies may not be applied to him at the FSA's discretion including: auditors' and actuaries' rules; control of information rules; financial promotion rules; general rules; insurance business rules; money-laundering rules; and price-stabilizing rules.

[26] 'An authorized person must not communicate an invitation or inducement to participate in a collective investment Compensation Scheme.'

An application for a waiver or a modification of rules must be made in the prescribed manner to the FSA. The FSA may not give a direction unless it is satisfied that:

(a) compliance with the rules or the modified rules would be unduly burdensome for the authorized person or would not achieve the purpose for which the rules were made; and

(b) that 'the direction would not result in undue risk to persons whose interests the rules are intended to protect'.[27]

A direction may be subject to conditions, but the Act does not provide for any particular forum in which a direction should be issued nor the conditions which may apply. In publishing a direction the FSA must consider whether its publication would prejudice to an unreasonable degree the commercial interests of those involved (section 148(7)(b)); furthermore, it must also consider whether it would be contrary to an international obligation of the UK, that is, whether the UK government has already concluded any treaty, in regard to non-disclosure of the commercial interests of authorized persons. However, the FSA could publish a direction without disclosing the identity of the authorized person concerned. Any decision as to the publication (or indeed the revokation or variation) of the direction is to be taken by the FSA alone.

A contravention of the provision under Part X (Rules and Guidance) by an authorized person is actionable by a private person who may have suffered losses as a result of the contribution.

When rules are published by the FSA, a copy must be provided to the Treasury without delay and in the event of a rule being altered or revoked the FSA must also give notice to the Treasury without delay giving the details of the alteration or revocation.

When the FSA proposes to make rules it must publish a draft version to bring it to the attention of the public. The draft of the proposals must be accompanied by a cost benefit analysis; a purpose of the proposals; the FSA's reasons for believing that the proposals would be compatible with its general duties; and notice that representations about the proposals may be made to the FSA within a specified time and in certain specified cases expected expenditure.

In the case of any difference between the proposed rules and the

[27] Section 148(4)(b)).

representations made, these differences must be published; costs are one of the main concerns.

The rule-making powers of the FSA are extensive; but the general view of the public is to be taken into account whenever necessary, and in particular under section 155 (Consultation Procedures). Part X of this Act clearly defines the various kinds of rules the FSA can make.

Conclusions

The FSA's plans are based on the contemporary needs of the financial markets and, for the reasons that were seemingly responsible for the collapse of BCCI and Barings Bank, the plans are much broader than those the Bank of England had. Although the plans might look overambitious, their implementation is essential for making the market as much risk-free as possible and developing consumer confidence. The plans cannot be successful unless sufficient resources, financial and otherwise, are available to the FSA and unless effective cooperation is extended to the FSA by all concerned.

9 Financial Services and Markets Act 2000

Introduction

By 1998 the powers of the Bank of England were finally transferred to the FSA. Governed by the Banking Act 1999, the FSA has been considering new legislation to cope with the demands and issues of the financial services market. This has now culminated in the Financial Services and Markets Act 2000 ('the FSMA' or 'the Act'), the objectives of which are:

- to make provisions for the regulation of financial services and markets; and
- to provide for the transfer of certain statutory functions relating to building societies, industrial, provident societies and certain other mutual societies, and for *'connected purposes'*.

The Act is comprehensive (30 parts, 425 sections and 22 schedules) in that it seems to have included most of the important aspects relating to financial markets and the markets of financial services. Below are detailed the titles of the Parts of the Act.

Part I	The Regulator
Part II	Regulated and Prohibited Activities
Part III	Authorization and Exemption
Part IV	Permission to Carry on Regulated Activities
Part V	Performance of Regulated Activities
Part VI	Official Listing
Part VII	Control of Business Transfers

Part VIII	Penalties for Market Abuse
Part IX	Hearings and Appeals
Part X	Rules and Guidance
Part XI	Information Gathering and Investigations
Part XII	Control over Authorized Persons
Part XIII	Incoming Firms: Intervention by Authority
Part XIV	Disciplinary Measures
Part XV	The Financial Services Compensation Scheme
Part XVI	The Ombudsman Compensation Scheme
Part XVII	Collective Investment Compensation Schemes
Part XVIII	Recognized Investment Exchanges and Clearing Houses
Part XIX	Lloyd's
Part XX	Provision of Financial Services by Members of the Professions
Part XXI	Mutual Societies
Part XXII	Auditors and Actuaries
Part XXIII	Public Record, Disclosure of Information and Co-operation
Part XXIV	Insolvency
Part XXV	Injunctions and Restitution
Part XXVI	Notices
Part XXVII	Offences
Part XXVIII	Miscellaneous
Part XXIX	Interpretation
Part XXX	Supplemental

These Parts are now discussed in the form of sections.

Definitions

Of the terms of which interpretations have been provided, the following need particular attention as per Part XXIX:

'Arrangement'	Any kind of arrangement for the performance of function of an authorized person or contract on his behalf with another person. It includes appointments of another person or a partner or an employee

	whether under a contract of services or otherwise.
'Authorized Person'	A person who is authorized for the purposes of this Act (section 29(2) of the Act), allowed to carry on the regulatory activities in the name of the firm[1]. An authorized firm's authorization must not be affected by any change in its membership.
	In the event of an authorized firm being dissolved this authorization continues to carry on to the successor's firm. A firm is a successor firm if the members are substantially the same as those of the predecessor firm; and succession may be relevant either to the whole or substantially the whole of the business of the predecessor's firm.
'Carrying on Regulated Activities by way of Business'	The Treasury may make provisions as to the circumstances in which a person who would otherwise not be regarded as carrying on a regulated activity by way of business is to be regarded as doing so or not doing so. An order under section 419(1) may be made by the Treasury so as to apply generally to all or to a specified category of regulated activities or to a particular regulated activity.
'Carrying on Regulated Activities in the United Kingdom'	A person who is carrying on a regulated activity but would not otherwise be regarded as carrying it on in the UK is, for the purposes of this Act, to be regarded as carrying it on in the UK is:

---

[1] Regulated activities are discussed in a separate section of this chapter.

(i) *'where a person has his registered office (or if he does not have a registered office his head office) in the UK; and*

(a) 'he is entitled to exercise rights under a single-market directive as a UK firm; and

he is carrying on in another EEA state a regulated activity to which that direction applies.'

(b) he is the manager of a Compensation Scheme which is entitled to enjoy the rights conferred on a relevant Community instrument for the purposes of Section 264 (Compensation Schemes constituted in other EEA states); and

Persons in another EEA state are invited to become participants in the Compensation Scheme.'

(c) or the day-to-day management of the carrying on of the regulated activity is the responsibility of his registered office (or head office) or another establishment maintained by him in the UK.

(ii) *'where the person's head office is not in the UK but the activity is carried on from an establishment maintained by him in the UK.'*

For the purposes of (i)(a) and (ii) it is irrelevant where the person with whom the activity is carried on is situate[2].

'Consent Notice'	Issued by an EEA firm's home state

[2] Section 418.

regulator in respect of the firm in order to enable it to establish a branch or an entity in the UK, in accordance with the relevant single-market directive. It must identify the activities to which the consent relates, and include such other information as may be prescribed.

Upon receipt of a consent notice, the FSA must prepare for the firm's supervision; notify the firm of the applicable provisions (within 2 months); or if the activity is direct insurance, the FSA must notify its home state regulator of the applicable provisions, if any, again, within two months.

'Firm'   A firm may mean a partnership or an incorporated association of persons. However, partnership must mean a partnership under the meaning of English law.

'Consumers'   *'"Consumers" means persons:*

(a) who use, have used, or are or may be contemplating using, any of the services provided by

(i) authorized persons in carrying on regulated activities; or

(ii) persons acting as appointed representatives; or

(b) who have rights or interests which

(i) are derived from, or are otherwise attributable to, or

(ii) may be adversely affected by, the use of any such services by other persons'.

'Controlled Activity'   An activity of a specified kind or which

	falls within a specified class of activity; or if it relates to an investment of a specified kind or to an investment that falls within a specified class of investment.
'Controlled Investment'	An investment of a specified kind or if it falls within a specified class of investment, includes any asset, right or interest specified by the Treasury by means of an order.
'Controller'	In relation to an undertaking ("A") means a person who falls within any of the cases in subsection 2 of section 422:

(a) where the person holds 10% or more of the shares in the undertaking; or

(b) he is able to exercise significant influence over the management of undertaking by virtue of holding shares in the undertaking; or

(c) he holds 10% or more of the shares in a parent undertaking ('B'); or

(d) he is entitled to exercise or control the exercise of 10% or more of the voting power in the undertaking; or

(e) he is able to exercise significant influence over the management of the undertaking by virtue of his voting power in that undertaking; or

(f) he is entitled to exercise or control the exercise of 10% or more of the voting power in the present undertaking; or

(g) he is able to exercise significant influence over the management of the parent undertaking by virtue of his voting power in the same undertaking.³

'Customer' A person *'who is using or who may be contemplating using any of the services provided by the authorized person'* (section 59(11)).

'EEA Firm' An EEA firm is a firm the head office of which is not located in the UK, but authorized in its home state. Such a firm may be an investment firm (as defined in Article 1.2 of the Investment Services Directive); or a credit institution (as defined in Article 1 of the First Banking Coordination Directive[4]); or an undertaking involved in direct insurance activity (within the meaning of Article 1 of the First Life Insurance Directive or of the First Non-Life Insurance Directive[5]) – or a financial institution (as defined in Article 1 of the Second Banking Co-ordination Directive[6]) which has also satisfied the conditions of Article 18 of the said Directive[7]. Although author-ization to EEA firms is granted by their home state authorities, hosts states have supervisory power over them, in order to ensure that the host market is not disturbed by any external or internal entity or person. Price movement of firms and the Right of Establishment within the

---

[3] See section 422.
[4] The Council Directive of 12 December 1977 on the coordination of laws, regulations and administrative provisions relating to the taking up and pursuit of the business of credit institution (No. 77/780/EEC).
[5] The Council Directive of 5 March 1979 on the coordination of laws, regulations and administrative provisions relating to the taking up and pursuit of the business of direct life assurance (No. 79/267/EEC).
[6] The Council Directive of 15 December 1989 on the coordination of laws, etc., relating to the taking up and pursuit of the business of credit institution and amending Directive 77/780/EEC (No. 89/646/EEC).
[7] Article 18 of the Second Banking Coordination Directive.

European Economic Area (EEA) are two very important foundations of the EEA, and they must be recognized and implemented for the operation of the single market.

Thus, each person or business entity has the right (EEA right) to establish a branch or provide services in another EEA state subject to the relevant single-market directives.

'Engaging in Investment Activity'	Either *'(a) entering or offering to enter into an agreement the making or performance of which by either party constitutes a controlled activity, or (b) exercising any rights conferred by controlled investment to acquire, dispose of, underwrite or convert a controlled investment'* (section 19(8)).
'Financial Crime'	Includes any offence involving fraud or dishonesty, misconduct in or misuse of information relating to a financial market or handling the proceeds of crime. Offence in this context would include any act or omission on the part of the regulated person.
'Financial System'	The system operating in the UK which would include financial markets, exchanges, regulated activities and other activities connected with financial markets and exchanges.
'Host State Rules'	These rules are made by a host state in accordance with the relevant single-market directive, and it is the responsibility of the host state (e.g. the UK) to implement those rules and to supervise compliance of these rules.

'Interested Parties'	(a) the applicant;
	(b) the person in respect of whom the application is made (the authorized person); and
	(c) the person by whom an authorized person's services are to be retained, if not the applicant (section 62(5)).
'Market Confidence'	The confidence that will be maintained in the financial system.
'Notices'	The Treasury may by regulations make provisions as to the procedure to be followed in regard to service of notices[8].
'Parent and Subsidiary Undertaking'	Except in relation to an incorporated friendly society *'parent undertaking'* and *'subsidiary undertaking'* have the same meaning as in Part VII of Companies Act 1985 (or Part VIII of the Companies (Northern Ireland) Order 1986). It is possible for an individual to have a business relationship that would be classified as a parent/subsidiary relationship.
	The definitions of parent/subsidiary undertaking are extended to cover any EEA undertaking that will be treated as a parent or subsidiary undertaking under the law of the EEA state in which the body is established[9].
'Permitted Activity'	These activities are identified in the regulator's notice; or where activities of an EEA firm are to be regarded as permitted by virtue of the 'notice of intention'.

---

[8] Section 414.
[9] See section 420; see also *Explanatory Notes* op. cit. at paragraphs 742 and 743.

'Public Awareness'	Its primary objective is to promote clear understanding of the financial system, and in particular, promoting awareness of the *'benefits and risks'* associated with different kinds of investment and other financial dealings (section 4(2)), and providing appropriate information and advice.
'Reasonably'	Whatever information may be required to satisfy the Authority for the purpose of section 59 approval.
'Regulated Activities'	Activities of a specified kind carried on by way of business and which relate to an investment of a specified kind, and in the case of activity falling under section 20(1) if carried on in relation to property of any kind.
'The Protection of Consumers'	The main objective is to secure the appropriate degree of protection for consumers with particular attention to the differing degree of risk associated with different types of investment; and the differing degrees of experience and expertise that different consumers may have with different kinds of regulatory activity. The consumers must have access to advice and adequate information so that they may take responsibility for their own decisions.

Inquiries about the FSA's performance and activities may be taken by the Treasury if (a) it appears to the Treasury that untoward events have occurred in relation to the Collective Investment Compensation Scheme or (b) a person who in the course of carrying out regulatory activity, whether or not as an authorized person, has posed, or is likely to pose, a grave risk to the financial system or (c) when events have occurred in relation to listed securities or when an issuer of listed securities which has caused or was likely to cause significant damage to holders of listed securities. The Treasury will determine the scope, duration and conduct of the inquiry as to the making of reports (sections 12 and 13) and meet all reasonable expenses. On completion the person holding the inquiry must submit a written report to the Treasury setting out the result and making such recommendations as he considers appropriate. The Treasury may publish the whole or any part of the report in such manner as it considers appropriate unless the Treasury thinks that it contains material that relates to the affairs of a particular person whose interest would be seriously jeopardised by the publication of the material or that the disclosure would be incompatible with the UK's international obligations.

The Regulator and Provisions about Regulated Activities and Prohibited Activities

The Regulator is the FSA. Its constitution has been set out in Schedule 1 to the Act. There shall be a chairman and a governing body which shall have its own chairman and other members appointed and removed from the office by the Treasury. The majority of the members of its governing body are to be non-executive members and a committee of its governing body consisting of its non-executive members shall discharge functions conferred by Schedule 1.

The members of the non-executive committee are appointed by the FSA, and the chairman of this committee will be appointed by the Treasury. The non-executive functions of this committee are:

- to keep under review whether the Authority in discharging its functions, is using its resources in the most efficient and economic manner, and
- to keep under review whether the FSA's internal financial controllers secure *'proper conduct of its financial affairs'*.

The FSA shall discharge its functions in accordance with the decision of its governing body. The non-executive committee shall also determine the remuneration of the chairman of the FSA's governing body and the executive members of that body.

All persons must be either authorized or exempt in order to carry on a regulatory activity under the purview of this Act in the UK unless authorization has been given to a person under Part IV ('*Permission to carry out Regulated Activities*') or resulting from any other provisions of this Act. Section 21 of the Act provides that no person shall 'in the course of his business' communicate an invitation or inducement to engage in investment activity (section 21(1)) unless that person is an authorized person or the consent to the communication is one which is approved for the purposes of this section by an authorized person. Section 21(3) provides that '*In the case of communications originating outside the UK subsection (1) applies only if the communication is capable of having an effect in the UK*'. The provision of this section can be repealed by order of the Treasury.

It is believed that the judicial meaning attached to '*in the course of business*' will be accepted[10]. Section 21(1) does not apply in relation to communications '*(a) of a specified description, (b) originated in a specified country or territory outside the UK, (c) originating in a country or territory which falls within a specified description of country or territory outside the UK, or (d) originating outside the UK*' (section 21(6)).

Contravention of any general prohibition under the Act will make the person concerned guilty of an offence and be liable on summary conviction to imprisonment for a term not exceeding 6 months or a fine not exceeding the statutory maximum, or both; on conviction or indictment such a person could be liable to imprisonment for a term not exceeding 2 years or a fine, or both. The only defence is for the offender to show that he took all reasonable precautions and exercised all due diligence to avoid committing the offence. A person who is neither an authorized person nor an exempt person will be guilty of offence if he so describes himself or holds himself out in a manner which indicates or which is likely to indicate that he is an authorized or exempt person and is liable on a summary conviction to imprisonment for a term not exceeding 6 months or a fine not exceeding level 5 under the standard scale, or both. But, if the offence included a public display

---

[10] *Johnson v Jewitt (H.M. Inspector of Taxes)*, CA, 40 Tax Cas 231, [1961] TR 81, [1961] TR 321, 40 ATC 109, 40 ATC 314; *Kenneth Gordon Coleman v The Commissioners*, London VAT Tribunal, [1976] VATTR 24; *J W Wilcox v The Commissioners*, Manchester VAT Tribunal, [1978] VATTR 79; *Church of Scientology of California v Customs and Excise Commissioners and another* QBD [1979] STC 297; *British Olympic Association v The Commissioners* London VAT Tribunal [1979] VATTR 122.

of any material, the maximum fine for any offence is level 5 *'multiplied by the number of days for which the display continued'*. Again, the only defence would be to show that he took all reasonable precautions and exercised all due diligence.

If a person contravenes restrictions on financial promotion (section 9(1)) he shall be guilty of an offence and liable on summary conviction as above (section 21(1)). The only defence that an accused can rely on is that he believed on reasonable grounds that the content of communication was prepared or approved for the purpose of section 19 (financial promotion) by an authorized person or that he took all reasonable precaution and exercised all due diligence to avoid committing the offence.

Agreements made by an authorized person in contravention of the general prohibition are unenforceable by the other party and in such a case the other party is entitled to recover any money or property paid or transferred by him under the agreement in addition to seeking compensation for any loss sustained by him (section 24), unless the regulatory activity is deposit-taking.

An agreement made by an authorized person in the course of business of carrying on a regulated activity not in contravention of the general prohibition but in consequence of some act or statement made by a third party in the course of a regulatory activity carried on by that party in contravention of the general prohibition is unenforceable against the other party ('the purchaser'), and the other party is entitled to recover any money or property paid or transferred by him in addition to seeking compensation for any loss sustained by him (section 25). This section does not apply if a regulatory activity is deposit-taking. If an agreement has been made unenforceable by section 24 or 25, the amount of compensation recoverable may be agreed by the parties or on an application of a party may be determined by the court. If the court is satisfied that in the circumstances of the case it would be just and equitable to enforce the agreement and to allow the retention of money and property paid or transferred under the agreement it may so order, under section 26. If an agreement is made between a depositor and a deposit-taker in contravention of the general prohibition, and if the depositor is not entitled under the agreement to recover quickly any money deposited by him, he may apply to the court for an order directing the deposit-taker to return the money to him. The court need not make any such order if it is satisfied that it would not be just and equitable for the money to be returned and if the deposit-taker reasonably believed that he was not contravening the general prohibition by making the agreement.

Authorization and Exemptions

Those involved in financial services have to be authorized (licensed) by the FSA to be able to participate in the market. Part III of the Act details the criteria that an institution or entity must satisfy for being *'authorized'* or being declared as an *'exempted'* person.

The following persons are regarded as *'authorized'* for the purpose of the Act:

(a) a person who has been authorized to carry on one or more regulated activities having been permitted under Part IV of the Act; or

(b) an EEA firm which qualifies for authorization under Schedule 3 (*EEA Passport Rights*); or

(c) a Treaty firm which qualifies for authorization under Schedule 4 (*Treaty Rights*), or

(d) a person who is already authorized or may be authorized under this Act.

An EEA firm qualifies for authorization in the UK if it seeks to establish a branch in the UK and satisfies the established conditions These conditions entail:

(a) receiving a *'consent notice'* from the firm's home state regulator whereby the firm has been allowed to establish a branch in the UK;

(b) upon receipt of the *'consent notice'*, the FSA must prepare for the firm's supervision; notify the firm of the applicable provisions, if any;[11]

---

[11] These provisions in this context stand for the host state rules with which an EEA firm must comply when carrying on a permitted activity as a legal entity in the United Kingdom.

(c) in the event of a firm pursuing the activity of direct insurance, the FSA must notify its home state regulator of the applicable provisions, if any. The notification period is limited to two months as from the day on which the FSA received the consent notice.

On the other hand, if an EEA firm seeks to provide services in the UK, it will qualify for authorization if it should satisfy the following *service conditions* in exercise of its EEA rights:

(a) that the firm must give its home state regulator a *'notice of intention'* indicating its intention to provide services in the UK;

(b) that in the event of a firm being an investment firm, the FSA must receive a *'regulator's notice'* from the firm's home state regulator containing such information as may be prescribed;

(c) that in the event of a firm being an investor firm, the home state regulator must notify the FSA that a regulator's notice has been served to it;

(d) that when the FSA has received a regulator's notice or has been notified of a firm's intention to provide services in the UK, it must prepare for that firm's supervision; and notify the firm of the applicable provisions[12], if any, within two months as from the date on which the FSA received the regulator's notice or was informed of the firm's intention.

Grant of Permission

An EEA business firm that qualifies for authorization under paragraph 12 of Schedule 3 (*Firms qualifying for authorization by virtue of establishing establishment conditions or service conditions*) cannot be subject to the provisions of sections 21, 39(5) and 147(1) of the Consumer Credit Act 1974 (business for which licences are required unless a Director-General has exercised the power conferred on him by section 203 of this Act).

---

[12] *'Applicable provisions'* in this context would include the rules of the host state with which the firm would be required to comply when carrying on a permitted activity by providing services in the United Kingdom.

EEA firms may be subject to continuing regulations and therefore they may be subject to any change in regard to the activity that it may carry on outside their home states. Of course, an EEA firm is at liberty to notify the FSA of its intention to cease to carry on a regulated activity in the UK. If a credit institution under the Second Banking Coordination Directive fails to satisfy the criteria of an authorized institution, then its authorization would be cancelled and it may seek to become an authorized person under Part IV of the Act (*Permission to carry on regulated activities*).

Exercise of Passport Rights by the United Kingdom

The provisions for the exercise of passport rights by UK firms have been detailed in Part III of Schedule 3. A UK firm may not exercise an EEA right to establish a branch unless the following conditions are satisfied:

(a) that the firm has given the FSA a notice of intention indemnifying the activities (may include those not of a regulated nature) which it seeks to carry on through the branch and provides such other information as may be specified;

(b) that the FSA has given a consent notice to the regulator in the home state;

(c) that the host state regulator has notified the firm of the applicable provisions or that two months have elapsed since the date on which the FSA gave the consent notice.

If the firm's EEA right is derived from the Investment Service Directive or Second Banking Coordination Directive and if the first condition is satisfied then the FSA must give a consent notice to the Regulator in the host state unless it has reason to doubt the adequacy of the firm's resources or its administrative structure.

Where a firm's EEA right is derived from any of the Insurance Directives when the first condition is satisfied, the FSA must give a consent notice unless it has reason to doubt the adequacy of the firm's resources or its administrative structure, or to question its reputation or the veracity or experience of directors or managers of that firm. If the

FSA proposes to refuse to give a consent notice, the firm concerned must be given a warning notice.

In the event of a firm's EEA right being derived from any of the Insurance Directives and the host regulator having been notified of the applicable provisions, the FSA must inform the firm of those provisions according to the prescribed rules. Consent notice of the FSA must be given in writing, and if refused, it must do so within three months from the date on which it received the notice of intention and the person concerned has the right to refer the matter to the Tribunal.

In order to provide services in exercise of its EEA right a UK firm must give the FSA a notice of intention to provide services identifying the activities (may include non-regulated activities) it intends to carry out and include such other information as may be specified.

If the firm's EEA right is derived from the Investment Services Directive or a Banking Coordination Directive, the FSA must within one month of the date of receipt of the notice of intention send a copy of it to a host state regulator, giving written notice to the firm concerned. However, if the firm's EEA right is derived from the Investment Services Directive it is not supposed to provide the services to which its notice of intention relates unless it has received written notice from the FSA.

A breach of the provisions of passport rights is a punishable offence. It its defence, a firm concerned is required to show that it took all reasonable precautionary means and exercised all due diligence in order to avoid committing an offence.

In order to maintain continuing regulation of UK firms, the UK Treasury may make changes relating to a UK firm or to an activity that it carries on or make provisions with respect to the consequences of the firm's failure to comply with the provisions of the regulations. A firm has a right to challenge a decision of the FSA as to refusal of consent or to any changes of regulations and may refer the matter to the Tribunal.

A UK firm operating in a host EEA state is subject to the regulations of that state and the FSA may impose any requirement in relation to the firm.

An authorization will terminate if an authorized person has no regulated activity to perform, and an EEA firm authorization ceases as the result of having its EEA authorization withdrawn or by virtue of ceasing to have an EEA right. In the case of a Treaty firm authorization will cease under Schedule 4 if its authorization is withdrawn by its home state, or if at the request of the treaty firm concerned, the FSA has given direction cancelling its Schedule 4 authorization. An authorized person may request the FSA under paragraph 1(a) of Schedule 5 to cancel its authorization.

It has already been discussed under Part II of Schedule 3 the circumstances in which an UK firm may exercise its EEA rights outside the UK. Section 38 of the Act provide for exemption orders by the Treasury, that is, the Treasury may by means of an exemption order exempt from the general prohibition any specified person or persons falling within a specified class but a person cannot be an exempt person if he has a Part IV permission. An exemption order can be issued in respect of all regulated activities or one or more specified regulated activities or only in specified circumstances or in relation to specified functions or subject to conditions.

Section 39 of the Act provides for exemption of appointed representatives. If an unauthorized person is a party to a contract with an authorized person (the principal) that allows him to carry on business of a prescribed description, and who complies with the prescribed requirements, and for whose business his principal has accepted responsibility in writing, he is to be regarded as an exempt person – that is, he is a person who is exempt from the general prohibition pertaining to *'any regulated activity comprised in the carrying on of that business for which his principal has accepted responsibility'* (section 39(1)(b). An *'exempt person'* is regarded as an *'appointed person'* under the Act. The principal of an appointed representative remains responsible for the activities of its agent (the appointed representative); the rules of the law of agency apply.

Permission to Carry on Regulated Activities

Part IV of the consisting of 16 sections (sections 40-55), states that it is for the following types of applicants to seek permission from the FSA to carry on one or more regulatory activities:

(a) an individual;

(b) a body corporate;

(c) a partnership;

(d) an unincorporated association.

The following persons need not apply for permission under section 40 if:

(i) it has already received permission from the FSA under this Part;

(ii) an authorized person who has a form of licence which amounts to giving permission under Part IV; and

(iii) an EEA firm if it is entitled otherwise to carry on a regulatory activity in exercise of its right.

Part IV also provides for threshold provisions that have been detailed in Schedule 6 to the Act. Where threshold conditions apply the FSA must ensure that the person concerned will satisfy the threshold conditions in relation to all the regulatory activities for which he has the permission.

If a regulatory activity relates to a contract of insurance the authorized person must be a body corporate, a registered friendly society or a member of Lloyd's. If the person concerned appears to the FSA to be seeking to be engaged in a regulatory activity constituting deposits, it must be a body corporate or a partnership, the accepting headquarters or registered office of which must be located in the UK. If the person concerned has its headquarters in the UK but it is not a body corporate, it must carry on business in the UK. Where a person has close links[13] with another, the FSA must ensure that effective supervision is carried out and if it appears to the FSA that the other person is subject to the laws of a non-EEA state, then neither the provisions in the other state nor any deficiency in their enforcement procedures would prevent the FSA from exercising its effective supervision of the person concerned. This provision may provoke controversy in that in such a situation the

---

[13] A person has close links with another person if that other person is a parent undertaking of that first person or that other person is a subsidiary undertaking of the first person, or the other person is a parent undertaking of a subsidiary undertaking of the first person, or the other person is a subsidiary undertaking of a parent undertaking of the first person or the other person owns 20% or more of the voting rights or capita of the first person or if the first person owns or controls 20% or more of the voting rights or capital of the other person.

FSA may exercise what is known as extra-territorial jurisdiction, which is currently exercised by many jurisdictions.

For the sake of defining a subsidiary undertaking the EC 7th Company Law Directive must be referred to. In order to satisfy threshold conditions the FSA must ensure that the resources (both human and capital) are adequate in relation to the regulatory activities for which it seeks permission, taking into account the applicant membership of the group and the effect that the membership may have and the means by which it manages risks in connection with its business. The criterion of fit and proper person will apply, as discussed in Chapter 7.

Performance of Regulated Activities/Prohibition Order

The FSA may issue a prohibition order on the basis that the individual concerned is not a *'fit and proper person'* to perform functions pertaining to a regulated activity that is carried on by an authorized person. In other words, this Part applies to an individual working for an authorized person. According to section 56(3), a prohibition order may relate to:

(a) any regulated activity, specified[14] or otherwise;

(b) *'an authorized person generally or any person within a specified class of authorized person.'*

A prohibition order must be preceded by a warning notice, setting out the terms of the prohibition, followed by a *'decision notice'*, which must name the individual, set out the terms of the order, and be served to the individual, who has a right to challenge it before the Tribunal.

Performance of any function in breach of a prohibition order will render a person guilty of an offence and liable to a fine not exceeding level 5 in the standard scale. The primary defence would be to prove that he took all reasonable precautions and exercised all due diligence to avoid committing an offence. An authorized person must ensure that a *'prohibited person'* does not perform any of his functions. A *'prohibited person'* may request the FSA to revoke the prohibition order, and the FSA may either revoke it or vary it. Section 58 of the Act states that if the FSA has decided to grant the application, it must give the individual concerned notice if the FSA proposed to refuse the application, a warning

---

[14] *'Specified'* means specified in the prohibition order (section 56(9)).

notice is made, then a decision notice must be issued to the applicant who may challenge the notice by referring the matter to the Tribunal.

An authorized person is required to take reasonable care in order to ensure that no person performs a controlled function under an arrangement entered into by an authorized person to carry on with a regulatory activity without the authority of the FSA. The same provision applies if an arrangement has been entered into by a contractor of an authorized person.

The FSA has the authority to approve particular arrangements, that is, it may specify *'a control function'* in relation to the performance of a regulated activity by an authorized person if it is satisfied that the following conditions are met:

(a) that the function is likely to enable the person responsible for its performance to exercise *'a significant influence on the conduct of the authorized person's affairs'* in relation to the regulated activity;

(b) that the function will involve *'the person performing it in dealing with customers of the authorized persons in a manner substantially connected with the carrying on of the regulated activity'*, and

(c) that the function will involve the person *'performing it in dealing with the property of customers of authorized persons in a manner substantially connected with carrying on of the regulatory activity'*.[15]

The FSA may grant an application under section 60 only if it is satisfied that the candidate is a fit and proper person to perform the function, most importantly whether he has obtained qualification and has undergone or is undergoing training or possesses a level of competence. The FSA has three months from the date on which the application was received to approve the application and if an application is not granted, a warning notice must be issued under section 62(2). It is possible for the FSA to impose a requirement under section 60(3), whereby the candidate will be required to provide more information.

All approval must be recorded in writing. If the FSA proposes to refuse an application it must give a warning notice to all the interested

[15] Section 59(5), (6) and (7).

parties, and if refused, it must give a warning notice to all the interested parties. Furthermore, it is also required to give a decision notice to each of the interested parties upon receipt of a refusal notice. Each of the interested parties may refer the matter to the Tribunal.

An approval under section 59 will be withdrawn by the FSA if it considered that a person who was approved is not a fit person to perform the function to which the approval related, taking into account any matter it would consider if an application was being made under section 60. If the FSA proposes to withdraw its approval, it must give each of the interested parties a warning notice and if the approval is withdrawn it must give each of the interested parties a decision notice. An interested party has the right to refer the matter to the Tribunal[16].

A certain standard of conduct is expected of approved persons and the FSA may issue statements of principle and a code of practice to help ascertain whether or not an authorized person's conduct complies with the statement of principle. The FSA has the discretion to alter or replace a statement or code issued under section 64, according to the exigencies of time and market. Such a code must be published by the FSA and brought to the attention of the public. However, any failure to comply with the Statement of Principle under section 64 does not automatically give rise to any right of action *'by persons affected or affect the validity of a transaction'* (section 64(8)), both of which will be determined objectively. The Treasury must be notified of a statement of principle or code.

Before issuing a statement of principle or code under section 64 the FSA must publish a draft version of it and bring it to the attention of the public together with a cost benefit analysis and a notice that representations about it may be made to the FSA within a reasonable period of time. Where the opinion may differ from the draft code or statement of principle, the FSA must publish details of the difference together with a cost benefit analysis.

Section 69 refers to the statement of policy which is different from the statement of principle. Whereas the conduct of an authorized person must be considered with reference to the statement of principle, the

---

[16] An interested party in this context would stand for the person on whose application authorization was given or the person in respect of whom it was given ('B'), the person by whom 'B' services are retained, if not 'A'.

statement of policy is predominantly concerned with considering whether any penalty may be imposed on an approved person by virtue of a breach.

Section 66 of the Act gives the FSA disciplinary powers to deal with a person guilty of misconduct if as an approved person[17] he fails to comply with a statement of principle issued under section 64 or he has been knowingly involved in the contravention *'by the relevant authorized person of a requirement imposed on that authorized person by or under this Act'* (section 66(2)(b)).

The limitation period for taking action under section 66 is two years as from the day on which the FSA comes to know of the misconduct unless proceedings in respect of it began before the end of that period. In fact, proceedings against a person in respect of misconduct *'are to be treated as begun when a warning notice is given to him under section 67'*.

Section 67 provides for disciplinary measures, procedures thereto and the right of an authorized person to refer matters to the Tribunal. When the FSA decides to take action under section 68 (Disciplinary Powers) it must give that person a warning notice containing a proposal for imposing a specialized penalty. Where the FSA may decided to take action under section 66, it must give that person a decision notice quoting the precise amount of the penalty imposed. The difference between a *'warning notice'* and a *'decision notice'* under section 67 is that a warning notice simply proposes to take action under section 66 whereas a decision notice actually imposes a penalty on a person. Under section 69 the FSA is required to issue a statement of its policy with regard to imposition of penalties under section 66 and the amount of penalties. In determining the amount of penalty regard is usually paid to the seriousness of the misconduct under the statement of principles; the extent to which misconduct was deliberate or reckless; and whether the penalty would be imposed on an individual. The FSA may at any time alter or replace a statement issued under section 69 and in that event it must notify the Treasury of such statement and draw its attention to the public.

Publication of a statement of policy must be preceded by a draft and

---

[17] An approved person under section 66 has the same meaning as an approved person under section 64, that is, a person who has been given approval under section 59.

the attention of the public must also be drawn to it. Again, the draft statement of policy must seek representations about the proposal within a specified time and upon receipt of representations the FSA must pay attention to such representations, and it must publish details of any difference.

Control over Authorized Persons

An *'authorized person'* in the context of this Part stands for an authorized person who is a body corporate or who is a body incorporated in or an unincorporated association formed under the law of any part of the UK[18].

It is for an authorized person to notify the FSA of the nature of the control he may wish to acquire by serving a notice of control. Control would include acquisition of control over a UK authorized person or any additional kind or increase kind of control UK which he already has over a UK person. The Act does not define the meaning of 'an additional kind of control'. However, in the case of any increase of control or any form of acquiring a new control over a UK authorized person, a controller (the person concerned) must notify the FSA before the end of 14 days as from the day on which he first became aware that he has acquired control. The notice of control must detail the nature of control that the person concerned has acquired.

For the purposes of Part XII of the Act a person becomes an acquirer (a person who acquires control over a UK authorized person) when he:

'The cases are where the acquirer

(a) holds 10%; or more of the shares in A;

(b) is able to exercise significant influence over the management of A by virtue of his shareholding in A;

(c) holds 10%; or more of the shares in a parent undertaking ('P') of A;

---

[18] Section 178(4). *'Authorized person'* in this context does not include persons who for the time being are operatives, trustees or depositories of a recognized investment Compensation Scheme.

> (d) *is able to exercise significant influence over the management of P by virtue of his shareholding in P;*
>
> (e) *is entitled to exercise, or control the exercise of 10%; or more of the voting power in A;*
>
> (f) *is able to exercise significant influence over the management of A by virtue of his voting power in A;*
>
> (g) *is entitled to exercise, or control the exercise of 10%; or more of the voting power in P; or*
>
> (h) *is able to exercise significant influence over the management of P by virtue of his voting power in P."*[19]

Control arises as the result of holding of shares in an authorized person in a parent undertaking and an entitlement or voting power in an authorized person and in a parent undertaking. For the purposes of section 179 (Part XII) the terms *'associate'*, *'shares'* and *'voting power'* have the same meaning. A controller of an authorized person who is a UK person increases his control as identified in section 180(2):

> *'The steps are*
>
> (a) *from below 10% to 10% or more but less than 20%;*
>
> (b) *from below 20% to 20% or more but less than 33%;*
>
> (c) *from below 33% to 33% or more but less than 50%;*
>
> (d) *from below 50% to 50% or more.'*

In the context of paragraphs (a) to (d) the term 'controller' means the controller, any of the controller's associates or the controller and any of the associates.

A controller of an authorized person can also reduce his control over an authorized person by decreasing the percentage of his shares and voting power by:

> *'The steps are*
>
> (a) *from 50% or more to 33% or more but less than 50%;*

---

[19] Section 179(2)(a)-(h). A stands for an authorized person and P for a parent undertaking.

(b) *from 33% or more to 20% or more but less than 33%;*

(c) *from 20% or more to 10% or more but less than 20%;*

(d) *from 10% or more to less than 10%…"*[20]

Again, for the purpose of section 181 (Reduction of Control) the term 'controller' means the controller, any of the controller's associates or the controller and any of its associates[21].

If the UK authorized person or controller proposes to reduce the extent of his control or cease to have control of a relevant kind over the authorized person, he must notify the FSA. A controller must do so within 14 days beginning with the day on which he first became aware that he has ceased to have control in question or he has reduced that control. A notice under this section must be given in writing detailing the extent of the control the person will retain over the authorized person. A person who fails to notify the FSA in the required circumstances or in respect of the required matters under this Part[22] is guilty of an offence unless he can show that he had, at the time of the alleged offence, no knowledge of the act or circumstances by virtue of which he was obliged to notify the FSA. Defence against an offence under section 178(1) or section 190(1) may also be available to a person if he notifies the FSA within 14 days beginning with the day on which he first became aware that a duty to notify arose under those provisions.

The Treasury has the power to change the definition of control (or increasing and reducing control), and may by order provide for exceptions from the obligations under section 178 and section 190; or amend section 179, section 180, section 181 or section 422 by varying or removing any of the cases in which a person is treated as having control over a UK authorized person or by adding a case.

A notice of objection must be accompanied by the relevant documents and given to the FSA in writing; however the FSA may require additional information or documents as it may reasonably consider necessary. Within three months of the receipt of the notice of control (the period for consideration) the FSA must determine whether to approve of the

---

[20] Section 181(2).
[21] Section 181(3).
[22] For example, section 178(1) or (2), or section 190(1) or (2), or section 183(3), or section 185(3).

acquisition of control by the person concerned with or without any conditions attached to it. The FSA may object to the authorized person's acquiring control on any of the following grounds: that the proposed acquirer is not a fit and proper person to have control over the authorized person, or that the interests of consumers would be threatened either by the acquirer's control or by his acquiring this control[23].

The FSA can also give a warning notice to the person concerned proposing that certain conditions be imposed on it. A notice of objection must be preceded by a warning notice. Where the FSA may decide to impose conditions on a person it must give a decision notice.

Where the FSA decides to approve the acquisition, it must notify the person concerned in writing, without delay. If the period of consideration is exceeded by the FSA then approval of control must be announced and the person concerned must be notified accordingly.

The FSA has the right to raise objections if an authorized person has failed to comply with the requirements of section 178 (Notice of Control), or if the FSA is satisfied that the approval requirements are not met with respect to the controller. The FSA can serve a notice of decision on the controller of the UK authorized person.

A person who is subject to a condition imposed in connection with the issue of acquiring control may apply to the FSA for the conditions to be varied or for its cancellation[24]. The FSA may on its own initiative cancel a condition imposed under section 185. An aggrieved person has the right to lodge its complaint with the Tribunal as to the imposition of the condition or refusal of an application pending seeking control.

Any notice of objection to be issued by the FSA under section 187b (Objection to existing control) must be preceded by a warning notice, issued before the end of the three months' period beginning with the date on which the FSA became aware of the failure (notice under section 187(1)) or of the matters in question (section 187(3)). The FSA has the right to request any additional information or documents it may deem appropriate.

Action under section 189 (Improperly acquired shares) can be taken only if a person has acquired or has confirmed his holding of any shares, even if relinquished at a later date, in contravention of a notice of

---

[23] Section 186.
[24] Section 186(5).

objection or a condition imposed on it by the FSA. The FSA must issue a 'restriction notice' in writing, pointing out that until further notice the shares specified in that notice shall be subject to any one or more of the following conditions:

(a) any transfer or agreement to transfer shares, issued or unissued (in the latter case the right to be issued with them) is void;

(b) no voting rights may be exercised;

(c) no further shares are to be issued *'in right of them or in pursuance of any offer made to their holder'*;

(d) the body corporate concerned must not pay any sum on those shares, except in a liquidation.

The FSA may request the court for an order for the sale of any shares to which section 189 applies. However, no order may be made by the court until the time for making a reference to the Tribunal in respect of the notice of objection has expired (section 189(4)(b). In the event of the shares being sold in pursuance of a court order, the proceeds of sale, less the costs of the sale, must be paid into the court 'for the benefit of the persons beneficially interested in them' (section 189(b)).

This section applies only

1. if an acquirer of control comes under section 178(1) to all the shares:

   (a) in the authorized person which the acquirer has acquired;

   (b) which are held by him or any of his associates; or

   (c) which were not so held immediately prior to his becoming a person with control over the authorized persons;

2. in the case of a person acquiring control or increased control after having notified the FSA (section 178(2)) to all the shares held by him or any of his associates when he became aware of his acquiring control over the authorized person;

3. to all the shares in an undertaking which are held by the acquirer or any of his associates, and which were not so held 'before he became a person with control in relation to the authorized person, but shares were acquired in that

undertaking by the acquirer or any of his associates and by virtue of which he became a person with control in relation to that authorized person' (section 189(7)(c).

The Treasury has the power to change the definition of control, and may by order provide for exemption from the obligations under section 178 and section 190, or amend section 179, section 180 or section 181 or section 422.

Revocation of Authorization Order Otherwise than by Consent

An authorization order may be revoked by the FSA, section 254, if it appears to it that:

(a) one or more of the requirements of the order are no longer satisfied; or

(b) that the manager or trustee of the scheme has contravened a requirement in this regard; or

(c) that the manager or trustee of the scheme has 'in purported compliance with any such requirement, knowingly or recklessly given the FSA information which is false or misleading in a material particular', or

(d) that no regulated activity has been carried out for the last 12 months; or

(e) that although none of the above applies it is nevertheless desirable to revoke the authorization order in order to protect the interests of participants, existent or potential, in the scheme.

In the event of the FSA proposing to make an order revoking an authorization order it must give the manager and the trustee of the scheme separate notices, but if the FSA decides to make an order to revoke it must issue a decision notice and the manager or trustee will have the right to refer the matter to the Tribunal. The manager or the trustee of the scheme has the right to request the FSA to revoke the order but the FSA has the right not to comply with such a request if it considers that:

(a) the public interest of the scheme should be investigated before a decision is taken in this regard; or

(b) that revocation would not be in the interests of the participants, or that it would be incompatible with community obligations.

If the FSA proposes to refuse the request it must give separate warning notices to the manager and the trustee of the scheme, but if it is refused, it must give them a decision notice with the right to refer the matter to the Tribunal.

The FSA's power of intervention in regard to authorized unit trust scheme is extensive. It may give directions if it believes that one or more requirements of the making of an authorization order are no longer satisfied; or that the manager or trustee of an authorized unit trust scheme has already contravened or is likely to contravene a requirement imposed on him under the Act; or that the manager or trustee has knowingly or recklessly given the FSA information which is false or misleading; or that in its opinion to protect the interests of participants, current and future. A direction may require the manager to cease the issue or redemption or both of units under the Scheme, or even require the manager or the trustee of the Scheme to wind it up. Section 150 of the Act will apply in the case of any contravention of any direction. The FSA may either on its own initiative or on the application of the manager or the trustee of the Scheme revoke or vary a direction if it is considered to be necessary.

Section 258 gives the FSA the power to apply to for a court order to remove the manager and/or the trustee or replace them by a suitable person or persons nominated by the FSA. However, before making an application for removal of a manager or a trustee, the FSA must given written notice of its intention to the manager and/or trustee of the scheme concerned[25].

Conclusions

Compared to the 1987 Act, the authorization system under the current Act is more extensive, although the basic ethos of authorization is very

---

[25] In regard to the procedure on giving direction under section 257 and varying them on the FSA's own initiative see sections 259-261.

similar. The Act of 2000 places more emphasis on the standard of conduct of approved persons than the 1987 Act, and for this reason the FSA has been endowed with extensive powers to monitor the standard of conduct of approved persons. The warning notice and the decision notice systems are novel ideas under the Act of 2000.

By the same token, the FSA's power of intervention in regard to authorized unit trust scheme is also extensive. Suitability of persons to operate a trust is one of the prime concerns of the FSA. Section 258 thus gives the FSA the power to apply to a court for an order to remove the manager and/or the trustee and to replace them by a suitable person or persons nominated by the FSA.

The FSA wishes to ensure that the authorization scheme is in place, otherwise one of the principal purposes of the Act will be defeated.

10 Collective Investment Schemes

Introduction

Part XVII of the Act, which has been allocated to collective investment schemes, deals with, among other issues, authorized unit trust schemes, open-ended investment companies, recognized overseas schemes – including the EEA states other than the UK – recognized Investment Exchanges and Clearing Houses.

The provisions have two aims: (a) to encourage such schemes; and (b) to promote such schemes within limits (restrictions) so that the interests of investors are protected. The Act provides for elaborate provisions for acceptance and refusal of applications. The FSA has the authority to make rules, known as *'scheme particular rules'*, requiring managers of authorized trust schemes to follow these rules. The FSA retains its right to intervene whenever it may appear to it that one or more requirements for the making of an authorization order are no longer satisfied.

Collective Investment Schemes

Section 235 of the Act defines a *'Collective Investment Scheme'* as:

> *'...any arrangements with respect to property of any description, including money, the purpose or effect of which is to enable persons taking part in the arrangements (whether by becoming owners of the property or any part of it or otherwise) to participate in or receive profits or income arising from the acquisition, holding, management or disposal of the property or sums*

paid out of such profits or income.'

The participants may provide directions or advice to management but need not have day-to-day control. The arrangements must have either or both of the following characteristics:

(a) that the contributions of the participants and the profits or income are pooled; and

(b) that the property is managed in its entirety by or on behalf of the operator of the Scheme.

It is out of the pooled resources that payments are to be made to the participants.

The Scheme provides for 'open-ended' companies as part of the collective investment scheme which must satisfy both the property conditions[1] and the investment conditions[2]. In determining whether the investment condition is satisfied, *'no account is to be taken of any actual or potential redemption or repurchase of shares or securities under-*

(a) *Chapter VII of Part V of the Companies Act 1985;*

(b) *Chapter VII of Part VI of the Companies (Northern Ireland) Order 1986;*

(c) *corresponding provisions in force in another EEA State; or*

(d) *provisions in force in a country or territory other than an EEA state which the Treasury has, by order, designated as corresponding provisions.'*[3]

'Unit trust scheme' is also another part of the collective investment scheme under Chapter XVII, whereby property is held in trust for the participants. An authorized person is usually prohibited from

---

[1] Under the property conditions the property will belong beneficially to and is managed by or on behalf of a body corporate for the purposes of investing its funds with the aim of spreading investment risks; and giving its members the benefit of the results of management of those funds.

[2] Under the investment condition, a reasonable investor would, if he were to participate in the Scheme, expect to realize, within a reasonable period of time, his investment in the Scheme by the value of shares in or securities of the body corporate held by him; and *'be satisfied that his investment would be realized on a basis calculated wholly or mainly by reference to the value of the property in respect of which the scheme makes arrangements'* (Section 236(3)(b).

[3] Section 236(4).

participating in a collective investment scheme when a communication of invitation or inducement to participate signifies that the scheme is outside the UK and the communication is capable of having an effect in the UK, unless the Treasury by regulations exempts single-property schemes under section 238(1), that is, a scheme which has the following characteristics and satisfies such other conditions as may be prescribed by the FSA:

(a) that the property subject to the scheme consists of:

    i. a single building, with or without ancillary buildings managed by or on behalf of the operator of the scheme; or

    ii. a group of adjacent buildings, with or without ancillary land or furniture, fittings, etc. managed by him or on his behalf as a single enterprise; and

(b) that the participants in the scheme are either dealt in on a recognized investment exchange or that any agreement for their acquisition is conditional on their admission to dealings on such an exchange.

Under this section, the Treasury has the power to make regulations exempting single-property schemes from section 238(1). The FSA may make rules imposing duties on the operator and trustee or depositary of schemes exempted under these regulations.

However, the restrictions on promotion (section 238(1)) do not apply to the following:

(a) an authorized unit trust scheme; or

(b) a scheme constituted by an authorized open-ended investment company; or

(c) a recognized scheme.

The Treasury has the power to specify circumstances in which section 238(1) does not apply, for example, in relation to communications of a specified description, or of origin in a location outside the UK.

Section 240 prevents an authorized person from approving a financial promotion under section 21[4] if the authorized person itself is prohibited

---

[4] *Restrictions on financial promotions.*

by section 238(1); if contravened, an action for damages may be brought against it in accordance with section 150.

Authorized Unit Trust Schemes

Chapter 3 of Part XVII deals with authorized unit trust schemes (sections 242-261). An application for authorization must be made to the FSA by the manager and trustee or proposed manager or trustee of the scheme. The FSA has the right to seek more information, and it may give different directions or impose different requirements in relation to different applications. A unit trust scheme may be declared an authorized scheme if the FSA is satisfied that the scheme complies with the requirements set out in section 243; that it is satisfied that the scheme complies with the requirements of the trust scheme rules; and that it has been provided with a copy of the trust deed and a certificate signed by a solicitor confirming that it complies with such of the requirements of section 243.

The manager and the trustee must be different people and independent of each other, each of them must be an authorized person with permission to act in that position a body corporate incorporated in the UK or another EEA state, have a place of business in the UK and that the affairs of each are administered in the country in which it is incorporated. Where the manager is incorporated in another EEA state, the scheme must not be one that satisfies the requirements of section 264 (which comes under recognized overseas schemes – Chapter 5). The name of the scheme must not be undesirable or misleading and the purposes of the scheme must be reasonably capable of being successfully implemented. The participants must be entitled to have their units redeemed at a price that is related to the net value of the property to which the units relate, in accordance with the scheme (section 243(10)). Those requirements will be treated as satisfied if the manager is required to ensure that a participant is able to sell his units on an investment exchange at a price that is not significantly different from that mentioned in subsection 10.

Section 242 prescribes the criteria that must be satisfied in making an application for authorization and states that an application must be determined by the FSA within six months of receipt. An applicant has the right to withdraw by giving written notice before the FSA determines it. If the FSA *proposes* to refuse an application it must give the applicant a decision notice drawing its attention to its right to appeal to the Tribunal. If the manager or trustee of a unit trust scheme that has satisfied the conditions of any relevant community investment so requires, the FSA may issue a certificate to the effect that the scheme complies with those conditions.

Under section 247 of the Act the FSA may make rules as to: the constitution, management and operation of an authorized unit trust scheme; the powers, duties, rights and liabilities of the manager and trustee of a scheme; rights and duties of the participants in any such scheme; and the winding up of such scheme.

These rules are to be known as trust scheme rules, and they may, in particular, make provisions:

a) as to the issue and redemption of units under the scheme;

b) as to the expenses of the scheme and the means of meeting them;

c) as to the appointment, removal, powers and duties of auditors of the scheme;

d) for restricting or regulating the investment and borrowing powers to be exercised in relation to the scheme;

e) requiring of record keeping with respect to transactions and for implementation of these records;

f) requiring of preparation of periodical reports with respect to the scheme and their submission to the FSA and their participants; and

g) with regard to amendment to the scheme.

Trust scheme rules, which may also make provisions as to contents of the trust deed, are binding on a manger, trustee and participants. The Treasury has the power to make modifications of the FSA's powers under the trust scheme rules if it is considered appropriate.

The FSA may also make *'scheme particulars rules'*[5] whereby the

---

[5] *'Scheme particulars'* means particulars in such form containing such information about the scheme as may be specified in the scheme particulars rules.

manager of an authorized unit trust scheme would be required to submit scheme particulars to the FSA and to publish them or make them available to the public on request, including revised or further scheme particulars in the event of a significant change affecting any matter which is contained in scheme particulars previously published or made available and the inclusion of which is required by the rules (section 248(3)).

Should a significant new matter arise, and the inclusion of information of that matter would have been necessary in previous particulars, the same rules will apply.

If it appears to the FSA that an auditor has failed to comply with a duty imposed on him by trust scheme rules, it may disqualify him from being the auditor of the Scheme or even of an authorized open-ended investment company.

The FSA may on application direct that all or any of these rules are not to apply in respect of a particular scheme.

Section 251 provides that the manager of an authorized unit trust scheme must give written notice to the FSA of any proposal to alter the scheme or to replace its trustee or manager. It is for the FSA to approve or disapprove changes of managers or trustees; and it shall not approve unless it is satisfied that, after replacement has taken effect, the scheme will continue to comply with the requirements of section 243(4)-(7) (Authorization Orders).

If, however, the FSA proposes to refuse approval of such a proposal, it must give a warning notice to the person concerned. If, however, the FSA proposes to refuse approval of a proposal to alter an authorized unit trust scheme, it must give separate warning notices to the manager and trustee of the Scheme. If after giving a warning notice to a person, the FSA decides to refuse approval, it must give him a decision notice and the person concerned may refer the matter to the Tribunal.

No provision of the Trust Deed of an authorized unit trust scheme may exempt the manager or trustee *'from liability for any failure to exercise due care and diligence in the discharge of its functions in respect of the scheme'*[6].

---

[6] Section 253.

Open-ended Investment Companies

Chapter IV of Part XVII deals with open-ended investment companies (sections 262-263). In order to facilitate the performance of collective investments by such companies, the Treasury may by regulations make provisions for such companies and the manner in which they will be regulated, in particular, they may make a provision for the incorporation and registration in UK of bodies corporate; the purposes for which such a body may exist, the investments it may issue, the management and operation, including the management of its property; the power, duties, rights and liabilities of such a body including its directors, shareholders, auditors or any person who may act or purport to act on its own behalf, and its depositary, if any; the merger of one or more of such bodies; appointment and removal of auditors, winding up and dissolution; its power to apply to act for an order removing and replacing a new director or depositary; its power to carry out investigation by persons appointed by the FSA or the Secretary of State, and corresponding to any provision made in relation to unit trust schemes included in this Scheme[7].

Regulations under this section may impose criminal liability, confer functions on the FSA, confer jurisdiction on any court or the Tribunal, modify, exclude, or apply any primary or subordinate legislation, make consequential amendments, repeals and revocations of any such legislation, and modify or exclude any rule of law. Section 263 amends section 716 of the Companies Act 1986 so that the prohibition on formation of companies with more than 20 members, other than under the Companies Act, will not apply to open-ended investment companies which may be incorporated by virtue of regulations made by the Treasury under section 262.

Recognized Overseas Schemes

Chapter 5 of Part XVII deals with recognized overseas schemes (sections 264-283), allowing a collective investment scheme constituted in other EEA states to be a recognized scheme if:

(a) it satisfies the requirements prescribed for the purposes of this section, that is by the Treasury regulations; and

---

[7] Section 262(2).

(b) that the operator of the Scheme has given notice to the FSA of not less than two months before inviting persons in the UK to participate, and specify the way in which the invitation is to be made. Failure to satisfy these requirements will disallow the scheme from recognition. A collective investment scheme is deemed to be constituted in another EEA state if it is constituted under the law of that state and is managed by a body corporate incorporated under that law, or if it takes the form of an open-ended investment company incorporated under that law[8]. The notice to be given to the FSA under section 264 must be accompanied by a certificate from the authority of the state concerned confirming that the scheme complies with the criteria necessary for it to enjoy the rights under any relevant community investment, in addition to containing the address in the UK for the service of the operator of notice or other documents. On the other hand, under the notice given by the FSA under section 264(2), that is, non-recognition of the scheme, the FSA must give reasons why the law in force in the UK will not be complied with and specify a period of not less than 28 days within which any person on whom the notice is served may make representations to the FSA. Upon receipt of representations, the FSA must decide within a reasonable period whether or not to withdraw its notice. If it should decide not to withdraw its notice, it must give a decision notice to each person and the operator of the scheme may refer the matter to the Tribunal.

An operator has the discretion to give written notice to the FSA that it does not desire the scheme to be recognized by the FSA.

Usually rules made by the FSA are not generally to apply to the operator, trustee or depositary of a recognized scheme under section 264. The FSA has the power to suspend an EEA scheme's promotion to the public if it appears that the operator has contravened promotional rules[9], after satisfying the procedures as to warning and decision notices, in addition to notifying the scheme's home state authority if it decides to give a direction under section 267[10]; the operator will have the right

---

[8] Section 264(5).
[9] Incidentally, the FSA cannot suspend an EEA scheme's recognition.
[10] This section is concerned with the power of the FSA to suspend promotion of schemes.

to refer the decision to the Tribunal. Section 267 also empowers the FSA to revoke or vary a direction suspending the promotion of an EEA scheme when the conditions specified in the direction have been complied with. Otherwise, a direction under section 267(2) has effect for a specified period, or until a specified event has occurred, or until specified conditions are complied with.

Section 268 of the Act details the procedures on giving directions under section 267 and varying them on the FSA's own initiative. If the FSA proposes to give any direction with immediate effect, it must give the operator of the scheme a written notice, and inform the home state of its proposal or direction.

The notice under section 268 must satisfy the following criteria:

a) give details of the directions;

b) inform the operator as to the date when the direction will take effect;

c) the reasons for the FSA's giving the directions;

d) inform the operator that he may make representations to the FSA within a specified period which can be extended by the FSA; and

e) inform him of his right to refer the matter to the Tribunal.

The FSA must also inform the competent authorities in the scheme's home state of the direction. After having considered any representations the FSA may decide not to give the direction in the way originally proposed, or to revoke a direction altogether.

It must give the operator of the scheme written notice and inform the competent authorities in the scheme's home state of its decision.

Section 269 details the procedure on application for variation or recognition of a direction. The FSA may propose to vary a direction or to refuse an application and give the operator of the scheme a warning notice. Where the FSA decides to vary a direction or to refuse the application, it must give a decision notice; however, the operator has the right to refer the matter to the Tribunal.

If on an application the FSA decides to grant the application, it must give the operator a written notice when it decides on its own initiative to revoke a direction issued under section 267, and it also must inform the competent authorities in the home state of the scheme of any notice given under section 269.

Section 270 considers whether a collective investment scheme managed under the law of a non-EEA countries may be recognized. It may be recognized if the country or territory is designated for the purposes of this section by an order of the Treasury, and the operator of the scheme must have given written notice to the FSA confirming that he wishes it to be recognized.

No order designating any country or territory for the purpose of section 270 may be made by the Treasury unless it is satisfied that: the law and practice under which the scheme is authorized and supervised in that foreign country or territory affords at least protection equivalent to that provided by the UK law on the collective investments scheme; and adequate arrangements already exist or will exist for cooperation between the authorities of a country or territory concerned and the FSA.

The Treasury may ask the FSA for a report of law and practice in that country or territory or any existing or proposed arrangements for cooperation between the foreign country or territory and the FSA. Again, if the FSA proposes to refuse approval of the scheme under section 270 it must go through the procedures of warning and decision notices, and in the case of a decision notice, it must provide the operator with an opportunity to refer the matter to the Tribunal.

Individually Recognized Overseas Schemes

The FSA may on the application of an operator of a collective investment scheme that is managed outside the UK and which does not satisfy the criteria of recognized organized overseas schemes under section 264, and is not managed in jurisdiction which is designated to countries or territories, but appears to it to satisfy requirements of section 272 (Individually recognized overseas schemes), make an order declaring the scheme to be a recognized scheme. The general criteria that such a scheme must satisfy are:

(a) participants in the scheme will have adequate protection;

(b) the arrangements for the scheme constitution must be adequate; and

(c) the powers and duties of the operator and, and if there is trustee or a depositary, of the trustee or depositary must be adequate.

However, an individually recognized overseas scheme must take the form of an open-ended investment company or the operator must be a body corporate. In the event of the operator being an authorized person, he must have permission to act as an operator and if he is not an authorized person, he must be a fit and proper person to act as an operator[11].

The FSA must ensure that the operator or the trustee or depositary must be able and willing to cooperate with it; that the name of the scheme is not undesirable or misleading; that the purposes of the scheme are such as may be reasonably capable of being successfully carried out; and that the participants must be entitled to have their units redeemed. In determining whether a person is a fit and proper person to act as a trustee or depositary, or an operator, the FSA may take into account any matter relating to the following:

'(a) any person who is or will be employed by or associated with the operator, trustee or depositary in connection with the scheme;

(b) any director of the operator, trustee or depositary;

(c) any person exercising influence over the operator, trustee or depositary;

(d) any body corporate in the same group as the operator, trustee or depositary;

(e) any director of any such body corporate;

(f) any person exercising influence over any such body corporate.'[12]

Application for a recognition of individual schemes must be made to the FSA who must decide on such applications within six months following the usual procedure of written notice, decision notice, and referred to the Tribunal. Under section 279 the FSA has the power to direct that a scheme be ceased to be recognized or be revoked if it appears to the FSA:

---

[11] The legal aspects of a fit and proper person have been discussed in Chapter 3.
[12] Section 273.

(a) that the operator, trustee or depositary of the scheme has contravened any requirement under this Act;

(b) that the operator, trustee or depositary has knowingly or recklessly given the FSA information which is false or misleading in any important respect;

(c) that, in the case of an order issued under section 272, that one or more of the requirements for the making of the order are no longer satisfied; or

(d) although none of the above may apply, but it is nevertheless undesirable for the interests of participants or potential participants that the scheme should be allowed to be continued to be recognized.

Again, in exercising this power the procedure of warning notice and decision notice applies. Directions may be issued by the FSA, under sections 281 and 282. The FSA must justify the reasons for giving the direction and inform the person concerned of his right to make representations to the FSA by a stipulated date, and also of his right to refer the matter to the Tribunal.

If the FSA should find the representations meritorious, then it may revoke a direction or refuse to revoke a direction, or can give a direction in a way other than that proposed.

Recognized Investment Houses and Clearing Houses

A recognized investment exchange or a recognized clearing house is exempt from the requirement of authorization. The Treasury may make regulations setting out the qualifications for recognition which must be satisfied by an investment exchange or a clearing house.

According to subsection (1) of section 286, 'default rules' are those rules of an investment exchange or a clearing house on the basis of which actions may be brought in the event of a person's appearing to be unable or likely to be unable to meet his obligations pertaining to a market contract connected with the exchange or clearing house[13].

[13] *'Market contract' means:*
(a) a contract to which Part VII of the Companies Act 1989 applies as a result of section 155 of that Act or a contract to which Part V of the Companies (No. 2)(Northern Ireland) Order 1990 applies as a result of Article 80 of that Order; and
(b) such other kind of contract as may be prescribed.' Section 286(4)).

Under section 287 any body corporate or unincorporated association may apply to the FSA for recognition. The application must be accompanied by:

(a) a copy of the applicant's rules;
(b) a copy of any guidance issued by the applicant;
(c) the required particulars; and
(d) such other information as the FSA may require for considering an application.

Usually, an applicant is required to provide information on arrangements for clearing services on the exchange or otherwise, and particulars of the criteria which the applicant will apply in determining to whom it will provide these services[14].

It is also possible to apply to the FSA for recognition as a clearing house under section 288 by applying similar criteria to investment exchange criteria described above[15]. The FSA can ask for supplementary information from an investment exchange or clearing house and make a recognition order or refuse to do so. It is important to note that:

> '(1) A recognized body and its officers and staff are not to be liable in damages for anything done or omitted in the discharge of the recognized body's regulatory functions[16] unless it is shown that the act or omission was in bad faith.'[17]

But this provision does not prevent an award of damages made in respect of an act or omission which would be regarded as unlawful under section 6(1) of the Human Rights Act 1998.

An overseas investment exchange or an overseas clearing house may also make an application under section 287 or 288, but it must have an address in the UK for the service of notices or other documents. In order to be recognized by the FSA, the following requirements must be satisfied:

---

[14] Section 287(3)(b).
[15] Section 288.
[16] 'Regulatory functions' means 'the functions of the recognized body so far as relating to, or to matters arising out of, the obligations to which the body is subject under or by virtue of this Act.'
[17] Section 291(1).

a) that investors are afforded protection in the same manner as a local body corporate;

b) that there exist adequate procedures for dealing with a person who is unable or likely to become unable to meet his obligations under market contracts connected with the investment exchange or clearing house concerned;

c) that the applicant is able and willing to cooperate with the FSA in sharing information and in respect of other relevant matters; and

d) that adequate arrangements exist for cooperation between the FSA and the supervisory authority in the home country of the overseas investment exchange or clearing house.

It is for the FSA to satisfy itself, and in its own interest, for the overseas institution to disclose all information and cooperate with the FSA in all possible ways. The FSA will have regard to the relevant law and practice of the jurisdiction in which the applicant's head office is situated, in addition to paying attention to the rules and practices of the applicant.

Under section 293, a recognized body may be required to provide any information the FSA may require of it. Section 293(3) provides that an obligation imposed by the rules *'extends only to a notice or information which the Authority [FSA] may reasonably require*[18] *for the exercise of its functions under this Act'*. However, if a recognized body alters or revokes any of its rules or guidance or makes new rules or issues new guidance it must give the FSA a written notice to that effect as soon as possible. By the same token, if a recognized investment exchange makes a change in the arrangement of clearing services or in the criteria it would apply in determining to whom it would provide clearing services, the FSA must be notified, in writing, accordingly as soon as possible[19].

A recognized body may request the FSA to modify or waive rules made under section 293 *(Notification Requirements)* or section 294 *(Notification: Overseas Investment Exchange and Overseas Clearing Houses)*. The FSA may not give a direction unless it is satisfied that the compliance with the rules by the recognized body would be unduly

---

[18] What is *'reasonably required'* will be determined by the FSA, although it may be subject to challenge by a recognized body.

[19] Section 293(5)-(7).

burdensome or would not achieve the purpose for which the rules were made, and that the direction would not result in an undue risk to persons whose interests the rules intend to protect[20]. Overseas investment exchanges and overseas clearing houses must submit to the FSA, at least annually, a report containing a statement as to whether any events have occurred that are likely to affect the FSA's assessment made under section 292 or to have any effect on competition; copies of the report must be submitted to the Treasury.

Should a recognized body fail or be likely to fail to satisfy the recognition requirements or has actually failed to comply with any other obligations imposed on it by the Act, the FSA may give that body directions for taking specified steps in order to secure compliance. A direction under section 296 is enforceable by an injunction or by an order for specific performance[21].

A recognition order may be revoked by another order made by the FSA if it appears to the FSA that a recognized body is failing or has failed to satisfy the recognition requirements or any obligation imposed on it by the Act. Usually, a three months' period is given for revocation. Before giving a direction order, or a revocation order, the FSA must give a written notice to the recognized body, or take steps to bring such notice to the attention of the members of that body, or to publish a notice to bring it to the attention of other persons who are likely to be affected, stating the reason for giving such direction or making such an order. It must allow a body concerned two months to make representations unless the FSA has allowed any longer period, and must have regard to any representations made. Where the FSA has decided to give a direction under section 296 or to make a revocation order it must give a written notice to that effect; and if a direction or order is made, then it must take such steps as will be considered reasonably practicable for bringing its decision to the attention of the members of a recognized body or other persons who are in the FSA's opinion likely to be affected.

The FSA has the power to a complaint which the Authority [the FSA] considers is relevant to the question of whether the body concerned should remain a recognized body,'[22] about a recognized body and must

---

[20] Section 294(4).
[21] In Scotland section 45 of the Court of Session Act 1988.

make arrangements for that purpose.

Where a decision has been taken to take disciplinary proceedings it will be referred to the Tribunal in light of the Human Rights Act 1998, and disciplinary proceedings in this context would mean *'proceedings under the rules of an investment exchange or clearing house in relation to market abuse by persons subject to the rules'*.[23]

The Treasury and the Secretary of State must be satisfied that it should be appropriate for the FSA to supervise settlement arrangements for non-investments contracts, and under subsection 4 of section 301 the Treasury must approve the conditions set by the FSA for admission to the list maintained by the FSA and the arrangements for admission to and removal from the list.

It is for the FSA to publish the list prevalent at a particular time, and provide a certified copy of it to any person who may wish to refer to it in legal proceedings. Section 301(10) allows the Treasury and the Secretary of State to make regulations that will apply to any of the provisions of this Act to the person settling non-investment contracts. This power is essential as otherwise it will be impossible for the FSA to regulate such persons on a statutory basis because they would not require authorization or exemption.

Competition Scrutiny

It is possible that regulatory provisions (rules, guidance, arrangements and particulars) can have an adverse effect on competition. Section 302(2) provides that regulatory provisions or practices have a significantly adverse effect on competition if:

'(a) they have, or are intended or likely to have, that effect; or

(b) the effect that they have, or are intended or likely to have, is to require or encourage behaviour which has, or is intended or likely to have, a significantly adverse effect on competition.'

The FSA is required to send to the Treasury and the Director General of Fair Trading copies of regulatory provisions and all information

---

[22] Section 299.
[23] Section 300(4).

received in support of an application for recognition, to enable the latter to ascertain whether any regulatory provision or practice has a significantly adverse effect on competition and if so, to make report, stating his reasons for reaching that conclusion. The Director General must send his report to the FSA, the Competition Commission and the Treasury. If the Competition Commission concludes that no significantly adverse effect on competition exists or if such effect does exist, but is justified, then the Treasury is required to approve the making of a recognition order unless exceptional circumstances exist to justify a refusal of the order. On the other hand, if the Competition Commission's report confirms that a significantly adverse effect on competition exists but is not justified, then the Treasury is required to refuse to approve the making of a recognition order unless exceptional circumstances exist.

Section 308 authorizes the Treasury to take action following an adverse report from the Commission other than a report on an application for a recognition order, by the Treasury issuing a remedial direction to the FSA. But, this does not apply if the Treasury considers it is unnecessary for it to give a direction or that the exceptional circumstances of the case would make it inappropriate or unnecessary for the Treasury to do so. If the action specified in a remedial direction is the giving by the FSA of a direction it must be compatible with the recognition requirements applicable to the recognized body.

'Remedial direction' means a direction whereby the FSA is required to revoke a recognition order for the body concerned, or to give such direction to the body concerned as may be specified in it[24]. Where, however, the Treasury gives a direction under section 308, the direction must detail the reason for it, place a copy of it before Parliament and publish a statement in the way that would best bring it to the attention of the public. The Treasury must provide an opportunity to those concerned to make a representation on any report made by the Director-General of Fair Trading under section 303 or 304 or by the Competition Commission under section 306, and must pay attention to the responses to representations.

---

[24] Section 308(8).

Conclusions

Under a collective investment scheme a participant will not have a day-to-day central role over the management of the property which is the subject matter of the investment. The basis of the scheme is that the property belongs to and is managed by or on behalf of a body corporate with the aim of spreading investment risk and providing its members with the benefit which may accrue from that management of those funds by or on behalf of that body[25].

The legislation is clear that an authorized person must not communicate an invitation or inducement to participate in a collective investment scheme[26]. The inclusion of unit trust schemes (provided they are authorized) in the collective investment scheme is a novel idea, and control by the FSA over all aspects of collective investment schemes should provide investors security of investment and confidence in the scheme.

---

[25] Section 236.
[26] Section 238.

11 Control of Business Transfers

Introduction

Part VII of the Act is concerned with the issues of control of business transfer schemes (sections 104-114) in relation to insurance business and banking business. Whereas control of insured business transfer schemes pertains to such businesses carried on, whether in whole or in part, in one or more of the EEA Member State(s), no such limitation exists in respect of banking business transfer schemes. Certain business, such as friendly societies or credit unions, are excluded from these schemes, as per section 105.

Control of Business Transfers

Section 104 of the Act provides that:

> 'No insurance business transfer Compensation Scheme or banking business transfer Compensation Scheme is to have effect unless an order has been made in relation to it under section 111(1).'

Section 111(1) sets out:

> '...the conditions which must be satisfied before the court may make an order under this section sanctioning an insurance business transfer Compensation Scheme or a banking business transfer Compensation Scheme.'

These conditions are that the court must be satisfied in regard to the appropriate certificates must have been obtained[1], and the transferee must have the required authentication for carrying on business in the place to which the business is to be transferred.

An *'authorized transfer'* stands for a transfer authorized in the home state of the EEA firm in accordance with Article 11 of the Third Life Directive[2]; or Article 12 of the Third Non-Life Directive[3]. In the case of an EEA firm, other than the UK firms, it must comply with Article 31(a) of the First Life Directive[4]; or Article 28(a) of the First Non-Life Directive[5].

Section 105 defines an insurance business transfer Compensation Scheme, which must satisfy one of the following conditions:

(a) that the business, whether in its entirety or in part, carried on in one or more Member States by a UK authorized 'person who has permission to effect or carry out contracts of insurance ("the authorized person concerned") is to be transferred to another body ("the transferee")' (section 105(2)(a)); or

(b) that in respect of a re-insurance business, it is carried on, whether in its entirety or in part, in the UK through an establishment there by an EEA firm qualified for authorization under Schedule 3 to effect or carry out contracts of insurance and is to be transferred to another body; or

(c) if an authorized person, who is neither a UK authorized person nor an EEA firm, but its business, whether in its entirety or in part, is carried on in the UK, and has permission to effect or carry out contracts of insurance, is to be transferred to another body.

A Compensation Scheme is also an insurance business transfer Compensation Scheme if it is a business actively operational and transferred from an establishment of the transferee (transferred to another body) in an EEA state, and it is not an excluded Compensation Scheme.

For the purpose of section 105, a Compensation Scheme is *an*

[1] See Parts I and II of Schedule 12.
[2] Article 11.
[3] Article 12.
[4] Article 31(a).
[5] Article 28(a).

'excluded Compensation Scheme' if it falls within any of the following cases:

1. if the authorized person concerned is a friendly society;
2. (a) if the authorized person concerned is a UK person;
   (b) if the business to be transferred under the Compensation Scheme is a business that effects or carries out contracts of re-insurance in one or more EEA states other than the United Kingdom; and
   (c) if the Compensation Scheme has been approved by a court in an EEA state other than a court in the UK or of the host state regulator;
(3) (a) where the authorized person is a UK authorized person;
   (b) the business to be transferred under the Compensation Scheme is operational/carried on in one country or more or territories, but not in an EEA state, and deals exclusively with re-insurance (but not with policies of insurance against risks arising in an EEA state); and
   (c) the Compensation Scheme has been approved by a court in a country or territory other than an EEA state or is approved by the supervisory authority in the country or territory in which the business is carried on.
(4) If the business transferred under the Compensation Scheme is to be the whole of the business of the authorized person concerned and consists solely of effecting or carrying out re-insurance contracts, or all policyholders are controllers of the firm or firms within the same group as the firm which is the transferee and in either case the policyholders who would be affected by the transfer must have consented to it (section 105(3) Case 4). The parties which come under Case 2, 3 or 4 may apply to the court seeking an order sanctioning the Compensation Scheme as if it were an insurance business transfer Compensation Scheme.
(5) A UK person in the context of section 105 means an authorized

person which is incorporated in the UK or is an unincorporated association formed under the law of any part of the United Kingdom.

The term *'establishment'* under this section means in relation to a person, its head office or a branch of establishment.

Any application for a court order sanctioning an insurance business transfer Compensation Scheme must be accompanied by a Compensation Scheme report prepared only by a person who, according to the Authority (presumably the competent authority), has the skills necessary for preparing such a report and who has been nominated as approved for the purpose by the Authority. The Treasury may impose requirements under section 107 and the court may not determine an application should the applicant fail to comply with a prescribed requirement. The Treasury's requirements may, in particular, include provisions as to the persons to whom and the duration for which notice of an application must be given and provision to enable the court to waive a requirement of the regulations in prescribed circumstances (section 108).

If a court order has been made under section 111(1) the court may appoint an independent actuary to investigate the business transferred under the Compensation Scheme, and to report to the FSA if any reduction in the benefits payable under policies issued by the authorized person concerned ought to be made. Section 114 gives certain policyholders certain rights in relation to an insurance business transfer Compensation Scheme if:

(a) the authorized person is not an EEA firm qualifying for authorization under Schedule 3;

(b) if the court has made an order under section 111 in relation to the Compensation Scheme; and

(c) if an EEA state other than the UK is the state of the commitment or the EEA state in which the risk is situated in relation to any policy included in the transfer which evidences a contract of insurance.

The court must direct that notice of the making of an order to give the effect of transfer must be published by the transferee in the EEA concerned specifying the period during which the policyholder may exercise his right to cancel his policy. Such an order does not bind the policyholder if the notice required under section 114(2) need not be published or the policyholder cancels the policy during the period specified in that notice.

Part III of Schedule 2 details the provision about certificates that the FSA may issue in relation to insurance business transfer effected outside the UK namely:

(a) the transferor is an EEA firm coming under paragraph (5)(d) of Schedule 3 and that the transferee is an authorized person where the solvency margin is supervised by the Authority;

(b) that *'the transferor is authorized in an EEA state other than the UK under Article 27 of the First Life Insurance Directive or Article 23 of the First Non-Life Insurance Directive and the transferee is a United Kingdom authorized person having been authorized under Article 6 of either of these directives'*; and

(c) that the transferor is a Swiss general insurer and the transferee is the UK authorized person having been authorized under Article 6 of the First Life Insurance Directive or the First Non-Life Insurance Directive.

The transferee must satisfy the conditions of the necessary margin of solvency[6] and the Authority shall issue a certificate to that effect.

Section 116 applies if as a consequence of the authorized transfer, an authorized company in an EEA state other than the UK under Article 27 of the First Life Insurance Directive or Article 23 of the First Non-Life Insurance Directive transfers to another body all its rights and obligations under any United Kingdom policy. If an appropriate notice of instrument has given effect to the transfer, that instrument has the effect in law of transferring to the transferee all the transferor's rights and obligations under the UK policy to which the investment applies[7].

Banking Business Transfer Compensation Schemes

Section 106 states that a Compensation Scheme is a banking business

---

[6] It means the margin of solvency which according to the Authority the transferee is required to maintain taking into account the proposed transfer of the business.

[7] See also Section 116(3)(b).

transfer Compensation Scheme if it satisfies one of the following conditions:

(a) that a business, whether in its entirety or in part, is carried on by a UK authorized person, which has permission to accept deposits (the authorized person) is to be transferred to another body (the transferee)[8], or

(b) where the business of an authorized person who is not a UK authorized person but who has permission to accept deposits (the authorized person concerned), whether in full or in part, is to be transferred to another body which will carry on the business in the UK (the transferee).

Furthermore, a Compensation Scheme is a banking business transfer Compensation Scheme if it is one 'under which the whole or part of the business to be transferred includes the accepting of deposits';[9] and is not an excluded Compensation Scheme. Under the excluded Compensation Schemes fall a building society or a credit union, as an authorized person, or if the Compensation Scheme is a compromise or an arrangement under section 427A(1) of the Companies Act 1985 or Article 420A of the Companies (Northern Ireland) Order 1986.

The 'UK authorized person' under this section has the same meaning as in section 105 of the Act. The term 'Building Society' is to be understood as an institution which is governed by the Building Society's Act 1986, and a 'credit union' means a credit union within the meaning of the Credit Unions Act 1979 and the Credit Union (Northern Ireland) Order 1985.

Common Provisions between an Insurance Transfer Compensation Scheme and Banking

An application in regard to an application for an order sanctioning a transfer Compensation Scheme may be made by either an authorized person concerned or a transferee, or both, provided that both are

---

[8] Section 106(4) provides however that: *'For the purposes of subsection (2)(a) it is immaterial whether or not the business to be transferred is carried on in the United Kingdom.'*
[9] Section 106(1)(b).

registered or their head offices are located in the same jurisdiction to the court. Where they are registered or have their head offices in different jurisdictions then the court can be in either jurisdiction. If the transferee is not registered in the UK nor does it have its head office here, then the court is that which has jurisdiction over the authorized person concerned. The Treasury may impose requirements on applicants and unless complied with the court may include provisions as to the persons and the periods by which notice of an application must be given or may allow the court to waive the requirement of the regulations in specified circumstances. Section 111 prescribes the conditions that must be satisfied before the court may make an order under this section sanctioning an insurance business Compensation Scheme or a banking business Compensation Scheme. The court has the ultimate discretion whether, by reference to the circumstances of the case, it would be appropriate to sanction the Compensation Scheme. Where the court may make an order under section 111(1) it may also make an order at its own discretion for the transfer of an undertaking in its entirety or in part and of any property or liabilities of the authorized person concerned to the transferee:

(a) '...for the allotment or appropriation by the transferee of any shares, debentures, policies or other similar interests in the transferee which under the Compensation Scheme are to be allotted or appropriated to or for any other person;

(b) ...for the continuation by (or against) the transferee of any pending legal proceedings by (or against) the authorized person concerned;

(c) *with respect to such incidental, consequential and supplementary matters as are, in its opinion, necessary to secure that the Compensation Scheme is fully and effectively carried out.*"[10]

Section 112(2) relates to transfer of property or liabilities. If any property or liabilities included in a court order are governed by the law of a country outside the UK, the order may require the authorized person concerned, to ensure that the transfer of the property or liability is fully effective under the law of that country.

[10] Section 112(b)-(d).

In the event of making an order under section 111(1) in relation to an insurance business Compensation Scheme, it has discretionary power to add by that or a subsequent order provision for dealing with the interest of any such person who may object to the Compensation Scheme or for a dissolution of the authorized person concerned or for the reduction of the benefits payable on such terms and conditions as it may think fit under any restriction or policy generally.

Conclusions

Part VII of the Act is, in reality, in conformity with the *'passport rights'* of EEA firms. The organization structure of the firm, and the permission to effect or carry out insurance and re-insurance contracts, prove to be important criteria for taking advantage of the provisions of this Act, in addition to satisfying in certain cases that all the policyholders are controllers of the firm or firms within the same group as the firm that is the transferee[11].

The Act makes provisions for the right of appeal of a policyholder in the case of an insurance business or of a person affected by a refusal of a banking business transfer scheme.

Like many other provisions of the Act, the issues of control of business transfers may need to be reviewed. Section 117(b) of the Act which comes under *Modifications* provides that the Treasury may by regulations:

> *'make such amendments to any provision of this Part as they consider appropriate for the more effective operation of that or any other provision of this Part.'*

---

[11] Section 105(4).

12 Official Listing

Introduction

This Part of the Act deals with the following items: the competent authority; the official list; listing; listing particulars; prospectuses; sponsors; compensation; penalties; competition and miscellaneous.

Under this Act, the FSA is the competent authority (see Schedule 7), and by Schedule 8 the Treasury may confer on the FSA any function under this Act.

In discharging its general functions, the competent authority (the FSA) must have regard to:

(a) the need to use its resources in the most economic and efficient way;

(b) that a burden or restriction which may be imposed on a person should be proportionate to the benefits which are expected to arise from the imposition of that burden or restriction;

(c) the need for facilitating innovation in respect of listed securities;

(d) the desirability of maintaining the international character of capital markets and the competitive position of the UK;

(e) the need to minimize the adverse effect on competition emanating from anything done in the discharge of those functions; and

(f) the desirability of facilitating competition pertaining to listed securities (section 73).

Under this Part, the general functions of the FSA are: the making of rules under this Part; the giving of general guidance in relation to this Part; and determination of the general policy and principles in regard to the functions performed under this Part.

The FSA must maintain the official list and confirm which securities may be admitted in conformity with the requirements of Part VI. The FSA has the authority to make rules (Listing Rules), and in context of this Part, 'security' would mean anything that has been or may be admitted to the official list, and listing would mean a security being included in the official list.

Application for admission to the official list must be made to the FSA, and may be entertained by the FSA only if it is made by, or with the consent of, the issuer of the securities concerned.

The FSA may not grant an application for listing unless it is satisfied that the requirements of the Listing Rules are complied with. One of the grounds for refusal would be that in the opinion of the FSA the granting of an application would be detrimental to the interests of investors. An application for listing securities that are officially listed in another EEA state may be refused if the issuer in the home state has failed to comply with any obligations to which he is subject as an entity of listing.

The decision of the FSA must be notified to an applicant within six months or if within that period the FSA required the applicant to provide further information in connection with the application then before the end of six months. Absence of notification by this period(s) would indicate that the FSA has decided to refuse the application. Where the FSA decides to grant an application for listing, a written notice must be given to the applicant, and if it proposes to refuse an application, a warning notice to that effect must be given to the applicant. Where, however, the an application for listing is refused, it must give the applicant a decision notice. The applicant has the right to refer the decision to the Tribunal. Where securities are admitted with the Official List, the question that the conditions for their admission have not been complied with cannot be raised, although it is possible to suspend or withdraw admission at a later date on breach of obligations by the applicant (section 77(1) and (2)). If, however, securities are suspended, for the purposes of section 96 (Obligations of Issuers of Listed Securities) and section 99 (Payment of Fees by Applicant for inclusion in the Listing Rules), they will still be treated as being listed. Suspension of listing of any securities may be challenged by the issuer and the matter will be referred to the Tribunal.

Listing Particulars

Listing particulars refers to a document containing information specified in the Listing Rules and these Particulars must be provided in the prescribed form. The persons who may be responsible for listing particulars are to be determined in accordance with regulations made by the Treasury. It is believed that eligibility for listing will be very similar to those currently listed in the Listing Rules.

General Duty of Disclosure

Section 80 of the Act provides that in order to protect the interests of investors, an issuer of securities has a general duty of disclosure in listing particulars of listed securities; professional advisers should be allowed to acquire information on securities to make an informal assessment of assets and liabilities, financial state of health, profits and losses and prospects of the issuer of securities and the rights attaching to the securities. The information is also required by the FSA as a condition of admission. *'Information'* means the information that is *'within the knowledge of any person responsible for the listing of particulars';* or *'which it would be reasonable for him to obtain'* [1].

In determining 'information' regard must be had, in particular, to the nature of securities and the standing of the issuer in the financial world; the nature of the persons who may consider acquiring them; the information that may reasonably be expected to be within the knowledge of professional advisers and the information which prospective investors may reasonably be expected to consult, and

> *'any information available to investors or their professional advisers as a result of requirements imposed on the issuer of the securities by a recognized investment*

---

[1] Section 80(3)(a) and (b).

exchange, by Listing Rules or by or under any other enactment.' [2]

If, after the listing particulars have been prepared and submitted to the FSA under section 79, and prior to commencing dealings, a significant change affecting those particulars was required by section 80[3], Listing Rules or the FSA or that a significant new matter has arisen which may have a significant effect on the securities, the issuer must submit supplementary listing particulars of the change or new matter to the FSA for its approval, and to allow it to publish them. The term *'significant'* in this context means: *'significant for the purpose of making informal assessment of the kind mentioned in section 80(1)'* [4].

Dispensation from Disclosure

Exemptions from disclosure may be allowed only on the grounds: that the disclosure would be contrary to the public interest; or that the disclosure of certain information would be seriously detrimental to the issuer of securities; or that in respect of securities of a kind specified in Listing Rules, their disclosure is unnecessary for persons *'of the kind who may be expected normally to buy or deal in securities of that kind'*[5].

But no dispensation from disclosure may be granted in respect of essential information, even when it may be maintained that disclosure would be contrary to the public interest or detrimental to the issuer. On the other hand, the Secretary of State or the Treasury may issue a certificate confirming that the disclosure of any information would be contrary to the public interest. *'Essential information'* in this context would mean the kind of information that a prospective acquirer of securities of the kind in question would require for making an informal assessment.

Particulars of listing are to be delivered for registration to the registrar of companies before they are published (including supplementary listing particulars) and details of their securities (failure to publish is a

---

[2] Section 80(4)(d).
[3] Disclosure in Listing particulars.
[4] Informal assessment of the assets and liabilities, financial position and losses, the prospects of the issuer of the securities and the rights attaching to the securities (section 80(1)).
[5] Section 82 (1) and (2) of the Act.

punishable offence). *'New Securities'* are those securities *'which are to be offered to the public in the United Kingdom for the first time before admission to the official list'* (section 84(2)), and to be admitted to the official list a prospectus must be prepared according to the requirements of the Listing Rules. The prospectus must be approved by the FSA in the following circumstances:

(a) if securities are to be offered to the public in the UK for the first time;

(b) if no application for listing of the securities has been made under Part VI of the Act *(Official Listing)*; and

(c) if the prospectus is submitted by or with the consent of the issuer of the securities.

A person may be required to make arrangements with a sponsor as may be specified in the Listing Rules. Sponsors must be approved by the FSA. Listing Rules may also specify the circumstances in which a person may be regarded as qualified for being approved as a sponsor. However, if the FSA proposes to refuse a person's application for approval as a sponsor or cancels a person's approval as a sponsor, it must give him a warning notice. Where, however, the FSA changes its decision, whether in the form of an approval or a reaffirmation of its previous finding, a decision notice must be served on the person concerned. The recipient of a decision notice has the right to appeal to the Tribunal.

In the event of a sponsor contravening a requirement imposed on him by rules made in pursuance of section 83(3)(c), a statement to that effect may be published, as a measure of public censure of the sponsor. A warning notice setting out the terms of the proposed statement is served on the sponsor and if the FSA decides to make the proposed statement it must give the sponsor a decision notice setting out the terms of the statement. A sponsor who receives a decision notice may refer the matter to the Tribunal.

Supplying any false or misleading information is a punishable offence incurring liability, and is liable to pay compensation to the person who has suffered losses in consequence thereof. Section 90(3) provides that:

'If listing particulars are required to include information

> *about the absence of a particular matter, the omission from the particulars of that information is to be treated as a statement in the listing particulars that there is no such matter.'*

Section 90(8) provides that:

> *'No person shall, by reason of being a promoter of a company or otherwise, incur any liability for failing to disclose information which he would not be required to disclose in listing particulars in respect of a company's securities-*
>
> *(a) if he were responsible for those particulars; or*
>
> *(b) if he is responsible for them, which he is entitled to omit by virtue of section 82.'*[6]

Section 91 is concerned with penalties for breach of Listing Rules.

Schedule 10 to the Act states that 'statement' in the context of compensation would mean any false or misleading statement provided in the listing particulars or any omission from listing particulars which was required to be included by section 80 or section 81 of the Act. The only exception on which such a person can rely is in paragraph 2 of Schedule 10, that is, primarily at the time of submission of listing particulars to the FSA the person concerned having made such inquires as were reasonable, reasonably believed that the statement was true and not misleading or that the matter which caused losses because of omission was properly omitted. Under Schedule 10 'statement' would also include statements by experts as well as statements made with the consent of another person, that is, an expert[7].

Paragraph 2 of Schedule 10 provides that:

> *'A person does not incur any liability under section 90(1) for loss caused by a statement if he satisfies the court that, at the time when the listing particulars were submitted to the competent authority, he reasonably*

---

[6] This section is concerned with *Exemptions from Disclosure*.

[7] *'Expert'* in this context would include any engineer, valuer, or other person whose profession, qualifications or experience authorizes him to make a statement under paragraph 8 of Schedule 10.

> *believed (having made such enquiries, if any, as were reasonable) that:*
>
> *(a) the statement was true and not misleading, or*
>
> *(b) the matter whose omission caused the loss was properly omitted,*
>
> *and that one or more of the conditions set out in sub-paragraph (3) are satisfied.'*

There will be no liability for losses caused by a statement if the court is satisfied that the statement was properly corrected before the securities were acquired and published in the manner calculated to bring it to the attention of a person likely to acquire the securities, or that he took all reasonable steps to secure such publication and reasonably believed that it had taken place before the securities were acquired. Similar protections are available in respect of expert reports or reports published with the consent of an expert.

Paragraph 5(b) states that if he satisfies the court that the statement is accurately and fairly reproduced, a person shall not incur any liability under section 90(1) or (4) provided the court is satisfied that the person who suffered losses acquired the securities in question in the knowledge that the statement was false or misleading or an important matter was omitted or a new matter introduced. By the same token, a person does not incur liability under section 90(4) if he satisfies the court *'that he reasonably believed a new matter in question was not such as to call for supplementary listing particulars.'*[8]

Under section 91 of the Act, the FSA has total authority to take any steps under Part VI, in addition to imposing a penalty of such amount as it may consider appropriate on the person concerned *'who was at the material time a director of the issuer or applicant who was knowingly concerned in the contravention'*. However, the FSA may not take action against a person under section 91 after two years after it knew of the contravention (section 91(6)).

If a decision has been made to take action against a person, then the section 92 procedure must be activated, initially by giving a warning notice, stating the proposal for imposing a penalty of a determined sum,

---

[8] Paragraph 7 of Schedule 10.

and that the FSA would publish a statement, and the terms of the proposed statement must also be set out in that notice. The affected person has the right to refer the matter to the Tribunal.

Under section 93 of the Act the FSA is required to issue a policy statement with respect to imposition of penalties under section 91 and the amount thereof. In determining the amount of penalty, the seriousness of contravention in question, the extent of that contravention, whether it was deliberate or reckless, and whether the person concerned is an individual or not may be considered. The FSA has the right to alter or replace its policy statement. The attention of the public must also be drawn to those statements. An altered or replaced statement must be preceded by a draft version of which must brought to the attention of the public for the purpose of seeking representations on the contents of such statements. Where the statement differs from the draft, the FSA must publish the details of the differences.

The Treasury has to prove to keep under review the practice of the FSA, in particular whether any regulatory provisions or practice has or may have a significantly adverse effect on competition.

Under section 97 of the Act the FSA may appoint persons to carry out investigations when, in its opinion, there may have been a breach of the Listing Rules, that a director at a material time in issuing securities has been knowingly concerned in a breach of Listing Rules, and the director of a person applying for admission of securities to official listing has been knowingly concerned in a breach of Listing Rules, and that there may have been a contravention of section 83 *(Registration of Listing Particulars)*, section 85 *(Obligation of Prospectus)* or section 98 *(Advertisement in connection with Listing Application)*.

Investigations or any publicity material in connection with listing applications may not be published in the UK unless the contents of an advertisement or other information has been approved by the FSA. A person who contravenes this condition is guilty of an offence, unless he shows that *'he believed on reasonable grounds that the advertisement or information had been approved, or is authorized by the competent authority'*[9].

Depending upon the case, the Listing Rules may make different provisions. The FSA may be authorized by the Listing Rules to dispense

---

[9] Section 98(3)).

with or modify the application of the Rules in particular cases.

The competent authority is immune from any liability in so far as its functions under Part VI are concerned. Section 102(1) provides that:

> 'Neither the competent authority nor any person who is, or is acting as, a member, officer or member of staff of the competent authority is to be liable in damages for anything done or omitted in the discharge, or purported discharge, of the authority's functions.'

There are two exceptions: if the act or omission is shown to have been in bad faith, or

> 'so as to prevent an award of damages made in respect of an act or omission on the ground that the act or omission was unlawful as a result of section 6(1) of the Human Rights Act 1998.'[10]

Discontinuance or Suspension

'Discontinuance' means a discontinuance of listing under section 77(1), that is, if the FSA is satisfied that because of special circumstances normal dealing with securities must be discontinued, whereas suspension means a suspension under section 77(2), that is, the FSA has a discretionary power but such power may be justified when considered in relation to the protection of investors. Both may take effect immediately or from the date stated in the notice.

In either case the FSA must give written notice to the issuer stating the reason therefor, the date on which it will take effect and specifying the date by which he must exercise his right to make representations to the FSA in addition to informing him of his right to refer this matter to the Tribunal.

However, where the FSA, having considered any representations made in response to a warning notice, decides to refuse an application, then it must give the issuer of the securities a decision notice, but if having considered a representation made in response to a decision notice, the Competent authority grants the application, it must give the

[10] Section 102(2)(b).

issuer of the securities a written notice of its decision. However, the applicant has the right to refer the matter of refusal or suspension to the Tribunal. It is to be emphasized that any decision by the FSA as to refusal or suspension or discontinuance of listing of securities is to protect the interests of investors.

Conclusions

Under the previous system, applications for admission to the Listing Rules were to be made to the London International Stock Exchange; under the Act of 2000, applications for admission to the Official List must be made to the FSA in the manner prescribed by Listing Rules; furthermore no application for admission to the Official List may be made to the FSA unless it is made by, or with the consent of, the issuer of the securities concerned. Again, in approving of an application for admission to the Official List, the protection of the interests of investors must be taken into consideration, along with the general duty of disclosure via listing particulars. Any new circumstances changing the strategy of the issuer and which would have an adverse effect on investors must also be disclosed by the issuer concerned. The power of the FSA in determining whether appropriate disclosure has been made by an issuer is absolute. It may also amend or alter its policy of disclosure. In view of the fact that one of the objectives of the Act is to protect the interests of investors, the provisions as to listing rules deserve appreciation.

Under the Act of 2000 there will be a single statutory regime for the Official Listing of all securities and other instruments. It is to be noted that the Treasury has the power to prevent a financial instrument from being admitted to the list if, in its opinion, it would pose undue risks to investors.

In order to protect the investors, a system of discontinuance and suspension of listing of securities and instruments has been devised. The general duty of disclosure in listing particulars[11] should be appreciated. Public censure of sponsors[12] is a novel provision under the current legislation. The ethos of public censure of sponsors has

---

[11] Section 80.
[12] Section 89.

been reinforced by the provision of compensation for false or misleading particulars[13].

Competition scrutiny[14] is another novel idea under the current legislation. It would be premature to comment fully on these provisions, as time alone will confirm whether they may be effectively implemented or not, and whether they will produce the intended results.

---

[13] Section 90.
[14] Section 95.

13 Provision of Financial Services by Members of the Professions

Introduction

Provision of financial services by members of the professions, such as accountants, actuaries and solicitors, has been included in Part XX of the Act, creating an exemption for member of the professions providing financial services to their clients, as set out in Section 327 of the Act. The FSA has the power to prohibit members of the professions who benefit from that exemption, if circumstances so justify. An exempt professional person has an obligation to disclose to its client that he is not regulated by the FSA. The grant of exemption is a discretionary power of the FSA. Claiming of exemption falsely by a member of a profession is a punishable offence.

Provision of Financial Services by Members of the Professions

As part of its general duty, the FSA must keep itself informed of the manner in which designated professional bodies supervise and regulate the carrying on of exempt regulated activities by members of the profession, as well as the manner in which the members of such professions are carrying on exempt regulated activities.

Under section 325 each designated professional body has an obligation to cooperate with the FSA in the form of sharing information and in any other manner that may be necessary in order to enable the FSA to perform its functions in Part XX of the Act.

The Treasury may by order designate professional bodies that would be responsible for regulating the practice of a professional. One of the basic conditions is that the professional body concerned has rules that are applicable to the carrying on of regulated activities by its members. The regulatory body must be recognized for the purpose of any enactment other than this Act, and if the professional body establishes in an EEA state other than the UK, the body has corresponding powers and status in that state. *'Enactment'* in this context includes an act of the Scottish Parliament, Northern Ireland legislation and subordinate legislation.

Section 327 provides for exemptions from the general principles, that is the general prohibition does not apply to the carrying on of a regulated activity by a person if the following conditions are satisfied:

(a) that the person is a member of a profession, and that he is controlled or managed by one or more such members;

(b) that he has not received from any person other than his client any unaccounted for pecuniary award or other advantage arising out of his carrying on any of the activities;

(c) that *'the manner of the provision by P (the person) of any service in the course of carrying on the activities must be incidental to the provision by him of professional services'* (section 327(4));

(d) that the person must carry on or hold himself out to be carrying on a regulatory activity that he is authorized to perform under section 332(3) or a regulatory activity in respect of which he is an exempt person;

(e) the activities must be of a description or relate to an investment of a description that has not been specified in an order made by the Treasury; and

(f) that the person must carry on only regulatory activities (that is those activities must be other than regulatory activities in relation to which he is an exempt person).

The FSA has the discretion to limit the application of the direction under section 327(1), that is, exemptions from the general prohibition. A direction under section 328(1) must be in writing and may be given in relation to different classes of person or different descriptions of regulatory activity, it must be published to bring it to the attention of the public, and a copy of the direction provided to the Treasury, and may be issued only if it is desirable to do so to protect the interests of the clients. In taking such a decision the FSA must have regard to compliance with rules made under section 332(1); for dealing with complaints against its members when they may carry on exempt regulatory activities; in order to offer redress to clients who have already suffered or may suffer losses by virtue of misconduct by a designated professional body member in carrying on exempt regulatory activities; or for cooperating with the FSA under section 325(4).

The term 'client' in this context would include persons who use or have used or may be contemplating using any of the services provided by a member of a profession in the course of carrying on exempt regulatory activities, or persons who have rights or interests that are either derived from or may be attributable to a use of any of the services by other persons or persons who have rights or interests that may be adversely affected by virtue of using of any of such services '*by persons acting on their behalf or in a fiduciary capacity in relation to them*' (section 328 (8)(c)), including when the professional is acting as a trustee.

When it may appear to the FSA that a person to whom general prohibition does not apply (section 327(1)) is not a fit and proper person to carry on regulatory activities, the FSA may make an order dis-applying section 327(1). The FSA may, however, on the application of the person concerned, vary or revoke it. If a partnership is named in an order under section 329, that order is not affected by any change by the membership of that partnership. If the partnership is dissolved, then the effect of the order will devolve on the successor partnership. A partnership is to be regarded as succeeding to the business of another if the members of the succeeding partnership are substantially the same as those of the former and the succession is to be the whole or substantially the whole of the business.

Prior to its issuing a direction under section 328(1) (*Directions in relation to General Prohibition*) the FSA must publish a draft version, which must be accompanied by a cost benefit analysis and a notice that a representation in connection with the proposed direction may be made to the FSA within a specified time. However, before giving the proposed direction the FSA must take notice of the representation, if any, already made to it. Where differences between the respondents and the FSA become evident, it must publish the details accompanied by a cost benefit analysis. However, those provisions do not apply if the FSA does not consider that the delay involved in complying with those differences would prejudice the interests of the consumers.

If the FSA proposes to make an order under section 329, it must give the person concerned a warning notice setting out the terms of the proposed order. Where it decides to make a section 329 order it must issue a decision notice setting out the terms of the order. Where the FSA decides to grant an application it must give the applicant written notice of its decision, and if it proposes to refuse that application it must also do the same, and the applicant may refer the matter to the Tribunal. The FSA may not make an order under section 329 unless:

(a) *'the period within which the decision to make the order may be referred to the Tribunal has expired and no such reference has been made; or*

(b) *if such a reference has been made, the reference has been determined.'*[1]

The primary purpose of Part XX is to make arrangements whereby professionals will be exempt from the requirement to obtain permission from the FSA in order to carry out certain regulated activities. Each professional will be required to qualify for the exception in accordance with the criteria set out in section 327 in order to protect the receivers of services to be offered by such professionals. Furthermore, the FSA will have the right to ban members of the profession who may benefit from the exemption from carrying on regulated activities where the circumstances justify that[2].

In this Part 'members' in relation to a professional would mean persons who are entitled to practise the profession concerned, and in doing so are subject to the supervisory and controlling body, whether or not they are members of that body. 'Exempt regulated activities' would mean activities carried on by members of a profession that are supervised

---

1 Section 331(10)(a) and (b).
2 See further *Explanatory Notes*, op. cit. at para 581.

and regulated by a designated professional body without breaching the general prohibition[3].

The Treasury may by order designate the bodies for the purposes of this Part only if it is satisfied that a body has rules applicable to the carrying on by members of the profession and that regulated activities would be exempt regulated activities; furthermore, the body must have power to regulate the practice of the profession; the body must have been recognized for the purpose of any enactment and its recognition not withdrawn; and if the body is established in an EEA state other than the UK, then it has power under any local enactment to regulate the practice of any profession; and that membership of a profession is essential and that the body is recognized for the purposes of any enactment and that its recognition[4] has not been withdrawn.

Section 327 sets out the criteria that must be met by a professional to qualify for the exemption. He must be a member of a profession, or controller or managed by one or more of such members; he must not receive from a person other than his clients any pecuniary reward or other advantage for which he does not account to his client; he must render only professional services. The Director-General is required to keep under review the regulatory provisions and practices of recognized bodies, and if he considers that a regulatory provision or practice has an adverse effect on competition he has the discretion to make or not to make a report; if the effect is significantly adverse he must make a report. The Director-General's report containing details of the adverse effect on competition is to be sent to the Treasury, the Competition Commission and the FSA, and must be published in a way that would bring them to the attention of the public. Absolute privilege is attached under Section 304 so that no action relating to the law of defamation may be brought against the Director-General.

In order to ensure that competition is not distorted the Director-General may initiate investigations, initially by notice in writing requiring a person to provide any document specified in the notice. The Director-General may by notice in writing require any person carrying on any business to provide any information specified in the

3 Section 325(1).
4 'Recognized' in so far as the United Kingdom is concerned means recognized by a minister of the Crown, Scottish minister or Northern Ireland minister or a Northern Ireland department or its head.

notice. Any refusal to comply with the Director-General's notice by the person concerned (the defaulter) will allow him to certify that fact to the court and the latter may inquire into the case. The court may deal with the defaulter as if it were a contempt[5].

The Competition Commission may propose its own report to confirm whether or not the regulatory provision and practice at issue has a significantly adverse effect on competition, and may direct the FSA and the Treasury as to what action ought to be taken by them.

However, the general prohibition or a core prohibition applies to the carrying on of an insurance market activity by a member of the Society of Lloyd's or the members of the Society taken together only if the FSA so directs[6]. A direction that relates to a core provision is referred to as '*an insurance market directive*', and a core provision means a provision that has been mentioned in section 317 of this Act, and these are Parts V, X, XI, XII, XIV, XV, XVI, XXII and XXIV, sections 384 to 386 and Part XXVI. In deciding whether to give a direction under section 316(1), the FSA must have particular regard to:

(a) the interests of actual policyholders and potential policyholders;

(b) any failure by the Society of Lloyd's to satisfy an obligation as a result of a provision of the law of another EEA state, which gives effect to an insurance directive; and that provision of law is applicable to an activity carried on in that state by a person to whom section 316 is applicable; and

(c) the need to ensure the effective exercise of the functions that the FSA does in relation to the Society of Lloyd's under section 315 of the Act.

The regulated activities must be provided only when they are incidental and complimentary to the provision of the professional services;[7] he must not carry on or hold himself out as carrying on a regulatory activity other than the one which he is allowed to carry on under section 332(3):

[5] Section 305(6).
[6] Section 316(1).
[7] *'Professional Services' means services 'which do not constitute carrying on a regulated activity and the provision of which is supervised and regulated by a designed professional body'* (section 327(8)).

'*(3) A designated professional body must make rules-*

(a) applicable to members of the profession in relation to which it is established who are not authorized persons; and

(b) governing the carrying on by those members of regulated activities (other than regulated activities in relation to which they are exempt persons).'

An exempt person's activities must not be of a description or relate to an investment of a description specified in an order made by the Treasury.

Section 328 allows the FSA to direct that the exemption from the general prohibition (section 327) is not to apply to certain classes of professional in order to protect the interests of clients. A determination of whether the interests of clients will be protected or not will be made by paying regard to the effectiveness of any arrangements made by a designated professional body for the following purposes:

(a) for securing compliance with rules made under section 332(1)[8];

(b) for dealing with complaints against its members arising from their carrying on with exempt regulated activities;

(c) for offering redress to clients who suffer or claim to have suffered loss as the result of the conduct of the members of the profession carrying out exempt regulated activities; and for co-operating with the FSA[9].

Under section 329 the FSA may make an order that would have the effect of prohibiting specified persons who are not fit and proper persons to carry on regulated activities. However, the FSA may be prepared to consider an application if made by the person concerned, in order to vary or revoke it. The general prohibition order on a partnership will continue to have an effect in relation to any partnership that may succeed to the business of a dissolved partnership. The FSA must publish a draft of the proposed direction with test benefit analysis allowing representations within a specified time, and before finalizing a direction

---

[8] Rules in relation to persons to whom the general prohibition does not apply.
[9] See section 325(4).

it must take into account the differences that may be revealed. If the FSA proposes to make an order under section 329 (*Orders in relation to General Prohibition*) it must give the person concerned a warning notice setting out the terms of the proposed order; and if the FSA decides to make an order under section 329 it must give a person concerned a decision notice.

If, on the other hand, the FSA decides to grant the application it must give the applicant a written notice of its decision. If the FSA proposes however to refuse the application it must give the applicant a warning notice accordingly. Again, if it decides to grant the application, it must give the applicant a decision notice and it may be referred to the Tribunal.

Section 332 authorizes the FSA to make rules applicable to persons to whom the general prohibition does not apply, to ensure that professionals carrying on exempt regulatory activities disclose to the clients that they are not authorized persons and that the professional bodies make rules to ensure that the exempted members will not carry on regulated activities that are not complementary to services to a particular client[10]. Rules made by a designated professional body must be approved by the FSA.

Mutual Societies

Under this Part the Treasury may order transfer of the functions of the Friendly Societies Commission and the Building Societies Commissions and functions under the Industrial and Provident Societies Act and the Credit Union Act 1979 to the FSA, under sections 334 to 339. The Treasury order may be extended to include Friendly Societies for Scotland. The Building Societies Investors Protection Board will cease to exist at a future date[11]. The Treasury may also by order provide for

---

[10] See further *Explanatory Notes*, op. cit. at para 590.

[11] '(1) The Treasury may by order provide for the transfer to the Authority of any functions conferred by:
  (a) the Industrial and Provident Societies Act 1965;
  (b) the Industrial and Provident Societies Act 1967;
  (c) the Friendly and Industrial and Provident Societies Act 1968;
  (d) the Industrial and Provident Societies Act 1975;
  (e) the Industrial and Provident Societies Act 1978;
  (f) the Credit Unions Act 1979' (section 338(1).

transfer to the Treasury of any functions under these enactments that have not been or are not being transferred to the FSA[12].

Auditors and Actuaries

This Part of the Act requires an authorized person to appoint an auditor or actuary who would produce periodic reports, subject to any rules that may be prescribed by the FSA, and their appointment must be notified to the FSA. An appointed auditor or actuary acting on behalf of an authorized person must have access at all times to that person's books, accounts and vouchers; he will also have the power to require such information and clarification as he may reasonably consider necessary for the performance of his duties and will not be in breach of confidentiality if he passes any information or gives an opinion to the FSA provided he does so in good faith and that he reasonably believes that the information or opinion so given is relevant to the functions of the FSA. The Treasury may make regulations prescribing the circumstances in which an auditor or actuary must submit information to the FSA. The same principle and practice shall apply to auditors and actuaries of persons who have close links[13] with authorized persons.

An auditor or actuary of an authorized person must notify the FSA without delay if he is removed from office or if he resigns or if he is not reappointed. Furthermore, if he ceases to act for an authorized person he must promptly notify the FSA of whether he was ceased for any reason to which, he believes, the FSA's attention ought to be drawn or without any reason therefor. If the FSA believes that an auditor or actuary has failed to comply with a duty under this Act, it can disqualify him from acting for any authorized person or a class of authorized person; and the usual system of issuing warning notice and decision notice will apply including the right to refer the matter to the Tribunal. An authorized person who knowingly or recklessly provides an auditor and actuary of an authorised person information that is false or misleading will commit a criminal offence.

[12] Section 338(2).
[13] An entity has close links with an authorized person if that entity is a parent undertaking of the authorized person or a subsidiary undertaking of the authorized person or a parent undertaking of a subsidiary undertaking of the authorized person or a subsidiary undertaking of a parent undertaking of the authorized person (see section 343(8)).

Public Reward, Disclosure of Information and Cooperation

The FSA shall maintain a record of: persons who may appear to be an authorized person; authorized unit trust schemes; authorized schemes; recognized investment exchanges; recognized clearing houses; individuals to whom prohibition orders relate; approved persons; and persons falling within such other class as the FSA may determine.[14]

Included in the records must be such information as the FSA may consider appropriate, and at least the following:

(a) in the case of a person appearing to be an authorized person

   (i) information as to the services for which he holds himself out as able to provide;

   (ii) any address at which a notice or other document may be served on him;

(b) in the case an authorized trust unit scheme, the names and addresses of the manager and trustee of the scheme;

(c) in the case of an authorized open-ended investment company, the name and address of the company; in the case of it having only one director, the name and address of the director; and if the company has a depository, its address;

(d) in the case of a recognized scheme, the name and address of the operator of the scheme and any representation of the operator in the UK;

(e) in the case of a recognized investment exchange or recognized clearing house, the name and address of the exchange or clearing house;

(f) in the case of an individual to whom a prohibition order relates, his name and details of the effect of the order;

(g) in the case of a person who is an approved person, his name; the name of the relevant authorized person; and in the event of an authorized person performing a controlled function under an arrangement with a contractor of a relevant authorized person, the name of the contract.

---

[14] Section 347.

It is for the FSA to decide whether or not to remove an entry from the record. When however the FSA decides not to remove the entry, it must make a note to that effect in the record, and justify its reason therefor. Records of the above-mentioned entities must be made available for inspection by members of the public. The FSA may publish the record, either in full or in part; or '*exploit commercially the information contained in the record, or any part of that information*'.[15]

A primary recipient or any person obtaining any information directly or indirectly from a primary recipient must not disclose any confidential information[16] without the consent of the person from whom the primary recipient obtained the information or the person to whom the information relates. It is immaterial whether the confidential information was received by virtue of a requirement for a person to so provide under the Act or for other connected purposes. Each of the following is to be regarded as a primary recipient:

(a) the FSA;

(b) any person exercising functions conferred on the competent authority by virtue of Part VI;

(c) the Secretary of State;

(d) any person appointed to produce a report under section 166 (*Reports by skilled persons*);

(e) any person who is or has been employed by a person at paragraphs (a), (b) and (c) above; and

---

[15] Section 347(6)).
[16] '*Confidential information*' in the context of this Part means information that relates to the business or other affairs of any person (the Act does not define what is meant by '*other information*') and which was '*received by the primary recipient for the purposes of, or in the discharge of, any functions of the Authority, the competent authority for the purposes of Part VI or the Secretary of State under any provision made by or under this Act*' and '*is not prevented from being confidential information ...*' (Section 348(2)(b) and (c). Part VI of the Act relates to Official Listing. Information is not confidential if: '*it has been made available to the public by virtue of being disclosed in any circumstances in which, or for any purposes for which, disclosure is not precluded by this section,*' (section 348(4)(a) or '*it is in the form of a summary or correction of information so framed that it is not possible to ascertain from it information relating to any particular person*' (section 348(4)(b).

(f) any auditor or expert[17] instructed by a person mentioned in paragraphs (a), (b) and (c).

Disclosure of confidential information is permissible in the following circumstances:

(a) if it is made for '*the purpose of facilitating the carrying out of a public function*'[18]; and

(b) if it is permitted by Treasury regulations made under section 349, which may permit disclosure of confidential information, whether of a general nature or of a prescribed kind by the following:

 (i) by recipients[19], prescribed or of a prescribed description, to any person in order to enable or assist the recipient to discharge prescribed public functions;[20]

 (ii) by recipients, prescribed or of a prescribed description, to prescribed persons or persons of prescribed descriptions in order to enable or assist those persons to discharge prescribed public functions;

 (iii) by the FSA to the Treasury or the Secretary of State for any purpose; and

 (iv) by any recipient if the disclosure is necessary for or in connection with prescribed proceedings[21]

---

[17] An expert in this Part would include:
(a) a competent person appointed by the competent authority under section 97 (*Persons appointed for carrying out investigations*);
(b) a competent person appointed by the FSA or the Secretary of State to conduct an investigation under Part XI (*Information gathering and investigations*); and any body or person appointed under paragraph 6 of Schedule 1 (*Monitoring and enforcement*) to perform a function on behalf of the FSA, see section 348(6).

[18] See section 349(1).

[19] A '*recipient*' in the context of section 349 would include a primary recipient or a person obtaining the information directly or indirectly from a primary recipient. See section 349(4).

[20] '*Public functions*' in the context of section 349 would include:
(a) functions conferred by any enactment or subordinate legislation;
(b) functions conferred by the Community Treaties or any Community instrument;
(c) functions conferred on persons by or under provisions having effect as part of the law of a country or territory outside the United Kingdom; and
(d) functions exercisable in relation to prescribed disciplinary proceedings; see section 349(5).

[21] Section 349(2).

Treasury regulations may make disclosure of confidential information subject to conditions or restrictions.

The Inland Revenue may disclose information to the FSA or the Secretary of State if disclosure is necessary for assisting in the investigation of a matter under section 168 (*Appointment of Persons to carry out Investigations in Particular Cases*). Section 348 (*Restrictions on Disclosure of Confidential Information by Authority*) does not apply to Revenue Information[22] obtained from the Inland Revenue which may not be used except in the following cases:

(a) when its use is needed for the purpose of deciding whether or not to appoint an investigator under section 168;

(b) in carrying out an investigation under section 168;

(c) in criminal proceedings brought against a person under this Act or the Criminal Justice Act 1993 which proceedings have been instituted as the result of an investigation under section 165;

(d) in order to take action under this Act against a person in consequence of an investigation under section 165;

(e) in proceedings before the Tribunal as a result of action taken in pursuance of an investigation carried out under section 168.

The purpose of section 351 is to protect the information obtained by the Director-General of Fair Trading and the European Union Commission in pursuance of their powers of competition scrutiny under the Act. According to section 351(1) a person will be guilty of offence if he holds competition information[23] but he improperly discloses it during the lifetime of the individual concerned or if it relates to a particular business of a body when that business is still operational.

A disclosure would be improper unless it is made with the consent of the person from whom it was obtained, and if that person is different

---

[22] '*Revenue Information*' in this context would mean the information held by a person and a non-disclosure of which would be an offence under section 182 of the Finance Act 1989 (section 350(7)).

[23] '*Competition Information*' means information which relates to the affairs of a particular individual or body and is not otherwise in a public domain and was obtained under or by virtue of a competition provision.

from the individual to whose affairs the information relates, the consent of the person for the time being carrying on the business to which information relates. Disclosure of competition information is regarded as necessary if it is disclosed in pursuance of the UK's obligations under the European Community law, or for the purpose of criminal proceedings in any part of the UK or in connection with the investigation of any criminal offence triable in order to institute civil proceedings, or for the purposes of civil proceedings brought under or in connection with the competition provision or a specified enactment.

It is an offence to disclose information without the consent of the Commissioners of the Inland Revenue, or in connection with criminal prosecutions unless such a person can successfully prove that he was not informed nor had he any reason to suspect that this information was confidential in nature, or that he took all reasonable precautions and exercised all due diligence to avoid committing the offence.

Section 353 allows the Treasury to make regulations permitting discharge of information held by third parties in order to assist the FSA to carry out its functions.

Under section 354 the FSA may take such steps as it may consider appropriate to cooperate with its counterparts, particularly in relation to prosecution or detection of financial crime, such as the sharing of information that the FSA is not prevented from disclosing.

The disclosure provisions are fundamentally important for the purpose of attaining transparency in the business of financial services, and also for the purpose of safeguarding the interests of investors. However, every precaution needs to be taken to ensure that disclosure powers do not lead to any abuse of authority.

Conclusions

From the point of view of protecting the interests of consumers, Part XX of the Act contributes significantly to the objectives of the FSA. It is the professionals to whom the typical consumer turns; Part XX should make professionals, accountants, actuaries and solicitors aware of their obligations towards their customers, and the action that the FSA can take against them if they derogate from their obligations

It is to be re-emphasized that exemption is not the general rule; each professional person is required to justify seeking exemption from the requirements of authorization. Thus, it may be concluded that authorization is the general rule, and exemption is the exception, and exemption may be withdrawn by the FSA at any time if it is satisfied that because of the kind of activities of the exempt person, exemption may not be allowed any longer.

14 The Financial Services Compensation Scheme

Introduction

Part XV is concerned with the issue of the financial services compensation scheme (sections 212-223), requiring the FSA to create a scheme, managed by an independent scheme manager, that would provide a system of payment of compensation to consumers who may suffer financial loss as a consequence of the inability of a relevant person to meet its liabilities. The scheme will not provide compensation for a regulatory breach by an authorized firm, but will do so in cases of the insolvency of such a person.

The Scheme Manager and his staff also enjoy immunity for actions for damages except where he may act in bad faith or where damages are sought under section 6(1) of the Human Rights Act 1998.

The Financial Services Compensation Scheme

For the operation of the Compensation Scheme a Compensation Scheme manager would assess and pay compensation, where appropriate, and will have the power to impose levies on authorized persons for the purpose of meeting its expenses[1] and recovering the costs of establishing the Compensation Scheme. In imposing levies on a particular class of authorized persons the FSA must ensure that it reflects as far as possible the amount of the claims made or likely to be made in respect of that class of persons.

The Compensation Scheme may, in particular, make provision in regard to the following:

---

[1] These expenses would include expenses incurred or expected to be incurred in paying compensation, borrowing or insuring risks.

(a) the circumstances in which a relevant person may be considered to be unable or likely to be unable to satisfy claims made against him;

(b) setting up different plans for meeting different kinds of claim;

(c) imposition of levies in each case;

(d) limiting the levy payable by a person for a specified period;

(e) repayment of the levy whether in full or in part in specified circumstances;

(f) entertainment of claims made only by a specified kind of claimant;

(g) consideration of a claim only if it comes under a specified category;

(h) the procedure to be followed making a claim;

(i) whether to make interim payments before a claim is finally determined;

(j) amount payable on a claim to a specified maximum amount, or a maximum amount calculated in a specified manner; and

(k) where payment is to be made in specified circumstances to a person other than the claimant.

The Compensation Scheme in its entirety or particular provisions of it may be applied only in relation to activities carried on by claimants; matters arising or events occurring in specified localities or areas. The decision whether a claimant should receive a payment in respect of his claim is to be taken by the Compensation Scheme manager and the claims may be satisfied under another Compensation Scheme or by virtue of a guarantee given by government or other authority (section 214(6)). The manager can recommend a full payment of compensation to the claimant and recover the money either in whole or in part from the other Compensation Scheme or under that guarantee.

In order to operate the Compensation Scheme, the FSA shall establish a body corporate, the management of which will consist of the chairman and a board, the members of which are the Compensation Scheme managers' directors, each appointed by the FSA with the approval of the Treasury. However, the terms of the appointment, especially those governing removal from office, must be such as to secure their independence from the FSA in the operation of the Scheme.

Section 215, which relates to the rights of the Compensation Scheme in relevant persons' insolvency, provides that:

> '(1) The Compensation Scheme may, in particular, make provision:
>
> > (a) as to the effect of a payment of compensation under the Compensation Scheme in relation to rights or obligations arising out of the claim against a relevant person in respect of which the payment was made;
> >
> > (b) for conferring on the Compensation Scheme manager a right of recovery against that person.
>
> (2) Such a right of recovery conferred by the Compensation Scheme does not, in the event of the relevant person's insolvency, exceed such right (if any) as the claimant would have had in that event.'[2]

One of the objectives of the Compensation Scheme is to allow the manager to recover the money from the authorized person, as per section 215(2). If a person other than a Compensation Scheme manager presents a petition under section 9 of the Insolvency Act 1986 or Article 22 of the 1989 Order concerning a company or a partnership that is a relevant person, the Compensation Scheme manager will have the same rights as are conferred on the FSA by section 362 of the Act[3].

In regard to the capacity to present a winding-up petition against a

---

[2] Section 215(1) and (2).

[3] (1)This section applies if a person other than the Authority presents a petition to the court under section 9 of the 1986 Act (or Article 22 of the 1989 Order) in relation to a company or partnership which:
  (a) is, or has been, an authorized person;
  (b) is, or has been, an appointed representative; or
  (c) is carrying on, or has carried on, a regulated activity in contravention of the general prohibition.
(2) The Authority is entitled to be heard:
  (a) at the hearing of the petition; and
  (b) at any other hearing of the court in relation to the company or partnership under Part II of the 1986 Act (or Part III of the 1989 Order).
(3) Any notice or other document required to be sent to a creditor of the company or partnership must also be sent to the Authority. (*Continued on p.310.*)

body that is a relevant person, the Compensation Scheme manager has the same rights as are conferred on the FSA by section 371, section 374 if an individual bankruptcy.

The Compensation Scheme may include provisions whereby the manager will be required to make arrangements for ensuring continuity of insurance for a policyholder or policyholders of a specified class, of relevant long-term insurers[4]. The manager may take such measures as appear to him appropriate for securing or facilitating the transfer of a relevant long-term insurer's business to another authorized person (section 216(3)(b)). The Compensation Scheme may authorize the manager to take measures for satisfying policyholders or policyholders of a specific class, of relevant insurers (i.e. relevant persons who are authorized to effect or carry out contracts of insurance, and are in financial difficulties). It is for the Compensation Scheme manager to take measures that he may deem appropriate for:

(a) securing or facilitating the transfer of a relevant insurer's business to another authorized person; and

(b) giving assistance to the relevant insurer in order to enable it to confirm to effect or carry out contracts of insurance[5].

The Compensation Scheme may provide that if measures as at (a) above are to be taken, they should be on terms that would appear to the

---

(4) The Authority may apply to the court under section 27 of the 1986 Act (or Article 39 of the 1989 Order); and on such an application, section 27(1)(a) (or Article 39(1)(a)) has effect with the omission of the words '(*including at least himself*)'.

(5) A person appointed for the purpose by the Authority is entitled:
 (a) to attend any meeting of creditors of the company or partnership summoned under any enactment;
 (b) to attend any meeting of a committee established under section 26 of the 1986 Act (or Article 38 of the 1989 Order); and
 (c) to make representations as to any matter for decision at such a meeting.

(6) If, during the course of the administration of a company, a compromise or arrangement is proposed between the company and its creditors, or any class of them, the Authority may apply to the court under section 425 of the Companies Act 1985 (or Article 418 of the Companies (Northern Ireland) Order 1986) (section 362).

[4] '*Relevant long-term insurers*' would mean relevant persons who are authorized '*to effect or carry out long-term insurance; and are unable or likely to be unable, to satisfy claims made against them*' (section 216(2)).

[5] Section 217(3)(a) and (b).

scheme manager the most appropriate[6]; if, on the other hand, measures of a kind as at (b) are to be taken, they should be *'conditional on the reduction of, or the deferment of the payment of'* items to which any eligible policyholder in relation to the relevant insurer is entitled in his capacity as such. The Compensation Scheme may also provide that measures of the kind mentioned at (b) do not benefit to any material extent *'persons who were members of a relevant insurer when it began to be in financial difficulties or who had any responsibility for, or who may have profited from, the circumstances giving rise to its financial difficulties, except the specified circumstances'*.[7] Any measures taken must be cost effective, in that it would cost less than it would cost to pay compensation if the relevant insurer became unable or likely to be unable to satisfy claims made against him[8].

The FSA will have power to give assistance to the Scheme Manager in order to assist it to determine what means would be most appropriate in respect of a particular relevant insurer; or the FSA may impose constraints on the manager in taking measures in respect of a particular relevant insurer. It may also require the manager to provide it with information in regard to any particular measures that the manager may propose to take. The manager may be allowed to make interim payments in respect of eligible policyholders of a relevant insurer, and to *'indemnify any person making payments to eligible policyholders of a relevant insurer'*.[9]

The scheme manager is required to submit its report on the progress made at least once a year to the FSA, including a statement identifying the value of each of the funds established of the Compensation Scheme, and justify that in discharging its functions it has complied with the requirement specified in the rules made by the FSA.

The Scheme Manager has the power to request the claimant to provide information or documents, within a reasonable period of time, and the manager may take copies or extracts from the document or require the person concerned to provide an explanation of the document. Where a

---

[6] This may include terms reducing or deferring payment of any of the items to which an eligible policyholder in relation to the relevant insurer is entitled in his capacity as such (section 217(4)).
[7] Section 217(4)(c).
[8] Section 217(4)(d).
[9] Section 217(6).

document may not be made available by the person concerned, the manager may require the person to state where the document is. However, the provisions of this section (section 110) do not apply to a relevant person who is insolvent, and to whom sections 220[10] or 224[11] apply.

In order to allow the Scheme Manager to discharge its functions pertaining to a claim in respect of an insolvent relevant person, the person concerned must permit a person authorized by the Scheme Manager to inspect the relevant documents and take copies of or extracts from the document. This section applies to: the administrative receiver, administrator, liquidator or trustee in bankruptcy of an insolvent relevant person[12], but not to a liquidator, administrator or trustee in bankruptcy, who is the Official Receiver, the Official Receiver for Northern Ireland, or the Accountant in Bankruptcy.

Should the person fail to comply with the requirement of section 219 (*Scheme Manager's power to require information*) or the requirements of section 220 (*Scheme Manager's power to inspect information held by liquidator etc.*), the Scheme Manager may apply to the court for an order for disclosure, and the court may enquire into the case. If the court is satisfied that the defaulter failed without reasonable excuse to comply with the requirement, it may deal with the defaulter[13] as if he were in contempt.

The Scheme Manager and the members of the board or officers or members of staff enjoy statutory immunity for '*anything done or omitted in discharge, or purported discharge, of the scheme manager's functions*'.[14] However, the provision does not apply if the act or omission is shown to have been in bad faith, or '*so as to prevent an award of damages made in respect of an act or omission on the ground that the act or omission was unlawful as a result of section 6(1) of the Human Rights Act 1998.*'[15]

---

[10] Section 220 deals with the Scheme Manager's power to inspect information held by the liquidator etc.
[11] Section 224 is concerned with the Scheme Manager's power to inspect documents held by the Official Receiver, etc.
[12] In Scotland, this section applies to the permanent trustee within the meaning of the Bankruptcy (Scotland) Act 1985, or the estate of an insolvent relevant person.
[13] In the case of a body corporate, any director or officer.
[14] Section 222(1).
[15] Section 222(2)(b).

Management expenses[16] allocated to a particular period may not exceed the amount fixed by the Scheme. The Scheme Manager has the power to inspect, make copies of or extracts from documents held by the Official Receiver in respect of a relevant person[17] who has become insolvent or bankrupt.

Other Provisions

Part XXVIII of the Act contains miscellaneous provisions including schemes for reviewing past business[18] whereby if the Treasury is satisfied that there is evidence suggesting the occurrence of a widespread or regulatory failure to comply with rules in consequence of which payments (Compensation Payments) may have to be made. In these circumstances the Treasury may by order (the scheme order) authorize the FSA to determine the nature and extent of the failure and to establish the liability of authorized persons to make compensation payments. This is another means of minimizing risks and protecting the interests of investors.

A scheme order may be made only if the FSA has given the Treasury a report about alleged failures, and if the Treasury is satisfied that the proposed scheme would be the most appropriate for dealing with failures.

Sections 405 to 408 are concerned with reciprocity powers.

Under section 405 the Treasury may direct the FSA to refuse an application for permission under Part IV (*Permission to Carry on Regulated Activities*)[19] made by a body incorporated in or formed under the law of the UK or to defer its decision on such application either indefinitely or for a specified period, or give a notice of objection to a person from a country which is the subject of a third-party decision acquiring a 50% share in an authorized person incorporated in or formed under the law of the UK irrespective of whether he has served the FSA

---

[16] These expenses stand for '*the expenses incurred or expected to be incurred by the scheme manager in connection with its functions under this Act other than those incurred (a) in paying compensation; (b) as a result of any provision of the Scheme made by virtue of section 216(3) or (4) or 217(1) or (b)*' (Section 223(3)).

[17] For the definition of a '*relevant person*' in the context of section 224, see paragraph 3 of the section.

[18] Section 404.

[19] Section 407 details the procedure the Authority must follow if the Treasury directs it to implement a third party decision.

with a notice of control as required under Part XXII of the Act. 'Third-party decision' means a decision of council or the Commission under Article 7(5) of the Investment Services Directive; Article 9(4) of the Second Banking Coordination Directive; Article 29(4) of the First Non-Life Insurance Directive; or Article 32(4) of the First Life Insurance Directive.

The circumstances in which a person may be regarded as acquiring a 50% share are detailed in section 406.

Section 408 is concerned with EFTA (European Free Trade Area) firms which may not exercise their passport rights if a third-party decision has been taken relating to the country of their parent. In such cases, the Treasury may make a determination whether a particular firm qualifies for authorization. However, if a subsidiary of a firm subject to a third-party decision is already authorized in a European Union Member State then its passport rights[20] to establish a branch or provide services in another Member State are not affected by the third-party decision.

The Treasury may withdraw a determination at any time; but whether a determination is in the affirmative or in the negative or whether a determination is to be withdrawn, in each case a written notice must be issued to the firm concerned, and any determination, whether in the form of acceptance or withdrawal, must be brought to the attention of those who are directly to be affected by it.

The Act has made special provisions for Gibraltar[21]. The Treasury may by order allow Gibraltar firms of a specified description for authorization. Schedule 4 to the Act and section 264 (*Schemes constituted in other EEA States*) may be amended in favour of Gibraltar firms.

Conclusions

The nearest analogy of the Financial Services Compensation Scheme will be with the Deposit Protection Scheme under the previous legislation. However, the Compensation Scheme is limited to providing compensation in the case of the insolvency of an authorized person.

---

[20] See Schedule 3 to the Act.
[21] Section 409.

Losses suffered by a customer as a consequence of a regulatory breach, for example mis-selling of investments, accrue liability for the authorized firm.

The rationale behind this Scheme is that no compensation may be allowed to an authorized person that may have been occasioned by its incompetence or lack of skills. Accepting that insolvency may also be occasioned by incompetence the Act makes provision for protecting the investors as much as possible. A situation such as that created by the Bank of Commerce and Credit International (BCCI) will be covered by the Compensation Scheme under the Act of 2000.

Membership of the Scheme is generally compulsory for authorized persons; and the Scheme is compatible with UK's obligations '*under EC Directives which make rules about the extent to which EEA firms can be required to join compensation schemes other than their home state scheme*'[22].

The Scheme provides for a safety net in so far as insurance contracts are concerned in that the Scheme Manager may provide assistance to an authorized person who is in financial difficulties, either by transferring that person's business to another insurer or by allowing the continuance of that business by another insurer. Payment to the firm concerned must not benefit any of its shareholders or company directors.

It is important to note that in order to allow him to perform his functions without any legal obstacle, the Scheme Manager and his staff are entitled to immunity, except where they act in bad faith or where damages may be sought under section 6(1) of the Human Rights Act 1998.

The FSA is virtually the watchdog of the financial markets, with the usual functions that a watchdog is required to perform: to watch, to bark and to bite. The latter represents its enforcement power.

Among other new aspects of regulatory activities, four very clearly stand out: control of market abuse; disciplinary measures; the Ombudsman Scheme and the Tribunal. It is also interesting to see that a 'totality of markets' view has been adopted by the current legislation, so that Lloyd's mutual societies and financial services by members of the profession have been embraced by it.

---

[22] Explanatory Notes, op. cit., at paragraph 426.

15 Insolvency

Introduction

The issue of insolvency becomes relevant to the FSA's activities for two main reasons: (a) the position of investors will be jeopardized if a financial service business becomes insolvent; and (b) a regulatory body may, in the light of under-performance of financial services business which may present risks to investors, be required to order the winding up of such a business. Save the particular provisions of Part VII of the Companies Act 1989 pertaining to transactions carried out on regulated markets, the general law of insolvency will continue to apply to most financial services business[1]. The power of the Secretary of State to petition the court to wind up an authorized business in justifiable cases remains intact[2].

The Building Societies Act 1986 will continue to apply to the relevant societies but the functions under that Act have been transferred to the FSA in accordance with the provisions of Part XXI.

Part XXIV has: voluntary arrangements; administration orders; receivership; voluntary winding up; winding up by the court; bankruptcy; and provisions against debt avoidance as the main sub-parts and these are now briefly explained.

Voluntary Arrangement

Section 356 applies if a voluntary arrangement has been approved under Part I of the Insolvency Act 1986 or Part II of the Insolvency (Northern Ireland) Order 1989 in respect of a company or insolvent partnership

---

[1] See further *Explanatory Notes*, op. cit. at paragraph 629.
[2] *Explanatory Notes*, ibid.

that is an authorized person. The FSA may make an application to the court for participation in the same way as a creditor in a company for voluntary arrangements or assignments in regard to an insolvent partnership under section 6 of the 1986 Act or Article 19 of the 1989 Order. In the event of a person other than the FSA making an application to the court in regard to the above matter, the FSA is entitled to be heard at any hearing relating to the application or an application made by an individual authorized person[3] under section 353 of the 1986 Act or Article 227 of the 1986 Order.

The FSA has the right to apply to the appropriate court, if it believes that a voluntary arrangement approved by a creditors' meeting would unfairly prejudice the interests of a creditor of the debtor[4]. The FSA is also entitled to be heard by the court if any other person makes such a challenge.

Whereas section 357 authorizes the FSA to participate in voluntary arrangements, corporate or otherwise, in England and Northern Ireland, similar authority is derived from section 358 in respect of Scotland, where a trust deed has been granted by or on behalf of a debtor of an authorized person. In Scotland, a debtor who is unable to pay his debts hands over his assets to a trustee, who may arrange a settlement with his creditors as an alternative to proceedings for sequestration under the Bankruptcy (Scotland) Act 1985. As soon as the trustee becomes aware that the debtor is an authorized person, it is required to send the FSA a copy of the trust deed and copy of the document or information sent to every creditor. The FSA has the same right as certain creditors who have not been sent a copy of the notice of the trust deed, or who have objected to petition for a sequestration order[5]. The FSA must be given the same notice as any other creditor.

Administration Orders

An administration order is an order whereby the court will place a company or partnership into administration, as an alternative to winding

---

[3] Individual voluntary arrangements whereby he may apply to the court for a moratorium for settling his debts, and protect himself against the prosecution of a bankruptcy petition.
[4] See section 262 of the 1986 Act (or Article 236 of the 1989 Order); or section 263 of the 1986 Act (or Article 237 of the 1989 Order).
[5] See paragraph 5(1)(c) of Schedule 5 to the 1985 Act.

up, in order to allow it to continue with its business under the supervision of an administrator. An administration order would seem to be appropriate in some cases as this would protect the interests of consumers which will not be damaged by winding up the business. Failure to pay a sum due and payable under an agreement is to be treated as its inability to settle its debts[6], and this is a sufficient ground for initiating administrative proceedings.

Section 360 is a novel section in that by virtue of this section insurance companies may also be subject to administration orders, which was not the case until this legislation was developed. This section therefore states that the *'Treasury may by order provide that such provisions of Part II of the 1986 Act (or Part III of the 1989 Order) as may be specified are to apply in relation to insurers with such modifications as may be specified.'*

If it should appear to the administrator of an existing administration order that the company or partnership is carrying or has carried on a regulated activity in breach of the general prohibition, then the administrator must notify the matter to the FSA without delay.

If a creditor other than the FSA presents a petition to the court under section 9 of the 1986 Act (or Article 22 of the 1989 Order) in relation to a company or partnership, which is or has been an authorized person or an appointed representative or is carrying on or has carried on a regulated activity in breach of that general prohibition, then the FSA is entitled to be heard at the hearing of the petition and at any other hearing of the court. The FSA must also receive all notices and other documents that are required to be sent to creditor(s).

A person appointed for the purpose of the FSA is entitled to attend any meeting of creditors of the company or partnership or any meeting of a committee established under section 26 of the 1986 Act (or Article 38 of the 1989 Order) and to make representations as to any matter for decision at such a meeting. Should during the course of the administration a compromise or arrangement be proposed, the FSA may apply to the court under section 425 of the Companies Act 1985 (or Article 418 of the Companies (Northern Ireland) Order 1986), with a proposal that the scheme be put to a vote of creditors.

---

[6] See section 8(1)(a) of the 1986 Act (or Article 21(1)(a) of the 1989 Order).

Receivership

If a receiver has been appointed in respect of a company that is or has been an authorized person or an appointed representative, or is carrying on, or has carried on, a regulated activity in breach of the general prohibition, the FSA is entitled to be heard on an application under section 35 or section 63 of the 1986 Act (or Article 45 of the 1989 Order), that is, at any hearings at which the receiver applies to the court for directions.

The FSA has also the right to receive any report or proposals sent by the receiver to creditors[7]. A person appointed by the FSA for the purpose is entitled to attend any meeting of creditors of the company concerned or to attend any meeting of a committee established under section 49 or 68 of the 1986 Act (or Article 59 of the 1989 Order), and to make representations as to any matter for decision at such a meeting.

Voluntary Winding Up

Section 365 gives the FSA powers to participate in voluntary winding-up proceedings that relate to an authorized person, but not a long-term insurer. Like general creditors, the FSA may ask the court to decide an any question arising under the winding up of a company[8]. Any notice or document which would be received by creditors must be sent to the FSA. A person appointed for the purpose by the FSA is entitled to attend any meeting of creditors of the company or to attend any meeting of a committee established under section 101 of the 1986 Act (or Article 87 of the 1989 Order), and to make representations as to any matter for decisions at such a meeting. If during the course of the winding up of the company, a compromise or arrangement or settlement of debts is proposed, the FSA may apply to the court under section 425 of the Companies Act 1986 (or Article 418 of the Companies (Northern Ireland) Order 1986) to propose that the arrangement be put to a vote of creditors.

If long-term insurance companies are allowed to seek voluntary winding up, then the policyholders, and in particular, endowment policyholders, would suffer most; such policies should be allowed to

---

[7] Under section 48(1)(a) or 67(1)(a) of the 1986 (or Article 58(1)(a) of the 1989 Order).

[8] Section 112 of the 1986 Act (or Article 98 of the 1989 Order).

run up to their maturity period, rather than requiring policyholders to accept the current value of such policies. Section 366 provides that such insurance companies may not be wound up voluntarily without the consent of the FSA; thus the legitimate expectations of policyholders may be respected, where possible[9].

If a resolution for voluntary winding up of a long-term insurance company has been adopted, a director of the company is required to notify the FSA as soon as possible; otherwise, he will be guilty of an offence. Section 378(3) and 381A of the Companies Act 1985 and articles 386(3) and 389A of the Companies (Northern Ireland) Order 1986[10] apply in relation to a winding-up resolution.

A copy of the winding-up resolution forwarded to the Registrar of Companies must be accompanied by a certificate issued by the FSA stating that its consents to the voluntary winding up of the insurer.

Winding Up by the Court

The FSA may present a petition to the court for the winding up of a body of an authorized person or an appointed person or a person that is carrying on or has carried on a regulated activity in breach of the general prohibition. The court may wind up the body if the latter is unable to pay its debts[11] or if it is of the opinion that it is just and equitable to do so. This allows the FSA to act on behalf of the consumers who may be unable to pursue winding-up proceedings owing to lack of resources.

The FSA may not however present a petition to the court under section 367 for the winding up of an EEA firm[12] or a Treaty firm[13] unless it has been asked to do so by the home state regulator of the firm concerned. This is because winding-up issues are generally matters of concern for the home state regulator.

Where a creditor or a third party presents a petition for the winding up of an authorized person who is in the insurance business, or applies to have a provisional liquidator[14] appointed, the applicant must serve a copy of the application on the FSA.

[9] See further *Explanatory Notes*, op. cit. at paragraph 646.
[10] See further *Explanatory Notes*, op. cit. at paragraph 646.
[11] See section 123 or 221 of the 1986 Act (or Article 103 or 185 of the 1989 Order).
[12] See Schedule 3 to this Act.
[13] See Schedule 4 to this Act.
[14] See section 135 of the 1986 Act or Article 115 of the 1989 Order.

The FSA is entitled to be heard at the hearing of the petition or at any other hearing of the court[15], and any notice or document required to be sent to a creditor of the body must also be sent to the FSA. A person appointed for the purpose by the FSA is entitled to attend any meeting of creditors of the body or those of a committee established for the purposes of Part V or VI of the 1989 Order under Article 87 of that Order or under Article 120 of that Order, and to make representations as to any matter for decision at such a meeting. If during the course of the winding up of the company a compromise or settlement or arrangement is proposed between the company and its creditors or any class of creditors, the FSA may, under section 425 of the Companies Act 1986 (or Article 418 of the Companies (Northern Ireland) Order 1986) ask the court to put the matter to a vote of creditors.

Bankruptcy

Section 372 gives the FSA the power to present petition for bankruptcy to the court in respect of sole traders engaged in financial services business, and correspondingly, in Scotland for the sequestration of his estate, on the ground that the individual appears to be unable to pay a debt arising in the performance of a regulated activity or that the individual '*appears to have no reasonable prospect of being able to pay a regulated activity debt*'. Whether or not an individual has any reasonable prospect of being able to pay such a debt is determined if any of the following criteria are satisfied:

(a) that the debtor has failed to establish upon receipt of a demand from the FSA, to the satisfaction of the FSA, that there is a reasonable prospect of his paying a sum when it falls due;

(b) that at least three weeks have lapsed since the demand was served; or

(c) that the demand has been neither complied with nor set aside in accordance with the rules.

If, however, a bankruptcy order or a sequestration award is already in

---

[15] By virtue of or under Part IV or V of the 1986 Act (or Part V or VI of the 1986 Order).

force, and it appears to the insolvency practitioner that the individual is carrying on, or has carried on, a regulated activity in breach of the general prohibition, the insolvency practitioner must notify the FSA accordingly. The FSA has the right to participate in such proceedings, that is, the right to be heard at the hearing of the petition or any other subsequent hearing pertaining to the petition under: Part IX of the 1986 Act; or Part IX of the 1989 Order; or The 1985 Act.[16]

A copy of the report prepared under section 274 of the 1986 Act (or Article 248 of the 1989 Order) must also be sent to the FSA. A person appointed for the purposes by the FSA is entitled to attend any meeting of creditors of the individual or entity or to attend any meeting of a committee established under section 301 of the 1986 Act (or Article 274 of the 1986 Order) or to attend any meeting of commissioners held under paragraph 17 or 18 of Schedule 6 to the 1985 Act; and to make representations as to any matter for decisions at such a meeting.[17]

Provisions against Debt Avoidance

Under section 375 the FSA has the right to apply to the court for an order[18] in relation to a debtor who was carrying on a regulated activity for setting aside a transaction which would appear to have been entered into to defraud creditors, by transferring assets as gifts or setting them at less than their full value.

Supplemental Provisions concerning Insurers

In order to protect the interests of policyholders, section 376 requires the liquidator to carry on the long-term insurers' business by transferring it to another company which may lawfully carry out those contracts. In order to protect the interests of creditors in respect of liabilities of the insurers pertaining to long-term insurance, he may apply to the court for the appointment of a special manager, and if such a person is appointed, he will have such powers, including any of the powers of a receiver or manager, as the court may direct.

---

[16] *Permission to Carry on Regulated Activities.*
[17] Section 375(4).
[18] See section 423 of the 1986 Act (or Article 367 of the 1989 Order).

The court may appoint an independent actuary to investigate the insurer's business and report on whether it would be desirable to allow the insurer's business to continue or *'on any reduction in the contracts of long-term insurance effected by the insurer that may be necessary for successful continuation of that part of the insurer's business'*.[19]

If an insurer has been proved to be unable to pay its debts, and if the court thinks fit, it may reduce the value of one or more of the insurer's contracts rather than making a winding-up order; this is how to a certain extent the interests of beneficiaries may be protected.

The Treasury may make regulations for the treatment of the assets of an insurer on its winding up. These regulations may, in particular, provide for: making particular assets to be more available for meeting liabilities attributable to specific part of the insurer's business; and separate general meetings of the creditors to take place in respect of liabilities attributable to a particular parts of the insurer's business.

Winding-up rules in the context of this Part would include provisions:

(a) for determining the quantum of liabilities of an insurer to policyholders of a particular class or description for the purposes of proof; and

(b) generally, for implementing the provisions of this Part with respect to the winding up of insurers.

Winding-up rules may make provisions for all or any of the following matters:

'(a) the identification of assets and liabilities;

(b) the apportionment, between assets of different classes or descriptions, of

  (i) the costs, charges and expenses of the winding up; and

  (ii) any debts of the insurer of a specified class or description;

(c) the determination of the amount of liabilities of a specified description;

(d) the application of assets for meeting liabilities of a specified description;

---

[19] Section 376(10)(b).

(e) the application of assets representing any excess of a specified description."[20]

Conclusions

Protection of customers' interest and confidence in the London Financial Market are the prime objectives of this current legislation. Where the winding up of an authorized business on the grounds of insolvency would appear to be most appropriate, the Act authorizes the FSA to initiate such action. A common approach in this regard is intended to be adopted in respect of all business coming under the purview of the Act. Of course, provision for alternative arrangements to insolvency have also been made in the Act[21] whereby the FSA may ask the court to make an administration order as an alternative to winding up. This Part of the Act should be read with Part XV – *Financial Services Compensation Scheme*; voluntary arrangement is also permissible under the Act.

The plan to transfer the interests of long-term policyholders in the event of the original insurer being insolvent is a novel one.

---

[20] Section 379(2).
[21] Section 359.

16 Lloyd's

Introduction

Part XX of the Act brings the Society of Lloyd's within the regulatory framework whereby it will be regulated and supervised by the FSA; as a body corporate, it must be authorized by the FSA to carry on certain regulated activities, as if authorization has been granted under Part IV of the Act[1]. The usual powers of the FSA, including its investigatory powers, will be applicable to the Society of Lloyd's.

The Explanatory Notes to the Act make it clear that:

> '*Members of Lloyd's will benefit from an exemption from the need to be authorized in relation to contracts of insurance effected or carried out at Lloyd's. They will, nonetheless, be subject to regulatory arrangements as directed by the Authority under powers contained in this Part, and subject to the powers of the Council. As a minimum, the Authority will need to require the members to meet the solvency requirements laid down under the relevant EC directive.*'[2]

Initially, Lloyd's will not be subject to the full regulatory framework, because certain regulatory functions will be left to the Lloyd's Council.

This chapter explains the nature of the power which the FSA may exercise over the Society of Lloyd's.

---

[1] See further *Explanatory Notes*, op. cit., at paragraph 563.
[2] *Explanatory Notes*, op. cit., at paragraph 564.

The Society

By this Part the Society of Lloyd's ('the Society' or 'Lloyd's') is brought within the general regulatory framework. The Society is an authorized person and has the permission to carry on regulatory activity of any of the following types:

(a) the basic market activity – that is arrangement of deals in respect of contents of insurance written at Lloyd's;

(b) the secondary market activity – that is arrangement of deals in participation in Lloyd's syndicates; and

(c) the combined activity – that is, the activities carried on in connection with or for the purposes of the basic or secondary market activities.[3]

The Society is not subject to any requirement of this Act concerning the registered office of a body corporate[4]. Lloyd's is regulated by the FSA for insolvency purposes in accordance with the provisions of Part IV of the Insurance Companies Act 1982. The regulation of the Society has, for most purposes, been taken up by the Council of Lloyd's, but the Act gives the FSA considerable discretion as to how it should discharge its obligations for the regulation of Lloyd's[5]. Under the current Act the FSA must keep itself informed of the way in which the Council of Lloyd's supervises and regulates the market at Lloyd's and the way in which regulated activities are being carried on in that market[6]. By virtue of Part XIX the Society is to be authorized to carry on certain regulated activities and permission will be defined by the FSA as if it has been granted under Part IV[7]. Activities include managing members carrying on of contracts of insurance, and thus underwriting agents will have relevant permission under Part IV. As authorized persons the Society and its agents will be subject to the full range of the FSA's powers under this Act including its power of investigation, discipline and even the power to withdraw authorization, if necessary.

---

[3] Section 315.
[4] Section 315(5).
[5] See further *Explanatory Notes*, op. cit. at para 562.
[6] Section 314.
[7] See further *Explanatory Notes*, op. cit. at para 653.

Members of Lloyd's will have an exemption from the requirement of authorization in relation to contracts of insurance effected or carried out at Lloyd's although they will be subject to regulatory arrangements directed by the FSA. The FSA will need to require the members to meet the solvency requirements laid down under the EC Solvency Directive[8]. However, a member of Lloyd's would need permission to carry out any other regulatory activity[9].

The FSA's General Powers

The power of direction is vested in the FSA by section 316, whereby the FSA may give directions applying the general prohibition to underwriters of Lloyd's or, where the general prohibition is not to be applied, then a core provision may be applied to the carrying on of an insurance market activity[10] by a member of the Society or the members of the Society taken together.

Section 317 has defined the core provisions. These are: Part V *(Performance of Regulated Activities)*; Part X *(Rules and Guidance)*; Part XI *(Information Gathering and Investigation)*; Part XII *(Control over Authorized Persons)*; Part XIV *(Disciplinary Measures)*; Part XV *(The Financial Services Compensation Scheme)*; Part XVI *(The Ombudsman Scheme)*, Part XXII *(Collective Investment Schemes)*; Part XXIV *(Insolvency)*; Part XXVI *(Notices)*; and Sections 384-386 *(Restitution Required by the FSA)*.

In deciding whether to give direction under Section 316, the FSA must have particular regard to: (a) the interests of the existing policyholders and potential policyholders; and (b) any failure by the Society to satisfy an obligation under the law of another EEA State giving effect to any of the insurance Directives, and which law was applicable to an act carried on in that State by a person to whom this Section applies (Section 316(4)).

Section 318 authorizes the FSA to give direction to the Council or the Society (acting through the Council) or to both (Section 318(1)), instead of giving a direction to the members. A direction may relate to

---

[8] Solvency Ratio Directive 89/647/EEC OJ L386/14 of 30 December 1989.
[9] See further *Explanatory Notes*, op. cit. at para 564.
[10] 'Insurance market activity' means '*a regulated activity relating to contracts of insurance written at Lloyd's*' (section 316(3)).

achieving or in support of a specified objective, or be given in respect of underwriting agents. A direction under section 318(1) must be published for the purpose of bringing it to the attention of the public and a copy sent to the Treasury.

Before giving a direction under section 316 or section 318, the FSA is required to publish a draft of the proposed direction, which will be accompanied by a cost benefit analysis[11] and a notice that representations, if any, about the proposed direction must be made to the Authority by a specified date. The FSA is required to pay attention to the representations made, and to publish the responses to its directions, including the details of the differences.

If, in the opinion of the FSA, the direction differs from the draft of the proposed direction, it must publish the details of the differences, together with a cost benefit analysis. However, the rigid rules of direction will not apply if the FSA believes that the delay that may be occasioned in complying with them would prejudice the interests of consumers. Publication of a document under section 319 *(Consultation)* must be done in the way that would appear to be the best calculated way of bringing the matter to the attention of the public.

Former Underwriting Members (Sections 320-322)

Irrespective of whether a person is an authorized person, a former underwriting member may carry out contracts of insurance that he underwrote at Lloyd's. In the event of his being an authorized person, any Part IV permission that he may have (permission to carry on regulated activities) does not extend to his activities in carrying out those contracts[12]. The FSA may by notice impose on such underwriting members any condition it may deem appropriate for the purpose of protecting the interests of policyholders against risks. Of course, a person on whom a condition/requirement is imposed may refer the matter to the Tribunal.

The notice must detail the requirement, and inform the person concerned of his right to make representations to the FSA within the

---

[11] Submission of a cost benefit analysis is not necessary if the FSA considers that there will be no increase in costs or that the increase in costs will be of minimal significance (section 319(7)).

[12] Section 320(2).

specified period; it must also inform him of the date on which the requirement/condition takes effect, and of his right to refer the matter to the Tribunal.

After having considered the representations, if any, the FSA may do any of the following:

(a) it may decide to impose the proposed requirement, or if the requirement has already been imposed, not to revoke it; or

(b) it may decide to grant an application made by an applicant for variation or revocation of a requirement; or

(c) it may propose to refuse an application made by the person concerned for variation or revocation of a requirement, but in that event it must serve a warning notice on the former underwriting member; or

(d) after having considered the representations, if any, made in respect of a warning notice, it may still decide to refuse an application, but it must give the person concerned a decision notice.

In respect of (a), (b) or (c) the FA must serve a notice on the former underwriting member informing him of its decision.

The general rule that will apply to former Lloyd's underwriters is that the FSA will have the power to impose requirements on them, until all their insurance liabilities have been discharged. In respect of any other regulated activities, they will be required to obtain permission from and be authorized by the FSA.

Conclusions

As stated in the *Introduction* to this Chapter, the FSA will not initially take over all aspects of supervisory and regulatory functions of the Council of the Society of Lloyd's. In view of the history and reputation of the Society of Lloyd's, section 315 states the Society is an authorized person without its requiring to submit an application[13]. The fact remains that the Society is the most experienced institution in its fields of activity.

---

[13] See *Explanatory Notes*, op. cit., at paragraph 315.

17 Notices

Introduction

The Act provides for various types of notice that the FSA is required to issue to persons, authorized or unauthorized. There are four types of notices with which the FSA is concerned: warning notice; decision notice; notice of discontinuance; and final notice.

Warning Notice

A warning notice, which must be in writing, shall state the action the FSA proposes to take, giving reasons for the proposed action. It must also state whether section 394 (*Access to the FSA's Material*) applies, and must allow at least 28 days within which time the person concerned will have an opportunity to make representations to the FSA. The FSA has the discretion to extend the period of representations in appropriate cases.

Decision Notice

A decision notice, which must be in writing, must provide the FSA's reasons for the decision to take the proposed action, stating whether section 394 (*Access to FSA's Material*) applies, and if it does apply, then it must describe its effect. A decision notice must also indicate whether the person concerned will have any right to refer the matter to the Tribunal, and if so, the procedure thereto.

Notice of Discontinuance

If the FSA should decide not to take the action proposed in a warning notice or the action to which a decision notice relates, it must give the person concerned a notice of discontinuance, identifying the proceedings that are being discontinued. The question of issuing a notice of discontinuance would not arise when the discontinuance of proceedings results in the granting of an application made by the person to whom the warning or decision notice was given[1].

Final Notice

If a person who received a decision notice did not refer the matter to the Tribunal within the period mentioned in section 133(1), the FSA will issue a final notice. But if the matter is referred to the Tribunal, the FSA must, on taking action in accordance with any directions from the Tribunal or by the court under section 137, issue a final notice setting out the terms of statement and give details of the manner in which, and the date on which, the statement will be published. A final notice about an order must set out the terms stating the date it will take effect, but a final notice about a penalty must state the amount of the penalty and the manner in which and the period within which the penalty must be paid and the proposed method of recovering it. If it is not paid within the stipulated date, the final notice in accordance with section 384(5)[2] must state the person to whom, the manner in which and the period within which it must be paid. In the case of a final notice about a penalty and a final notice about a requirement to make payment or distribution, the period of the notice may not be less than 14 days beginning with the date on which the final notice was given. If any other required payment or distribution has not been made within the period stated in the final notice about a requirement to make payment or distribution, the obligation will be enforced on the application of the FSA by injunction or, in Scotland, by an order under section 45 of the Court of Session Act 1988.

Publication

Neither party to a warning notice or decision notice may publish the

---

[1] Section 389.
[2] Section 384 is concerned with the restitution required by the FSA.

notice or any details therein. In respect of a notice of discontinuance, the FSA, with the consent of the person to whom the notice is addressed, may publish such information. But the Authority must publish the information about the matter to which a final notice relates. Where a supervisory notice takes effect, the FSA must publish such information as it may consider appropriate[3].

But the FSA may not publish information under section 391 if publication of it would, in its opinion, be unfair to a person against whom action was taken as prejudicial to the interests of consumers. Under section 391(7) it is for the FSA to determine which information would be appropriate to publish.

If any of the reasons contained in a warning or decision notice relates to a matter which identified a third party, and if that matter is prejudicial to that party, then a copy of the notice must be given to the third party, giving it an opportunity to make representations within not less than 38 days. A third party need not be given a copy of a notice if a separate warning or a decision notice has been given to him. Section 392 gives third party's right to seek disclosure of the FSA's material. Section 392 lists the particular sections of the Act where a third party's rights in relation to sections 393 and 394 apply.

Section 394 deals with the issue of access to the FSA's material. If the FSA gives an authorized person a notice, it must allow that person access to the material on which it relied in taking the decision as well as to secondary material which, in the opinion of the party, might undermine that decision, but the FSA is not required to allow access to an authorized person's material if the material is *'excluded material'*[4] or it relates to a case involving a person other than the authorized person, and *'was taken into account by the Authority [the FSA] in A's case only for purposes of comparison with other cases'*.[5]

[3] *'Supervisory notice'* means a notice given in accordance with section
   (a) 53(4), (7) or (8)(b);
   (b) 78(2) or (5);
   (c) 197(3), (6) or (7)(b);
   (d) 259(3), (8) or (9)(b);
   (e) 268(3), (7)(a) or (9)(a) (as a result of subsection (8)(b));
   (f) 282(3), (6) or (7)(b);
   (g) 321(2) or (5)' (section 395(13).
[4] Section 394(7)(a)-(d).
[5] Section 394(2)(b).

The FSA may refuse an authorized person access to particular material if, in its opinion, access to that material would be contrary to public interest or could cause potential prejudice to the *'commercial interests of a person other than an authorized person which would be caused by the material's disclosure'.*[6]

Where the FSA would refuse the authorized person access to material because it is excluded material, it must give the authorized person a written notice of the protected item. It is for the FSA to decide on its procedures, but under section 395(2) the FSA, in order to avoid prejudice, should develop a procedure which would ensure that the decision whether to issue a warning or a decision or a supervisory notice should be carried out by different people. However, section 395(4) provides that this requirement may be waived for supervisory notice if it appears to be necessary to do so in order to protect the interests of consumers. The FSA must issue a statement of the procedure and that statement must be brought to the attention of the public and a copy of it must be submitted to the Treasury.

Statements made under section 395 must go through a consultation procedure, that is, the draft version must be brought to the attention of the public and they must be provided with an opportunity to make representations. If a statement or procedure differs from a draft version to a significant extent, when the representations are taken into account the details of the differences must be published.

Conclusions

In various Parts of the Act, provisions for notices have been included. This is because the FSA, in taking its decisions as to whether to grant or to withdraw authorization and approvals or to take action on information, has decided to serve warning notices and decision notices on authorized persons concerned.

The primary purpose of a *'warning notice'* in particular, as its title suggests, is to warn an authorized person as to suspected derogation from the regulatory framework, so that it may correct its position. This system has two advantages:

(a) that the authorized person concerned can still carry out

---

[6] Section 394(3)(b).

corrective or remedial work to ensure the confidence of its customers; and

(b) the protection of any financially devastating event from taking place on the market.

An authorized person should really avoid creating a situation whereby it will be served with a decision notice or final notice. It is to be emphasized however that the third-party rights to receive copies of notices[7] is a signal to prepare themselves for their remedial rights as to the loss of their investments.

---

[7] Section 393.

18 Investigations and Control

Introduction

Investigation is to be regarded as a component of control. The Act authorizes the FSA to retain information on authorized persons and if information on them causes concern, to carry out investigations on them. The purpose is to protect the interests of investors and customers and a means of reminding authorized persons of the need for conforming to the regulatory framework.

The FSA's decision to exercise its power under Part XI must be regarded as an indication of a derogation from the regulatory framework by an authorized person, and it must cooperate with the FSA in providing information, or be compelled to provide information, of documents under the coercive procedure available to the FSA.

Investigations

Either the FSA or the Secretary of State can appoint a person to carry on the investigations into collective investment schemes, not open-ended investment companies, or provisions concerning those investigations that can be made by the Treasury's regulations[1]. The powers extend to investigating the affairs of all of the managers or trustees of authorized unit trust schemes, or operator, trustee or depositary of any recognized scheme in relation to its activities carried on in the UK, or an operator, trustee or depositary of any other collective investment scheme except a body incorporated by virtue of regulations under section 262. An investigation can be initiated if deemed desirable

---

[1] Section 262.

to do so in the interests of participants, actual or potential, or that the matter is of public concern.

The provisions of section 170 generally apply and the statements made to the investigator may be based as admissible evidence in proceedings[2]. The power of entry under section 176 is also available to an investigating authority along with the power to investigate persons other than those mentioned, when necessary. Failure to comply with the requirement of an investigation may be referred to a court, and misrepresentation or concealment of a fact will be construed as an offence[3].

Information Gathering and Investigations

Section 165 of the Act authorizes the FSA to obtain information from an authorized person on its business activities, but it does not identify the circumstances in which the FSA may exercise this power. The FSA has unlimited power in this regard whereby it may require an authorized person to provide it with information or documents, whether specified or of a type, without delay. Section 196(4) provides that this section applies '...*only to information and documents reasonably required in connection with the exercise by the Authority of functions conferred on it by or under this Act*'. The FSA's decision on 'reasonably required' is final.

The same power may be exercised by the FSA in regard to persons who are connected with the authorized person, or an operator, or trustee, or a depositary of a Compensation Scheme recognized under sections 270 or 272, who is not an authorized person, or a recognized investment exchange or a clearing house.

For the purpose of section 165 a person is 'connected with an authorized person' if he is or has at any material time been a member of the authorized person's group, or a controller of an authorized person, or any other member of a partnership of which an authorized person, or any other member of a partnership of which an authorized person is a member, or in relation to an authorized person, a person mentioned in Part of Schedule XV[4].

---

[2] Section 174.
[3] See further paragraphs 5.1.2 and 5.1.3, *Explanatory Notes, Financial Services and Markets Act 2000*, Chapter 8, the Stationery Office Ltd, London, 2000.
[4] Schedule XV (Information and Investigation: Connected Persons).

Under section 166 the FSA may, by notice in writing, require provision of reports by a skilled person in a prescribed form. Such skilled persons must be deemed to have the skills necessary to make a report on the matter concerned and be nominated or approved by the FSA.

If it appears to the FSA or the Secretary of State (the Investigating Authority) that it has not got resources for appointing persons to carry on the general investigations, the Investigating Authority may appoint one or more competent persons to conduct that investigation on its behalf. All investigation must be carried out upon written notice to the authorized person concerned or a person who is connected with an authorized person. Investigations into the affairs of a former authorized person or its appointed representatives may be only in relation to the business carried on at the material time to which the investigation relates.

'*Business*' in this context includes any part of the business even if it does not relate to carrying on regulated activities.

In fact, the FSA has very broad powers of investigation under various sections, namely 142, 177, 191, 346, 398, Schedule IV, 24(1) or 397, or under Part V of the Criminal Justice Act 1993, or section 21 or 239, or if a breach of general prohibition or a market abuse has taken place, the Investigating Authority may appoint one or more persons to conduct investigation on its behalf.

In addition to the above, persons can be appointed to carry out investigations if it appears to the FSA that there are circumstances suggesting that:

a) a person may have contravened section 20; or

b) a person will be guilty of an offence relating to money laundering; or

c) an authorized person may have contravened a rule made by the FSA; or

d) an individual person may have contravened a rule made by the FSA; or

e) an individual may not be a fit and proper person to perform functions in relation to a regulated activity carried on by an authorized or exempt person; or

f) an individual has already performed or agreed to perform a function in breach of a prohibition order; or

g) an authorized or exempt person may have failed to comply with section 56(6)[5]; or

h) an authorized person has failed to comply with section 59(1) or (2)[6]; or

i) a person who has been given approval under section 59 may not be a fit and proper person to perform the function to which the approval relates; or

j) a person may be guilty of misconduct for the purpose of section 66 of the Act[7].

---

[5] 'An authorized person must take reasonable care to ensure that no function of his, in relation to the carrying on of a regulated activity, is performed by a person who is prohibited from performing that function by a prohibition order' (section 56(6)).

[6] '(1) An authorized person ("A") must take reasonable care to ensure that no person performs a controlled function under an arrangement entered into by A in relation to the carrying on by A of a regulated activity, unless the Authority approves the performance by that person of the controlled function to which the arrangement relates.

(2) An authorized person ("A") must take reasonable care to ensure that no person performs a controlled function under an arrangement entered into by a contractor of A in relation to the carrying on by A of a regulated activity, unless the Authority approves the performance by that person of the controlled function to which the arrangement relates.'

[7] '(1) The Authority may take action against a person under this section if
 (a) it appears to the Authority that he is guilty of misconduct; and
 (b) the Authority is satisfied that it is appropriate in all the circumstances to take action against him.

(2) A person is guilty of misconduct if, while an approved person
 (a) he has failed to comply with a statement of principle issued under section 64; or
 (b) he has been knowingly concerned in a contravention by the relevant authorized person of a requirement imposed on that authorized person by or under this Act.

(3) If the Authority is entitled to take action under this section against a person, it may
 (a) impose a penalty on him of such amount as it considers appropriate; or
 (b) publish a statement of his misconduct.

(4) The Authority may not take action under this section after the end of the period of two years beginning with the first day on which the Authority knew of the misconduct, unless proceedings in respect of it against the person concerned were begun before the end of that period.

(cont. on p.339)

Investigations in support of Overseas Regulators

At the request of an overseas regulator, the FSA may exercise its power to gather information (section 165) or to investigate any matter. Section 169(3) provides that:

> *'If the request has been made by a competent authority in pursuance of any Community obligation the Authority must, in deciding whether or not to exercise its investigative power, consider whether its exercise is necessary to comply with any such obligation.'*

In deciding whether or not to exercise its investigative powers, the FSA has a wide discretion, but it may take into account, in particular, the following:

(a) whether a reciprocal system of assistance would be operational, if necessary, between the overseas regulator concerned and the UK regulatory activity;

(b) whether, in the case of breach of law, any close parallel of the breach exists in the UK jurisdiction that is not recognized by the UK;

(c) the seriousness of the case and its implications to persons in the UK; and

(d) whether in the public interest it might be appropriate to give the assistance sought.

The FSA may not exercise its investigative power unless the overseas regulator undertakes to make contributions the costs as the FSA may consider appropriate. Those conditions, of course, do not apply if the FSA exercises its investigative power to comply with the community

(5) For the purposes of subsection (4)
  (a) the Authority is to be treated as knowing of misconduct if it has information from which the misconduct can reasonably be inferred; and
  (b) proceedings against a person in respect of misconduct are to be treated as begun when a warning notice is given to him under section 67(1).
(6) 'Approved person' has the same meaning as in section 64.
(7) 'Relevant authorized person', in relation to an approved person, means the person on whose application approval under section 59 was given.' (section 66 of the Act).

obligations. The investigator appointed may permit a representative of the overseas regulator to take part in any interview conducted for the purposes of the investigation[8]. No investigation can be conducted unless the investigative authority has given a written notice which must specify the provisions under which, and the reason for which, an investigator is appointed. An investigator's report must be submitted by an investigator to the investigating authority, who has the power to determine the scope of investigation, the duration of the investigation, the conduct of the investigation and the manner in which it will be reported, along with interim reports, if necessary. In the event of any change in the scope of the conduct of the investigation that might significantly prejudice the position of a person subject to an investigation, then that person must be given written notice of the change. The provisions of the conduct of investigations, in general, do not apply if an investigator is appointed as the result of section 168(1) or 168(4) and the investigating authority believes that the carrying out of the investigation will be frustrated[9].

An investigator may require the person to be investigated to attend before itself at a specified time and place, and answer questions and submit documents of a specified description or provide such information as required. Only the information and the document(s) that are relevant to the purposes of investigation may be called for. For the purpose of carrying out an investigation, a person is connected to the person under investigation ('the authorized person') if he is or at any material time has been a member of the authorized person or with the partnership of which the authorized person is a member or has been in relation to the authorized person as a person mentioned in Part I and II of Schedule XV. Part I of Schedule XV provides for additional rules in respect of a person who is or at the material time has been a partner, manager, employee, agent, appointed representative, banker, auditor, actuary or solicitor of an authorized person under investigation, a parent or subsidiary undertaking of the authorized person, or a parent undertaking of a subsidiary undertaking of an authorized person. An investigator may also require any other person to attend before the investigator at a

[8] Such a direction cannot be given unless the FSA is satisfied that any information obtained by the overseas regulator will be subject to safeguards equivalent to those contained in Part XXIII.
[9] Sub-sections 168(1) and 168(4) have already been discussed in this chapter.

specified time and place and answer questions or otherwise provide such information as the investigator may require. These requirements are equally applicable to investigations which have particularly a hint of criminal offence[10].

Any statements made by a person under an investigation to an appointed investigator will be regarded as admissible evidence in any legal proceedings, provided it complies with any requirements governing the admissibility of evidence[11]. However, no evidence relating to the statements made by a person who is under investigation or a person who is accused of market abuse[12] may be advised or asked by or on behalf of the prosecution or the FSA, unless '...*the evidence relating to it is addressed or a question relating to it is asked, in the proceedings by or on behalf of the person*'.[13]

All powers to provide documents may be extended to include a third party who may be in possession of such documents. The FSA or an appointed investigator has the authority to take copies or extracts from the document that has been produced or to require the person producing the document or any relevant person[14] to provide an explanation of the document[15]. Should a person fail to produce a document, the FSA or an investigator may require him to state, to the best of his knowledge and belief, where the document is. A person may not be required to disclose information or produce a document if he owes an obligation of confidentiality by virtue of carrying on the business of banking unless:

(a) he is the person who is subject to an investigation procedure or he is a member of that person's group; or

(b) the person to whom the obligation of confidentiality is owed is also the person under investigation or a member of that person's group; or

---

[10] See section 168(2).
[11] Section 174(1).
[12] Section 123.
[13] Section 174(2).
[14] A *'relevant person'* in this context would include: a person who has been or is proposed to be a director or controller of the person who is required to produce a document; an auditor of that person; or has been or is an actuary or an accountant or a lawyer instructed by that person; or has been or is an employee of that person.
[15] Section 175(2).

(c) the person to whom the obligation of confidentiality is owed has consented to the disclosure of information or production of documents; or

(d) the investigating authority has specifically authorized the imposition of the requirements of disclosure of information or production of documents.

For a document on which a lien has been created, its production will not affect the lien.

Disclosure of information and/or production of documents may be obtained even by entering the premises of a person on the basis of a warrant issued by a justice of the peace (under section 176), providing he is satisfied by information on oath provided by or on behalf of the Secretary of State, the FSA or an investigator that there are reasonable grounds for believing that the first, second or third set of the conditions is satisfied.

The First Set of Conditions

(a) the person concerned has failed, wholly or in part, to comply with the requirement of disclosure of information or production of documents; and

(b) that the documents or information which are required are available on the premises specified in the warrant.

The Second Set of Conditions

(a) that the premises are those specified in the warrant of an authorized person or appointed representative; and

(b) that the documents or information in relation to which an information requirement could be imposed are on the premises; and

(c) if such a requirement were to be imposed it would either not be complied with or the documents or information without the warrant would be removed, tempered with or destroyed.

The Third Set of Conditions

(a) that the person concerned has already committed the offence mentioned in section 168, and that the maximum sentence has been imposed on him;

(b) that there are on the premises specified documents or information relevant to whether that offence has been or is being committed;

(c) that the requirement of seeking information could be imposed in relation to these documents or information;

(d) that if such a requirement were to be imposed the person concerned would not comply with it or that the documents or information to which the warrant relates would be removed, tampered with or destroyed.

A constable can only enter a premises with a warrant authorizing the constable to search the premises for any documents or information in respect of which a warrant is issued; to take any other steps which may be deemed necessary for preserving them or preventing interference with them; to take copies of or extracts from any documents or information which may be deemed relevant and to require any person on the premises to provide any explanation of any documents or information which may appear to be relevant. Section 176 also authorizes the constable to use force for the purpose of seeking information or obtaining documents but force must be reasonable.

In relation to entry and search, in England and Wales sections 15(5) to (8) and section 16 of the Police and Criminal Evidence Act 1984 (Execution of Search Warrants and Safeguards) apply to warrants issued under section 176 of the Act[16].

A person who knows or suspects that an investigation is being or is likely to be conducted under Part XI is guilty of an offence, if:

'(a) he falsifies, conceals, destroys or otherwise disposes of a document which he knows or suspects is or would be relevant to such an investigation, or

---

[16] In Northern Ireland, Articles 17(5) to (8) and 18 of the Police and Criminal Evidence (Northern Ireland) Order 1989 apply to warrants issued under this section. In relation to Scotland, the references to a justice of peace are to be replaced by reference to a justice of the peace or a sheriff, and references to information on oath by evidence on oath.

(b) he causes or permits the falsification, concealment, destruction or disposal of such a document..."[17]

unless he is able to establish that he had no intention of concealing the documents from the investigator.

A person who, in purported compliance with the requirements of Part XI, knowingly provides information that is false or misleading, or recklessly provides information which is false or misleading, is guilty of an offence.

Conclusions

Compared to the 1987 Act, the FSA's powers of investigation and search are more extensive and draconian in nature.

Some of the measures provided by the Act, for instance investigation of suspected 'market abuse', might provoke controversy. The issue of transparency has received much attention in this legislation. The question remains whether transparency of information and/or documents to its extreme might violate some of the provisions of the Human Rights Act 1998.

In regard to 'assistance to overseas regulators' it may be pointed out that mutual assistance may be expected only when the standards and systems of the two parties are similar. The 'catch all' clause *'whether it is otherwise appropriate in the public interest to give the assistance sought'* may in certain cases restrict the scope of assistance, although the need for such a clause may not be overemphasized.

---

[17] Section 177(3)(a) and (b).

19 Intervention and Disciplinary Measures by the FSA

Introduction

'Intervention' in this context stands for the power of the FSA to intervene in the business of EEA and Treaty firms that have been authorized by virtue of Schedules 3 and 4 – the incoming firms. Part XIII (section 194) details the grounds on which the FSA may exercise its power to intervene in the way an EEA firm conducts its business. The FSA's intervention power may be exercised in support of an overseas regulator only if requested, because the regulation of EEA firms is primarily the responsibility of the home country competent authority.

'Disciplinary measures' stands for the measures that the FSA may take in the form of public censure, public statements or financial penalties because of breach of rules or other requirements by authorized persons, all subject to the notice procedure.

Intervention of the FSA in respect of the Incoming Firms

An incoming firm is an EEA firm that is exercising or has exercised its right to carry on a regulated activity in the UK in accordance with Schedule 3, that is, in the exercise of its EEA passport rights, or a treaty firm, that is, a firm as above but in accordance with Schedule 4. The FSA's powers of intervention under section 194 seem to be broad, and, in particular, it may exercise this power if it appears to the FSA that:

   i. the firm has already contravened or is likely to contravene a requirement under the Act in a case where the FSA is responsible for enforcing compliance in the UK; or

ii. in its purported compliance with any requirements under this Act, the firm has knowingly or reluctantly given the FSA false or misleading information on a matter on which it is required to provide information; or

iii. in order to protect the interests of customers, actual or potential, it is desirable to intervene.

The FSA may exercise its powers of intervention if the Director-General of Fair Trading has notified the FSA that an EEA firm or any of its employees, agents or associates whether past or present, or if the firm is a body corporate, a controller of the firm or an associate of such a controller has done any of the things specified in paragraphs (a) – (d) of section 25(2) of the Consumer Credit Act 1974 or in respect of an incoming firm at the request of or for the purpose of assisting an overseas regulator.

The FSA's function under section 195 also extends to include investigations of conduct of a kind prohibited under Part V of the Criminal Justice Act 1993 (Insider Dealing) or the enforcement of rules relating to such conduct or any other function that may be prescribed by regulations under section 195(4) which in the opinion of the Treasury relates to the companies or financial services.

If in pursuance of the community obligations a home state regulator requests the FSA to exercise its power of intervention, or notifies the FSA that an EEA firm's authorization has been withdrawn, then the FSA must consider whether exercising its power of intervention is necessary to comply with a community obligation. In deciding if it should intervene it may take into account, in particular, whether in the jurisdiction concerned corresponding assistance would be given or whether this is a case of breach of the law or another requirement, which has no close parallel in the UK, or which involves assertion of jurisdiction not recognized by the UK, or whether it is otherwise appropriate in the public interest to render the assistance sought. In the case of the FSA's intervention in response to a request by an overseas regulator the costs must be borne by the overseas regulator; however, the issue of costs does not arise when the FSA exercises its power to comply with a community obligation, being able to impose any requirement on the firm which it could impose if the firm was to have a Part IV permission.

A notice is necessary for activating the intervention powers of the FSA. This notice must:

(a) give details of the requirement under section 196;

(b) inform the firm when the requirement takes effect;

(c) state the FSA's reason for imposing the requirement;

(d) inform the firm of its right to make representation to the FSA within the period specified in the notice; and

(e) inform the firm of its right to refer the matter to the Tribunal.

The FSA has the discretionary power to extend the period under the notice for making representations.

If, after consideration of the representations made by the firm, the FSA decides to impose the requirement or not to rescind a requirement, it must give the firm a written notice to that effect; on the other hand, if it should decide not to impose the requirement or vary it or to rescind it, it must also give similar notice, clearly indicating that it has the right to refer the matter to the Tribunal.

The FSA also has power to apply to the High Court in England and Wales or the Court of Session in Scotland for an injunction in respect of certain overseas insurance companies if it receives a request in respect of an incoming EEA firm in accordance with Article 20.5 of the First Non-Life Insurance Directive or Article 24.5 of the First Life Insurance Directive. The court may grant an injunction (in Scotland it is known an interdict) whereby the firm will be restrained from disposing of assets or dealing with any of its assets henceforth; the court has also power to make a supplemental order regarding incidental and consequential matters. Under section 119 the FSA has the power to intervene in relation to an incoming EEA firm that has been in breach of a requirement imposed by the FSA and a requirement under any single-market directives, instructing the firm in writing to remedy the situation. Should the firm fail to rectify the situation within a reasonable period of time, the FSA is required to give a notice to the firm's home state regulator requesting it to take all appropriate measures for remedying the situation, informing the FSA of the measures it proposes to take or has taken; or the reasons for not taking any measures. Generally, the FSA may not exercise its power of intervention unless it is satisfied that either the firm's home state regulator has failed or refused to take measures for remedying the situation, or that the measures taken by the home state regulator have proved inadequate. In the event of emergency the FSA has the power of intervention in order to protect the interests of consumers even prior to notifying the firm and the home state regulator, notifying the home state regulator and the commission at the earliest possible opportunity. The Commission has the power under any of the single-market directives to decide whether the FSA must rescind or vary any requirement imposed in the exercise of its power of intervention.

The FSA has the discretion to rescind or vary a requirement imposed in exercise of its power of intervention either on the basis of an application made by the person concerned, or on its own initiative. If the requirement is rescinded or varied a person concerned must be notified accordingly. Where the FSA proposes to refuse an application for a variation or rescission of a requirement, it must give the applicant a warning notice, but where it decides to refuse an application made for these purposes the FSA must give the applicant a decision notice, and the person concerned has the right to refer the decision to the Tribunal. A contravention of a requirement imposed under Part XIII does not make a person guilty of an offence, nor does it make a transaction void or unenforceable, or give rise to any right of action for breach of statutory duty[1].

Under section 203 the Director-General of Fair Trading has powers to prohibit carrying on a business under the Consumer Credit Act 1974 if it appears to him that a firm[2] has contravened, or is likely to contravene, that Act; he may serve notice on the firm imposing a consumer prohibition or a restriction. A prohibition under section 203 would have

---

[1] In certain prescribed cases, however, a contravention is actionable at the suit of a person who has suffered loss as a result of the contravention, but in order to bring such an action defences applied to action of breach of statutory duty should be looked into.

[2] 'Firm' in this context would also include any of its employees, agents or associates, past or present or if the firm is a body corporate any controller of the firm or an associate of any such controller. Contravention in this context principally relates to the matters referred to in paragraphs (a)-(d) of section 25(2) of the Consumer Credit Act 1974.

the effect of disallowing the firm from carrying on or purporting to carry on in the UK any Consumer Credit Act business 'which consists of or includes carrying on one or more listed activities'.[3]

A consumer credit prohibition may be either absolute or it may be imposed for a limited period of time, and until the conditions are complied with, the Director-General has the discretion to vary any period, event or condition or he may even withdraw the prohibition if he is satisfied that variation or withdrawal would be justified. Contravention of provisions under section 203 will make a person guilty of an offence[4]. The firm must be given an opportunity to submit representations in accordance with paragraph 4 of Schedule 16, and a prohibition or restriction must not come into force before the end of an appeal period. A copy of the prohibition or restriction must be submitted to the FSA and the EEA firm's home state regulator.

The Director-General has the power to impose restrictions instead of a prohibition if it appears to be appropriate to do so, and a restriction may be withdrawn or varied with the agreement of the firm concerned, confirmed by written notice which will take effect on the date specified in the notice. A firm contravening a restriction is guilty of an offence.

Disciplinary Measures

In addition to the various types of controlling powers, namely, supervisory, and interventionary, the FSA has also the power to take disciplinary measures against authorized persons. These measure progress through stages:

(a) public censure;

(b) financial penalties; and

(c) disciplinary measures.

Public censure takes place when the FSA considers that an authorized person has contravened a requirement imposed on him, and it may

---

[3] Section 203(3).
[4] *'A firm contravening a prohibition under this section is guilty of an offence and liable (a) on summary conviction, to a fine not exceeding the statutory maximum; (b) on conviction on indictment, to a fine'* (section 203(9)).

publish a statement in order to make the contravention public (section 205) and the FSA may also impose a financial penalty, payable to the FSA, of such amount as it may consider appropriate (section 204). However, a penalty will not be accompanied by withdrawal of the authorization under section 33. Disciplinary measures, public censure or a penalty must be preceded by a warning notice. Whereas a warning notice of public censure must set out the terms of the statement, the precise amount of the penalty must be shown in the warning notice of a proposal to impose a penalty.

If the FSA decides to publish a statement under section 205 or to impose a penalty under section 206, it must promptly serve on the authorized person concerned a *decision notice*, setting out the terms of the statement and the amount of the penalty, as the case may be. The authorized person has the right to refer the decision to the Tribunal. A copy of the published statement must be sent to the authorized person or to any person on whom a copy of the decision notice was served under section 393(4).

In developing a policy in regard to the amount of penalty, the authority would have regard to:

(a) the seriousness of the contravention in question pertaining to a requirement;

(b) whether the contravention was deliberate or reckless; and

(c) whether the person on whom the penalty is to be imposed is an individual.

The FSA is required to issue a statement of policy regarding the imposition and amount of penalties, but can alter or place it. A copy of the altered or replaced statement must be sent to the Treasury and must be published in a way that would bring the matter clearly to the public. A publication of a further version of the statement must be preceded by a draft version which would also be brought clearly to the attention of the public and which would invite representations from the public within specified period of time. Prior to its issuing the final version of the statement the FSA must pay attention to representations; and in the event of significant differences, the FSA must publish details of the difference.

Injunctions and Restitutions

The FSA and, in certain cases, the Secretary of State may seek injunctions or restitutions orders from the High Court (in Scotland, the Court of Session) against authorized and unauthorized persons if, in their opinion, certain requirements have already been or might be contravened. Under section 380 they may make an application for an injunction if the court is satisfied that there is a reasonable likelihood that the person may contravene a requirement or that the person who has already contravened is likely to contravene a again. The court may make an order restraining (in Scotland, interdict prohibiting the contravention) if it is satisfied that a person has actually contravened the relevant requirement and that steps could be taken for remedying the contravention. If the court is satisfied that a person may have contravened or been knowingly concerned in the contravention of such a requirement, it may make an order (or in Scotland an interdict-prohibit) restraining him from disposing of or otherwise dealing with any assets that he is reasonably likely to dispose of or otherwise deal with. Under section 380 the court may exercise two types of power: preventative and curative. The term *'restraining a person from disposing of his assets'* would mean an order to freeze a person's assets in the way a Mareva injunction used to be applied for such purposes. The likelihood of disposing of assets would need to be established before the court; otherwise the relevant provisions of the Human Rights Act 1998 may be used as a defence.

The Act gives the FSA the authority to make an application to the court for grounds of injunctions in cases of market abuse. The FSA is required to satisfy the court that there is a reasonable likelihood that the person will engage in a market abuse or that a person is or has actually engaged in market abuse, and that there is a reasonable likelihood that the market abuse will continue or will be repeated. If by applying an objective test the court is satisfied that the person has actually been engaged or is engaged in market abuse, then the court may make an order restraining (in Scotland an interdict) the market abuse and, secondly, it may require the market abuser to take such steps as the court may require to remedy it. Again, along the lines of section 380, the court under section 381 may make an order restraining the abuser from disposing of its assets (a freezing order). Any references to remedying any market abuse would also include references to mitigating its effect.

Section 382 is concerned with restitution orders. This section allows the FSA or the Secretary of State to make an application to the court for a restitution order, and the court may issue such an order if it is satisfied that a person has contravened a relevant requirement or been knowingly concerned in the contravention of such a requirement, and if the court is also satisfied that profits had accrued to him or the result of contravention is that one person or more have suffered losses or been otherwise adversely affected as the result of contravention the court may order the person concerned to pay such sum as may appear to it to be just having regard to the profits accrued to the person, the extent of the loss and other adverse effects, or both. However, these criteria must be satisfied by objective evidence.

Any amount paid to the FSA must be paid by the latter to such qualifying persons or distributed among such qualifying persons as the court may direct. *'Qualifying persons'* in this context would mean persons who would appear to the court to be these to whom profits are attributable or who have suffered loss or adverse effect as the result of the contravention[5]. The court may require such a person to submit such accounts and information for establishing whether any and, if so, what profits are accrued to him and whether any person or persons have suffered any loss or adverse effect. The court may also require such person to submit accounts or other information for verification of the liability.

Section 382(7) provides that the fact that the FSA or the Secretary of State has made an application for a restitution order does not affect the right of any person other than the FSA or the Secretary of State to bring proceedings under this Part.

Section 383 is concerned with restitution orders in cases of market abuse. The court may on the application of the FSA make an order. If it is satisfied that a person has engaged in market abuse or has encouraged another person to be engaged in similar behaviour the court may on the application of the FSA make an order whereby the person concerned would be required to pay to the FSA such sum as it would appear to the

---

[5] Section 382(8).

court to be just, having regard to the profits that would appear to the court to have accrued or to the extent of the loss or other adverse effect or both. The only conditions that must be satisfied before such an order is issued is that the profits have accrued to the person concerned as the result of market abuse or that one or more persons have suffered losses or have been otherwise adversely affected as a result.

The court may not make a restitution order in cases of alleged market abuse if it is satisfied that the person concerned believed on reasonable grounds that its behaviour did not fall in any of the categories of market abuse or that it took all reasonable precautions, and exercised due diligence[6], to avoid behaving in a way that would make him responsible for market abuse. The court may order the person concerned to pay the FSA such sum as it may appear to it to be just having regard to the profits it has accrued or the extent of the losses or other adverse effects suffered by consumers, or both, and any amount that may be paid to the FSA in pursuance of the court order must be paid by the FSA to such qualifying persons as the court may direct. *'Qualifying persons'* in this context would mean the person to whom profits are attributable or the person who suffered losses or adverse effect occasioned by the conduct of the authorized person.

Again, the court may require the person concerned to submit to it accounts or other information to establish whether any and, if so, what profits have accrued to the person concerned and whether any person or persons have suffered losses or adverse effect, or both. Again, the extent of loss or adverse effect must be established by objective evidence.

Section 384 gives the FSA power to require restitution if it is satisfied that an authorized person has engaged in, or encouraged another to engage in, market abuse or contravened a relevant requirement and that profits have accrued to him as the result of the contravention or market abuse and that one or more persons have suffered losses or have otherwise been adversely affected as the result of the contravention or market abuse.

The only defence that the person concerned may have is that he believed on reasonable grounds that his behaviour did not fall within the criteria of market abuse or that he took all reasonable precautions and exercised all due diligence to avoid being accused of abuse of market

---

[6] See Chapter 3.

behaviour. However, if the section 384 criteria are satisfied the FSA has the power to require the person concerned to pay such amount as it appears to the FSA to be just having regard to the profits already accrued and the extent of the losses and other adverse effects.

There are some points that need to be highlighted in this context:

(a) the Secretary of State has no direct powers under this Part to require restitution;

(b) the extent of losses suffered must be objectively established;

(c) if the FSA wishes to exercise its power under section 384(5) (Payment to the Appropriate Persons or Distribute among the Appropriate Persons), it is required to issue a warning notice specifying the amount which he will be required to pay or distribute, and where a decision notice is to be issued, it must state the amount that he is required to pay or distribute, identify the person or persons to whom the amount is to be paid or distributed and state the arrangements in accordance with which the payment or distribution is to be made[7]. There is the right to refer the matter to the Tribunal.

The Enforcement Manual

In the Consultation Paper 30 entitled *The FSA's Regulation of Professional Firms* the FSA set out proposals for the future regulation of firms the investment business of which is normally regulated by Recognized Professional Bodies (Disapplication Orders against members of the professions). The issue is whether the FSA should be allowed to apply direct regulation to professional firms carrying out certain regulated activities. Members entitled to an exemption will be able to conduct certain regulated activities without the FSA's authorization, under section 326 and 327.

However, the FSA's power to disqualify in certain circumstances professional firms from carrying on regulated activities is derived from section 329 of the Act, and as a consequence it will be able to prevent such firms from carrying on that regulated activities to which a *'disapplication'* order applies. In the event of a firm persisting in carrying

---

[7] Section 386.

out the regulated activities to which the disapplication order relates, a breach of the general prohibition will take place. The FSA maintains however that it shall consider whether a prohibition order against those individuals should be made rather than disapplying the firm's exemption, liasing closely with relevant designated professional bodies when deciding, taking into account: whether any disciplinary action has been taken by a designated professional body as to the fitness and propriety of the firm; what kinds of risk the firm presents to its clients; and the extent to which the firm concerned has complied with the FSA's rules.

In determining whether to vary or reverse an order disapplying an exemption, the FSA proposes to consider the following factors:

- the nature of steps taken by the firm to rectify the circumstances that gave rise to the original order;
- whether the firm has ceased to present any risks to clients and consumers or to the FSA's regulatory objectives;
- the circumstances that gave rise to the original order; and
- the time that has elapsed since the order was made[8].

The FSA also proposes to maintain a record of disapplication orders on the FSA website in accordance with the requirement of section 347(1)(i) of the Act, and the FSA must also maintain a public record of every person who has been subject to disapplication orders[9].

Conclusions

According to the FSA, the purposes of the Enforcement Manual are twofold: (a) to provide guidance on the proposed policies in the exercise of its range of enforcement powers[10]; and (b) to demonstrate compatibility with its general duties. The FSA further maintains this Manual will provide greater certainty as to how it will exercise its powers, and provide help with compliance costs and costs of regulation, maintaining consistent standards in the UK financial markets, and

---

[8] See the *Enforcement Manual*, op. cit., at paragraph 3.172.
[9] See further the *Enforcement Manual,*, op. cit., at paragraph 3.174.
[10] *The Manual*, op. cit., at Annex A, p.7.

increase the level of confidence in users in those markets.

The key policy proposals are:

(a) the decision-making powers – decision notice or supervisory notice, with provision to appeal to the Financial Services and Markets Tribunal; the establishment of a Regulatory Decisions Committee (RDC) to take decisions on behalf of the FSA in order to achieve an early resolution of the issues, instead of referring matters to the Tribunal; the RDC will separate the investigators and decision makers and incorporate provision for mediation in disciplinary and market abuse cases; and

(b) financial penalties – which entail a tariff-based system, a flexible system (case by case determination).

The FSA maintains that the Enforcement Manual is compatible with: the market confidence objective; the public awareness objective; the protection of consumers objective; and the reduction of financial crime objective.

The FSA believes that the draft Enforcement Manual is compatible with the general duty to have regard to:

(a) the need to use its resources in the most efficient and economic way;

(b) the responsibilities of those who manage the affairs of authorized persons;

(c) the principle that a burden or restriction should be proportionate to the benefits, considered in general terms, which are expected to result from the imposition of that burden or restriction;

(d) the desirability of facilitating innovation in connection with regulated activities;

(e) the international character of financial services and markets and the desirability of maintaining the competitive position of the UK;

(f) the need to minimize the adverse effects on competition that may arise from any exercise of its general functions; and

(g) the desirability of facilitating competition between those who are subject to any form of regulation by the FSA[11].

In May 2000, the FSA published the feedback statements on its Consultation Paper 33, and draft rules regarding complaints-handling arrangements. It is to be pointed out at the outset that the various aspects of the Financial Ombudsman Service Limited (FOS) are to be shared between the FSA and the FOS, on a date ('N2') not yet been finalized.

FOS will be made available to small businesses among other parties, the FSA has decided not to apply an employees' test during the initial period of the Scheme, but to apply a single £1 million annual turnover test[12], to be kept under review. The FSA will usually rely on self-certification by a firm, but it will have the right to ask the firm to provide evidence in confirmation of its turnover. A subsidiary of a corporate group may avail itself of the Scheme only if the group as a whole meets this test.

Consultation Paper 33 also proposed that the FOS should be made available to: private individuals, small businesses, and third parties, the latter particularly in the insurance industry[13]; but, in effect, these are all private customers.

In Consultation Paper 33, the FSA also proposed that all authorized firms should be subject to the Compulsory Jurisdiction; exempt firms would be required to certify to the FSA on an annual basis. Mortgage lenders will require authorization by the FSA (as soon as N2 is determined) and be subject to the Compulsory Jurisdiction of the Scheme. Although credit unions will be regulated by the FSA, they may not be subject to the Compulsory Jurisdiction until the final quarter of 2001.

The FSA also proposed that professional firms requiring authorization should be subject to the Compulsory Jurisdiction of the Scheme in respect of their regulated activities; exempt firms need not seek any

---

[11] See further *The Manual*, op. cit., Annex A at pp.1-6. As these proposals and the issue of compatibility are of a fundamental nature, the authors decided to reproduce them *ad verbatim*, rather than translating them or distorting them, without any intention whatsoever to reproduce them for any other purpose.[12] Charities will be subject to this £1 million test in relation to their income, but in the case of trustees, to the net assets of the trust.

[13] An insured person may have legal rights to enforce under the Contracts (Rights of Third Parties) Act 1999, or under other legislation.

authorization by the FSA. In order to ensure consistency of treatment the FSA proposed that complaints pertaining to professional bodies should be dealt with by the relevant professional body. The Society of Lloyd's will be subject to the Compulsory Jurisdiction of the Ombudsman Scheme in respect of complaints from personal policyholders and small businesses only. Complaints about the conduct of regulated activities within Lloyd's market will not come under the Scheme; thus Lloyd's will be required to maintain their own dispute-settlement machinery for dealing with complaints about the Society of Lloyd's and underwriting agents. By virtue of the *'passport'* system, EEA firms that may establish branches in the UK will be subject to the Compulsory Jurisdiction of the Scheme.

As to the territorial scope of the Ombudsman Scheme, the general view of the respondents was that the Scheme should cover authorized firms doing business in or from the UK. One of the concerns of the respondents was whether providing services to the United Kingdom through the Internet would require authorization. The FOS decided not to open the Voluntary Jurisdiction to such firms at present, but this matter will be kept under review[14].

As to the standard terms, the consensus was that there should be a harmonized set of rules for both the Compulsory and Voluntary Jurisdictions. In the case of the Voluntary Jurisdiction the FSA need not be notified by firms, which would however be required to give the FOS notice prior to their withdrawing from the Scheme.

With regard to complaint-handling by firms, the main concerns expressed by firms were: the definition of *'complaint'* for record keeping and reporting purposes; the time limits for dealing with complaints; and the time limit for keeping records of complaints.

Consultation Paper 33 proposed that the definition of a *'complaint'* for the purposes of firms' internal complaint-handling procedures should include any written or oral expression of dissatisfaction, whether justified or not[15].

Although the FSA continues to believe in the merits of adopting a wide definition of the term *'complaint'*, it recognized the concerns expressed by firms, and concluded that:

[14] Consultation Paper, op. cit., at paragraph 1.47.
[15] Consultation Paper, op. cit., at paragraph 1.68.

'... the wider definition of complaint should apply for the purposes of the general requirement on firms to have appropriate procedures for handling complaints, but that authorized firms should be required to keep records of – and report to the FSA on – complaints if they involve an allegation of financial loss and/or material distress or material inconvenience and relate to an activity within the Jurisdiction of the Scheme.'[16]

Controversy arose as to the time limits that should be allowed to deal with complaints; three principal proposals were put forward:

(a) a total of eight weeks for a firm to deal with and resolve a complaint under its internal procedures prior to its referring to the Scheme;

(b) a maximum of six months for referring a complaint to the Scheme; and

(c) to adopt the English law of limitations in respect of the time limit for making a complaint to the Scheme.

The proposed six-month time limit for complainants to refer cases to the Scheme met with general approval, allowing the Ombudsman a right to exercise his discretion to extend this time limit in appropriate cases.

A significant number of firms approved the requirement of reporting on a bi-annual basis[17]; and the FSA also proposed that firms should keep records of complaints for a minimum period of six years, but this requirement should not apply to Voluntary Jurisdiction participants, who should keep complaint records for a sufficient period in order to enable them to cooperate with the Ombudsman where complaints may be referred to the Scheme[18].

Consultation Paper 49 contains a chapter entitled *'Statement of Compatibility with the FSA's General Duties'*[19], in which it is attempted

---

[16] Consultation Paper, op. cit., at paragraph 1.70.
[17] According to this requirement the firms would be required to provide the FSA with the number of complaints received, the percentage of complaints resolved within a four-week and an eight-week period, and a breakdown according to the subject matter of those complaints.
[18] Consultation Paper 33, op. cit., at paragraph 1.87.
[19] Chapter 3.

to justify that the complaint-handling arrangements are compatible with the FSA's general duties and its consumer protection objective, its public awareness objective, and the market confidence and reduction of financial crime objectives.

The Consultation Paper (*Compulsory Jurisdiction*) maintains that the extension of the Scheme to small businesses would not result in significant costs, nor would the costs be significantly raised by making investment trust shareholders eligible for the Compulsory Jurisdiction. The Consultation Paper also maintains that the proposal for a monetary limit on Ombudsman awards of £100,000 would not create material costs. This observation is based on the fact that all but one of the existing complaints-handling schemes has an upper monetary limit of £100,000 on an award[20].

As to the compliance costs, the FSA maintains that costs on each case will depend on the size of the firm and the type and volume of business it does, and it estimated costs may vary between £50 and £1,700 per case and that awards by the FOS would not entail any significant additional costs. The incidence of complaints may be diminished by the fact that firms are required to satisfy compliance in respect of the following: *time limits* (by which complaints must usually be dealt with within four weeks); *access* (firms must publish their complaints-handling procedures and allow complainants access to them); *reporting* (whereby firms would be required to report twice yearly on the level and types of complaints received by them and provided to the FSA); *recording* (firms should make and retain records of any complaints for a certain fixed period); and *handling* (firms should ensure that complaints are adequately reviewed and that consumers are kept informed of the progress made about their complaints).

In its Consultation Paper 49 the FSA also identified the benefits that may arise from the single Ombudsman Scheme, which, in the main, are the following:

- as a result of increased consistency and uniform access to the Scheme, the quality of the complaints-handling process should improve;

- in view of a clearer access procedure, if the number increases,

---

[20] See the *Consultation Paper*, op.cit., at paragraph 4.17.

consumers will directly benefit by learning what they may expect of the system;

- a greater level of efficiency of operation will be achieved, particularly because of the standardization of procedures; and

- the extension of the Voluntary Scheme, where possible, should at least initially cater for all regulated firms, and the Compulsory Jurisdiction may be allowed to evolve at a reasonable pace[21].

Consultation Paper 49 also incorporated Draft Rules on complaints-handling procedures for firms, Jurisdiction rules, complaints-handling procedures of the Financial Ombudsman Services, and Standard Terms for Voluntary Jurisdiction. These rules were published by the FSA in May 2000. Schedule 17 to the Financial Services and Markets Act 2000 details the procedural aspects of the Ombudsman Scheme, and one is now required to follow the statutory provisions and the provisions of the Schedule.

---

[21] *Consultation Paper 49*, op. cit., at paragraph 4.8.

20 Dispute Settlement Procedures

Introduction

Part IX of the Act entitled *Hearings and Appeals* and Part XVI entitled *The Ombudsman Scheme* provide the dispute settlement procedures. Basically, the Ombudsman Scheme must be activated, where possible; but Part IX of the Act also sets up the Financial Services and Markets Tribunal. Whereas the principal purpose of the Ombudsman Scheme is to resolve disputes by an independent person, the Tribunal will be required to act when the FSA has decided to take regulatory action under the various powers conferred by the Act.

PART I
The Ombudsman Scheme

The principal purpose of the Ombudsman Scheme is to allow certain disputes to be resolved quickly and with minimum formality by an independent person. The Scheme is to be administered by a body corporate, to be known as the '*Scheme Operator*'. This Scheme has been further debated by Schedule 17.

Under the Scheme there are two jurisdictions: compulsory and voluntary; and two types of rule: '*compulsory jurisdiction rules*' and '*voluntary jurisdiction rules*'. Whereas compulsory jurisdiction rules are made by the *FSA* and are to be applied to specified activities; voluntary jurisdiction rules are made by the *Scheme Operator* and are to be applied to specified activities.

The Ombudsman has the power to seek a court order to compel a party to provide information and/or produce documents. Section 233 requires a new subsection to be added to section 31 of the Data Protection Act 1998 to ensure that the Scheme Operator would not be required to disclose information obtained when considering a complaint if disclosure would be likely to prejudice the proper discharge of its functions. The FSA has the authority to levy fees on authorized persons to meet the costs of establishing the Ombudsman's fee for running the compulsory jurisdiction. The costs of the voluntary jurisdiction will be met by fees determined under the voluntary jurisdiction rules.

The Scheme Operator

The Scheme Operator will have a chairman and a board (which must include the chairman), and its directors are its members. The FSA will be the appointing authority for the Chairman and the members of the board and will have the authority to remove them from their office. However, the terms and conditions of their appointment '*must be such as to secure their independence from the Authority [the FSA] in the operation of the Scheme*' (Schedule 17, clause 3(3)).

It is for the Scheme Operator to appoint and maintain a panel of qualified and appropriate persons to act as Ombudsmen for the purposes of the Scheme. In selecting such persons, the Scheme Operator must pay particular attention to the independence of the person, and shall appoint one member of the panel to act as the Chief Ombudsman, on such terms as it considers appropriate. Neither the Scheme Operator, Ombudsmen, members of the board nor staff of the Scheme Operator may be regarded as Crown Servants, and the Scheme Operator is not to be regarded as one who exercises his functions on behalf of the Crown (Schedule 17, Clause 6).

Both Scheme Operator and the Chief Ombudsman must publish and submit their reports to the FSA at least once a year, containing therein the functions performed in respect of both the compulsory jurisdiction and the voluntary jurisdiction.

The annual budget that will be adopted by the Scheme Operator and any variations must be approved by the FSA. Expenditures pertaining to the operation of both compulsory jurisdiction and voluntary jurisdiction must be shown separately.

The Scheme Operator has also the power to make what are known as '*Scheme Rules*' for setting procedure for reference of complaints and their investigation and determination by the Ombudsman. A complaint may be dismissed without consideration of its merits if:

(a) if the Ombudsman considers that a complaint is frivolous or vexatious; or

(b) that the legal proceedings that have already been brought on the subject matter of the complaint would be the preferred course of action; or

(c) according to the Ombudsman there are other compelling reasons for which it would be inappropriate to deal with the complaint under the Ombudsman Scheme.

Under the scheme rules the respondent may be required to pay the Scheme Operator as may be specified by those rules, or may provide for waiver or reduction of fees or a set of different fees or provide for a refund of fees altogether. Costs under the scheme will have the force of a county court order in England and Wales and be recovered by execution, or will have the force in Northern Ireland of a money judgement under the Judgements Enforcement (Northern Ireland) Order 1981 or in Scotland as if it were a Sheriff's Order.

The Scheme Operator may confer on the Ombudsman the award costs in relation to a complaint brought under the compulsory jurisdiction scheme, under cost rules approved by the FSA. Cost rules may not provide for the making of an award against the complainant in respect of the respondent's costs (Section 230(3)). But, these rules may '*provide for the making of an award against the complainant, if in the opinion of an Ombudsman, the complainant's conduct was improper or unreasonable or the complainant was responsible for an unreasonable delay*'.[1] The amount payable under the award will bear interest at a rate and as from a date specified in the order.

In sum, under section 230 (*Costs*), the Scheme Operator may make rules concerning the amount of costs that an Ombudsman may award. If a complaint is settled in favour of the complainant, the firm concerned will be required to meet the costs of the complainant and the Scheme Operator.

---

[1] Section 230(4).

Jurisdiction

The Compulsory Jurisdiction

In order to activate the compulsory jurisdiction, a complaint must relate to an act or omission of a person (the respondent) in carrying on an activity, and compulsory jurisdiction rules be applicable to it, in addition to satisfying the following conditions:

(a) that the complainant is eligible, and wishes to refer the dispute to the Scheme;

(b) that the respondent was an authorized person at the time the act or omission to which the complaint relates took place; and

(c) that at the material time of the act or omission compulsory jurisdiction rules were in force pertaining to the activity at issue.

The eligibility of a complainant has been discussed earlier, but may not provide for authorized persons to be eligible other than in specified circumstances or in relation to complaints of a specified kind[2], but compulsory jurisdiction applies only to persons authorized at the time the 'offence' was carried out.

Under the compulsory jurisdiction scheme it is to be determined if the complaint is, in the opinion of the Ombudsman, fair and reasonable in the circumstances of the case. When determined the Ombudsman must give a written statement of his determination, and the reasons, to both the respondent and the complainant. The complainant is required to notify the Ombudsman in writing by a stipulated date whether he accepts or rejects the determination; if accepted, it is binding on the respondent and the complainant. But if he has not notified the Ombudsman of his acceptance or rejection, then it will be assumed that he has rejected it. The Ombudsman will notify the respondent of the outcome. If a complaint is determined in favour of a complainant, the determination will include a reward against the respondent of such monetary amount as the Ombudsman may consider fair compensation for loss or damage suffered by the complainant, or give a direction requiring the respondent to take such steps as he considers just and appropriate, and the direction is enforceable by injunction proceedings.

[2] Section 226(7).

(In Scotland, an order may be brought only by the complainant.)³ The FSA may specify the maximum amount that may be regarded as fair compensation for a particular kind of loss or damage.

The FSA shall make rules whereby no complaint would be entertained unless the complainant has referred it under the Ombudsman Scheme. The FSA may also make rules providing that a complainant must communicate the substance of its complaint to the respondent in order to provide him an opportunity to deal with it.

It is for the FSA to make rules providing that no complaint may be determined unless it is referred to under the Ombudsman Scheme by the stipulated date. The Ombudsman will have discretionary power to extend the time limit in specified circumstances. It is for the FSA to make rules determining which activities of an authorized person may fall within the compulsory jurisdiction.

The Voluntary Jurisdiction

Voluntary jurisdiction under the Scheme may be activated when a complaint relates to an act or omission of a person (the respondent) in carrying on any activity, but only if the following conditions are satisfied:

(a) that the complainant is eligible, and that he wishes to refer the dispute to the Scheme;

(b) that the act or omission to which the complaint relates took place at a time when the respondent participated in the Scheme;

(c) that at the time when the complaint is referred to the Scheme, the respondent has not withdrawn from the Scheme;

(d) that the act or omission took place at a time when voluntary jurisdiction rules were in force in relation to the activity in questions; and

(e) that the complaint is one that cannot be dealt with under the compulsory jurisdiction.

The voluntary jurisdiction rules require the FSA's approval. A

---

[3] In Scotland it is enforceable by an order under section 45 of the Court of Session Act 1988.

complainant is eligible to refer a matter under the voluntary jurisdiction of the Ombudsman Scheme if he comes under a class of eligible persons. Provisions may be made in the rules for persons other than authorized persons to participate in the Ombudsman Scheme.

The standard terms by reference to which complaints are to be dealt with under the voluntary jurisdiction are to be fixed by the Scheme Operator with the approval of the FSA and cannot add or remove them without FSA approval. Different standard terms may be fixed with respect to different matters or in relation to different cases[4]. These standard terms may, in particular, require the making of payments to the Scheme Operator by participants as the Scheme Operator may determine; these terms may also make provisions as to the award of costs on the determination of a complaint (see Schedule 17, clause 8(3)(a) and (b)). The following will not be held liable in damages for anything done or omitted in the discharge of their functions pertaining to the voluntary jurisdiction:

(a) the Scheme Operator;

(b) any member of the governing body of the body corporate (the Scheme Operator);

(c) any member of its staff; and

(d) any person acting as an ombudsman for the purpose of the Scheme.

The Scheme Operator is required to publish a draft of the proposed rules in order to bring them to the attention of the public in the best possible way. The draft proposal must be accompanied by an explanation of the proposed rules, and a statement that representations about the proposal may be made to the Scheme Operator within a specified time. In the event of any significant difference between the proposed rules and the representations thereto, the Scheme Operator must publish a statement of the difference.

Comments

The Ombudsman Scheme is a laudable scheme in that it provides

[4] See Schedule 17, clause 18(2).

opportunities to settle disputes in an amicable manner and without delay. It remains to be seen how the two jurisdictions, in reality, function. Clause 10 of Schedule 17 provides that:

> '(1) No person is to be liable in damages for anything done or omitted in the discharge, or purported discharge, of any functions under this Act in relation to the compulsory jurisdiction.
>
> (2) Sub-paragraph (1) does not apply
>
> (a) if the act or omission is shown to have been in bad faith; or
>
> (b) so as to prevent an award or damages made in respect of an act or omission on the ground that the act or omission was unlawful as a result of section 6(1) of the Human Rights Act 1998.'

It remains to be seen how these provisions develop in practice. Clause 11 of Schedule 17 to the Act provides that:

> 'For the purposes of the law relating to defamation, proceedings in relation to a complaint which is subject to the compulsory jurisdiction are to be treated as if they were proceedings before a court.'

PART II

The Tribunal Procedure

The Financial Services and Markets Tribunal ('the Tribunal') (section 132(2)) deals with legal issues that may be referred to it. The Lord Chancellor's Office has the authority to make such provisions as may appear to him necessary. The Tribunal shall assume jurisdiction generally 'if a matter is referred to it within 28 days beginning with the day on which a decision notice or supervisory notice is issued or such other provision as may be specified by Lord Chancellor from time to time under section 132'. However, the Tribunal has the discretion to allow a reference to be made after the end of this period. It is for the Tribunal to determine what would be the appropriate action for the

FSA with such directions as it may consider appropriate for enforcing its determination.

The FSA must not take the action specified in the decision notice until the period for referring the matter to the Tribunal has expired, and if the matter is referred to the Tribunal until the reference and any appeal has been finally reached. The FSA must act in compliance with the Tribunal and the Tribunal's order is to be regarded as an order of a county court or an order of a Court of Session in Scotland. The Lord Chancellor may by regulation establish a legal assistance Compensation Scheme. This has not yet come into force but naturally the Compensation Scheme must contain the basic terms and conditions for availing of the assistance it may provide. Section 135 states that the legal assistance Compensation Scheme may make provision in regard to the following: the kinds of legal assistance that the Compensation Scheme may provide; the persons who may be eligible for it; the manner in which applications for such assistance should be made; the criteria by which eligibility for legal assistance is to be determined; the person or business who may have the authority to consider eligibility for applications made; the procedures for appeals against refusals of applications; the instances in which decisions on such applications may be varied or revoked; and the enforcement of the provisions of the Compensation Scheme.

The Lord Chancellor appoints a panel of persons for the purposes of serving as Chairman of the Tribunal. Membership of the panel of Chairmen is open to a person who has seven years' general qualification within the meaning of section 71 of the Court and Legal Services Act 1990[5]; or is an advocate or solicitor in Scotland, a member of the Bar of Northern Ireland, or a solicitor of the Supreme Court of Northern Ireland each of at least seven years' standing.

The Lord Chancellor appoints one of the members of the panel as chairman to preside over the Tribunal's functions, known as the President of the Tribunal.

Furthermore, a 'lay panel' of persons who may appear to the Lord Chancellor as qualified by experience or otherwise to deal with matters coming under the provisions of the Act, must also be appointed by him.

[5] According to section 71 of the 1990 Act, a person has a general qualification *'if he has a right of audience in relation to any class of proceedings and any part of the Supreme Court, or all proceedings in county courts or magistrates' courts.'*

The President or Deputy President should satisfy the following criteria:

(a) has ten years' general qualification within the meaning of section 71 of the Courts and Legal Services Act 1990; or

(b) is an advocate or solicitor in Scotland of at least ten years' standing; or

(c) a member of the Bar of Northern Ireland of at least ten years' standing; or

(d) a solicitor of the Supreme Court of Northern Ireland of at least ten years' standing.

If the President or the Deputy President ceases to be a member of the panel of Chairmen, he/she also ceases to be the President or Deputy President.

The constitution of each tribunal will depend upon the nature of the matter referred to it. According to Part III of Schedule 12 clause 7(1), it does not seem to be obligatory to choose a member from the lay panel, although it is obligatory to select at least one member from the panel of Chairmen; the president has the discretion to determine the number of members of the Tribunal. The relevant provision provides that:

> *'On a reference to the Tribunal, the persons to act as members of the Tribunal for the purposes of the reference are to be selected from the panel of chairmen or the lay panel in accordance with arrangements made by the President for the purposes of this paragraph ("the standing arrangements").'*[6]

However, it is for the Tribunal to appoint one expert or more to provide assistance, if necessary, Clause 7(4) of Schedule 13, Part III, if it appears to the Tribunal that a matter before it involves a question of fact of special difficulty, it may appoint one or more experts to provide assistance.

'Assistance' in this context would mean expert opinion(s) in regard to technical issues, but not to questions of law.

The Lord Chancellor, who determines the terms of appointment of

---

[6] Part III, Schedule 13, clause 7(1).

the members of the Tribunal, may also remove a member of either panel, including the President, on the ground of incapacity or misbehaviour. A member is eligible for re-appointment and he/she may at any time resign office by notifying the Lord Chancellor in writing.

The remuneration and expenses of the members of the Tribunal, including service as the President or Deputy President, will be determined by the Lord Chancellor, along with appointing such staff for the Tribunal as he may determine, but remuneration of the Tribunal's staff and expenses of the Tribunal will be defrayed by the Lord Chancellor.

It is for the Lord Chancellor to prescribe (a) the manner in which references are to be instituted; (b) the circumstances in which hearings should be held in private; (c) the persons who may appear on behalf of the parties; (d) the circumstances in which a member of the panel of Chairmen may hear and determine interlocutory matters arising on a reference; (e) the conditions and circumstances under which decisions of the FSA that have already taken effect may be suspended; (f) the situations in which references may be withdrawn and (g) the procedure for registration, publication and proof of decisions and orders[7].

The Tribunal has been given power comparable to a court in relation to taking evidence or producing by means of summons documents, which may be in the custody or under the control of the person concerned, and to require the person to attend at such time and place to give evidence or produce any document for that purpose. Evidence may be taken on oath and may require the person concerned to make and subscribe a declaration of the truth. Unless there exists any reasonable excuse, any failure or refusal to attend the Tribunal, where summons has been issued or evidence has been asked for, is a punishable offence. By the same token, a person who may alter, support, create, destroy or refuse to produce a document which he may be required to produce in connection with the proceedings before the Tribunal shall be guilty of a punishable offence[8].

Decisions of the Tribunal, which may be taken by a majority, must state whether the decision was taken unanimously or by a majority, and must state the rationale of the decision thereof, and be signed and

[7] See also section 132.
[8] Schedule 13, clause 11(3)(b).

dated by the member of the panel of Chairmen dealing with the reference. Each party and the Treasury must be informed by the Tribunal of its decision.

If the Tribunal considers that a party to any proceedings has acted vexatiously, frivolously or unreasonably it may order that the party to pay the other party to the proceedings the whole or part of the costs or expenses incurred. Or it may order the FSA to pay the other party the whole or part of the costs or expenses incurred in connection with the proceedings, if it considers the FSA has been unreasonable.

Conclusions

In August 2000 the FSA published a Consultation Paper entitled *The Enforcement Manual* seeking comments from the relevant authorities by 31 October 2000.

The purpose of this Consultation Paper, which contains a draft enforcement manual, is to provide proposals on how the FSA may wish to exercise its enforcement powers under the Act of 2000. The enforcement manual in conjunction with the Authorization Manual and Supervision Manual will constitute the Regulatory Processes block of the FSA's Handbook of Rule and Guidance[9].

The Manual puts forward proposals for a mediation scheme which would be used when settlement discussions break down during the FSA disciplinary process. The Manual also contains proposals on the following, among others:

(a) how financial penalties for disciplinary breaches and market abuse might be imposed;

(b) how the FSA will exercise its powers to vary and cancel a firm's permission and intervene against incoming EEA firms;

(c) how the FSA will use its powers in relation to insolvency proceedings;

(d) how it will exercise its enforcement powers in relation to collective investment schemes, the disqualification of auditors and actuaries who may act on behalf of authorized firms, and

---

[9] See further Consultation Paper entitled *The Enforcement Manual*, London, the FSA, 2000, at p.3.

dis-application orders against members of the profession.

The Enforcement Manual in its draft form contains the following chapters:

1 Executive Summary
2 Introduction
3 Commentary on the draft Enforcement manual
4 Next steps

Annex A Explanation of purpose and compatibility with the FSA's general duties

Annex B List of questions

Annex C List of respondents to Consultation Papers 17 and 25

Annex D Further information about the Regulatory Decisions Committee

The Enforcement Manual will form part of the FSA's Handbook which was published in April 1998 (Designing the FSA's Handbook of Rules and Guidance). The FSA has already produced separate *Authorization, Supervision and Enforcement Manuals* for different types of readership. The Enforcement Manual also contains guidance in accordance with section 157(1) of the Act on the FSA's use of its enforcement powers, including its power to vary permission or to apply to court for an injunction or to obtain restitution and the power to prosecute for certain criminal offences.

It is to be borne in mind that whereas the Act and the Schedules provide for the power of the FSA, the Enforcement Manual primarily provides the method by which any departure from the statutory provisions will be dealt with. The Manual therefore starts with the FSA's power of information gathering and investigative power in relation to the following:

(a) authorized firms, approved persons, individuals involved in authorized firms, and appointed representatives;

(b) suspected market misconduct;

(c) unauthorized business;

(d) assistance to overseas regulations; and

(e) collective investment schemes.

The firms concerned will be requested to provide reports by skilled persons in the usual circumstances, but the FSA may be required to appoint an investigator and may require the production of documents.

The draft Manual points out that the FSA's primary aim in exercising its investigative powers will be to protect the interests of its consumers[10]. For the same reasons investigation of overseas authorities and collective investment schemes will be carried out.

The Manual clearly proposes that there should be a separation of the FSA's investigative process from its decision-making process when issuing warning notices, decision notices and supervisory notices. The proposed Regulatory Decision Committee (RDC) will act on behalf of the FSA's Board but as an independent body outside the FSA's management structure, and apart from the Chairman, none of the members of the RDC panel will be employed by the FSA. The other members of the RDC will be drawn from a pool of market practitioners and other public investment representatives[11]. It is proposed that the RDC will be responsible for the issue of warning and decision notices in regulating enforcement cases and the issue of supervisory notices where the FSA exercises its own initiative power to vary a firm's Part IV permission which would lead to a fundamental change in the nature of the firm's permission, its power to intervene against incoming firms in a way which would amount to making a fundamental change to the nature of the permission, its power to give directions in relation to collective investment schemes and its power to impose requirements on former underwriting members of Lloyd's[12].

In this draft Enforcement Manual the FSA promotes the idea of mediation by experts who are independent of the FSA and that this method of settling of disputes must be flexible, although the FSA does envisage that mediation may not be appropriate in all cases.

Chapters IV, V and VI of the draft Manual deal with the issue of variation of Part IV permission on the FSA's own initiative, intervention

---

[10] *The Enforcement Manual*, op. cit., at paragraph 3.19.
[11] See further *The Draft Enforcement Manual*, op. cit., at paragraph 3.27.
[12] *Draft Enforcement Manual*, op. cit., at paragraph 3.40.

against incoming firms and cancellation of Part IV permission and withdrawal of authorization. Chapter VII identifies the circumstances in which the FSA may apply to court for injunctions and interdicts, and section 7.6 contains a list of factors which the FSA should take into account to decide whether an application for injunction or interdict should be made to court. Chapter VIII contains a statement of its proposed policy on the use of its power to withdraw approval from approved persons. Briefly, a withdrawal may be proposed upon: lack of the qualification, training and level of competence of an authorized person; lack of honesty, integrity and reputation, and whether and to what extent the approved person has failed to comply with the Principles for Approved Persons and has been knowingly concerned in a relevant firm's contravention of a requirement imposed by the Act.

In regard to prohibition orders in relation to individuals, authorized persons or exempt persons, the Enforcement Manual maintains that they may be issued upon breach of a general prohibition order under the Act. According to the FSA, its power to prohibit individuals is protective and preventive in that it will reduce the risk of consumers suffering losses as a result of dealing with such individuals[13]; consequently confidence in the market will be promoted and the incidence of financial crime will be reduced.

In its Consultation Paper 25 entitled *Enforcing the New Perimeter* the FSA proposed the factors that would be taken into consideration in order to determine whether to vary or revoke a prohibition order. These criteria also appear in the schedules to the Act and are:

(a) the seriousness of the misconduct that resulted in the prohibition order;

(b) whether sufficient time has elapsed since the original order was made;

(c) the nature of steps subsequently taken by the individual concerned to remedy the misconduct;

(d) evidence of his honesty, integrity or competence once the order was made;

(e) whether the finding of unfitness arose out of the individual's

---

[13] *The Enforcement Manual*, op. cit., at paragraph 3.80.

incompetence rather than his dishonesty or lack of integrity;

(f) the financial soundness of the individual concerned; and

(g) whether the individual is still a risk to consumers or market confidence.

The Enforcement Manual confirms that in the event of a consumer or a market counterparty suffering losses or other adverse effects as a result of an individual's or firm's conduct, the FSA will have powers to obtain restitution for such affected persons, via the court for an order for restitution where a firm or individual, authorized or not, has engaged in or encouraged market abuse or has been in breach of a provision for requirement under the Act. The FSA proposes to take into account the following in determining whether to seek or require restitution:

- any identifiable person who has suffered quantifiable losses or other adverse effects;
- the number of persons who have suffered losses and the extent of such losses;
- whether it would be cost-effective for the FSA to seek or require restitution;
- whether redress would be available through the Ombudsman Scheme or the Financial Services Compensation Scheme;
- whether redress would be available through any other scheme, namely, the Takeover Panel;
- whether the persons who have suffered losses are in a position to institute civil proceedings on their behalf;
- whether the FSA may obtain a compulsory insolvency order against the firm or unauthorized person concerned;
- the conduct of the persons who have suffered losses; and
- the context of the particular case, for example, a takeover bid situation[14].

The Enforcement Manual details the FSA's proposal as regards insolvency proceedings and order against debt avoidance. The FSA wishes to seek:

---

[14] *The Manual*, op. cit., at paragraph 3.91.

(a) insolvency orders from the court;

(b) its right to be heard in regard to petitions by third parties for insolvency orders; and

(c) its right to be involved in insolvency regimes affecting firms or individuals who carry on a regulated activity.

The Manual makes it clear that recourse to insolvency shall only be taken for the benefit of creditors as a whole, and it would be the most appropriate measure to take. The FSA would initially seek an administrative order in relation to the firm concerned rather than a winding-up order[15]. The following are the principal factors the FSA proposes to consider before seeking an administrative order or a winding-up order in relation to firms:

- the circumstances in which the FSA might seek a winding-up order even where the firm concerned is solvent (the Manual does not clearly spell out the circumstances in which the FSA can decide to do so);

- the circumstances in which the FSA would seek its right to appear on petitions by third parties relating to firms or individuals; and

- the circumstances in which it would seek its right to attend and make representations at meetings of creditors.

In petitioning the court for an order the FSA maintains that it would consider whether it would be just and equitable for a firm to be wound up, and the FSA would consider whether there is a need for a firm to cease operating or whether there is a need to protect the claims and assets of consumers, the extent to which the firm has derogated from the general prohibitions under the Act and whether the firm is or may be involved in any financial crime.

As regards the FSA's general approach to the discipline of firms and approved persons, it wishes to rely on its private warning system initially, and thereafter enforcement policies in relation to approved persons. The disciplinary action is a consequential action in that it will be taken only if the warning system has failed; the criteria that must be satisfied

---

[15] *The Manual*, op. cit., at paragraph 3.95.

in taking discretionary action have been proposed by the FSA in its Consultation Paper 17 entitled *Financial Services Regulations: Enforcing the New Regime 1998*. The proposed criteria are:

- the nature and seriousness of the breach;
- the conduct of a firm or of the approved person after the breach;
- the extent of guidance given by the FSA and disregarded by the firm;
- action taken by the FSA in the past; and
- action taken by other regulatory authorities.

The FSA shall consider whether the disciplinary action should be taken against the approved person where he is personally culpable rather than against the firm. The FSA's proposed test points out that personal culpability would arise in two circumstances: where the breach was deliberate; or where the individual's standard of behaviour was below that which would be ordinarily expected. This is an objective test.

The factors the FSA would like to consider in determining whether to impose a public statement of misconduct or public censure, as an alternative to financial penalties, are:

- if a firm or an approved person earned a profit or avoided a loss as a result of misconduct (which may be a factor in favour of a financial penalty);
- if the misconduct is more serious in the nature of a claim (which can be a factor in favour of a financial penalty);
- if the firm or approved person has admitted a misconduct and fully cooperates with the FSA;
- if the firm or approved person has a poor disciplinary or compliance record; and
- if the firm or approved person has inadequate means to pay the financial penalty (which may be so in the case of public censure or public statement).

In determining the amount of penalty the FSA must have regard to the statutory criteria (sections 69 and 210) that is: the seriousness of the contravention in relation to the nature of the requirement contravened; the extent to which the contravention is deliberate or reckless; and whether the person on whom the penalty is to be imposed is an individual.[16]

In addition to the statutory criteria the FSA proposes a policy of looking into additional factors which was suggested in its Consultation Paper (No. 17) entitled *Financial Services Regulations: Enforcing the New Regime*:

- the amount of profits accrued or losses avoided;
- the conduct of the firm or approved person following the contravention;
- the nature of action taken by the FSA in relation to similar behaviour in the past; and
- the nature of action taken by other regulatory authorities[17].

The FSA reserves its right to determine a penalty in certain circumstances that would be lower or higher than the one suggested by the scale. As to its power to impose sanctions for market abuse[18], the principal type of action would be public statements and financial penalties. The factors which the FSA would take into account in determining whether or not to impose sanction in cases of market abuse are: the nature and seriousness of the contravention; the behaviour of the person concerned; the degree of sophistication of the users of the market, its size and liquidity; the extent to which the market abuse can be adequately addressed by other regulatory bodies; the nature of action taken by the FSA in similar cases in the past; and the impact that any sanction may have on financial markets or on the interests of consumers[19].

Under section 123 of the Act the FSA has the authority to decide not to impose a financial penalty if following representations it is satisfied that that person either (a) believed on reasonable grounds that its behaviour did not constitute market abuse or (b) that he took all

---

[16] *The Manual*, op. cit., at paragraph 3.119.
[17] *The Manual*, op. cit., at paragraph 3.120.
[18] See the FSA's *Code of Conduct* (Consultation Paper 59).
[19] *The Manual*, op. cit., at paragraph 3.128.

reasonable precautions and exercised due diligence to avoid market abuse. The following are the factors the FSA may take into account in deciding whether (a) or (b) is met, although they are not to be treated as exclusive criteria:

- whether, and if so, the extent to which the person concerned took reasonable care to avoid engaging in market abuse;
- whether the behaviour of the person concerned was analogous to that described in the Code of Market Conduct, as amounting or not amounting to market abuse;
- the extent to which the person concerned has followed the guidance issued by the FSA;
- whether and the extent to which the behaviour of the person concerned has complied with the rules of any relevant market or other regulatory requirements or codes of conduct or best practice;
- the standard of knowledge, skill and experience to be expected of the person concerned;
- whether the person can demonstrate that he/it was pursuing a legitimate purpose;
- whether the person concerned has followed established internal consultation and '*escalation*' procedures;
- whether the person concerned has at all sought appropriate legal advice, including advice from the market authorities of any relevant market and the Takeover Panel, where relevant; and
- whether the guidance issued by the FSA has been followed by the person concerned.

It is clear that sanctions for market abuse may generally take two forms: financial penalty; or issuance of a public statement.

In determining whether it would be more appropriate to make a public statement than to impose a financial penalty, the FSA will take into account the following:

- whether the person has made a profit or avoided a loss as a

result of market abuse;
- if the market abuse is of a serious nature, then the sanction should reflect the seriousness of the conduct;
- whether the person concerned has taken remedial measures to prevent the abuse and to rectify the consequences of the behaviour;
- whether it would be consistent for the FSA with its own system of imposing a penalty, that is whether it has done so in respect of such behaviour in the past; and
- the impact of a financial penalty on the person concerned, that is, when the person has inadequate means to pay a financial penalty it will be more appropriate for the FSA to issue a public statement.

The following are the factors that the FSA will take into account when determining the level of financial penalty to impose in cases of market abuse:
- the relevant circumstances of the case which would be consistent with the FSA's general approach to imposing financial penalties on firms and approved persons[20];
- whether the imposition of a penalty would have an adverse effect on the market in question, and if so, the extent of that effect;
- whether the behaviour was deliberate or reckless; and
- whether the person on whom the penalty to be imposed is an individual.

The FSA also refers to the conduct of the firm or individual following the market abuse, the previous disciplinary record, and the previous action taken by the FSA and other regulatory authorities.

In so far as the behaviour of a firm outside the UK amounts to market abuse, the FSA will consider in each case whether it is appropriate for it or another enforcement agency to take action, or whether joint action should be taken. The FSA has the power to bring criminal proceedings

---

[20] The FSA does not propose to adopt a tariff-based approach.

for offences under the Act and other legislation. In determining whether civil or regulatory action would be appropriate the FSA will take the following factors into account:

- whether the taking of civil or regulatory action might unfairly prejudice the prosecution or proposed prosecution of criminal offences;
- whether the taking of such civil or regulatory action might unfairly prejudice the defendants; and
- having regard to the scope of the criminal proceedings and the powers of criminal courts, whether it would be appropriate to take such civil or regulatory action;
- the seriousness of misconduct; whether any victims may be identified to evidence that they have suffered losses as the result of misconduct;
- the extent of the misconduct on the market;
- the extent of any profits accrued or loss avoided as a result of misconduct;
- whether there are reasons for believing that the misconduct is likely to be repeated;
- whether the person concerned has been previously cautioned or convicted in relation to such misconduct;
- the extent to which redress has been provided to those who have suffered losses as a result of misconduct; and whether any steps have been taken to remedy any failures;
- the effect of a criminal prosecution on the prospects of securing redress;
- whether the person concerned has voluntarily cooperated with the FSA to take corrective measures;
- whether the individual's misconduct may be construed as dishonest or as an abuse of a position of authority or trust;
- whether this conduct was carried out by a group;

- whether a particular individual played a leading role in the commission of misconduct; and
- the relevance of the personal circumstances of an individual to deciding whether or not to commence criminal prosecution.

The Enforcement Manual also contains proposed guidance on the use of the FSA's enforcement powers in relation to authorized unit trusts, authorized open-ended investment companies and recognized overseas schemes, including powers to revoke authorization of a scheme otherwise than by consent, to give directions to the manager and trustee of a scheme and to apply to court for the removal of the manager or trustee or for the winding up of a scheme[21]. The FSA would consider whether it would be appropriate to exercise one or more of those powers:

- the seriousness of the contravention by a manager or a trustee of a requirement under the Act;
- the consequences of a failure to satisfy a requirement for authorizing the Scheme;
- whether it would be necessary to suspend the issue and redemption of units in order to protect the interests of existing or potential participants;
- whether enforcement action against a manager or a trustee would resolve the problem;
- whether there is evidence to suggest that a manager or a trustee has knowingly or recklessly given the FSA false information;
- the conduct of the manager or a trustee in relation to the matter in issue;
- the compliance history of a manager or a trustee; and
- whether there is evidence to suggest that the scheme is being used for criminal purposes and/or the manager or the trustee are themselves involved in financial crime.

The FSA proposes to exercise its enforcement powers related to authorized unit trusts individually or in combination with each other. The guidance also suggests that in cases where the FSA may consider,

[21] *The Enforcement Manual*, op. cit., at paragraph 3.150.

if appropriate, the revocation of an authorization order, it will generally first require the manager or trustee to wind up the scheme, or alternatively, it will seek a court order for the appointment of a firm to wind up the scheme[22].

The FSA also has the power to suspend promotion of an EEA Scheme where the operator has breached the FSA's rules on financial promotion. In order to determine whether a suspension order would be appropriate, the FSA may take into account the following general factors: the seriousness of the contravention of financial promotion rules, and the conduct of the operator after the contravention was identified[23].

In regard to disqualification of auditors and actuaries of authorized unit trust schemes or authorized open-ended investment companies, the following are the factors that the FSA is proposing to take into account when considering whether or not to disqualify an auditor or an actuary under section 345 of the Act, following a failure to notify the FSA of certain circumstances as to disclosure of certain information of a serious nature which may include:

(a) information related to the fitness and propriety of approved persons;

(b) information relating to a firm's financial soundness; and

(c) information or circumstances which might indicate that a firm is in breach or is likely to be in breach of any requirement under the Act;

(d) that the firm or auditors or actuaries concerned have disclosed to the FSA information which is false, inaccurate or misleading;

(e) that the accounts do not provide a true and fair view in relation to the state of affairs of the firm, or in the case of an actuary any information or circumstances that would have led to a qualification of his opinion;

(f) the effect of the non-disclosure of particular information;

(g) the nature and seriousness of any breach of rules under the Act;

---

[22] See further *the Manual*, op. cit., at paragraphs 3.151 and 3.152.
[23] See further *the Manual*, op. cit., at paragraph 3.154.

(h) the nature of action taken by the auditor or the actuary to remedy the non-disclosure or breach; and

(i) action taken by professional bodies against the auditors or the actuaries.

In considering whether to disqualify auditors under section 249 of the Act, the FSA may want to look at the following factors:

- the effect of a breach of trust scheme including losses to consumers and damage to the integrity of the market;
- the nature of action taken by the auditor to remedy the breach; and
- the nature of action taken by professional bodies.

When deciding whether to grant a request to remove a disqualification made in relation to an auditor or an actuary the FSA proposes to take into account: the seriousness of the breach of duty that resulted in the disqualification; the amount of time that has elapsed since the original disqualification took place; and the nature of steps taken after the disqualification took place to remedy breach of duty[24].

---

[24] See *the Manual*, op.cit., at paragraphs 3.162 and 3.163.

Overall Conclusions

Although this work attempts to trace the growth and development of the supervision and surveillance powers of the Bank of England, now entrusted to the Financial Services Authority (FSA), it was essential to briefly examine the nature of the historical growth and development of the business of banking since the evolution of the Bank of England. In carrying out this research, it became manifest that the nature of early legislation for regulating the money market, albeit unsophisticated, was meant for dealing with internal conflicts between official authorities and the commercial institutions, which were engaged in activities similar to those that were performed by the Bank of England. Until about 1944, banking regulations were primarily aimed at resolving conflicts between institutions engaged in monetary and financial activities, and also at consolidating the position of the Bank of England, by allowing it to be involved in the issues of the British economy and to influence the government's monetary policy.

Although British industries had consolidated their position in various parts of the world by the 19th century, the British government, could not and did not consolidate its position in developing an international monetary policy. During the post-1945 years a new type of banking legislation was developed with provisions that were meant for dealing with international transactions and conforming to the international monetary policy developed by the International Monetary Fund.

The nature and characteristics of all banking and banking-related legislation, except the Financial Services and Markets Act 2000, shows that until the Banking Act 1979, the issue of developing and operating formal supervision and surveillance systems did not receive much attention, although by that time the Bank of England, as the government's bank, did have the authority to control the money market, and also to supervise the activities of actors on that market.

Until the Banking Act 1979, the basis for supervision and surveillance was the assumed belief that accountability and trust would be sufficient to keep the market regulated. It is to be noted, however, no major bank collapses took place in London, although the Bank of England undertook rescue operations in certain cases.

The issue of the protection of depositors does not seem to have received much attention by the government or the Bank of England until the Banking Act 1987. By the 1970s the issue of the protection of depositors and the need for developing a supervision and surveillance system became crucial as otherwise the market would not have been able to attract investors and depositors. The 1979 Act could not prevent two bank collapses, pointing to the fact that regulatory measures, perhaps, had their limits. The 1987 Act contained very elaborate provisions for authorization, including suspension and revocation, and the deposit protection scheme; it also placed emphasis on the very crucial issues of the integrity of bank officers and the duties of internal and external auditors. But again the Baring Bank collapsed when the 1987 Act was in force.

One is not to be solely concerned with the comprehensiveness of the regulatory measures, but in that the complex organizational structures of banks and a sense of responsibility on the part of bank officials should ensure that depositors' and investors' interests are protected; this is a crucially important issue in maintaining the integrity of capital markets.

By the 1998 Act the Bank of England transferred its supervision and surveillance power to a new body called the Financial Services Authority. It is premature to comment on the justification for creating a separate body. Both the FSA and the Act of 2000 will pass through an evolutionary process; indeed the FSA is still developing various rules and guidance for a successful implementation of the legislation. The current legislation is also based on responsible opinions in many cases, in particular consumer protection[1] and jurisdiction of the Ombudsman Scheme. Protection of small businesses and investors has been one of the main concerns of this legislation. One can only hope that the new body may develop an enriched pool of resources. So long as a sense of responsibility and the importance of accountability remain a low priority

---

[1] See Consultation Papers Nos 4 and 33.

in the minds of officers of banks, any attempt to effectively control the money market solely by regulatory measures could prove to be futile.

Annexes

Annex 1: Section 187 of the Consumer Credit Act 1974

Arrangements between creditor and supplier

> '(1) A consumer credit agreement shall be treated as entered into under pre-existing arrangements between a creditor and a supplier if it is entered into in accordance with, or in furtherance of, arrangements previously made between persons mentioned in subsection (4)(a), (b) or (c).
>
> (2) A consumer credit agreement shall be treated as entered into in contemplation of future arrangements between a creditor and a supplier if it is entered into in the expectation that arrangements will subsequently be made between persons mentioned in subsection (4)(a), (b) or (c) for the supply of cash, goods and services (or any of them) to be financed by the consumer credit agreement.
>
> (3) Arrangements shall be disregarded for the purposes of subsection (1) or (2) if:
>
> > (a) they are arrangements for the making, in specified circumstances, of payments to the supplier by the creditor; and
> >
> > (b) the creditor holds himself out as willing to make, in such circumstances, payments of the kind to suppliers generally.
>
> [(3A) Arrangements shall also be disregarded for the purposes of subsections (1) and (2) if they are arrangements for the

electronic transfer of funds from a current account at a bank within the meaning of the Bankers Books Evidence Act 1879.]

(4) *The persons referred to in subsections (1) and (2) are:*

   (a) the creditor and the supplier;

   (b) one of them and an associate of the other;

   (c) an associate of one and an associate of the other.

(5) *Where the creditor is an associate of the supplier, the consumer credit agreement shall be treated, unless the contrary is proved, as entered into under pre-existing arrangements between the creditor and the supplier.*

Annotations:

Sub-s (3A): added by the Banking Act 1987, s 89.

Annex 2: Section 183 of the Financial Services Act 1986

Reciprocal facilities for financial business

'(1) *If it appears to the Secretary of State or the Treasury that by reason of:*

   (a) the law of the country outside the United Kingdom; or

   (b) any action taken by or the practices of the government or any other authority or body in that country, persons connected with the United Kingdom are unable to carry on investment, insurance or banking business in, or in relation to, that country on terms as favourable as those on which persons connected with that country are able to carry on any such business in, or in relation to, the United Kingdom, the Secretary of State or, as the case may be, the Treasury may serve a notice under this subsection on any person connected with that country who is carrying on or appears to them to intend to carry on any such business in, or in relation to the United Kingdom.

(2) *No notice shall be served under subsection (1) above unless the Secretary of State or, as the case may be, the Treasury consider*

it in the national interest to serve it; and before doing so the Secretary of State or, as the case may be, the Treasury shall so far as they consider expedient consult such body or bodies as appear to them to represent the interests of persons likely to be affected.

(3) A notice under subsection (1) above shall state the grounds on which it is given (identifying the country in relation to which those grounds are considered to exist); and any such notice shall come into force on such date as may be specified in it.

(4) For the purposes of this section a person is connected with a country if it appears to the Secretary of State or, as the case may be, the Treasury:

- *(a) in the case of an individual, that he is a national of or resident in that country or carries on investment, insurance or banking business from a principal place of business there;*
- *(b) in the case of a body corporate, that it is incorporated or has a principal place of business in that country or is controlled by a person or persons connected with that country;*
- *(c) in the case of a partnership, that it has a principal place of business in that country or that any partner is connected with that country;*
- *(d) in the case of an unincorporated association which is not a partnership, that it is formed under the law of that country, has a principal place of business there or is controlled by a person or persons connected with that country.*

(5) In this section "country" includes any territory or part of a country or territory; and where it appears to the Secretary of State or, as the case may be, the Treasury that there are such grounds as are mentioned in subsection (1) above in the case of any part of a country or territory their powers under that subsection shall also be exercisable in respect of any person who is connected with that country or territory or any other part of it.

Bibliography

Textbooks

Stephen Fay *Portrait of an Old Lady, Turmoil at the Bank of England*
   Harmondsworth, Middlesex, England, Penguin Books Ltd, 1987

John Giuseppi *The Bank of England*
   London, Evans Brothers Limited, 1966

Margaret Reid   *All Change in the City, The Revolution in Britain's Financial Sector*
   Houndmills, Basingstoke, Hampshire, The Macmillan Press Limited (1988)

R D Richards *The Early History of Banking in England*
   London, Frank Cass and Company Ltd, 1958

Richard Roberts and David Kynaston (ed.) *The Bank of England: Money, Power & Influence 1694-1994*
   Oxford, Clarendon Press, 1995

The Stationery Office Ltd under the authority and superintendance of Carol Tulla, Controller of Her Majesty's Stationery Office and Queen's Printer of Acts of Parliament, 2000
   Explanatory Notes, Financial Services and Markets Act 2000, Chapter 8

Consultation Papers Issued by the FSA

CP01   *Consumer involvement*, October 1997
CP02   *Practitioner involvement*, October 1997

CP04	*Consumer complaints*, October 1997
CP05	*Consumer compensation*, October 1997
CP10	*Market abuse*, June 1998
CP13	*The FSA Principles for Businesses*, October 1998
CP16	*The Future Regulation of Lloyds*, November 1998
CP20	*The Qualifying Conditions of Authorization*, March 1999
CP24	*Consumer Compensation: A Further Consultation*, June 1999
CP33	*Consumer Complaints and the New Single Ombudsman Scheme*, November 1999
CP43	*Consultation paper 43: Customer classification*, February 2000
CP45	*The Conduct of Business Sourcebook*, February 2000
CP53	*The Regulation of Approved Persons: Controlled Functions*, June 2000
CP58	*Financial Services Compensation Scheme Draft Rules*, July 2000
CP59	*Market Abuse: A Draft Code of Market Conduct*, July 2000
CP64	*The Supervision manual*, August 2000
CP65	*The Enforcement manual*, August 2000

Index

A

Abu Dhabi
 and BCCI 120, 125
 Investment Authority 125
Abu Nhield organization and BCCI 120
accountants and banking supervision 70
actuaries as recognized professionals 300
adequate capital 74
administration order 317
advertisement regulations 61
applicable provisions 238
Asset and Liabilities Committee (ALCO) 153
Asset Identification Rules and FSA 220
auditors
 and banking supervision 70
 of members of professions 300
auditors' reports and collapse of JMB 109
audits, external, at Barings 158
authorization
 and exemptions, Financial Services and Markets Act 2000 237
 grant and refusal 41
 minimum criteria for 72
 order, revocation of 252
 restrictions 47
 revocation of restrictions 51
 v licence 98
authorized
 institutions 181
 person 247
 Lloyd's 326
 trading activities of BFS 143
 unit trust schemes 258
Ayr Bank 11

B

Baker, Ron 137
bank, reservation of title 181
bank collapses, examination 107–171
Bank of America and BCCI 111, 112
Bank of Credit and Commerce International (BCCI) 110–136
 Abu Nhield organization 120
 and
  Bank of England 128, 130
  Bank of America 111, 112
 Bank of England
  consultation exercises 114
  failure to revoke licence 115
  initiation 111
  licensing 113
  monitoring liquidity 119
  not informed of activities 116
  overseas supervision 113
  supervision of BCCI 112

UK supervision of BCCI 124
Banking Act 1979 111
 and failure 114
Banking Act 1987 128
Basle Concorde 112
City of London Fraud Squad 117
collapse 110
Crown Prosecution Service (CPS) 131
Depositor Protection Scheme prior to BCCI 135
Ernst & Whinney (E&W) 117
Federal Reserve Board 124
further reflections 127
initiation of prudential interviews by Bank of England 111
Inland Revenue 131
Luxembourg Banking Commission (LBC) 111
Noriega, General 119
Office of Fair Trading (OFT) 132
Price Waterhouse (PW) 114, 117, 121, 123, 126
Treasury
 deauthorization of BCCI 130
 ignorance in BCCI case 130
 knowledge in BCCI case 121
 warnings of BCCI 127
Bank of England
 1800-1914 14
 1918 and 1945 17
 and
  BCCI 128, 130
  Board of Banking Supervision 94
  British Government 14–21
  East India Company 11
  Federal Reserve Board 124
  FSA 175
  Hudson's Bay Company 11
  initiation of BCCI 111
  JMB, prudential interviews 108
  South Sea Company 11
  the British economy 14–21
  consultation 179
  exercises for BCCI 114
  criticized in JMB case 110
  evolution
   1735 -1801 7
   19th century 11
  failure to revoke BCCI licence 115
  Foreign Exchange Joint Standing Committee 180
  foundation 1, 4
  gold standard 12
  'Grocers' Hall' period 6
  JMB rescue operation 108
  licensing of BCCI 113
  monitoring liquidity of BCCI 119
  not informed of BCCI activities 116
  overseas supervision of BCCI 113
  paper money 10
  post-1945 18
  PW audit of BCCI 123
  receiving adverse reports on BCCI 118
  relationship with FSA 178
  reliance on auditors in JMB case 109
  representation overseas 179
  responsibilities for Barings 167
  responsibility for UK financial stability 175
  specific responsibilities 175
  Stock Lending and Repo Committee 180
  supervision of
   BCCI 112
   JMB 108
  UK supervision of BCCI 124
Bankers' Industrial Development Company 18
banking
 early history 1
 growth and development 1–13

statutory provisions analysed 22–83
Banking Act 1979
  and BCCI 111
  failure 114
  and JMB 108
Banking Act 1987
  accountants 70
  adequate capital 74
  advertisement regulations 60
  analysis 32
  and BCCI 128
  auditors 70
  authorization 47
    minimum criteria 72
    grant and refusal 41
  composition of the board of directors 80
  deposit 32
  deposit-taking business 33
  directions 56
  essential features 35
  exempted
    persons 34
    transactions 34
  fit and proper person 80, 182
  integrity and skill 76
  investigations 68
  objections to controllers 57
  prudent conduct criteria 74
  revocation of restrictions on uthorization 51
  seeking information 63
  Statement based on Section 16 72
  supervision by FSA 79
Banking Advisory Committee 184
banking book 75
banking business
  supervision of risk-based 79
  transfer compensation schemes 277

banking supervision
  and accountants 71
  and auditors 70
  by FSA 180
Banking Supervisory Board 185
bankruptcy 321
Baring Brothers & Co (BB&C) 136
Baring Futures (Singapore) Pte Ltd (BFS) 136
  and SIMEX 143
  in 1993 audit 160
  setting up 136
  unauthorized trading 147
Baring Investment Bank (BIB) 136
Baring Securities (Hong Kong) Ltd (BSHK) 146
Baring Securities (Japan) Ltd (BSJ) 136
  operations 145
Baring Securities Limited (BSL) 136
  and audit 161
Baring, Sir Francis 10
Barings
  see also Leeson, Nick
  1993 audit 159
  1994 audit 159
  account number 88888
    internal audit 157, 158
  Asset and Liabilities Committee (ALCO) 153
  audit of futures and options settlements 163
  authorized trading activities 143
  Bank of England's responsibilities 167
  collapse 136–171, 148
    specific issues relating to collapse 140
  Coopers and Lybrand
    London 137, 159
    Singapore 160
  Deloitte Touche 159
  external audit 158, 160

Index 397

futures and options settlement audit 163
internal
  audit 155, 157
  control system 152
  controls 154
Internationale Nederlanden Groep (ING), purchase 139
issue of supervision 166
Management Committee (MANCO) 153
matrix structure 153
Nikkei 225 contracts 145
Osak Securities Exchange (OSE) 143
purchase 139
recognized regulators and supervisors 167
reporting duty 164, 166
risk
  control 141
  management 140
Securities and Futures Authority (SFA) 169
self-regulatory organizations (SRO) 168
Singapore 143, 152
Standard Portfolio Analysis of Risk (SPAN) 163
supervision, lack 152
supervisors and regulators 167
switching 142
trading activities, authorized 143
Basle
  Accord 76
  Committee 185
    Core Principles 133, 185
  Concorde 112
    and BCCI 112
  Supervision Committee 180
Bax, James 137

BCCI *see* Bank of Credit and Commerce International International Holdings (Luxembourg) SA 110
BECOM factors (business, controls, organization, management) 78, 79
BFS *see* Baring Futures (Singapore) Pte Ltd
Bingham Report 112, 114, 115, 118, 124, 130, 134
Board of Banking Supervision 34, 94, 144, 168
board of directors, composition 80
book
  banking 75
  trading 75
BSJ *see* Baring Securities (Japan) Ltd
BSL *see* Baring Securities Limited
Building Societies Commission 60, 62
  FSA 299
Building Societies Investors Protection Board 299
business
  risk 198
  transfers, control of 273–280

C

CAMEL factors (capital, assets, market risk, earnings) 78, 79
Capital Adequacy Directive 75
Cayman Islands 111
Child 5
City of London Fraud Squad and BCCI 117
clearing houses, recognized 266
client and professions 294
Code of
  Banking Practice 77, 81
  Market Conduct 380
Collective Investment Scheme, definition 255

collective investment schemes 255–272
  authorized unit trust schemes 258
  competition scrutiny 270
  definition 255
  individually recognized overseas schemes 264
  open-ended investment companies 261
  recognized
    clearing house 266
    investment houses 266
    overseas schemes 261
Companies Act – external audit 158
compensation payments 91
  to depositors 86
Compensation Scheme 369
  excluded 275, 278
  scheme manager 311
Competition
  Commission 296, 297
  information 304
  scrutiny 270
compulsory jurisdiction, FSA 365
conditions
  for issuing a warrant to FSA 342
  sets of 342
confidential information 302
consultation 179
  between agencies 179
consumer compensation and FSA 210
consumer complaints
  and
    FSA 206
    New Ombudsman Scheme
  publication 206, 209
Consumer Involvement
consumer protection and FSA 191, 203
consumer relationship risk 198
contributions, contributory and initial 89

contributions
  further 89
  special 90
contributory institutions 88
Control of Information Rules and FSA 221
control risk 198
controllers, objections to 58
Convention for the Protection of Human Rights and 207, 208
cooperation
  and Bank of England 179
  between agencies 179
Coopers & Lybrand
  London and Barings 137, 159
  Singapore and Barings 160
core capital 74
Core Principles 185
Council of Mortgage Lenders 207
crime, financial and FSA 205
crime prevention, FSA's role in 191
Crown Prosecution Service (CPS) and BCCI 131

D

debt avoidance 322
decision notice 330, 350
definition
  deposit 32
  deposit-taking business 33
  exempted persons 34
  exempted transactions 34
Deloitte Touche and Barings 159
Delta risk 148
deposit 32
  Banking Act 1987 32
Deposit Protection
  Board 29
  Fund 29, 85
  Scheme 84–95, 92
    Board of Banking Supervision 94
    compensation payments 91

compensation payments to depositors 86
contributory institutions 88
further contributions 89
initial contributions 89
insolvency 85
joint deposits 88
protected deposits 87
recovered money 93
special contributions 90
transferee institutions 90
trustee deposits 88
deposit-taking business 33
and Banking Act 1987 33
Depositor Protection Scheme prior to BCCI 135
Derivatives Joint Standing Committee 180
Dillon Read & Co Inc 136
direction, remedial 271
directions under Banking Act 56
Directive, Second Council 96
analysis 97
authorization conditions 98
freedom of establishment 102
freedom to provide services 102
harmonization 99
disciplinary measures of FSA 345–361
disclosure
and FSA 202
dispensation from 284
general duty of 283
discontinuance 289
dispute settlement procedures 362–386
FSA 362

E

East India Company and Bank of England 11
EFTA (European Free Trade Area) 314

EMI Banking Supervision Sub-Committee 180
enactment 293
Endorsing Rules and FSA 220
Enforcement Manual 354, 372, 383
Enforcing the New Perimeter 375
Ernst & Whinney (E&W) and BCCI 117
European Union Treaty, Article 108 173
exchange, historical concept 2
exchange of information, Second Council Directive 104
exempted
persons 34
transactions 34
expert 303

F

Federal Reserve Board 124
and BCCI 124
final notice 331
Financial Promotion Rules and FSA 221
Financial Services and Markets Act 2000 224–254
authorization and exemptions 237
control over authorized persons 247
definitions 225
EFTA (European Free Trade Area) 314
Gibraltar 314
grant of permission 238
objectives 189–223
open-ended investment companies 261
passport rights 239
performance of regulated activities 243
permission to carry on regulated activities 241

prohibited activities 234
prohibition order 243
recognized overseas schemes 261
regulated activities 234
regulator 234
revocation of authorization order 252
Financial Services and Markets Tribunal 368–372
Financial Services Authority (FSA) 79, 172–188
  actuaries 300
  adequate
    capital 186
    provisions for debt 187
  administration order 317
  and
    Maastricht Treaty 188
    Bank of England 175, 178
    Second Council Directive 104
  Approaches to Regulations 194
  Asset Identification Rules 220
  auditors 300
  authorized person (ex-Lloyd's) 328
  Banking Act 1987 supervision
  banking supervision 180
  bankruptcy 321
  Bank of England, relationship with 178
  Building Societies Commissions 299
  Code of Conduct 379
  Compensation Scheme 369
  compulsory jurisdiction 365
  conditions
    for obtaining a warrant to enter 342
    sets of 342
  Consultation Paper
    33 209
    4 209
  consumer
    compensation 206, 210
    complaints 206
    involvement 212
    protection 203
    protection role 191
  Control
    of Information Rules 221
    system 186
  cooperation 179, 301
  crime
    prevention 191, 205
    financial 205
  debt avoidance 322
  decision
    notice 350
    or regulatory response 201
  Derivatives Joint Standing Committee 180
  disciplinary measures 345–361
  disclosure 202
    of information 301
  dispute settlement procedures 362–388
  Endorsing Rules 220
  Enforcement Manual 354, 372
    draft 374
  EU powers 105
  financial crime 205
  Financial Promotion Rules 221
  financial services compensation scheme 307–315
    other provisions in the Act 313
  Financial Services and Markets Tribunal 368–372
  Financial Supervision Directorate 180
  fit and proper persons 187
  four statutory objectives 190
  Friendly Societies Commission 299
  General Duties 216
  Handbook 373
  implementation of role 218
  information gathering and investigations 336

injunction 347, 351
intensive research 199
intervention 345
 in new firms 345
 notice 347
investigations 335
 and control 335–344
jurisdiction 365
Lloyd's 325
market
 abuse 203
 confidence 201
Memorandum of Understanding 175
money laundering 205
 rules 221
National Criminal Intelligence Service 205
New Operating Framework 197
Notices 330–334
operating framework 189-223
powers of search 336
practitioner involvement 195
Price-Stabilizing Rules 220
Principles for Business 191, 194
Principles of Good Regulation 190
probability measures 201
public
 awareness 202
 reward 301
publication of notices 331
receivership 319
reciprocity powers 313
record of authorized person 301
Regulation of Professional Firms 354
Regulatory Tools 214
relationship with Bank of England 178
remote monitoring 199
reports to Treasury 194
representation overseas 179
responsibilities 177

restitution orders 352
restitutions 351
risk 197
 assessment 199
 identification 197
Rule-Making 218
sequestration rights 317
Sterling Joint Standing Committee 180
supervision 184, 185
supporting overseas regulators' investigations 339
Treasury
 appointment of members 234
 approval of consumer panel members 217
 inquiries into activities 233
 power to direct 313
 power to modify powers 259
 submission of publications to Tribunal Procedure 368
viable business plan 186
voluntary
 insolvency arrangements 317
 jurisdiction 366
 winding-up 319
winding up by the court 320
Financial Services Ombudsman Scheme 206
Financial Services Regulations: Enforcing the New 378, 379
Financial Supervision Directorate of FSA 180
First American Bank 129
fit and proper persons 73, 80, 187
 in professions 294
Foreign Exchange
 Brokers Association 20
 Joint Standing Committee 180
Friendly Societies Commission and FSA 299
FSA *see* Financial Services Authority
Further Contributions 94

Banking Act 1987 90
futures and options settlements,
  audit of in Barings 163

G

Gamma 148
general guidance 217
Gibraltar and Financial Services and
  Markets Act 2000 314
gold standard 12
government debt, management 8
grant of permission 238
'Grocers' Hall' period 6

H

Handbook of FSA 373
Hoares 5
  goldsmiths 3
Hudson's Bay Company and Bank of
  England 11

I

ICFC (Industrial and Commercial
  Finance Corporation) 18
implementation of FSA objectives
  218
incoming firm 345
information
  acquisition and exchange by
    agencies 178
  banking control by supply of 64
  disclosure of 301, 342
  gathering and investigations 336
initial contributions 89
injunction, FSA 347, 351
Inland Revenue and BCCI 131
insolvency 85, 316–324
  administration order 317
  bankruptcy 321
  debt avoidance 322
  receivership 319

voluntary
  arrangement 316
  winding-up 319
  winding up by the court 320
Institut Monetaire Luxembourg
  (IML) 114
Insurance Directives 239
insurance market activity 327
Insurance Ombudsman 207
  Bureau (IOB) 210
insurance transfer compensation
  scheme 278
insurers, suppplemental provisions
  on bankruptcy 322
integrity and skill (Banking Act) 76
internal
  audit, Barings 155
  control system, Barings 152
International Convergence of
  Capital Measurement 76
International Monetary Fund 12
Internationale Nederlanden Groep
  NV (ING), purchase of Barings
  139
intervention
  by FSA 345
  notice, FSA 347
investigation and information
  gathering 336
investigations 335
  and control 335–344
  banking supervision by 69
  with overseas regulators 339
investment houses, recognized 266
Investment Services Directive 93/22/
  EEC 44

J

JMB *see* Johnson Matthey Bankers
  Limited
Johnson Matthey Bankers (JMB) 31
  Bank of England supervision 110
  examination of collapse 107

Index   403

joint deposits 88
Joint Money Laundering Steering
   Group's Guidance Notes 81
Jones, Simon 137
jurisdiction of FSA 365, 366

L

Land Bank 6
Lawson, Nigel 110
LBC *see* Luxembourg Banking
   Commission
Leeson, Nick 137
   see also Barings
   account number 88888 138, 148
   error accounts 146
   internal audit reports 155
   Nikkei 225 futures contracts 147
   Nikkei trading 145
   reporting lines 137
licence v authorization 98
liquidity, adequate 186
listing particulars 283
Listing Rules 284
   breach 286, 288
Lloyd's 325-329, 374
   authorized person 326
   former underwriting members
      328
   FSA's general powers 327
   The Society 326
London Capital Market 28, 31, 53
London Code of Conduct for the
   Wholesale Market in 77, 81
London Commodity Market 20
London International Capital Market
   185
Luxembourg Banking Commission
   (LBC) 111
   and BCCI 111, 113

M

Maastricht Treaty and FSA 188
Mareva injunction 351

market abuse and FSA 203
Martins, goldsmiths 3
matrix structure at Barings 153
members of professions as
   authorized person 301
money laundering 205
money-laundering rules and FSA
   221
money lenders 3
Morgan Stanley 137
mutual societies 299

N

National Criminal Intelligence
   Service 205
*New regulator for the new
   millennium* 189
Nikkei 225 contracts at Barings 145
non-voting shareholders, influence
   82
Noriega, General and BCCI 119
Norris, Peter 138
notice of discontinuance 330
notices 330-334
   decision notice 330
   final notice 331
   notice of discontinuance 330
   publication 331
   warning notice 330
Notional Risk Weighted Assets 75

O

Office of Fair Trading and BCCI 132
Office of the
   Banking Ombudsman (OBO) 210
   Building Societies Ombudsman
      (OBSO) 210
   Investment Ombudsman (OIO)
      210
official listing 281
Ombudsman Scheme
   362, 366, 367
Operator 363

rules 364
open-ended investment companies (OEIC) 261
Osaka Securities Exchange (OSE) 143
   Barings activities on 139
overseas
   regulators and investigations 339
   schemes, individually recognized 261, 264

P

Panel on Takeovers and Mergers 20
paper money, history of 10
passport rights 240, 314
   exercise of 239
past business, reviewing 313
Personal Insurance Arbitration Service (PIAS) 210
Personal Investment Authority (PIA)
   Consumer Panel 213
   Ombudsman Bureau 210
persons, fit and proper 80, 187
Practitioner Involvement 195
Price Waterhouse (PW) 114
   and BCCI 114, 117, 121, 123, 126
Price-Stabilizing Rules and FSA 220
Principles for Business, FSA 191
Principles of Good Regulation, FSA 190
professional services 297
professions
   actuaries acting for members of 300
   and client 294
   auditors of members 300
   fit and proper person 294
   members of providing financial services 292–306
prohibition order 243
protected deposits 87
prudent
   conduct criteria 74

supervision 182
public
   functions 303
   reward, FSA 301
publication of notices 331

R

receivership 319
recipient 303
reciprocity powers 313
recognized
   overseas schemes 261
   professional bodies 354
recovered money 93
regulated activities, performance 243
regulations, FSA and 194
regulators and supervisors, Barings 167
Regulatory Decision Committee (RDC) 374
regulatory functions 267
Regulatory Tools, FSA 214
relevant
   long-term insurers 310
   person 313, 341
remedial direction 271
Report of the Board of Banking Supervision 137, 142, 147, 148, 149, 153, 154, 164, 166
response, decision or regulatory, FSA 201
responsibilities
   Bank of England 175
   FSA 177
   Treasury 177
responsibility, distribution between agencies 178
restitution orders 352
restitutions from FSA 351
revenue information 304
revocation of authorization order 252

Revocation or Restriction, Notice of 47
risk
　assessment, FSA 199
　business 198
　consumer relationship 198
　control 198
　　and Barings collapse 141
　identification
　FSA 197
　management
　　and Barings collapse 140
　risk-based banking business supervision 79

S

scheme
　operator, Ombudsman Scheme 363
　particulars 259
　rules 259
　rules, Ombudsman 364
search, FSA powers of 336
Securities and Futures Authority (SFA) and Barings 169
Securities and Futures Authority Complaints Bureau 210
Securities Management Trust 18
securities, new 285
self-regulatory organizations (SRO) and Barings 168
sequestration 317
　FSA rights 317
SIB Principles 193
SIMEX *see* Singapore International Monetary Exchange
Sinagapore and Barings 143, 152
Singapore International Monetary Exchange (SIMEX) 137, 143
　and BFS 143
Solvency Ratio Directive 77
South Sea Bubble 6

South Sea Company 6
　and Bank of England 11
Special Areas Reconstruction Association Limited 18
Special Contributions 94
Standard Portfolio Analysis of Risk (SPAN) and Barings 163
state lottery 7
Sterling Joint Standing Committee 180
Stock Lending and Repo Committee 180
supervision
　adequate capital 186
　by FSA 184
　elements of 186
　　adequate capital 186
　　adequate control system 186
　　adequate liquidity 186
　　adequate provisions for bad and doubtful debts 187
　　fit and proper persons 187
　　integrity and skill 187
　　viable business plan 186
　lack of in Barings 152
　reporting duty of Barings 164
supervisors and regulators at Barings 167
supervisory notice 332
supplementary capital 74
suspension 289
switching, Barings 142

T

Takeover
　Code 77, 81
　Panel 380
third-party decision 314
Tokyo
　International Financial Futures Exchange (TIFFE) 143
　Stock Exchange (TSE) 143

Touche Ross and BCCI 127
trading activities, authorized, of Barings 143
trading book 75
transfer compensation scheme
 banking business 277
 insurance 278
transferee institutions 90
transfers, control of business 273–280
transnational corporation, problems of size 141
Treasury 175
 and
  Competition Commission 297
  mutual societies 299
  recognition process 270
 appointment of FSA members 234
 approval of
  Compensations Scheme's directors 309
  FSA consumer panel members 217
 auditors and actuaries 300
 de-authorization of BCCI 130
 defining regulated activity 226
 designating
  countries or territories 264
  professional bodies 293
 distribution of responsibilities 178
 exemption
  of single property schemes 257
  orders 241
 FSA 175
  penalty policy statements to 350
  reports to 194
 further contributions 89
 ignorance in BCCI case 130
 imposition of compensation scheme requirements 276
 in relation to Bank of England's supervisory power 128
 informed of Tribunal decisions 372
 inquiries into FSA activities 233
 knowledge of BCCI 121
 notices 232
 notification to from FSA 246
 OEICs 261
 orders applying to insurers 318
 power to
  direct FSA 313
  modify FSA's powers 259
 powers
  in a regulatory failure 313
  of exception 249
  of repeal of section 21(3) 235
 prescription of markets under section 118 204
 regulations 305
  for recognition 266
  on assets of an insurer 323
 responsibilities 128, 177
  in relation to Bank of England 130
 setting contributions amendments 89
 special contributions 90
 specifying controlled investment 229
 submission of FSA publication to 333
 warnings of BCCI 127
Tribunal 371
 President 369
Tribunal Procedure 368
trustee deposits 88

U

unauthorized trading by BFS 147
underwriting members, former Lloyd's 328

unit trust scheme
   authorized 258
   definition 256

V

value of money, origin of term 3
voluntary
   jurisdiction of FSA 366
   winding-up 319

W

warning notice 330
warrant issue
   first set of conditions 342
   second set of conditions 342
   third set of conditions 342
winding up by the court 320